ONE NATION MANY PEOPLE

VOLUME TWO

THE UNITED STATES SINCE 1876

Consultants

Juan García
University of Arizona

Sharon Harley
University of Maryland

John Howard
State University of New York, Purchase College

GLOBE FEARON
Educational Publisher
Paramus, New Jersey

Paramount Publishing

Juan García is Associate Professor of History and the Director of the University Teaching Center at the University of Arizona. He received his Ph.D. from the University of Notre Dame. The focus of his research is Mexican and Mexican American history, U.S. history, and ethnic studies.

Sharon Harley is Associate Professor of Afro-American Studies and History at the University of Maryland. She received her Ph.D. from Howard University. She has conducted extensive research in African American women's history, focusing on the history of women workers.

John Howard is a Distinguished Service Professor at the State University of New York, Purchase College. He received his Ph.D. at Stanford University and a J.D. at Pace Law School. He is a professor in the social science department with a particular focus on law-related topics.

Executive Editor: Stephen Lewin
Senior Editor: Francie Holder
Editors: Helene Avraham, Kirsten Richert
Editorial Assistant: Mindy DePalma
Production Manager: Penny Gibson
Manufacturing Supervisor: Della Smith
Senior Production Editor: Linda Greenberg
Production Editor: Alan Dalgleish

Art Director: Nancy Sharkey
Senior Product Manager: Elmer Ildefonso
Book Design: Carole Anson
Electronic Page Production: Margarita Giammanco and IMPRESSIONS A Division of Edwards Brothers, Inc.
Photo Research: Jenifer Hixson
Maps: Mapping Specialists Limited
Cover Design: Richard Puder Design

Photo Credits: **Cover:** Reuters/Bettmann; **Cover:** The Jesus Colon Papers. Centro de Estudios Puertoriquenos, Hunter College, CUNY; Beningo Giboyeaux for the Estate of Jesus Colon; **Cover:** UPI/Bettmann; **Cover:** Courtesy of The Detroit Institute of Arts, Detail of "The Detroit Industry" - North Wall, by Diego Rivera. Photographed by Dirk Bakker; **6:** Library of Congress; **7:** Bettmann Archive; **8:** The Granger Collection; **11:** Library of Congress #305334; **12(l):** Library of Congress #3455 -LC-D4-14278; **12(r):** Library Of Congress #60239-262-12318; **15:** Library Of Congress #60239-11202; **19:** Los Angeles County Museum of Natural History; **20:** Folsom Historical Society, Collection of the City of Sacramento, History and Science Division, Sacramento Archives and Museum Collection Center; **23:** Library of Congress #33903-2248; **27:** The Schomberg Center for Research in Black Culture; **31:** Photograph by James Caldwell Burnes, Harper'sWeekly in Centro de Estudios Puertorriquenos, Hunter College, CUNY; **32:** The Postcards and Steroecards Collection, Centro de Estudios Puertorriquenos, Hunter College, CUNY; **34:** Florida Photographic Collection, Florida State Archive; **36:** Museum of New Mexico; **39:** Brown Brothers; **40:** National Archives; **42:** Library of Congress-Lot 5799; **44:** FPG International; **47:** Library of Congress # 5762-22262; **48:** The George Eastman House; **51:** Library of Congress; **55:** The Granger Collection; **56:** UPI/Bettmann; **60:** Culver Pictures, Inc.; **61:** Culver Pictures, Inc.; **64:** The Granger Collection; **66:** Culver Pictures, Inc.; **69:** The Postcards and Steroecards Collection, Centro de Estudios Puertorriquenos, Hunter College, CUNY; **72:** The Bettmann Archive; **75:** The Granger Collection; **76:** The Bettmann Archive; **81:** Culver Pictures, Inc.; **86:** National Archives; **90:** FPG International; **91:** UPI/Bettmann; **94:** UPI/Bettmann; **95:** Library of Congress; **96:** Bettmann Archive; **97:** The Schomberg Center for Research in Black Culture; **100:** Courtesy of the NAACP; **102:** The Schomberg Center for Research in Black Culture; **104:** Courtesy of the NAACP; **105:** The Schomberg Center for Research in Black Culture; **108:** National Archives; **111:** Franklin D. Roosevelt Library; **113:** Library of Congress; **117:** Courtesy of TOLA Productions; **120:** UPI/Bettmann; **123:** UPI/Bettmann; **126:** U.S. Army Photograph; **131:** The Schomberg Center for Research in Black Culture; **134:** The Bettmann Archive; **137:** National Archives; **140:** UPI/Bettmann; **142:** LT Thomas Devine, Department of the Army; **143:** The Bettmann Archive; **149:** US Army Photograph; **151:** The Bettmann Archive; **152:** UPI/Bettmann; **154:** The Bettmann Archive; **155:** Library of Congress; **156:** UPI/Bettmann; **159:** Wide World Photos; **162:** The Bettmann Archive; **163:** The Bettmann Archive; **164:** UPI/Bettmann; **165:** Wide World Photos; **168:** U.S. Army Photograph; **172:** UPI/Bettmann; **173:** Reuters/Bettmann; **176:** The Justo A. Marti Photographic Collection. Centro de Estudios Puertorriquenos, Hunter College, CUNY; **178:** UPI/Bettmann; **180:** UPI/Bettmann; **181:** John Pearson; **184:** Bettmann Archive; **185:** UPI/Bettmann; **186:** Wide World Photos; **189:** The United Nations; **190:** UPI/Bettmann; **191:** Reuters/Bettmann; **194:** Reuters/Bettmann; **196:** Martha Swope; **199:** Reuters/Bettmann; **202:** UPI/Bettmann; **205:** FPG International; **206:** UPI/Bettmann Newsphotos; **208:** Reuters/Bettmann; **211:** George Ballis, TakeStock; **212:** AP/Wide World; **214:** George Ballis, Take Stock; **215:** AP/Wide World Photos; **216:** AP/Wide World; **219:** The Justo A. Marti Photographic Collection, Centro de Estudios Puertorriquenos, Hunter College, CUNY; **222:** UPI/Bettmann; **224:** Raul Rubiera, Miami Herald; **227:** The Justo A. Marti Photographic Collection. Centro de Estudios Puertorriquenos, Hunter College, CUNY; **231:** © Beryl Goldberg; **232:** © Beryl Goldberg; **235:** Wide World Photos; **240:** UPI/Bettmann; **241:** Courtesy of Mary Ross; **243:** Martha Cooper, City Lore; **246:** Adam Stoltzman; **248:** UPI/Bettmann; **252:** © Tom Sobolik, Black Star; **255:** AP/Wide World; **256:** Reuters/Bettmann; **257:** AP/Wide World; **260:** Melanie Carr, Zephyr Pictures; **261:** Pete Sousa/ The White House; **264:** UPI/Bettmann Newsphotos; **265:** AP/Wide World; **266:** UPI/Bettmann Newsphotos; **269:** Reuters/Bettmann; **274:** © Cindy Karp, Black Star; **277:** UPI/Bettmann; **278:** UPI/Bettmann; **280:** UPI/Bettmann; **282:** Martha Cooper, City Lore; **284:** F.A.S.E.; **286:** Pam Sciosia, Habitat for Humanity; **291:** UPI/Bettmann; **294:** J. Howard, FPG International; **296:** Reuters/Bettmann; **298:** Telegraph Colour Library, FPG International; **299:** NASA; **302:** Melanie Carr, Zephyr Pictures; **306:** Beringer-Dratch/The Picture Cube.

Printed in the United States of America

4 5 6 7 8 9 10   02 01 00 99 98

ISBN: 0-835-90801-1

CONTENTS

Unit 1 Into the Twentieth Century (1876-1914)

CHAPTER 1 The United States Faces the 1900s. (1876-1914) (7)

1 The United States Becomes an Industrial Giant. (8)
2 Workers Suffer from Bad Conditions. (10)
3 U.S. Cities Grow. (12)

CHAPTER 2 New Immigrants Contribute to the Nation. (1880s-1920s) (15)

1 A New Era of Immigration Opens. (16)
2 Immigrants Add to U.S. Life. (18)
3 Asians Find New Homes in the United States. (19)
4 The Gates Close. (20)

CHAPTER 3 African Americans Move North. (1900-1914) (23)

1 African Americans Settle in Northern Cities. (24)
2 African Americans Organize for Their Rights. (27)
3 African Americans Advance in Education, Science, and the Arts. (28)

CHAPTER 4 Latinos Build New Communities. (1896-1914) (31)

1 United States Gains Control of Puerto Rico. (32)
2 Cuba Wins Independence. (34)
3 New Mexico Becomes a State. (35)

CHAPTER 5 Workers Fight for Improved Conditions. (1886-1914) (39)

1 The Union Movement Grows Stronger. (40)
2 Many Workers Are Not Welcome in the Labor Movement. (42)
3 Workers Succeed in Improving Working Conditions. (44)

CHAPTER 6 Reformers Work to Improve American Life. (1876-1920) (47)

1 Reforms Are Needed. (48)
2 Reformers Work to Improve Society. (49)
3 The Women's Movement Works for Change. (51)

Unit 2 Becoming a World Power (1900-1920s)

CHAPTER 7 The United States Is a Power in the Pacific. (1897-1914) (56)

1 The Philippines Resist. (57)

2 The United States Competes in Asia. (59)

3 Racism Grows in the United States. (61)

CHAPTER 8 The United States Controls Cuba and Puerto Rico. (1898-1920s) (64)

1 The United States Controls Cuba. (65)

2 Puerto Rico Becomes a U.S. Colony. (67)

CHAPTER 9 The United States Is Involved in Latin America. (1900-1920) (72)

1 The United States Builds the Panama Canal. (73)

2 The United States Carries a "Big Stick." (75)

3 The United States Invades Mexico. (76)

4 Mexicans Find Homes in the United States. (77)

CHAPTER 10 The United States Fights World War I. (1914-1918) (81)

1 The United States Goes to War. (82)

2 All Americans Help in the War Effort. (84)

3 Americans See Action at Home and Abroad. (85)

Unit 3 Times of Trial (1920s-1940s)

CHAPTER 11 The 1920s Are a Time of Change. (1920-1929) (91)

1 A Slump After the War Creates Fears. (92)

2 Business Booms in the 1920s. (94)

3 Ways of Life Change. (96)

CHAPTER 12 African American Culture Thrives in the Jazz Age. (1919-1929) (100)

1 Marcus Garvey Appeals to Black Nationalism. (101)

2 African Americans Create the Harlem Renaissance. (103)

CHAPTER 13 A Great Depression Takes Hold. (1929-1933) (108)

1 Millions Are Without Work. (109)

2 The Depression Hits Some Groups Hardest. (112)

3 The Government Fails to Meet the Challenge. (114)

CHAPTER 14 The New Deal Brings New Hope. (1933-1938) (117)

1 President Roosevelt Launches the New Deal. (118)

2 The New Deal Continues. (122)

3 The New Deal Includes More Americans. (122)

CHAPTER 15 The Nation Fights Another War. (1933-1945) (126)

1 The United States Joins the Fight. (127)

2 The Allies Defeat the Axis. (128)

3 All Americans Participate in the War. (131)

CHAPTER 16 Americans Support World War II on the Home Front. (1941-1945) (134)

1 World War II Ends the Depression. (135)

2 The War Effort Enlists Women. (136)

3 African Americans and Latinos Contribute to the War Effort. (137)

4 Japanese Americans Are Interned. (138)

Unit 4 A Challenging Period (1945-1980)

CHAPTER 17 The United States and the Soviet Union Fight a Cold War. (1945-1962) (143)

1 The Cold War Breaks Out. (144)

2 The United States Fights Communism. (145)
3 The Cold War Turns Hot in Korea. (147)
4 The Cold War Spreads to Cuba. (148)

CHAPTER 18 The Years After World War II Bring Prosperity and Problems. (1946-1956) (151)

1 The Nation Adjusts to Peace. (152)
2 Fear of Communism Causes Panic. (154)
3 The Civil Rights Movement Gets Under Way. (155)

CHAPTER 19 Five Presidents Shake Up the Nation. (1960-1980) (159)

1 President Kennedy Sets New Goals for the Nation. (160)
2 President Johnson Tries to Build the "Great Society." (162)
3 A Scandal Leads to the Downfall of President Nixon. (163)
4 Troubles Hurt Presidents Ford and Carter. (165)

CHAPTER 20 The United States Fights a War in Vietnam. (1960-1975) (168)

1 The Cold War Leads the United States into War in Vietnam. (169)
2 Americans Are Divided on the War. (170)
3 Americans Look Back on the Vietnam War. (173)

CHAPTER 21 Changes in the American Way of Life Take Place. (1945-1980) (176)

1 Large-Scale Shifts of People Take Place. (177)
2 New Styles Become Popular in the Arts. (178)
3 Young People Explore New and Old Ways. (181)

Unit 5 The Struggle for Equality (1960-1990s)

CHAPTER 22 African Americans Struggle for Rights and Equality. (1960-1990s) (185)

1 The Civil Rights Movement Advances. (186)
2 African Americans Explore New Paths in the Search for Equality. (188)
3 African Americans Struggle With Changing Attitudes Toward Civil Rights. (191)

CHAPTER 23 African Americans Score Successes in Many Fields. (1950-1990s) (194)

1 African Americans Contribute to the Arts and Sports. (195)
2 African Americans Make Economic Leaps. (196)
3 African Americans Fill Political Offices. (198)

CHAPTER 24 Women Fight for Their Rights. (1950-1990s) (202)

1 Women Face Unequal Treatment. (203)
2 The Women's Rights Movement Gets Under Way. (205)
3 Women Take More Important Roles in Society. (207)

CHAPTER 25 Mexican Americans Struggle for Equal Rights. (1950-present) (211)

1 Farm Workers Form a Union. (212)
2 Mexican Americans Expand the Civil Rights Movement. (214)
3 Mexican Americans Face New Challenges. (215)

CHAPTER 26 A Cuban Presence Grows in the United States. (1959-present) (219)

1 Many Cubans Flee Communist Rule in Their Homeland. (220)
2 Cuban Exiles Make New Homes in the United States. (223)

CHAPTER 27 Puerto Ricans and Dominicans Strive to Succeed. (1950s-1990s) (227)

1 Life Changes in Puerto Rico. (228)
2 Puerto Ricans Meet New Challenges. (229)
3 Dominicans Come to the United States. (232)

CHAPTER 28 Native Americans Fight for Their Rights. (1950-present) (235)

1 Native Americans Face More Government Policy Changes. (236)
2 Native Americans Take Direct Action. (238)

CHAPTER 29 Americans from Asia Are a Fast–Growing Part of the U.S. Population. (1940s-present) (243)

1 U.S. Policy Changes Encourage Immigration from Asia. (244)
2 An End to Exclusion Brings Many Chinese to the United States. (246)
3 Many Changes Affect the Lives of Japanese Americans. (247)
4 Korean and Filipino Immigrants Build New Lives in the United States. (248)

CHAPTER 30 Immigrants from Europe and the Middle East Make New Lives in the United States. (1945-present) (252)

1 Immigration from Europe Continues. (253)
2 Arab American Communities Grow. (256)

Unit 6 Facing a Changing World (1980-present)

CHAPTER 31 New Leaders Search for New Solutions. (1981-present) (261)

1 The United States Turns More Conservative. (262)
2 George Bush Tries to Become "the Education President." (264)
3 Bill Clinton Charts a New Direction for Americans. (266)

CHAPTER 32 The United States Is Challenged by World Problems. (1980-present) (269)

1 The United States Sees the Soviet Union Collapse. (270)
2 The Middle East and Africa Demand U.S. Attention. (272)
3 Latin America Challenges the United States. (273)
4 U.S. Power in Trade is Threatened. (275)

CHAPTER 33 New Immigrants Make the United States a More Diverse Nation. (1970-present) (277)

1 Vietnamese Escape from Communism to the United States. (278)
2 Indians from Asia Find Opportunity in the United States. (281)
3 Newcomers Arrive from South America. (282)

CHAPTER 34 The United States Faces Challenges. (1990-present) (286)

1 Americans Try to Improve Their Environment. (287)
2 Poverty and the Homelessness Remain Problems. (288)
3 Americans Fight Against Drugs and Crime. (290)

CHAPTER 35 Science Changes the Way Americans Live. (1990-present) (294)

1 Computers Create a Revolution. (295)
2 Advances in Medicine Save Lives. (298)
3 Space Travel Aims High. (299)

CHAPTER 36 The American People Face the 21st Century. (1990-present) (302)

1 The United States Has More Diversity Than Any Other Nation. (303)

2 New Voices Speak Up. (304)

3 Is the United States Like a Melting Pot or a Mosaic? (306)

Maps

Immigrants in the United States, 1920   16

Migration of African Americans to Cities, 1910-1920   26

African American Colleges and Universities, 1865-1915   28

Woman Suffrage to 1919   52

The United States in the Pacific Region, 1914   59

The United States in the Caribbean, 1898-1917   68

The Panama Canal   73

The Mexican Revolution and Mexican Migration to the United States   78

World War I in Europe   84

Europe After World War I   87

The Dust Bowl   114

Tennessee Valley Authority   121

World War II in Europe and North Africa   129

World War II in the Pacific   130

Internment Centers for Japanese Americans, 1942-1946   139

The Cold War Divides Europe   146

The Korean War   148

The Vietnam War   170

African American Population in the United States Today   198

The United States and Cuba, 1960s-1970s   220

Latino Population in the United States Today   230

Native American Population in the United States Today   238

Asian American Population in the United States Today   249

The Breakup of the Soviet Union, 1991   270

The Middle East and North Africa   272

The United States Today   307

Charts, Tables, and Graphs

Immigration to the United States, 1840-1900   18

Money Spent on Education in the South   24

Crash and Depression   118

The Election of 1960   160

African American Voter Registration Before and After the Voting Rights Act of 1965   188

Women Working Outside the Home   207

Cuban Americans in the Labor Force, 1991   225

Immigrants from the Caribbean   233

Quality of Life for Native Americans Compared to Other U.S. Citizens   236

Asian Immigration to the United States, 1961-1990   244

Federal Budget Showing Deficit/ Surplus, 1980-1990   262

South American Immigration to the United States, 1961-1990   283

The Global Environment   288

Percentage of Public Schools Using Microcomputers, 1981-1990   295

Population Age Distribution of Males and Females, 1990   305

Unit 1
Into the Twentieth Century
(1876-1914)

Chapters

1 The United States Faces the 1900s.
2 New Immigrants Contribute to the Nation.
3 African Americans Move North.
4 Latinos Build New Communities.
5 Workers Fight for Improved Conditions.
6 Reformers Work to Improve American Life.

THE UNITED STATES FACES THE 1900s. (1876—1914)

What changes affected life in the United States in the late 1800s and early 1900s?

By working on a moving assembly line, these workers at the Ford Motor Co. could make automobile parts in 5 minutes instead of 20 minutes.

Looking at Key Terms

- mass production • assembly line

Looking at Key Words

- **monopoly:** complete control of a whole industry
- **sweatshop:** crowded room in which dozens of workers make clothing or other products
- **discriminate:** to treat a person or group unfairly

- **reservoir:** a place for collecting fresh drinking water
- **tenement:** a rundown building divided into many small apartments

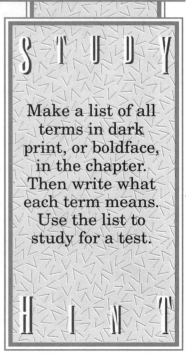

STUDY

Make a list of all terms in dark print, or boldface, in the chapter. Then write what each term means. Use the list to study for a test.

HINT

The floor of the steel mill seemed to stretch forever. Open furnaces lined one wall. In each furnace, 64 tons (58 metric tons) of iron boiled. Heat filled the air with steam. Tired workers sweated in the heat. They looked tiny in the huge mill. Yet workers such as these turned the United States into a great economic power.

1 The United States Becomes an Industrial Giant.

What were some of the problems caused by big business?

Industries grew fast in the late 1800s and early 1900s. Products poured out of U.S. factories. Thousands of yards of

African American inventor Elijah J. Mc Coy created a device that oiled machines while they were running. His was one of many ideas that led to mass production.

cloth, tons of steel bars, and thousands of cars were produced very quickly. This was made possible by new inventions.

New ideas and inventions By the early 1900s, new inventions were dramatically changing worklife. In 1880, Thomas Edison developed the electric light. Owners put lights in their factories. Factories could stay open all night.

In the past, factory workers had to stop machines to oil them. Then, an African American inventor, Elijah McCoy, created a new device. It oiled machines while they were still running. Machines could now run day and night. This helped factories turn out more goods than ever before.

New ideas also changed the way goods were made in factories. These new ideas and inventions led to **mass production.** Mass production is making large quantities of goods quickly. Since goods were made fast, they were cheaper to make. Big business owners could charge less for their products and still make a profit.

Henry Ford used one new idea, the **assembly line,** to mass produce cars. In an assembly line, each worker makes only one part of the product. The assembly line allowed cars to be made much faster. In 1913, it took 14 hours to build a Model T. Then in 1914, Ford introduced the assembly line. As the frame of a car moved down the line, each worker added a part until the car was finished. Now workers could make a Model T in 93 minutes! Cars were made so quickly that the price went from $845 to $290.

Other businesses copied Ford's assembly line. Mass production and the assembly line made some people very rich.

Dirty business Unfortunately, some of these rich business owners were ruth-

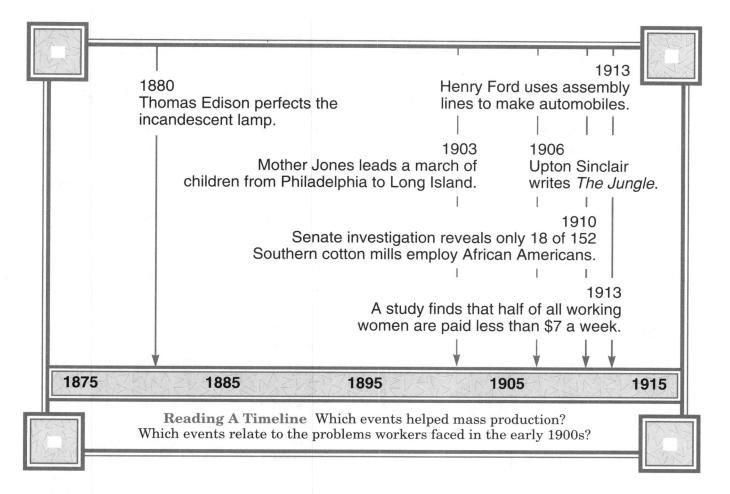

1880
Thomas Edison perfects the incandescent lamp.

1913
Henry Ford uses assembly lines to make automobiles.

1903
Mother Jones leads a march of children from Philadelphia to Long Island.

1906
Upton Sinclair writes *The Jungle*.

1910
Senate investigation reveals only 18 of 152 Southern cotton mills employ African Americans.

1913
A study finds that half of all working women are paid less than $7 a week.

1875	1885	1895	1905	1915

Reading A Timeline Which events helped mass production? Which events relate to the problems workers faced in the early 1900s?

less. John D. Rockefeller owned the Standard Oil Company. He used bribery and spying against other oil companies. He lowered the price of his oil so much that other companies were forced to go out of business. Soon Rockefeller was able to get control of many other oil companies.

By the late 1890s, Rockefeller controlled nearly all U.S. oil companies. He had created a **monopoly** in the oil industry. A monopoly is complete control of a whole industry. He no longer had any competition. He could charge whatever prices he wanted. Rockefeller became very rich.

A duty to society Rockefeller was one of a new class of millionaires. American business leaders in the early 1900s created companies worth over a billion dollars. Some used their money for luxuries, such as $14-million-dollar mansions. Others used their money to improve people's lives. Andrew Carnegie was one such person.

Carnegie bought many steel companies. He then made them into one huge company, U.S. Steel. The company made steel very cheaply. Carnegie could sell steel for half the price his competitors charged. He became one of the richest people in the United States. He used some of this money to help others.

Carnegie believed wealthy people had a duty to society. In 1902, he retired and sold his business. Carnegie spent his last years giving his fortune away. Many public libraries in the United States were built with Carnegie's money.

Greed and cruelty Unlike Carnegie, most big business owners cared only about profits. In 1906, Upton Sinclair wrote a book called *The Jungle*. The book focused on the meat-packing industry.

Sinclair showed that meat packing plant owners did not care about consumers. Sickly cattle were used. What consumers thought was waste such as blood and guts was actually used to make sausages. Rats and other vermin were often ground up with the beef. Plant managers bribed inspectors. Americans were disgusted by *The Jungle*. Many vowed to improve conditions.

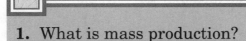

1. What is mass production?
2. What did *The Jungle* reveal about the meat-packing industry?

2 Workers Suffer from Bad Conditions.

What were working conditions like in the early 1900s?

Upton Sinclair's *The Jungle* described how horrible it was to work in a meat-packing plant. Work hours were long and the pay was low. Slaughterhouses were dirty and dark. Workers risked disease. Some spent their days shoveling animal blood and intestines. When these workers cut themselves, they often got blood poisoning. Equipment was dangerous. Many workers were injured or killed.

Miserable conditions The new factories changed the lives of U.S. workers. Most factory jobs paid very little. Workers struggled just to survive. In 1913, a study found that half of all working women were paid less than $7 a week. Men made about twice as much.

One woman was asked how she lived on so little. She said she shared a bed with her landlady's children. Others only ate one meal a day.

Working hours were long. Emma Goldman described working in a coat factory in Rochester, New York. One girl fainted from overwork. The manager did not care. Instead, he yelled at everyone to get back to work. In Southern factories, supervisors often threw cold water in workers' faces to keep them alert during the night shift. In the North, some managers forced employees to go outside at midnight for a short break. They hoped the cold air would keep workers awake.

Not surprisingly, factory work was not safe. Mill workers often got lung disease from breathing in lint. Thousands of workers lost fingers and limbs in cloth-making factories. Others lost their lives. In a single year in the early 1900s, 195 workers died from accidents in Pittsburgh's steel plants. Worker deaths did not make factory owners change anything. When workers were killed or injured, the owners simply hired new workers.

Child labor Children were the most tragic victims of this system. Some factories hired very young children. They often worked at very dangerous jobs. They had no chance to go to school. Children were paid the lowest wages.

In the early 1900s, a writer named Marie Van Vorst disguised herself as a factory worker in a cotton mill. She found that workers were as young as 7 years old. Even the youngest worked 10 to 12 hours a day. The poor children were exhausted. Many fell asleep at lunch between bites of food. Others went hungry.

Some people protested this abuse of children. One such person was Mary Harris Jones. She was known to her fol-

This young girl worked in a textile factory in 1911. Many factories hired children as young as 7 years old to work long hours in dangerous conditions for very little pay. Working children had little time for food or rest and no time for school or play.

lowers as Mother Jones. She demanded laws to protect children who worked. In 1903, Mother Jones led a march of children. They marched from Philadelphia to President Theodore Roosevelt's summer home in Long Island, New York. Her efforts made a difference. Tougher child labor laws were passed in Pennsylvania, New York, and New Jersey.

Unfair treatment   Big business owners often **discriminated** against immigrants and African Americans when hiring workers. To discriminate is to treat a person or group unfairly. In the meat packing industry, some jobs such as labeling cans were considered "clean." These jobs were given to white women born in the United States. Employers hired immigrant women for the "dirty" jobs—cutting beef and stirring boiling pots of animal parts.

Many immigrant women worked in **sweatshops.** These are crowded rooms in which dozens of workers make clothing or other products. Conditions in the sweatshops were even worse than in the factories. Bosses pushed workers to go faster. In their hurry, workers often caught fingers in their sewing machines and needles went through them. Some lost fingers. Immigrant women often worked in sweatshops for less than $2 a week.

Most business owners refused to hire African Americans for any job. In 1890, only 7 percent of all African American men worked in industry.

One of the few jobs open to African American women was in laundries. This was difficult work. Workers stood over very hot machines for up to 17 hours a day. Harsh chemicals were used. These affected workers' health. Other African American women worked at home,

The Flatiron Building in New York City, one of the first skyscrapers, was built with modern building materials. But the city's crowded Mulberry Street shows improvements did not extend to the slums and tenements where the poor lived.

sewing or doing laundry. African American women earned about one third what white women earned doing the same work.

Fighting back Working conditions continued to get worse in the early 1900s. They were so bad that many workers were ready to risk their jobs, even their lives, to try to improve them. They joined a movement of workers who fought for better conditions. However, changes would come slowly and only after much tragedy.

1. Who was Mother Jones?
2. What was one industrial job open to African American women?

3 U.S. Cities Grow.

How were cities changing by the early 1900s?

By the early 1900s, people crowded the cities of the United States. There they hoped to find jobs. The populations of U.S. cities soared. In 1860, there had only been nine cities with more than 100,000 residents. By 1910, there were 50! City dwellers saw many improvements in city life. But they also faced problems such as crowding and disease.

Modern improvements In the early 1900s, cities began to be better places to live and work. Most American cities had paved streets and running water. Cities began to use electricity to light their streets. Many buildings and homes were lit by electric lamps.

Electricity also improved public transportation. First Boston and then other big cities built subways. Subways are railroads that run underground on electric rails. Above ground, electric streetcars carried people through the crowded city streets.

Cities became healthier, cleaner, and safer. City governments built **reservoirs.** A reservoir is a place for collecting fresh drinking water. Underground pipelines brought this clean water to the cities. Diseases caused by drinking impure water became rare. Sanitation departments kept the streets clean. This also stopped the spread of disease. Cities formed police departments to keep order. They formed fire departments to improve safety.

Life in the tenements However, the cities' poor did not benefit from many of these improvements. The poor were usually crowded into slums. These neighborhoods were usually made up of **tenements.** A tenement is a rundown building divided into many small apartments. As many as eight families lived on one floor of these buildings. Usually the tiny apartments had only one room with a window. Many tenements had only one or two bathrooms on each floor. Some were even worse.

Tenements were so crowded that they were unhealthy. They were also built very close together. This cut off light and fresh air. Rotting garbage piled up in alleys between the tenements. Rats feasted on the garbage. Diseases could spread to all the residents of the tenements. Children were lucky to live past the age of five. Many of the children died.

Poor neighborhoods were usually the last to receive services from city governments. As a result, these areas suffered most from crime and disease. Middle and upper class people rarely went into these unsafe areas. Many had no idea how bad life could be for the poor.

1. How did electricity change cities in the early 1900s?
2. Why were tenements unhealthy?

CHAPTER 1
KEY IDEAS

- In the late 1800s and early 1900s, American industry grew fast.
- Many big business owners did not care about their workers or the consumers of their products. They only cared about making profits.
- Workers suffered from poor working conditions and low wages.
- Cities had many modern improvements by 1900. However, poor city dwellers still had many problems.

I. Reviewing Vocabulary

Match each word or term with its meaning.

1. reservoir
2. discriminate
3. monopoly
4. sweatshop
5. tenement

a. complete control of a whole industry
b. crowded room where dozens of workers make clothing or other products
c. to treat a person or group unfairly
d. a rundown building divided into many small apartments
e. a place for collecting fresh drinking water

II. Understanding the Chapter

1. What new ideas and inventions changed the way products were made in the late 1800s and early 1900s?
2. How did Rockefeller create a monopoly?
3. What were working conditions like in the early 1900s?
4. How did big business owners discriminate against immigrants and African Americans?
5. What kind of improvements did city governments make in the early 1900s?

III. Building Skills: Reading a Time Line

Use the time line on page 9 to answer these questions.

1. In what year was the electric light perfected?
2. Which came *first*: Upton Sinclair writes *The Jungle* or Mother Jones leads a children's march?
3. What new idea changed the way goods were made in 1913?

IV. Writing About History

1. **What Would You Have Done?** If you were one of the new millionaires of the early 1900s, how would you try to improve people's lives? Explain.
2. Pretend you are a child working in a factory in 1910. Write a diary entry about one day in your life.

V. Working Together

1. Choose several classmates. Work together with them to make a chart. On one side of the chart, list the benefits of the growth of U.S. industries in the late 1800s and early 1900s. On the other side of the chart, list the problems. Share your chart with the class.
2. **Past to Present** With a group, discuss improvements in city life during the 1900s. Then talk about city life today. List five ways cities are better today.

NEW IMMIGRANTS CONTRIBUTE TO THE NATION. (1880s—1920s)

How did new immigrants add to the United States?

Immigrants arriving in New York Harbor aboard the *S. S. Patricia* hope to begin a new life in a new land. Ships like this one brought waves of new immigrants to the United States from the 1880s to the 1900s.

Looking at Key Terms

- Chinese Exclusion Act • Gentlemen's Agreement
- Self-help groups

Looking at Key Words

- **persecution:** harsh treatment of people because of their religion, race, or political ideas
- **ghetto:** a separate section of European cities where Jews were forced to live
- **industrial:** working in industry such as manufacturing

- **urban:** having to do with a city
- **prejudice:** an unfair opinion about a person made without knowing much about him or her

STUDY

List each new immigrant group. Then give their reasons for coming to the United States.

HINT

On a foggy morning in October 1907, Edward Corsi got his first view of the United States. After two weeks at sea, the steamer *Florida* entered New York Harbor. The 14-year old watched as the ship headed towards New York City.

Then he saw the Statue of Liberty. It was a sight young Corsi never forgot. The giant statue was the symbol of the country that he would soon call home.

1 A New Era of Immigration Opens.

How were the new immigrants different from the early immigrants?

Millions of immigrants like Edward Corsi entered the United States from 1880 to 1920. They helped make the United States the great mix of peoples it is today.

A land of immigrants People from Europe, Africa, and Asia had long come to the United States. From the 1600s, they had settled the English colonies. Millions of Africans were brought to the colonies as slaves. In the early part of the 1800s, a famine drove Irish immigrants to the United States. Poverty and violence also drove immigrants from other European countries. After gold was discovered in California in 1848, many Chinese came to live on the U.S. West Coast.

New immigrants However, this early immigration was small compared

Reading a Map. What does this map show? In which states did the largest percentage of immigrants settle? In what area did immigrants from Italy settle? from Canada? from Mexico?

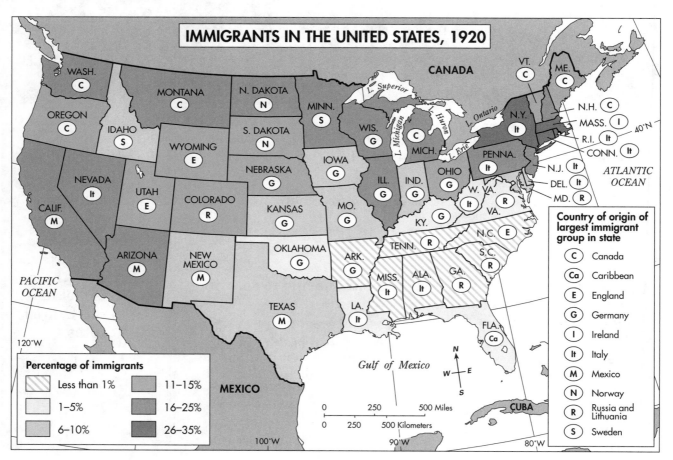

IMMIGRANTS IN THE UNITED STATES, 1920

Country of origin of largest immigrant group in state
- C Canada
- Ca Caribbean
- E England
- G Germany
- I Ireland
- It Italy
- M Mexico
- N Norway
- R Russia and Lithuania
- S Sweden

Percentage of immigrants
- Less than 1%
- 1–5%
- 6–10%
- 11–15%
- 16–25%
- 26–35%

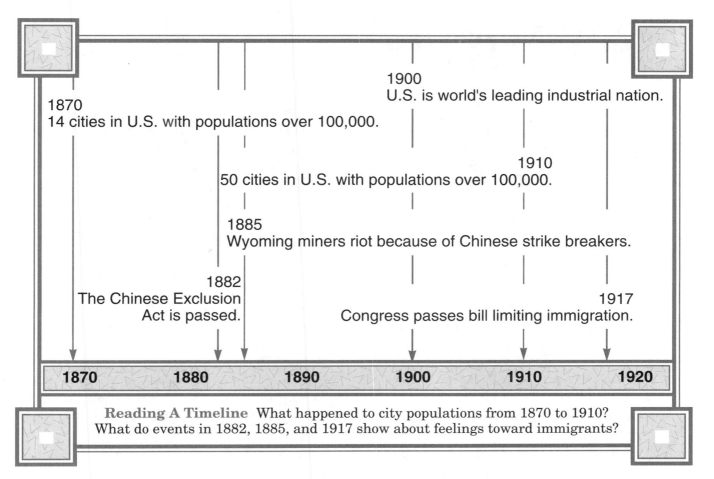

1870
14 cities in U.S. with populations over 100,000.

1900
U.S. is world's leading industrial nation.

1910
50 cities in U.S. with populations over 100,000.

1885
Wyoming miners riot because of Chinese strike breakers.

1882
The Chinese Exclusion Act is passed.

1917
Congress passes bill limiting immigration.

| 1870 | 1880 | 1890 | 1900 | 1910 | 1920 |

Reading A Timeline What happened to city populations from 1870 to 1910? What do events in 1882, 1885, and 1917 show about feelings toward immigrants?

to what started in the 1880s. In the 50 years from 1820 to 1870, about five million immigrants came to the United States. During the next 50 years, more than 25 million people entered the country. This was the largest movement of people in the history of the world!

Before the 1880s, immigrants to the United States came mainly from northern and western Europe. By the 1880s, many newcomers were from southern and eastern Europe. The new immigrants were from many ethnic groups. Some were Poles, Italians, Jews, Czechs, Hungarians, Portuguese, and Greeks.

Reasons to come There was no one reason why these people left their homes in Europe. Most, however, were escaping poverty. They had decided that they could make a better life for themselves in the United States.

Many of the immigrants were farmers. Many could no longer feed their families on their worn-out farms. Moving to the United States seemed the only answer.

Others were fleeing from **persecution** (pur-seh-KYOO-shun). Persecution is harsh treatment of people because of their religion, ethnic group, or political ideas. Millions of Jews left eastern Europe at this time. Most of them came from Russia and Poland. In those places, Jews were forced to live in certain parts of the country. In the cities, they had to live in separate sections, called **ghettoes** (GET-ohz). They were not allowed to own land.

In the 1880s, there were bloody masacres of Jews in Europe. Mobs in more than 200 Russian cities and towns attacked Jews and destroyed their property in 1881. Millions of Europe's Jews

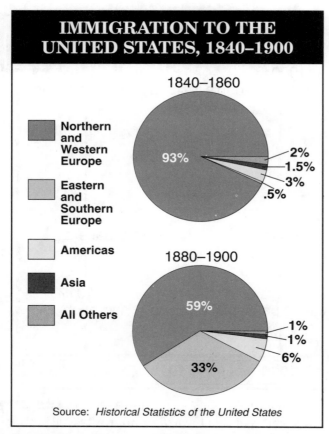

IMMIGRATION TO THE UNITED STATES, 1840–1900

1840–1860

Northern and Western Europe

Eastern and Southern Europe

Americas

Asia

All Others

93%
2%
1.5%
3%
.5%

1880–1900

59%
1%
1%
6%
33%

Source: *Historical Statistics of the United States*

Reading a Chart. What percentage of immigrants came from Eastern and Southern Europe from 1840 to 1860? from 1880 to 1900? What does this show about how immigration patterns changed?

looked for a place where they could be safe. For most of these people, the United States was that place.

Armenians also came to the United States to escape persecution. From 1915 to 1918, almost three million Armenians died in what is now Turkey. Many were killed. Others were left to starve. A few lucky ones fled to other countries in the Middle East. Then they came to the United States.

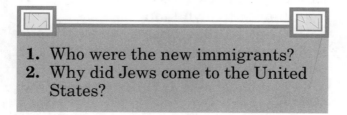

1. Who were the new immigrants?
2. Why did Jews come to the United States?

2 Immigrants Add to U.S. Life.

What did the new immigrants bring to the United States?

Between 1880 and 1920, millions of people suffered through the boat trip to the United States. Teodor Matropoulis (mah-TROP-uh-lis), a 17 year old, described the trip: "The rooms held about 150 people, sometimes more. There was no fresh air. After about three days, the smell was terrible. I don't believe I have ever felt worse in my life."

Most of the immigrants had little money. They needed work right away. However, they had almost no job skills. Only a few knew English. Thus the immigrants had to take jobs in the hardest, lowest-paying industries. Because they were so poor, almost all members of a family had to work. Many made their living in dark, dirty factories called sweatshops.

Immigrants helped make the United States an **industrial** nation. In an industrial nation, most people work by making goods. By 1900, the country was the world's leading industrial nation.

To the cities The new immigrants also helped make the United States an **urban** nation. Urban means having to do with a city. For almost all the newcomers, home was a busy U.S. city. Cities were where the jobs were.

The great age of immigration made U.S. cities grow. In 1870, there were only 14 cities in the United States with populations over 100,000. By 1910, that number had grown to 50. Between 1870 and 1910, Chicago's population doubled. New York City in 1910 had more foreign-born residents than any other city in the world. Other large cities also had great numbers of foreign-born residents. These included Cincinnati, Chicago, St. Louis, and San Francisco.

Immigrants lived in neighborhoods near other people from their homeland. Many Jewish immigrants from Russia lived and worked on Hester Street in New York City.

The immigrants moved into neighborhoods with other people from their homeland. Ethnic neighborhoods sprang up. There might be a Polish section next to an Italian section. Next might be a Jewish neighborhood. In these neighborhoods, almost everyone spoke the same language and followed the same customs.

Life was hard for the poor immigrants. Most lived in slums. Often a whole family had only one room. Windows were a luxury. Sometimes there was no heat or running water. Many slums did not have sewers. Waste poured into gutters in the streets.

Helping each other From their first days, immigrants formed **self-help groups** to improve conditions. These were clubs where immigrants could discuss issues, study English, and play sports. Immigrants learned about their adopted country. Self-help groups even bought plots in cemeteries, so members could be buried near each other.

Many immigrant groups quickly rose in U.S. society. The Armenians, for example, began coming to the United States about 1920. Within 20 years, most had joined the middle class. Almost all of their children attended college. There were many well-known writers and business people who were Armenian American.

1. Where did many new immigrants settle when they arrived in the United States?
2. What did self-help groups do?

3 Asians Find New Homes in the United States.

What did immigrants from east Asia find when they arrived in the United States?

Sometime in the 1880s, a young girl in China ran away from home. Her name was Mary Bong. She found work as a clerk in a Chinese port city. There she saved her money.

A success story Finally she had enough to come to the United States. In 1892, Bong married a man who owned a restaurant in Sitka, Alaska. She was the only Chinese woman in all of Alaska. She soon learned enough English to run her husband's restaurant. However, when he died, she lost the restaurant. To support her two daughters, she became a housekeeper.

Several years later, Bong married again. When gold was discovered in Alaska in 1899, Bong and her husband went to the gold fields. She dug for gold and used blasting powder.

These Japanese American women are packing grapes at a fruit-processing plant in Sacramento, California around 1900. Men and women of Japanese descent helped to build California's great agriculture industry.

At the age of 70, Bong was asked if she would ever return to China. She said, "I'll never go back. China seems like a faraway dream to me." For her, as for many other Chinese, the United States had become home.

There were many Chinese, like Mary Bong, who made their mark in the United States. In the late 1800s, the only jobs open to Chinese in the United States were jobs no one else wanted. Yet, time after time, a Chinese person managed to turn these jobs into new opportunities. Some Chinese in the U.S. West became peddlers. They sold small articles, dishes, pots, and pans. When they found a good location, they sometimes opened a store. They helped to build up the economy of the U.S. West.

Japanese in the United States
Around 1900, thousands of Japanese arrived on the U.S. mainland. The Japanese immigrants took jobs on fishing boats, in lumber camps, with railroads, and on farms.

The Japanese were excellent farmers. They bought or leased lands that white farmers thought were useless. The Japanese built these lands into prosperous farms. In 1910, the Japanese were only two percent of California's population. Yet, they produced 13 percent of its food. It took hard work and careful management. In the end, the Japanese made these lands profitable.

1. What kind of jobs were open to the Chinese in the United States in the late 1800s?
2. When did Japanese begin arriving in the United States?

4 The Gates Close.
How did Americans react to the new immigrants?

One of the biggest problems immigrants faced was **prejudice.** Prejudice is an unfair opinion about a person. It is made without knowing much about that person. Many Americans looked down on the newcomers. The immigrants seemed different. They spoke different languages and had different customs.

U.S. workers also were angry because the newcomers were willing to work at lower wages than native-born workers. They thought immigrants were taking jobs away from them.

Immigrants from China, Japan, and Korea faced special problems. Their language, clothing, and customs set them apart. The Chinese were the first to come to the United States in large numbers. So they were the first Asians to feel prejudice and violence. In the 1880s, gangs attacked and sometimes killed Chinese. In 1885, white miners in Wyoming rioted because Chinese were used as strike breakers. More than 30 Chinese were killed.

Shutting the door   Some Americans attempted to keep immigrants out of the country. In 1895, a bill was introduced in the Senate to cut back on immigration. It would keep out any person over the age of 14 who could not read or write. The bill did not pass. But supporters continued to introduce it.

Finally in 1917, the bill passed. In the 1920s, Congress cut back even further on immigration. (See Chapter 11.)

State laws barred Asians from owning land. In 1882, Congress passed a law known as the **Chinese Exclusion Act.** Exclusion means to keep out. The act barred immigration from China. Immigration of other Asians was limited later. Bans on Asian immigration lasted until 1952.

The American dream   By 1920, the United States was no longer open to anyone who had a dream. Yet nothing could change most immigrants' faith in the United States. Most immigrants believed that they would have better lives here. If their lives were not better, immigrants were sure that their children would have better lives. In most cases, that promise came true.

1. Why did U.S. workers fear immigrants?
2. Why did Asian immigrants have special problems?

CHAPTER 2
KEY IDEAS

- Immigration increased greatly from the 1880s to the 1920s.
- Immigrants came to escape poverty and persecution. Many came from southern and eastern Europe and Asia.
- Immigrants helped to build an urban, industrial nation.
- Beginning in 1895, Americans pushed to limit immigration.

I. Reviewing Vocabulary

Match each word on the left with the correct definition on the right.

1. persecution	**a.** having to do with a city
2. ghetto	**b.** harsh treatment of people because of their religion, race, or political ideas
3. industrial	**c.** working in industry such as manufacturing
4. urban	**d.** an unfair opinion about a person made without knowing much about him or her
5. prejudice	**e.** a separate section of a city where Jews were forced to live

II. Understanding the Chapter

1. What is similar about the reasons Jews and Armenians came to the United States?
2. Why did immigrants take low-paying jobs?
3. What did immigrants do to improve their situation?
4. Why did Americans want to cut back immigration?
5. What changes did immigrants help to make in the United States?

III. Building Skills: Interpreting a Chart

Study the pie charts on page 18. Think about what you read in the chapter. Then answer the questions below.

1. Which immigrant group shows the greatest increase in numbers from 1860 to 1900?
2. Which immigrant group shows the greatest decrease?
3. Where did the majority of immigrants come from between 1840–1900?

IV. Writing About History

1. **What Would You Have Done?** If you had been an immigrant in the United States in 1900, where would you have settled? Why?
2. Write an editorial that opposes limitations on immigration.

V. Working Together

1. With a group, interview someone in your community who immigrated to the United States from another country. Ask about the person's reasons for coming. Also find out about first impressions of the United States and special experiences. Present your findings to the class.
2. **Past to Present** With a group, research to find what countries immigrants have come from in the 1990s. Also find out how many came from each country. Then make a pie chart like the ones on page 18 to display your information. What conclusions can you make?

AFRICAN AMERICANS MOVE NORTH. (1900–1914)

What advances did African Americans make in the early years of the 1900s?

George Washington Carver's discoveries revolutionized Southern agriculture. Booker T. Washington convinced Carver to teach at his Tuskegee Institute.

Looking at Key Terms

- Great Migration • Jim Crow laws • National Association for the Advancement of Colored People (NAACP)
- National Urban League

Looking at Key Words

- **sharecropper:** person who farms a plot of land owned by another in exchange for a share of the crop
- **segregation:** separation of one group from others by law
- **lynch:** to murder by a mob
- **agriculture:** the science of farming

S T U D Y

Copy down each of the key ideas on page 29. Under each key idea, write the facts from the chapter that support it.

H I N T

On a cotton plantation in Georgia in 1910, 15 African American families tried to make a living. However, the Harrisons, the Battles, and 13 other families barely earned enough to feed themselves. By the end of 1917, not a single family remained. Like thousands of other African Americans, they had gone north. There they hoped for a better life.

1 African Americans Settle in Northern Cities.

What conditions were faced by African Americans who moved to Northern cities?

Beginning in 1910, great numbers of African Americans from the South moved to the North. This movement was called the **Great Migration.** This migration went on for more than 20 years. Over a million African Americans left the South. There were several causes of this migration.

Hardship in the South In the early 1900s, life was very difficult for African Americans in the South. Many earned their living farming cotton. Most African American farmers were **share-croppers.** A sharecropper farms a plot of land owned by another. In exchange, the owner gets a share of the crop.

Sharecroppers borrowed plows, seeds, and even their houses from white landowners. They went into debt when they planted a crop. After the crop was harvested, it was sold. Then sharecroppers paid their debts. They lived on what little was left. Usually they had to borrow more. So sharecropping was a cycle of poverty and debt.

No way out but North Share-croppers were trapped. Laws in the Southern states often worked against them. In Georgia, sharecroppers could not leave their fields until they paid their debts. If they moved to another town, local sheriffs could bring them back.

Laws that discriminated against African Americans were called **Jim Crow laws.** Jim Crow laws **segregated** African Americans. Segregation is separation of one group from others by

Reading a Chart. What does this chart show about money spent on education in the South for whites and African Americans in 1890? How does this change in 1910? Why did this change occur?

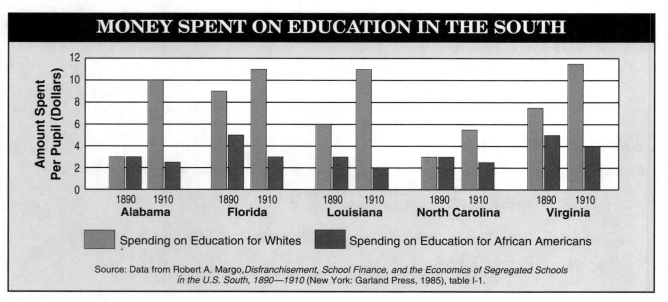

MONEY SPENT ON EDUCATION IN THE SOUTH

Amount Spent Per Pupil (Dollars)

Alabama: 1890, 1910
Florida: 1890, 1910
Louisiana: 1890, 1910
North Carolina: 1890, 1910
Virginia: 1890, 1910

■ Spending on Education for Whites ■ Spending on Education for African Americans

Source: Data from Robert A. Margo, *Disfranchisement, School Finance, and the Economics of Segregated Schools in the U.S. South, 1890—1910* (New York: Garland Press, 1985), table I-1.

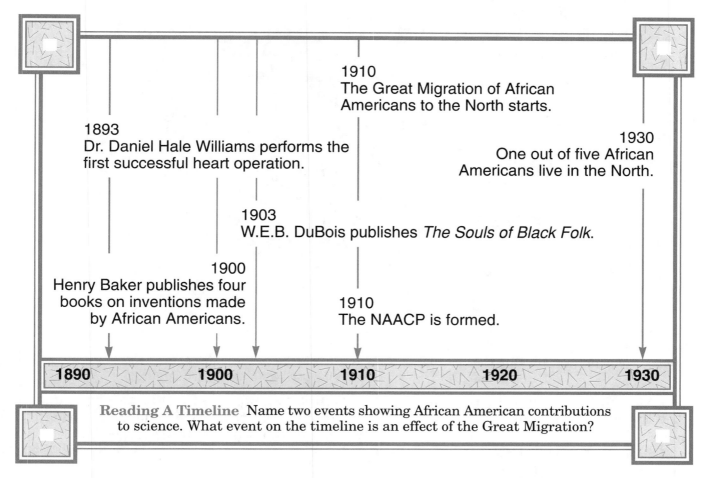

1910
The Great Migration of African Americans to the North starts.

1893
Dr. Daniel Hale Williams performs the first successful heart operation.

1930
One out of five African Americans live in the North.

1903
W.E.B. DuBois publishes *The Souls of Black Folk.*

1900
Henry Baker publishes four books on inventions made by African Americans.

1910
The NAACP is formed.

| 1890 | 1900 | 1910 | 1920 | 1930 |

Reading A Timeline Name two events showing African American contributions to science. What event on the timeline is an effect of the Great Migration?

law. These laws forced African Americans to live in separate neighborhoods. They could not go to the same schools as whites. Many parts of their daily lives were restricted.

African Americans were given only the lowest paying jobs. An African American field worker made $1 a day. Factory workers made $.14 an hour. As a result, most African Americans in the South were poor.

They also faced violence. African Americans were often beaten by angry whites. **Lynching,** or murder by a mob, was common. Southern police did not help. There was no justice for African Americans in the South.

Promise and problems in the North By 1910, thousands of African Americans headed north. They wanted to find good jobs. They also hoped for a bet-

ter life. They had heard that African Americans were treated better in the North. By 1930, one out of five African Americans lived in the North.

In the North, African Americans faced new problems. Most of them lived in all-African-American neighborhoods due to discrimination. These neighborhoods were very poor. Housing was run-down and crowded. City services, such as sanitation, police, and health inspections, often did not cover these poor areas.

African Americans from the South also had trouble finding good jobs. Most did not have the skills needed for high-paying jobs in Northern factories and businesses. Northern employers also discriminated against African Americans. They hired African Americans for only the hardest labor. African Americans often got jobs white

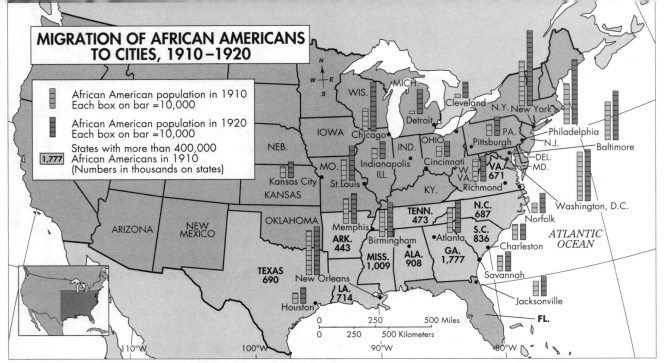

Reading a Map. What does this map show? How had the African American population in cities changed from 1910 to 1920? What three cities gained the most African American population during that period?

workers did not want. They usually had the lowest-paying jobs.

Creating a new life Despite these problems, African Americans created lives for themselves in the North. They set up their own churches. Many of these churches helped new arrivals from the South. They offered food, housing, and advice. These churches provided both spiritual comfort and community support.

African Americans also created new businesses. Some started small businesses to serve their neighborhoods. Restaurants, beauty parlors, drugstores, groceries, and other stores sprang up. African American banks and insurance companies opened. Successful business owners joined a small but growing African American middle class.

Some African Americans were very successful. Madame C.J. Walker was one such person. Walker created a hair conditioner for African Americans. She sold it door-to-door. The product was a big success. Walker then developed a complete line of cosmetics. By 1910, her company employed 5,000 saleswomen. Walker was the first African American woman to become a millionaire.

African American newspapers African Americans also founded their own newspapers. They read news that concerned them in the *New York Age*, the *Washington Bee*, and the *Cleveland Gazette*. One of the most famous of these newspapers was the *Chicago Defender*.

The *Defender* was founded in 1905 by Robert S. Abbott. The paper was sold from Chicago to New Orleans. Every week, 300,000 people read it. The *Defender* attacked racial discrimination. It also reported lynchings. Newspapers like the *Defender* played a key role in African Americans' fight for equal rights.

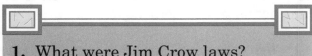

1. What were Jim Crow laws?
2. What problems did African Americans face in the North?

2 African Americans Organize for Their Rights.

How did African Americans win greater civil rights in the early 1900s?

In the early 1900s, it was clear that African Americans in both the North and the South faced discrimination and violence. They did not have basic civil rights. However, African Americans had different ideas about what should be done. Two African American leaders represented these different ideas. One of these leaders was Booker T. Washington. The other was W.E.B. DuBois.

Different views   Booker T. Washington headed Tuskegee Institute. At Tuskegee, African Americans learned skills used in industry. Washington believed African Americans should be trained so they could get better jobs. He did not believe oppression would benefit African Americans or whites. Washington argued African Americans should be able to earn a living and buy property. He believed this would help African Americans more than being able to vote.

Madame C. J. Walker was the first woman to earn a million dollars! She employed 5,000 saleswomen by 1910.

W.E.B. DuBois attacked Washington's ideas. He was the first African American to receive a doctoral degree from Harvard University. In 1903, he published a book, *The Souls of Black Folk*. Soon after, DuBois gave up teaching to fight for civil rights.

DuBois wanted more than better jobs for African Americans. He demanded equality. DuBois believed in using education as a way to achieve civil rights. He wanted African Americans to take pride in their rich culture and in their abilities. He wanted them to develop an art and literature of their own. Most important of all, said DuBois, African Americans had to organize.

The NAACP   In May 1909, such an organization began. Nearly 300 African Americans and whites met in New York City. They gathered to discuss African American rights. W.E.B. DuBois was there. Other African American leaders such as Ida B. Wells also attended. Wells was known in America and Europe for her fight against lynching. Many leaders of white churches were present.

At that meeting, a committee was created. In 1910, this committee founded the National Association for the Advancement of Colored People (NAACP). Its objective was to win "equal rights and opportunities for all." The NAACP quickly built a strong national organization. After ten years, it had over 400 local branches, with more than 91,000 members.

The NAACP became a powerful voice for justice. It tried to change public opinion about discrimination. The NAACP took out ads in newspapers. These ads described lynchings and other violence against African Americans. It also published studies on African American living conditions.

The NAACP also fought for justice in the courts. It attacked laws that dis-

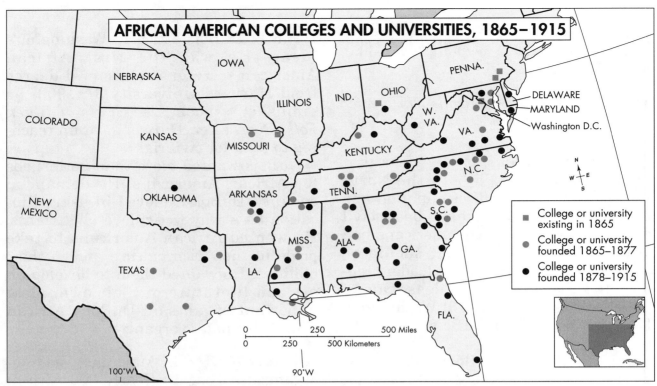

AFRICAN AMERICAN COLLEGES AND UNIVERSITIES, 1865–1915

Legend:
- College or university existing in 1865
- College or university founded 1865–1877
- College or university founded 1878–1915

Reading a Map Where were the most African American colleges and universities located during the time shown on the map? What does this tell you about where most African Americans lived during 1865–1915?

criminated against African Americans. Over the years, the NAACP won important court victories in fair housing, education, and voting rights.

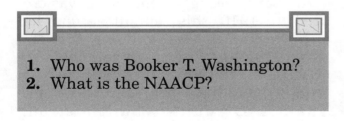

1. Who was Booker T. Washington?
2. What is the NAACP?

3 African Americans Advance in Education, Science, and the Arts.

What were some achievements of African Americans in the early years of the 1900s?

In spite of many difficulties, African Americans made great progress in the 1900s. In education, science, and the arts, African Americans succeeded.

Education blossoms By 1910, over 70 percent of African Americans could read. This was more than twice as many as 50 years before. Over 1,700,000 African Americans attended public school. There were 35,000 African American teachers.

Many of these teachers had graduated from African American colleges. Spelman College produced thousands of teachers. Other colleges also graduated many African Americans. Hampton Institute and Tuskegee Institute trained thousands in skills for industry. Howard University turned out African American doctors, lawyers, and engineers. These graduates contributed a great deal to U.S. society.

Scientific discoveries Many of these graduates made major scientific breakthroughs. George Washington Carver changed **agriculture** in the

South. Agriculture is the science of farming. Carver told farmers to plant peanuts, sweet potatoes, and soybeans. These plants made the soil rich. To make these crops profitable, he found new uses for them. He invented 300 uses for the peanut, over 100 for the sweet potato, and many for the soybean.

African Americans were active in the field of medicine. Dr. Daniel Hale Williams founded Chicago's Provident Hospital. This hospital trained African Americans to be doctors and nurses. In 1893, Williams performed the first successful heart operation there.

In 1900, Henry Baker of the United States Patent Office published four thick books. They described inventions made by African Americans. These inventions helped bring about the amazing growth of U.S. industries.

The arts   African Americans also contributed to the development of the arts in the United States. In the late 1800s and early 1900s, African American artists struggled for proper recognition. Edmonia Lewis was one of the few women sculptors of her time. African American

painters such as Henry Ossawa Tanner received praise in Europe.

African American writers of this period produced a variety of works. William Wells Brown wrote about the years of slavery. The experiences of African Americans in the early 1900s were described by Charles W. Chesnutt.

In the late 1800s and early 1900s, African Americans created new forms of music—ragtime and blues. These were very popular. African American musicians, performers, and composers worked all over the country. African American composer Scott Joplin's "Maple Leaf Rag," was the first piece of sheet music to sell a million copies. African American music became part of the culture of the whole nation. However, many white Americans still held strong prejudices against African Americans.

1. How had education changed for African Americans by 1910?
2. Why is George Washington Carver famous?

CHAPTER 3
KEY IDEAS

- In the early 1900s, thousands of African Americans moved from the South to the cities of the North in search of better lives.
- African Americans faced discrimination in the North as well as in the South.
- African Americans organized to fight for equal civil rights. One such organization was the NAACP.
- African Americans made progress in education, business, science, and the arts.

REVIEWING CHAPTER 3

I. Reviewing Vocabulary

Match each word on the left with the correct definition on the right.

1. segregation
2. sharecropper
3. agriculture
4. Jim Crow
5. lynch

a. murder by a mob
b. separation of one group from others by law
c. laws in the South that discriminated against African Americans
d. a person who farms a plot of land owned by another in exchange for a share of the crop
e. the science of farming

II. Understanding the Chapter

1. Why was it difficult for an African American sharecropper to make a living?
2. What problems did African Americans face in the North?
3. How did the NAACP fight for African American rights?
4. What scientific breakthroughs did African Americans make?
5. What new forms of music created by African Americans became popular in the late 1800s and early 1900s?

III. Building Skills: Comparing Points of View

Make a chart to compare the ideas of Booker T. Washington and W.E.B. DuBois. At the top of one column, write Booker T. Washington. At the top of the other column, write W.E.B. DuBois. Under each name, write what the person believed African Americans should or should not do to change their lives.

IV. Writing About History

1. **What Would You Have Done?** If you were an African American sharecropper living in the South in 1910, would you go North? Explain.
2. Suppose that you are an editor of the *Defender*. Write an editorial telling African Americans why they should vote.

V. Working Together

1. Form a small group. Choose ragtime or blues. Research the music's roots, famous composers and performers, and popular songs. If possible, find an audiotape of your form of music. Present what you have found to the class.
2. **Past to Present** With a group, discuss the contributions of African Americans in the arts, education, business, and science. Working together, create an advertisement that the NAACP could place in a newspaper showing these contributions.

LATINOS BUILD NEW COMMUNITIES. (1896–1914)

Why did Puerto Ricans, Cubans, and Mexicans build new lives in the United States during the early 1900s?

The Annual Spring Field Day in Ponce, Puerto Rico, was a time for people to enjoy themselves. Puerto Ricans continued celebrations like this on the mainland.

Looking at Key Terms

- *el Grito de Lares* • Foraker Act • Jones Act
- *nuevomexicano* • *Las Gorras Blancas*

Looking at Key Words

- ***barrio:*** a section of a city where large numbers of Latinos live
- ***bodega:*** a Spanish word meaning "a small grocery store"
- ***lector:*** a reader hired by cigar workers to read to them as they worked

STUDY HINT

Write down the questions that appear at the beginning of each section. After you read each section, answer the question. Then answer the question at the beginning of the chapter.

At one time, Spain controlled a huge empire in Latin America. By 1898, Spain had lost most of that empire. All that remained was Puerto Rico and Cuba—two islands in the Caribbean Sea. Spain was determined to keep the two colonies. But the people of both islands had had enough of Spanish rule. They had already begun to fight for freedom.

1 United States Gains Control of Puerto Rico.

What were the effects of U.S. control of Puerto Rico?

Puerto Rico was conquered by Spain in the early 1500s. It remained a Spanish colony for almost 400 years. By 1898, the number of people on Puerto Rico was nearly one million. Most people earned their livings on small farms.

El Grito de Lares   In 1868, Puerto Ricans in the town of Lares rose up against Spanish rule. The uprising was called **el Grito de Lares**, or "the cry of Lares." Its goal was to gain independence for Puerto Rico. Spanish troops quickly put the uprising down.

Puerto Ricans continued to press for freedom. Finally, in 1897, Spain gave Puerto Rico some self-rule. Just as Puerto Rico was enjoying its new freedoms, Spain and the United States went to war. The Cuban-Spanish-American War began in April 1898.

As a colony of Spain, Puerto Rico became involved in the war. However, by the time U.S. soldiers arrived in Puerto Rico, Spain had lost the war. In just 17 days, Puerto Rico was under U.S. control.

Puerto Rico under U.S. control Most Puerto Ricans welcomed the Americans. They believed that the United States would give them more freedom than Spain had. Many hoped that Puerto Rico would gain complete independence.

The U.S. government, however, decided to keep the island under U.S. control. In 1900, the **Foraker Act** was passed by the U.S. Congress. It gave Puerto Ricans the right to elect some representatives to their government. The U.S. President, however, would appoint the rest of the representatives as well as the governor.

In 1917, Congress passed the **Jones Act.** The Jones Act gave U.S. citizenship to all Puerto Ricans who wanted it. It also gave Puerto Ricans the right to elect all their representatives. The governor and other top officials, however, would continue to be appointed by the U.S. President. Puerto Rican leaders asked for greater self-rule. It would be many more years before they got it.

A postcard printed at the time of the Cuban-Spanish-American War shows the San Juan, Puerto Rico harbor. What does it tell you about the port city?

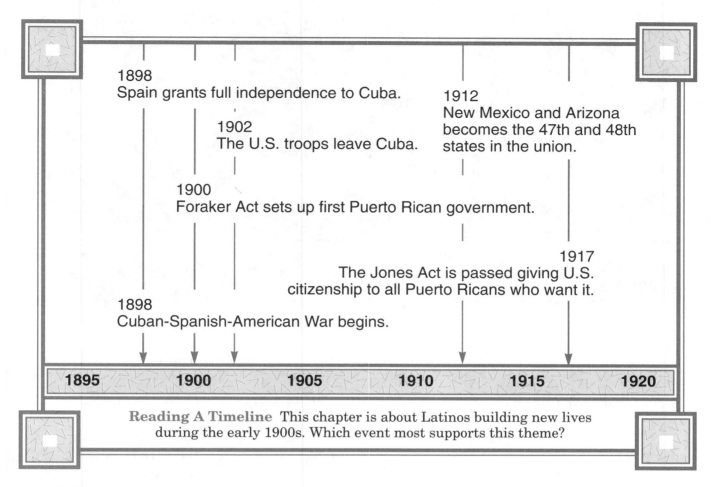

1898
Spain grants full independence to Cuba.

1902
The U.S. troops leave Cuba.

1912
New Mexico and Arizona becomes the 47th and 48th states in the union.

1900
Foraker Act sets up first Puerto Rican government.

1917
The Jones Act is passed giving U.S. citizenship to all Puerto Ricans who want it.

1898
Cuban-Spanish-American War begins.

| 1895 | 1900 | 1905 | 1910 | 1915 | 1920 |

Reading A Timeline This chapter is about Latinos building new lives during the early 1900s. Which event most supports this theme?

U.S. rule also brought economic changes to Puerto Rico. Wealthy people bought small farms and turned them into large sugar or tobacco plantations. The result was that a few families became very wealthy. Most of the people became poorer and poorer. Under these conditions, many workers moved to the United States in search of a better life.

Puerto Ricans on the mainland
Most Puerto Ricans who moved to "mainland" United States went to New York City. There were already some Puerto Ricans there who had left their homeland after the failure of *el Grito de Lares*. Many found work as cigar makers in the city's cigar factories. In 1894, there were 3,000 cigar factories in New York City. Five hundred of them were owned by Latinos.

Puerto Ricans continued to move to New York in the early 1900s. Not all of them could get work in the cigar industry. However, most found good work for steady wages. Wherever they went to live in the great city, Puerto Ricans brought their culture and customs with them. They lived in neighborhoods that became known as ***barrios*** (BAHRR-ee-ohs). The streets of the barrios were lined with colorful grocery stores called ***bodegas*** (boh-DEH-gahs). The barrios also had Puerto Rican restaurants and boardinghouses.

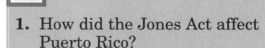

1. How did the Jones Act affect Puerto Rico?
2. Why did many Puerto Ricans move to the mainland?

In Tampa, Florida, cigar workers roll tobacco as they listen to the *lector* read. El *lector* is the Spanish word for reader. The *lector* used his voice to express the meaning of a story or news article. What might he be reading to these workers?

2 Cuba Wins Independence.

How did Cuba gain independence?

Like Puerto Rico, Cuba struggled to win independence from Spain in 1868. For ten years, Cubans fought a bitter war for freedom. During those years, 100,000 people left Cuba for the United States. Some went to the cities in the North. But most went to Florida.

Cubans in Key West Many Cubans settled in Key West, Florida. Key West is only 90 miles (145 kilometers) from Cuba. It also has a climate like Cuba's.

In Cuba, cigar making was an important industry. Cubans brought the industry to Key West. Wages were low, however. Cubans organized unions to protect their jobs and wages. They held several strikes in the cigar factories. Then, in 1886, a huge fire swept through Key West. It destroyed 16 factories and left many people homeless.

Ybor City, Florida Conditions in Key West were bad. One cigar manufacturer decided to move his factory. His name was Vicente Martinez Ybor (mahr-TEE-nes ee-BOHR).

Ybor bought 40 acres (16 hectares) of cheap, swampy land near the small city of Tampa. On this land, Ybor built his factory. He also built a town where his employees could raise their families. Ybor sold houses to his workers at low prices. If workers needed money, Ybor would give them some of their pay ahead of time. He threw picnics for workers and their families.

Even so, cigar workers did not want to depend on Ybor. Cigar workers continued to organize unions. In 1887, Ybor's workers went on strike for higher wages. Ybor hired new workers to replace the strikers. Fighting broke out, leaving one worker dead and three wounded.

As time went on, cigar factories were built in other Florida cities, such as Jacksonville and Ocala. Thousands more Cubans came to Florida. Their skill at making tobacco into high-grade cigars won them jobs.

The role of the lector Almost every cigar factory had a *lector* (lek-TOHR). A *lector* was a reader who read to the workers as they made the cigars. *Lectores* were hired and paid by the workers themselves, not by the factory owners.

Lectores read both political articles and popular novels to the workers. As the struggle for independence grew in Cuba, they became a powerful voice in its support.

Cuban independence from Spain In 1895, Cubans began a new attempt to win freedom from Spain. Spain sometimes used harsh and brutal methods to try to crush the rebellion. Many Americans became angry at what Spain was doing.

Early in 1898 a U.S. ship, the U.S.S. *Maine*, blew up in the harbor of Havana, Cuba's capital. The explosion killed 260 Americans. Americans blamed Spain for the disaster. In April, Congress declared war.

The Cuban-Spanish-American War was brief. The U.S. army defeated the Spanish army in Cuba. It took Puerto Rico with almost no opposition (see page 32). The U.S. Navy won battles in the Caribbean and in the Pacific. At the end of the war, a defeated Spain turned over to the United States its colonies of Cuba and Puerto Rico in the Caribbean and the Philippines and Guam in the Pacific. (See the maps on pages 59 and 68.)

The United States had fought to free Cuba. However, the United States occupied the island until 1902. Before the United States agreed to leave, it pressed Cuba to make the **Platt Amendment** part of Cuba's constitution. The Platt Amendment allowed the U.S. Army to

return to Cuba if U.S. interests there were threatened. It also gave the United States the right to build and rent a naval base at Guantánamo (gwahn-TAH-nuh-moh) Bay, Cuba. The Cubans were eager to see the U.S. army leave, so they agreed to the Platt Amendment.

1. Who was Vicente Martinez Ybor?
2. What was the Platt Amendment?

3 New Mexico Becomes a State.

How did the movement of new people into the U.S. Southwest affect New Mexico?

In 1848, the United States signed a treaty with Mexico ending a two-year war. The treaty gave the United States a huge amount of Mexican territory. This territory included New Mexico. The treaty also protected the rights of Mexicans who chose to stay in these territories.

The Mexicans who lived in New Mexico were called ***nuevomexicanos*** (NWEH-voh-meh-hee-KAH-nohs). The *nuevomexicanos* were guaranteed "all the rights of citizens of the United States." Soon, however, the *nuevomexicanos* found their rights being ignored time and again.

People from the East For many years, the *nuevomexicanos* made up the largest part of the population of New Mexico. By 1880, however, they were beginning to lose this position.

In the 1880s, the Atchison, Topeka and Santa Fe Railway came to New Mexico. The railroad linked New Mexico with the East. Large numbers of settlers from the East began to arrive. The newcomers

Latinos kept their traditions long after the U.S. takeover of New Mexico. Here *nuevomexicanos* watch the Corpus Christi procession, a religious celebration, in Santa Fe in 1895. What other Latino traditions do they carry on?

looked on the *nuevomexicanos* and their culture as strange and inferior.

The *nuevomexicanos* believed in progress, too. But for them, progress meant having enough land to farm and enough food to eat. They disliked the practices of the Easterners. Many of the *nuevomexicanos* withdrew to their farms and villages.

Nuevomexicanos and Easterners clash By the 1880s, the cattle business was booming in New Mexico. Easterners bought up or stole *nuevomexicano* lands for grazing their cattle. They put up barbed-wire fences to keep their cattle in and people out. *Nuevomexicanos* called the fences "the devil's hat band."

Some *nuevomexicanos* decided to fight back to protect their way of life. At night, groups of them would ride across the countryside. They cut fences, wrecked rail lines, and destroyed property. The most famous of these groups was **las Gorras Blancas**, or "the White Caps," after the masks they wore. In 1890, they ruined 9 miles (14.5 kilometers) of barbed wire in just one night.

Many *nuevomexicanos* saw *las Gorras Blancas* as heroes who were fighting for their land and homes. But to most Easterners, they were a lawless mob. The governor threatened to call out the army to halt the raids. *Las Gorras Blancas* gave up their raids and turned to politics.

Statehood As New Mexico's population grew, more and more people wanted it to become a state. Congress, however, refused to act. It argued that New Mexico had too few people. Congress also said New Mexico did not have enough development for statehood.

New Mexicans thought those arguments made no sense. Territories with far fewer people had been admitted as states. The truth was that Congress did not want to admit New Mexico while most of its people were Spanish-speaking Catholics of Mexican descent.

In 1910, Congress finally agreed to split New Mexico territory into two states, New Mexico and Arizona. First, however, the territories had to draw up state constitutions. The New Mexico convention met at Santa Fe in October 1910.

Larrazolo and the constitution
One of the delegates to the convention was Octaviano Larrazolo (lah-rrah-SOH-loh). Larrazolo was born in the Mexican state of Chihuahua (chih-WAH-wah). His family moved to New Mexico when he was 15. Larrazolo studied at college. He became a teacher, then a principal, and finally a lawyer. He was a brilliant speaker in both Spanish and English. After New Mexico became a state, he served as a governor and as a senator.

One-third of the 100 delegates to the constitutional convention were *nuevomexicanos*. They were led by Octaviano Larrazolo. They were determined that the new constitution would protect their rights, and they succeeded.

One of the constitution's articles protected *nuevomexicanos'* right to vote. The right of "children of Spanish descent" to "enjoy perfect equality with other children in all public schools" was also protected. Another part of the constitution made Spanish as well as English an official language.

On January 6, 1912, New Mexico became the 47th state of the union. Arizona was admitted as the 48th state just a few weeks later. However, the struggle for equality for *nuevomexicanos* was not yet over.

1. Who were *las Gorras Blancas*?
2. How did New Mexico's constitution protect the rights of *nuevomexicanos*?

CHAPTER 4
KEY IDEAS

- In 1898, the United States won control of Cuba and Puerto Rico.
- Thousands of Puerto Ricans moved to New York City in the early 1900s in search of a better life. Many became U.S. citizens after the Jones Act was passed.
- Many Cubans moved to Florida during the rebellion against Spanish rule in the 1870s.
- The United States occupied Cuba until 1902. After Cuba adopted the Platt Amendment, U.S. forces left the island nation.
- As more Easterners moved to New Mexico territory, they came into conflict with *nuevomexicanos*. In 1912, New Mexico territory was organized into the states of New Mexico and Arizona.

I. Reviewing Vocabulary
Match each word on the left with the correct definition on the right.

1. *barrio*
2. *bodega*
3. *nuevomexicano*
4. lector
5. *las Gorras Blancas*

a. Spanish-speaking residents of New Mexico
b. a section of a city where large numbers of Latinos live
c. a Latino protest movement in New Mexico
d. a grocery store
e. reader in a Cuban-American cigar factory

II. Understanding the Chapter
1. How did Puerto Rico become a U.S. possession?
2. Why did many Puerto Ricans move to the United States?
3. What industry did Cubans bring to Florida?
4. What was the role of the United States in bringing independence to Cuba?
5. What guarantees did the treaty between Mexico and the United States make *nuevomexicanos*?

III. Building Skills: Identifying Fact and Opinion
Read the statements below. On a separate piece of paper decide which statements are fact and which are opinion.
1. Many Puerto Ricans came to New York City after the Cuban-Spanish-American War.
2. *Bodegas* are the best kinds of grocery stores.
3. The workers of Ybor City had no right to strike because Ybor treated them well.
4. The Platt Amendment allowed the United States to rent a naval base in Cuba.
5. New Mexico's constitution guarantees certain rights to Spanish-speaking people.

IV. Writing About History
1. Imagine that you are a Cuban who has moved to Ybor City. Write a letter to your family in Cuba about your life in Ybor City.
2. **What Would You Have Done?** If you had been a *nuevomexicano* in the 1880s, would you have joined *las Gorras Blancas*? Why, or why not?

V. Working Together
1. Working with three or four other students, prepare a report on the kinds of foods that you would find in a *bodega* that would not be in most other U.S. grocery stores. Visit a *bodega* if there is one near you, and interview the owner. If there is not, do your research in the library. Report also on recipes made with these ingredients.
2. **Past to Present** Larrazolo was one of the first Latino governors in the United States. With a group, find out about Latino politicians today. List who they are, what job they fill, and what state they are from.

WORKERS FIGHT FOR IMPROVED CONDITIONS. (1886—1914)

How did workers manage to improve working conditions?

In 1911, the National Women's Trade Union League of America held their Convention of Congress in Kansas City. This organization united women from different trades and different social classes.

Looking at Key Terms

- Knights of Labor • American Federation of Labor (AFL)
- Japanese-Mexican Labor Association
- National Women's Trade Union League (NWTUL)
- International Ladies Garment Workers' Union (ILGWU)

Looking at Key Words

- **union:** a group of workers organized to protect their rights and improve work conditions
- **strike:** refusal to work until demands are met
- **general strike:** a strike of all workers in the same industry

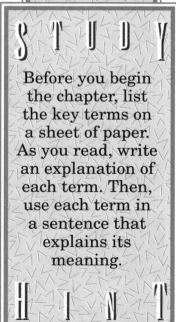

STUDY

Before you begin the chapter, list the key terms on a sheet of paper. As you read, write an explanation of each term. Then, use each term in a sentence that explains its meaning.

HINT

As you read in Chapter 1, U.S. industry had changed a great deal from the 1800s to the 1900s. Huge factories and assembly line production changed working conditions forever. These changes brought factory owners great profit. However, many of these changes made conditions worse for workers.

1 The Union Movement Grows Stronger.

How did labor unions help workers?

Workers had tried to form groups to improve working conditions during the early 1800s. A group of workers who

Women worked long hours under difficult conditions sewing garments in factories. Workers had no health or safety protection.

organize to protect their rights and improve work conditions is called a **union.** Early unions were not very successful, however. The first successful union was formed in 1869. It was called the **Knights of Labor.**

The Knights of Labor The Knights of Labor was the first nationwide labor union. It was also the first union that allowed women, immigrants, and African Americans to join. The Knights accepted skilled workers as well as unskilled workers. They worked to win equal pay for men and women and shorten the work day. However, the Knights did not believe in using **strikes.** A strike is a form of protest. During a strike, union members refuse to work until their demands are met.

At first, the Knights met in secret. They did this because factory owners fired employees who joined unions. Factory owners had no desire to pay workers more money or to shorten the work day. Later, the Knights ended their secrecy. Thousands joined the union. In 1886, however, the Haymarket Riot brought an end to the Knights' success.

The Haymarket Riot On May 3, union members staged a strike at their factory in Chicago. The Knights of Labor did not call for the strike. However, the strikers were members of the Knights. During the strike, the police shot four workers and wounded several others. The following day, thousands of union members gathered in Haymarket Square to protest.

As police tried to break up the gathering, someone threw a bomb into the crowd. Eight police officers were killed. More than 60 others were injured. Then, police shot into the crowd. A number of people were killed. Others were injured. The protest had turned into a riot.

The Haymarket Riot turned many people against the Knights of Labor.

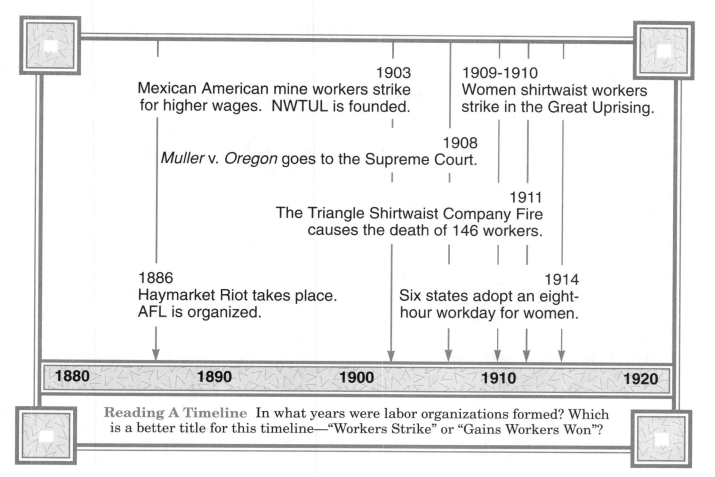

1903
Mexican American mine workers strike for higher wages. NWTUL is founded.

1909-1910
Women shirtwaist workers strike in the Great Uprising.

1908
Muller v. *Oregon* goes to the Supreme Court.

1911
The Triangle Shirtwaist Company Fire causes the death of 146 workers.

1886
Haymarket Riot takes place. AFL is organized.

1914
Six states adopt an eight-hour workday for women.

1880   1890   1900   1910   1920

Reading A Timeline In what years were labor organizations formed? Which is a better title for this timeline—"Workers Strike" or "Gains Workers Won"?

Membership in the Knights declined quickly. The popularity of other unions also suffered.

Samuel Gompers and the AFL
The **American Federation of Labor (AFL)** was founded in 1886 by Samuel Gompers. Gompers was a member of the cigar-makers' union. He wanted to organize all the unions of skilled laborers into one large organization.

Gompers contacted the unions for bricklayers, plumbers, carpenters, and other skilled trades. He did not include unskilled workers in his plan, however. Gompers felt that skilled workers were harder to replace than unskilled workers. Therefore, a strike of skilled workers would be very effective.

Gompers' main goals for the AFL included winning higher wages, better working conditions, and shorter hours

for workers. Gompers was president of the AFL from 1886 to 1924. Under his leadership, membership grew to about three million. Wages of skilled workers rose 25 percent. The work day was shortened to nine hours. Working conditions, however, remained poor.

The Women's Alliance While things got better for skilled workers, things stayed the same or got worse for unskilled workers. Certain skilled workers usually were not allowed to join skilled trade unions. Women, Latinos, and African Americans were often not allowed as members. Also, child labor was still a problem.

Elizabeth Morgan, a skilled factory worker, spoke out for women and children laborers. She organized an AFL union for women in 1888. Then, she brought together women from this union and other groups and formed the Illinois Women's Alliance.

The Women's Alliance began an investigation into Chicago's sweatshops. It found women and children working from 14 to 16 hours a day in filthy shops for very low wages. Morgan told government officials what she had found. In 1893, the Illinois government passed laws that improved sweatshop conditions. Other laws banned child labor and made an eight-hour workday for women.

1. Why did the membership of the Knights decline after 1886?
2. What gains did the AFL win for workers?

2 Many Workers Are Not Welcome in the Labor Movement.

What groups did not share in the gains won by unions?

Often, immigrants, women, African Americans, Latinos, and Asians faced discrimination at work. In addition, many were also rejected by the unions.

Mexican and Japanese Americans In the U.S. West, thousands of Mexican Americans worked on railroads, farms, and in factories. Often they were paid less for the same job than non-Latino workers.

In 1903, Mexican members of the United Mine Workers went on strike. They won a pay increase and an eight-

Workers often called strikes to protest poor working conditions and low wages. Here, New York garment workers carry strike signs in three languages.

hour day. That same year, Japanese and Mexican farm workers joined together to fight for better conditions. They formed the **Japanese-Mexican Labor Association.** It was the first time in California's history that two minority groups joined forces to create a union. The association used a strike to win better wages for farm workers.

Women organize Mary Kenney O'Sullivan was determined to do more for women workers. O'Sullivan had worked for the AFL in 1892. She unionized women garment workers, printers, textile workers, and shoemakers. After just five months, however, the AFL decided it could not pay her salary.

For the next ten years, O'Sullivan continued to organize women workers. On November 14, 1903, her dream came true. She founded the **National Women's Trade Union League (NWTUL).** This organization united women from different trades and different social classes.

Just a few years before the NWTUL, the **International Ladies Garment Worker's Union (ILGWU)** had been formed. This union organized men and women in the women's garment, or clothing, industry. In 1909, the ILGWU put together the biggest labor strike New York had ever seen. It was called the Great Uprising.

The Great Uprising The Triangle Shirtwaist Company in New York employed hundreds of women workers. When the company found that some women had joined unions, it fired them. In protest, the women went on strike. These women were joined by women workers in another shirtwaist, or blouse, factory.

The workers struck for two months. They were about to give up. Then, the ILGWU called for a **general strike,** or a strike of all workers in the same industry. Within 24 hours, nearly 30,000 garment workers joined the strike.

Strikers marched in front of their work places through the cold winter. They held signs declaring: "We Are Striking for Human Treatment." The ILGWU and the NWTUL supported the strikers with money and food. However, by February 1910, the ILGWU ran out of money. After 13 weeks, it had to call the strike off. The workers won higher wages but no union recognition. However, the strike did prove women to be loyal union members. A song the women sang put it this way:

In the black of the winter of nineteen nine,
When we froze and bled on the picket line,
We showed the world that women could fight
And we rose and won with women's might.

Triangle shirtwaist tragedy Just a year later, a tragedy occurred. On March 25, 1911, New Yorkers heard a great explosion from the Triangle Shirtwaist Company. The company was located on the top three floors of a ten-story building. It was on fire!

A crowd watched as smoke and flames poured out from the building. Then, they saw dark packages falling from the windows. At first, people thought these were batches of cloth. But with horror, they realized that the bundles were young women. The women were jumping to try to save themselves.

A total of 146 of the company's 500 workers died in the fire. Later it was revealed that the factory owners were at fault for the workers' deaths. They had kept the doors of the factory locked. The owners wanted to stop the workers from

Bodies of some of the 146 young women workers killed in a tragic fire at the Triangle Shirtwaist Factory lay on the sidewalk. Many jumped from the burning building. The horrors of the fire brought about improved working conditions for working women.

taking breaks. When the fire broke out, many workers were trapped. Those who did not jump burned to death.

1. How did Mexican and Japanese workers cooperate to win better wages?
2. What organization did Mary Kenney O'Sullivan found?

3 Workers Succeed in Improving Working Conditions.

What laws were passed to benefit workers?

The Triangle Shirtwaist Fire proved that many factory owners did not care about their workers. People were out-raged. They called for action. Soon after the fire, New York State set up the Factory Investigating Commission. One of the investigators was a woman named Frances Perkins.

Frances Perkins At a time when few women went beyond elementary school, Perkins had received several college degrees. She devoted her life to improving conditions for the poor.

Perkins had witnessed the Triangle Fire. As a member of the Factory Investigating Commission, she spent four years checking factories. Members of the commission were shocked by what they found. They saw children as young as five cutting vegetables with sharp knives. They saw dangerous machinery that could "cut off a man's arm." Commission members climbed down ice-covered fire escapes that ended 12 feet above ground.

Based on the commission's report, New York State passed laws to improve working conditions for women and children. New laws limited the work week to 54 hours.

Going to court   The commissions, unions, and strikes helped workers win new rights during the early 1900s. Another way workers were able to win rights was in court. In court, judges decided on a number of labor issues.

In 1908, two reformers, Florence Kelley and Josephine Goldmark brought a labor case to the Supreme Court. The case concerned an Oregon law that limited women's workdays to ten hours. Factory owners said this law was unjust. They believed workers and factory owners should be allowed to set the length of the workday. Kelley, Goldmark, and others said that factory owners only wanted to force women to work long hours.

Kelley and Goldmark convinced Louis Brandeis (BRAND-eyes) to represent women workers in the case. Brandeis was a well-known lawyer. In the case, called *Muller* v. *Oregon*, Brandeis convinced the Supreme Court that longer hours were harmful to women. The Court ruled in favor of limiting women's workday to ten hours.

More laws   Workers were encouraged by the result of *Muller* v. *Oregon*. A Chicago union of waitresses fought for improved conditions in 1909. Elizabeth Maloney led the fight. The union called for an eight-hour workday. They put their suggestion before the Illinois state government. The union's plan was called "the Girls Bill."

"The Girls Bill" sparked a heated debate. In the end, the union had to compromise. It got its bill passed into law by agreeing to a ten-hour workday. However, the NWTUL began a nationwide drive for the eight-hour workday. By 1914, six states had adopted it.

1. What did the Factory Investigating Commission find in New York City factories?
2. What issue did *Muller* v. *Oregon* bring to the Supreme Court?

CHAPTER 5
KEY IDEAS

- In the early 1900s, labor unions grew stronger and achieved many gains for their members.
- Many unions did not allow women, African Americans, Latinos, or Japanese Americans to join. These groups formed their own unions to fight for better working conditions.
- Labor unions worked to pass many laws. These laws improved working conditions for all workers, including women and children.

I. Reviewing Vocabulary

Match each word on the left with the correct definition on the right.

1. Knights of Labor
2. union
3. strike
4. general strike
5. AFL

   a. a refusal to work until demands are met
   b. a group that organized trade unions of skilled laborers
   c. a union of skilled and unskilled workers that also accepted women, immigrants, and African Americans
   d. a group of workers organized to protect their rights and improve work conditions
   e. a strike of all workers in the same industry

II. Understanding the Chapter

1. What risks did workers take by joining a union?
2. Why did Samuel Gompers include only skilled laborers in his organization?
3. How did the Women's Alliance affect labor laws in Illinois?
4. What gains did shirtwaist workers win as a result of the Great Uprising?
5. How did each of the following ways help workers gain rights: unions, strikes, commissions, and courts?

III. Building Skills: Expressing Your Opinion

Agree or disagree with the statements listed below. Explain your opinion in a written paragraph.

1. Parents should decide whether or not their children should work, not the government.
2. It is wrong for the government to limit the number of hours people may work.
3. The government should inspect every factory to see how workers are treated.

IV. Writing About History

1. **What Would You Have Done?** Imagine that you are working in a sweatshop and are asked to join a union. The conditions in the shop are terrible. However, if you join the union you may lose your job. In addition, your family depends on the money you earn. Would you join the union or not? Explain your feelings in a letter.
2. Imagine that you are a member of a commission that inspects factories. Write a report that describes what you have seen and what laws you think the government should make to protect workers.

V. Working Together

1. Work with two or three classmates. Think of a school rule or program that you think needs improvement. Write a plan of action to change the rule or program. Write up this plan and present it to your classmates.
2. **Past to Present** With a small group of classmates, look through recent newspapers to find an article about a union. Then, prepare an oral report that summarizes what the article says about the union.

REFORMERS WORK TO IMPROVE AMERICAN LIFE. (1876–1920)

How did reformers bring about change in American life?

Parades drew attention to the issue of voting rights for women. Women renewed their struggle for equal rights during the 1890s.

Looking at Key Terms

- muckrakers • Progressives • Sherman Anti-Trust Act

Looking at Key Words

- **bribery:** making illegal payments to officials
- **primary election:** an election that lets voters choose their party's candidates for office
- **recall:** a special election that allows voters to remove an elected official from office

- **trust:** a group of corporations managed by a single board of directors
- **conservation:** preservation of natural resources
- **suffrage:** the right to vote

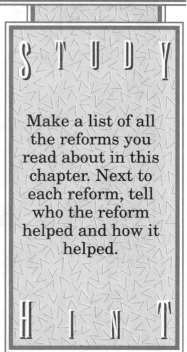

STUDY

Make a list of all the reforms you read about in this chapter. Next to each reform, tell who the reform helped and how it helped.

HINT

A huge reform movement swept the country as the 20th century began. Reformers, or people who worked for change, brought many of America's problems to public attention. Women played leading roles in the reform movement. At the same time, however, women were fighting for greater equality.

1 Reforms Are Needed.

Who were the Progressives, and what problems did they find in society?

Imagine that you are living in 1900. You are hopeful as the 20th century begins. You are a person who believes in progress. For you, life in the United States has never been better.

But all around you see problems. Poor people live in slums. Garbage flows in the streets. Drunks lie in doorways. Children as young as ten work in mines and factories.

A rear tenement bedroom shows the miserable living conditions of many poor people. A room like this was often the only space a family had to live in.

Muckrakers Such problems were real. New magazines brought such problems to people's attention. They printed articles that exposed serious problems. The writers had plenty of targets. Ida Tarbell wrote about the evils of big business. Lincoln Steffens discussed corrupt city governments. Upton Sinclair told of diseased meat being sold to consumers. (See Chapter 1.)

President Theodore Roosevelt gave a name to writers who exposed society's problems. He called them **muckrakers.** They were stirring up the muck, or dirt, beneath the surface.

The muckrakers wanted to stir their readers to action. Print the facts, they thought. Get the people to understand the problems. Then let the people attack the problems. In a democracy, after all, the people can change things.

Progressives Those who joined the crusade to improve the United States were called **Progressives.** They believed that problems like poverty and misery were not just problems of individuals. They were problems of all Americans. So government action was part of the cure.

In some ways the Progressives were like earlier reformers. However, the Progressives tended to come from cities rather than rural areas. Most were from the middle class. Most were white and Protestant. They had a strong religious faith. They believed that they knew what was right for other people.

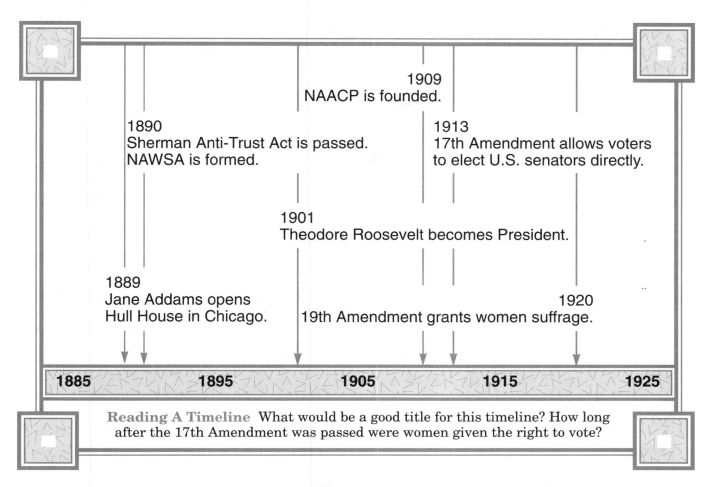

1909
NAACP is founded.

1890
Sherman Anti-Trust Act is passed.
NAWSA is formed.

1913
17th Amendment allows voters
to elect U.S. senators directly.

1901
Theodore Roosevelt becomes President.

1889
Jane Addams opens
Hull House in Chicago.

1920
19th Amendment grants women suffrage.

| 1885 | 1895 | 1905 | 1915 | 1925 |

Reading A Timeline What would be a good title for this timeline? How long after the 17th Amendment was passed were women given the right to vote?

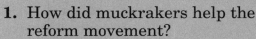

1. How did muckrakers help the reform movement?
2. What problems did Progressives hope to solve?

2 Reformers Work to Improve Society.

How did the Progressive movement try to improve society?

The Progressives attacked problems with great energy. They tried to make government more democratic. They wanted to control big business.

Fighting corruption Muckraker Lincoln Steffens exposed corruption in city after city. In St. Louis, he told how **bribery,** or making illegal payments to officials, was a way of life. If you wanted a new sign, you had to bribe someone to get a permit. If you wanted the city government to pass a bill, you had to pay the right people. "Nothing was passed free of charge," Steffens wrote.

The Progressives struggled to vote corrupt politicians out. They supported "good government" candidates in local and state elections. Progressives elected Tom Johnson mayor of Cleveland. He swept out corruption. Robert "Battling Bob" La Follette served many years as Progressive governor of Wisconsin.

Government reforms Progressives introduced new methods to give people a greater say in government. These methods are still in use today in many states.

An initiative allows voters to pass laws directly. If enough people sign a petition, or written request, the law is put to a vote. A referendum allows voters to strike down a law they think is wrong.

Other Progressive reforms include the **recall** and the **primary election.** The recall is an election that allows voters to remove an elected official from office. The primary is an election that allows voters to choose their party's candidates for office. Before, only party leaders would choose the candidates.

Progressives also changed the way U.S. senators gained office. The old way was for state legislators to name senators to office. In 1913, the 17th Amendment to the U.S. Constitution allowed voters to elect senators directly.

Trust busting The Progressives wanted the people to have a say in the economy, too. They worried that large corporations were becoming too powerful. If left unchecked, giant **trusts** might end up with too much money and power. A trust is a group of corporations managed by a single board of directors.

Theodore Roosevelt was the first Progressive President. He was in office from 1901 to 1909. Roosevelt became known as a *trust buster.* He took action to break up giant trusts. Roosevelt did not oppose big business in general. He was only against "bad" trusts. Such companies forced competitors out of business or charged people too much.

Efforts to control big business began in the 1880s. In 1887, Congress set up a commission to control railroads. Congress tried to stop businesses from becoming too big. The **Sherman Anti-Trust Act** of 1890 banned monopolies and trusts. Such laws were weak.

Progressives supported stronger measures. Under Roosevelt, Congress tightened the control of railroads. It passed laws to make sure that food products like meat and milk were safe.

Conservation Roosevelt pushed for another Progressive goal—preserving natural resources, or **conservation.** Roosevelt loved the great outdoors. He urged Congress to protect trees on millions of acres of federal lands. Loggers, or tree cutters, would no longer be allowed to cut them.

Protecting workers The Progressives also won new protections for workers. Massachusetts was the first state to adopt a minimum-wage law. Maryland was the first state to adopt a workers' compensation law. The law required employers to pay into a fund. The fund paid workers who were hurt on the job.

Progressives won a victory in 1916 when Congress outlawed child labor. But the Supreme Court later threw out the law. The Court said it unfairly denied children the right to hold a job.

Other Progressive goals One group of middle-class reformers moved into poor sections of cities. They started neighborhood centers called settlement houses. Centers offered many services. Working women could drop off children. Young people could play sports. Immigrants could learn English.

Jane Addams ran one of the most famous settlements. Started in 1889 in Chicago, it was called Hull House. Addams tried to improve the lives of her neighbors. When she noticed that rotting garbage was not being collected, she complained to the city. The mayor named her garbage inspector for the district. Addams got up before dawn to follow the garbage wagons. She also organized the neighborhood to fight for better housing and parks.

Progressives and African Americans Most Progressives paid little attention to African Americans. But African Americans also wanted reforms. Most of all they wanted a federal law against lynching. Lynching is when a mob murders someone accused

In the 1900s, new job opportunities opened for women. Here African American women are learning clerical skills at the National Training School for Women and Girls. What types of jobs might these women be training for?

of a crime before he or she has been brought to trial. White mobs lynched many African Americans in the late 1800s and early 1900s.

In 1909, African Americans formed the National Association for the Advancement of Colored People (NAACP). The NAACP went to court to help African Americans who were treated unfairly. It won many cases. But it did not get an anti-lynching law.

1. How did Progressives try to control big business?
2. What services did settlement houses offer?

3 The Women's Movement Works for Change.

How did opportunities for women increase in the early 1900s?

The women's movement gained new energy during the Progressive period. Most women still identified themselves mainly as homemakers and mothers. But more and more women were taking jobs outside the home.

New kinds of jobs By 1900, two inventions had opened new jobs for women. One was the telephone. The other was the typewriter. Thousands of women became switchboard operators or office secretaries.

Meanwhile, women continued to find jobs in factories and schools. Many became maids or cooks in other people's homes. African American and immigrant women were most likely to take such jobs. Few other jobs were open to them. Between 1890 and 1910, the number of working women jumped from 3.7 million to 7.6 million.

A few women managed to enter professions. By 1900, the nation had about 1,000 female lawyers and 7,000 female doctors. One of the lawyers was Belva Ann Bennett Lockwood. In 1906, at the age of 76, she appeared before the Supreme Court. She won her case on behalf of Cherokee Native Americans.

Winning more rights The drive to expand women's rights went on. By 1917, many states had dropped laws that limited the rights of married women. Illinois allowed wives to keep their own earnings. It also permitted women to serve on school boards.

In a few places, women were allowed to vote in school elections. However, before 1900, only four states let women vote in all elections. They were Wyoming, Utah, Colorado, and Idaho.

The women's suffrage movement The right to vote is called **suffrage.** The campaign for women's suffrage began in the 1840s. But it really began making progress after 1890. Earlier, many women believed that the demand for suffrage was too extreme. However, as women took on new roles in society, more wanted the right to vote.

In 1890, the National American Women's Suffrage Association (NAWSA) was founded. Its leaders included two women who had been fighting for women's suffrage since the 1850s. One was Elizabeth Cady Stanton. The other was Susan B. Anthony. Both were growing old. In 1900, a younger woman, Carrie Chapman Catt, took over. She became leader of the suffragists, as supporters of women's suffrage were called.

Under Catt, the suffragists' goal was an amendment to the U.S. Constitution that would allow all women to vote. However, a long struggle seemed likely. So as a first step, the suffragists fought

Reading a Map. What state was the first to give women the right to vote? In what section of the U.S. were women granted suffrage by 1919? What states had no statewide suffrage by 1919? What was the voting status of women in Texas?

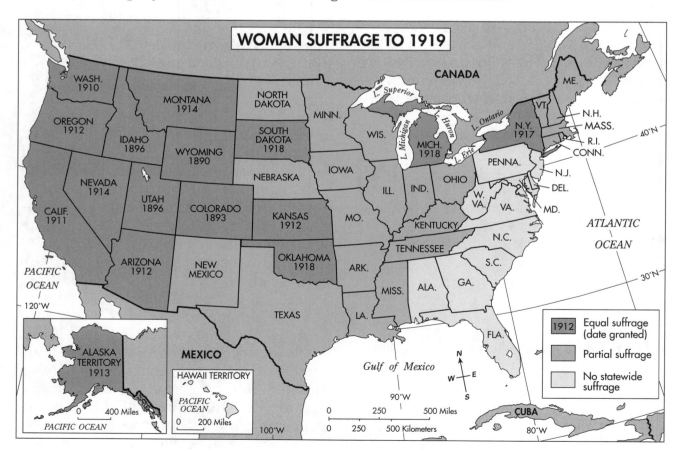

WOMAN SUFFRAGE TO 1919

to amend state constitutions. By 1915, women had won the right to vote in seven more states.

Getting attention   A young Quaker named Alice Paul wanted to draw attention to the suffragists and their goals. She staged parades in the nation's capital. Her methods were too strong for Catt and other NAWSA leaders. So Paul and her supporters started their own suffrage group.

Paul's group stood outside the White House day after day, asking for women's suffrage. The President, Woodrow Wilson, ignored them. When the United States entered World War I in 1917, the women kept protesting.

Some people thought the women were unpatriotic. Bystanders attacked them. Police arrested hundreds of women for "blocking the sidewalk." In jail, Alice Paul went on a hunger strike.

The 19th Amendment   The public attention helped the woman suffrage movement. Catt urged women to help the war effort. She appealed to people's sense of fair play. Did it make sense for the nation to deny women the vote when female nurses were risking their lives on the battlefronts? Such arguments won over many people—including President Wilson.

In 1919, at Wilson's urging, Congress approved an amendment for women's suffrage. The 19th Amendment went into effect in 1920. After more than 70 years of struggle, women had won the right to vote.

1. What sorts of jobs did women hold in the early 1900s?
2. How did the methods used by Carrie Chapman Catt and Alice Paul differ?

CHAPTER 6
KEY IDEAS

- In the early 1900s, Progressives began to look for ways to solve the problems of society.
- Progressives fought government corruption by supporting candidates who wanted reform. They gave people more say in government.
- Progressives tried to limit the power of big business by outlawing monopolies and trusts.
- During the 1900s, women gained new opportunities at work. They also increased their efforts to gain the right to vote. In 1920, women won a Constitutional amendment granting them suffrage.

I. Reviewing Vocabulary

Match each word on the left with the correct definition on the right.

1. conservation
2. suffrage
3. bribery
4. recall
5. primary election

   a. the right to vote
   b. making illegal payments to officials
   c. a special election that allows voters to remove an elected official
   d. preservation of natural resources
   e. an election that lets voters choose their party's candidates for office

II. Understanding the Chapter

1. What problems did the muckrakers write about?
2. Describe three reforms that Progressives used to reform government.
3. What type of trusts did President Roosevelt try to break up?
4. What role did African Americans play in the Progressive era?
5. How did suffragists win the right to vote for women?

III. Building Skills: Analyzing a Map

Study the map on page 52. Then, answer the questions below.

1. In what year did California allow equal suffrage?
2. In which region of the United States were most of the states that granted no suffrage before 1920?
3. In which region of the country were most of the states that granted equal suffrage before 1920?

IV. Writing About History

1. Imagine that you are a muckraking journalist today. Think of a problem in your community that you would like to solve. Then, write an article describing the problem and suggesting solutions.
2. **What Would You Have Done?** Suppose you were a man living in the early 1900s. Would you support or oppose woman suffrage? Why?

V. Working Together

1. Form a group with two or three classmates. Together, write the script for a brief "television documentary" about one of the people described in the chapter. What did the person do to bring about change? Was the person successful? Perform your documentary for the class.
2. **Past to Present** With a group of classmates, research to find out if your state uses any of the government reforms described on pages 49 to 50. Create a poster that describes the reforms your state uses and when it began using each reform.

Unit 2
Becoming a World Power
(1900-1920s)

Chapters

7 The United States Is a Power in the Pacific.
8 The United States Controls Cuba and Puerto Rico.
9 The United States Is Involved in Latin America.
10 The United States Fights World War I.

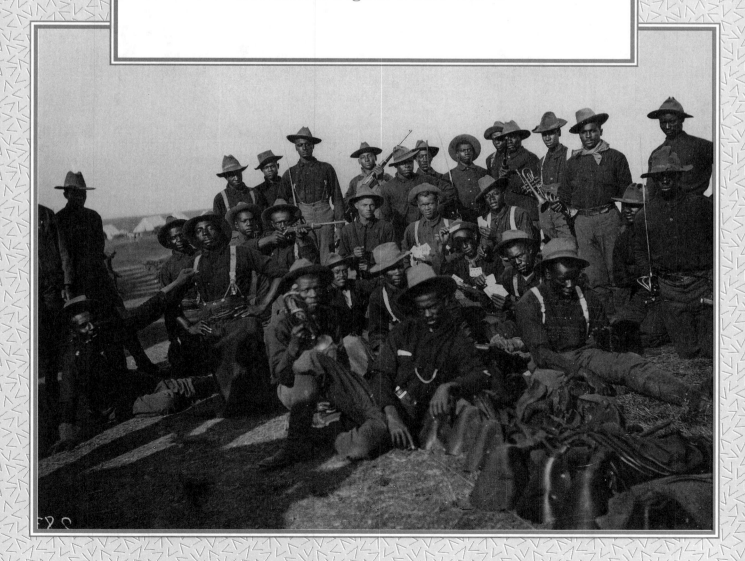

THE UNITED STATES IS A POWER IN THE PACIFIC. (1897—1914)

Why did the United States expand into the Pacific?

Emilio Aguinaldo led Filipinos in the fight for independence from Spain and then the United States. He held off the United States Army for four years.

Looking at Key Terms

- Open Door Policy • Gentleman's Agreement

Looking at Key Words

- **colonialism:** taking over of foreign countries as colonies
- **imperialism:** building of empires

- **compromise:** an agreement that gives each side part of what it wants

S T U D Y

Make a timeline with the dates 1897 and 1914 on each end. As you finish a section, list the important events on the timeline.

H I N T

What happened in the Philippines in 1898 changed U.S. history. Before that year, the United States owned little land beyond its borders. After 1898, the United States owned many islands in the Pacific. The nation also became involved in eastern Asia. By 1900, the United States was a world power.

1 The Philippines Resist.

Why did Filipinos object to U.S. control of their islands?

The Philippines is an island nation in Asia. Its 7,000 islands are in the Pacific Ocean about 500 miles (800 km) east of China and Vietnam. Almost 19 out of every 20 Filipinos live on the 11 largest islands. About one-half of them live on the largest island of Luzon (LOO-zon).

In 1721, Ferdinand Magellan claimed the islands for Spain. About 50 years later, the Spanish built the capital city of Manila. In the years that followed, Spain took over the rest of the islands.

Fighting the Spanish In the 1890s, a movement for independence from Spain began in the Philippines. By 1897, a young Filipino named Emilio Aguinaldo (ah-gwee-NAHL-doh) became the leader of this fight. Aguinaldo and his small army were a threat to Spanish rule. The Spanish government was then fighting a war in Cuba. (See page 35.) It did not want to fight another war in the Philippines. Spain forced Aguinaldo to leave the country.

Aguinaldo did not give up. He went to Hong Kong. There he started shopping for weapons. When there was another chance to fight for Philippine independence, he wanted to be ready.

In April 1898, the United States declared war on Spain. On the first day of May, ships from the U.S. Navy arrived in Manila Bay, near the Philippine capital. They were led by Admiral George Dewey. The Americans quickly sank every one of the Spanish ships. Then guns on shore began firing at the American ships. Dewey threatened to flatten the city unless it stopped. The firing stopped.

Neither Dewey nor anyone in the U.S. government was sure what to do next. Should the United States take control of the Philippines from Spain? Many people favored such a move. It seemed like an important step in the growth of U.S. power. Many others argued that the United States had once fought to free itself. **Colonialism,** or the taking over of foreign countries as colonies, would go against everything the United States stood for.

Although Dewey's ships controlled Manila harbor, he did not have the troops to capture the city. While he waited for soldiers to arrive from the United States, he sent weapons to Aguinaldo and his band. The freedom fighters prepared to attack Manila.

Taking over the Philippines Two months later, U.S. forces landed in the Philippines. The Spanish position was hopeless. Dewey's warships cut off escape by sea. Aguinaldo's army surrounded the city. The U.S. troops were ready to attack. Manila surrendered on August 13, 1898. A treaty ended the Cuban-Spanish-American War.

According to the U.S. government, Filipinos were not ready to govern themselves. So the United States took over the Philippines. The U.S. government had chosen colonialism.

Beginning in 1899, the United States sent more and more troops to the Philippines. In 1900, a civilian governor, William Howard Taft, took over. He cooperated with the Filipinos. He included some Filipinos in the new gov-

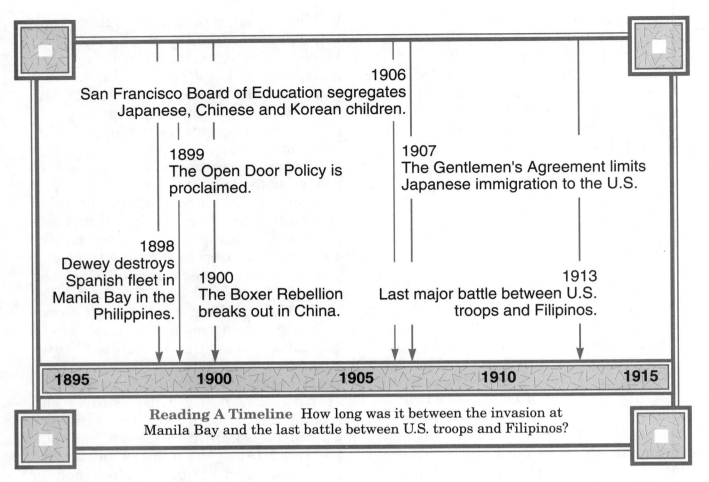

1906
San Francisco Board of Education segregates Japanese, Chinese and Korean children.

1899
The Open Door Policy is proclaimed.

1907
The Gentlemen's Agreement limits Japanese immigration to the U.S.

1898
Dewey destroys Spanish fleet in Manila Bay in the Philippines.

1900
The Boxer Rebellion breaks out in China.

1913
Last major battle between U.S. troops and Filipinos.

| 1895 | 1900 | 1905 | 1910 | 1915 |

Reading A Timeline How long was it between the invasion at Manila Bay and the last battle between U.S. troops and Filipinos?

ernment. But control of the Filipino people was not that easy. It turned out to be harder than defeating the Spanish.

Fighting the United States Throughout this period, Aguinaldo's army continued its battle for independence. 70,000 U.S. troops fought against Aguinaldo. It took 175 million dollars and three years to defeat him.

Aguinaldo's headquarters were based in the mountains of the island of Luzon. They were far from the capital of Manila. The enemy—the U.S. army—was located in that city. A small squad of troops protected Aguinaldo. Maybe, though, there were not enough of them, he thought. He wrote an order asking for 400 more soldiers. A messenger went off with the order.

In March 1902, Aguinaldo learned that some Filipino troops were nearby.

He thought the troops were the soldiers he requested. They were not. They had brought five American prisoners with them. The Filipino commander went to Aguinaldo's office. Then Aguinaldo heard shooting outside. He thought his troops were celebrating. But the shooting came from the visiting troops. The commander shot two of Aguinaldo's lieutenants and arrested the rebel leader.

How had this happened? U.S. troops had captured Aguinaldo's messenger. A U.S. Army officer thought of this plan to capture Aguinaldo. His arrest ended the most serious threat to U.S. control of the Philippines.

Under U.S. control The war had taken the lives of an estimated 200,000 Filipino civilians and 20,000 Filipino soldiers. 4,234 U.S. soldiers also died. On July 4, 1902, President Theodore

Roosevelt announced that the fighting was over. However, smaller groups continued to fight until as late as 1913. It was not until 1946 that the Philippines became a free nation.

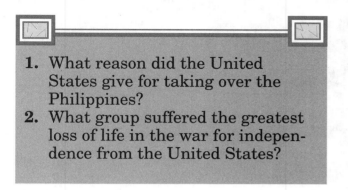

1. What reason did the United States give for taking over the Philippines?
2. What group suffered the greatest loss of life in the war for independence from the United States?

2 The United States Competes in Asia.

How did the United States become a major force in east Asia?

In the late 1800s, the Japanese emperor wanted to make his country stronger. So he decided to copy the European nations. Japan changed its government. It quickly built up its industries. Soon it was a military power equal to European countries.

Japan first showed the world its new power in 1894–95. It easily defeated China in a war over control of Korea. In the peace treaty, Japan took Korea and some of China.

Reading a Map. What lands in the Pacific were U.S. possessions by 1914? What four islands were acquired in 1898 by the United States? What countries are closest to the Philippines? What American island is farthest south?

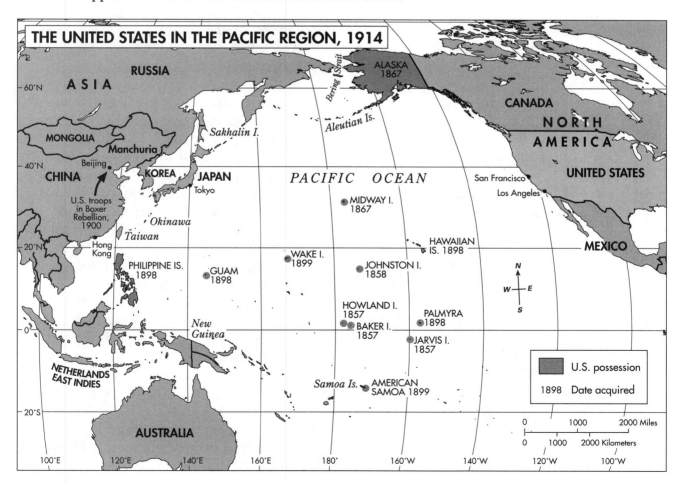

THE UNITED STATES IN THE PACIFIC REGION, 1914

After foreigners divided China into spheres of influence, a secret group called "Boxers" worked to force them out of China. During this uprising, many foreigners were killed. The United States and Europe sent troops in to suppress the rebellion.

The Japanese action upset the powerful countries of Europe. European countries made a lot of money trading in China. They wanted pieces of China for themselves. By 1900, France, Russia, Germany, and Italy, as well as Japan had control of areas of China. Because these areas were still part of China, they were called "spheres of influence." They were a first step in dividing up China. This was **imperialism**—building empires to control trade. Many European countries practiced imperialism.

The United States did not want China divided. It wanted Chinese ports to be open to all countries for trade. The U.S. government also wanted to protect its new possessions in the Pacific. It feared that the European nations would want more than pieces of China. The European powers might try to take the Philippines and other U.S. islands.

The Open Door policy   In 1899 Secretary of State John Hay announced the **Open Door** policy. He asked for a guarantee. He wanted all nations to have equal trading rights throughout China. By 1900, most of the European powers agreed.

Later that year, the Open Door policy took on a new meaning. Some Chinese formed a secret military group. The Chinese name for the group meant "fist." Europeans nicknamed members of the group "Boxers." The Boxers were angry. They did not like what foreigners were doing to their country. They wanted to force all foreigners out of China. In the spring of 1900, the Boxers attacked. They killed about 300 foreigners. Many other foreigners fled to Beijing. They locked themselves in a British government building.

Several countries, including the United States, sent an army to rescue them. Secretary of State Hay was afraid that the other countries would use their troops to divide China further. He said that the purpose of the army was to keep China together. The other countries had to agree. So for the next 30 years, China remained weak. However, it was in one piece.

A grateful China Because of these actions, many Chinese saw the United States as their friend. The Chinese government sent thousands of students to U.S. colleges. These students helped to build greater understanding between the two countries. Americans took a new interest in China. Over the next 40 years, thousands of them moved to China. They brought medical help and care. Some also wanted the Chinese to become Christians.

Japan and the United States The United States was friendly toward China. But it was uneasy with Japan. Japan was increasing its military and economic power. In 1904, Japan challenged Russia. Russia had pushed into Korea and northern China. Japan wanted the same territory. So Japan declared war. In a little over a year, its army drove Russia from Korea and China. Meanwhile a large Russian fleet was sailing halfway around the world to attack Japan. It arrived in May 1905. The Japanese Navy wiped it out in one battle. Japan had defeated a major European power in battle!

The U.S. government was concerned about the war. The war was fought in China. That threatened U.S. trading interests. It also went against the Open Door policy.

President Theodore Roosevelt offered to help end the war. The offer was accepted. Officials from Japan and Russia traveled to Portsmouth, New Hampshire. They met with the President. In September 1905, a peace treaty was signed at Portsmouth. In 1906, Theodore Roosevelt received the Nobel Peace Prize for ending the war.

The treaty was a success for the United States. It kept the Open Door policy alive. No nation had control of China. Americans could still trade in eastern Asia and the Pacific. The United States was becoming more and more powerful in the eastern Pacific.

1. How did the Open Door policy protect China?
2. Why was the United States uneasy with Japan?

3 Racism Grows in the United States.

Why did the U.S. government limit immigration from Asia?

Roosevelt admired the Japanese. However, many Americans did not

In 1907 in San Francisco, a Japanese American boy is denied permission to enter school. Japanese, Chinese, and Koreans were all forced into segregated schools.

share his feelings. Japanese immigrants had settled in California. Dislike of the Japanese was strong there.

Segregation   In 1906, an incident in San Francisco brought these feelings to the attention of the whole country. In San Francisco, the children of Chinese immigrants had to go to segregated schools. In September of that year, the school board ordered all children of Japanese and Korean immigrants to attend the same segregated schools.

Japanese parents protested. When the board paid no attention, some parents wrote to newspapers in Japan. The Japanese government saw the papers. It did not like the way its citizens' children were being treated.

President Roosevelt called the school board's action "wicked." He ordered the federal government to sue the school district. He learned, however, that many Californians supported the school district. Large numbers of them were very loud in their support.

A Gentlemen's Agreement   Roosevelt had to quiet these people and satisfy the Japanese government. So he made a **compromise.** That is an agreement that gives each side part of what it wants. The school board had to back down. Then, he stopped Japanese immigrants from entering the United States from Canada, Mexico, and Hawaii. Next, he reached a quiet **"Gentlemen's Agreement"** with the Japanese government. It would not allow Japanese laborers to leave for the United States. These policies reduced the number of Japanese immigrants. In the interest of peace, the United States closed its gates to Asian immigrants.

1. What did the San Francisco school board force Japanese students to do in 1906?
2. What compromise did Roosevelt make with Japan?

CHAPTER 7
KEY IDEAS

- The United States had acquired the Philippines after the Cuban-Spanish-American War.
- By 1900, the United States became a major force in east Asia. The Open Door policy allowed China to remain a nation. Theodore Roosevelt persuaded Russia and Japan to end their war.
- Prejudice against Japanese immigrants grew in the United States. President Roosevelt created the Gentlemen's Agreement with Japan to reduce immigration.

REVIEWING CHAPTER 7

I. Reviewing Vocabulary

Match each word on the left with the correct definition on the right.

1. Open Door Policy
2. compromise
3. imperialism
4. colonialism
5. Gentleman's Agreement

   a. an agreement that gives each side part of what it wants

   b. taking over of foreign countries as colonies

   c. restricted Japanese immigration to the United States

   d. U.S. policy that trade with China be open to all nations

   e. building of empires

II. Understanding the Chapter

1. What cause did Emilio Aguinaldo fight for?
2. Why did the United States take control of the Philippines?
3. What events led to the United States declaration of the Open Door policy?
4. What was the U.S. role in the Boxer Rebellion?
5. What was the attitude of many Californians toward immigrants from Japan?

III. Building Skills: Understanding Cause and Effect

Tell whether each phrase below is a cause or an effect.

1. Spanish-American War ends; United States takes over the Philippines.
2. Boxer Rebellion begins; European nations carve up China into spheres of influence.
3. Japan and Russia sign a peace treaty; Open Door Policy is declared.

IV. Writing About History

1. **What Would You Have Done?** If you had been an advisor to the President of the United States, how would you have advised him to deal with Emilio Aguinaldo? Explain.
2. Imagine that you are a Japanese parent in 1906. Write a letter to a newspaper in Japan telling about the San Francisco school board's actions.

V. Working Together

1. With a group, prepare a wall map of east Asia in 1900, including China, Japan, and the Philippines. Show which neighboring countries were independent and which were colonies. Within China, show the spheres of influence of Great Britain, France, Germany, Russia, Japan, and Italy.
2. **Past to Present** Beginning in the 1890s, the United States involved itself in the affairs of foreign countries. With a group, discuss times that the United States has involved itself in other countries' affairs today. List those times and the reasons why.

THE UNITED STATES CONTROLS CUBA AND PUERTO RICO. (1898–1920s)

How did U.S. control of Cuba and Puerto Rico affect the people of these islands?

U.S. forces were rescued from this fort in Cuba by African American troops in the 24th and 25th U.S. Infantry, during the Cuban-Spanish-American war.

Looking at Key Terms

- Platt Amendment • Foraker Act • Jones Act

Looking at Key Words

- **protectorate:** a weak country that is under the control of a stronger country

- **cultural imperialism:** the desire to replace the culture of a colony with that of the ruling country

On December 10, 1898, Spain and the United States signed a peace treaty ending the Cuban-Spanish-American War. Under the terms of the treaty, Cuba gained its freedom from Spain. Puerto Rico, the Philippines, and the Pacific islands of Guam and Wake were turned over to the United States. In exchange, the United States paid Spain 20 million dollars.

Many people worried about the U.S. victory. They wondered if the United States would let Cuba and Puerto Rico become independent countries.

1 The United States Controls Cuba

How did the United States control Cuba in the early 1900s?

The Cuban-Spanish-American War of 1898 left the United States in control of Cuba. (See page 35.) The first thing that the United States did in Cuba was set up a military government. It ruled the country. The goals of this government were to improve living conditions in Cuba and to make Cuba ready for independence. General Leonard Wood was the head of this government. Under his leadership, employment rose and education improved. New roads, bridges, and sewer systems were built.

By 1900, Cuba was worn out by years of warfare. 200,000 fewer people lived in Cuba than five years earlier. The greatest problem was the deadly disease yellow fever or "yellow jack." Each year the disease killed thousands of people in Cuba and other tropical countries. In the Cuban-Spanish-American War, many more U.S. soldiers died of yellow fever than died in battle.

A cure for yellow jack A Cuban doctor, Carlos Juan Finlay, found the key to the disease. As early as 1881, he said that yellow fever was spread by mosqui-

toes. Scientists in both the United States and Cuba rejected his idea. In 1900, however, army doctor Walter Reed and his team decided to test Finlay's idea. Finlay gave Reed some mosquito eggs. Reed grew mosquitoes from them. These mosquitoes were then allowed to bite soldiers who had volunteered for the experiment. Every one of the soldiers came down with yellow fever.

Now there was proof that mosquitoes caused yellow fever. A push to wipe out the dangerous mosquito began. Thanks to Finlay's and Reed's pioneering work, the terror of yellow fever was ended.

Meanwhile, Cubans wanted to end U.S. occupation. They continued to press for full independence. In 1902, U.S. troops finally pulled out. The United States, however, was not willing to give up all of its power in Cuba.

A U.S. protectorate Cubans knew that they needed a system for self-government. So they wrote a constitution. The United States insisted that the new constitution give certain rights to the United States. These U.S. rights were spelled out in the **Platt Amendment.** It became part of the Cuban constitution. Under the Platt Amendment, the United States could send its army into Cuba to keep order. It also gave the United States the right to establish a navy base in Cuba.

The Platt Amendment made Cuba a **protectorate** of the United States. A protectorate is a weak country that is under the control of a stronger country. Many Cubans were unhappy with the Platt Amendment. However, they accepted it as the price of independence. On May 20, 1902, Cuba's first president took office.

The new president was a member of the Moderate party. The Liberal party opposed him. In 1906, the Liberals rebelled. The president asked the

United States for help. The United States sent in troops and set up a temporary government. This temporary government lasted until 1909. Then Cuba returned to Cuban control.

A second Cuban republic was established in 1909. José Miguel Gómez, head of the Liberal Party, was president. Gómez announced, "Once again we are completely free." Gómez was a popular president. However, he was not sensitive to the needs of many of the Cuban people, especially those of African descent.

U.S. troops again   In 1912, African Cuban sugar workers revolted. Cuba was filled with panic. The United States sent marines to protect U.S.-owned sugar mills. Cuban troops put down the revolt, and the marines left.

In 1917 and again in 1921, the United States sent diplomats to Cuba to settle election disputes. After that, there was no direct control of the Cuban government by the U.S. government.

A sugar economy   Much of the Cuban economy, however, continued to be controlled by U.S. companies. U.S. companies owned most of the sugar industry. Sugar went from being an important export to almost the only product made.

During World War I, sugar production in some other countries was shut down. Cuba became the major producer of sugar in the world. Sugar cane was planted everywhere on the island. Sugar prices zoomed from 6½ cents per pound (.45 km) to 22½ cents in just five months. Cuban landowners and sugar

President Palma reviews a parade in Havana. The parade was held to celebrate Cuban independence. Although Cuba was independent, the United States maintained control over the island. Many Cubans were unhappy with this.

LESLIE'S WEEKLY

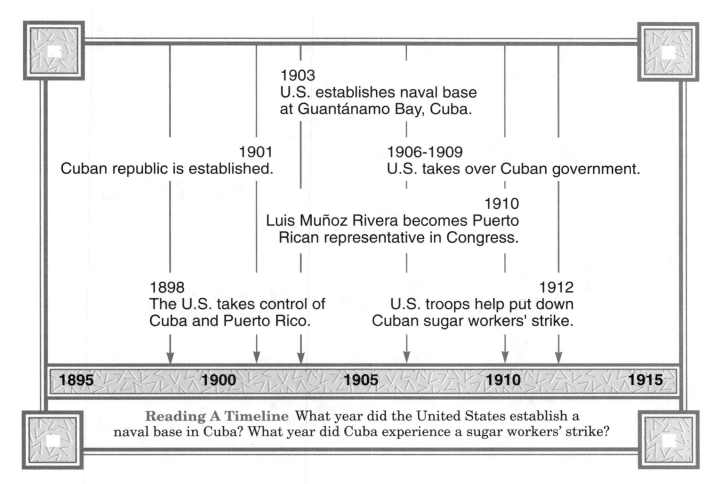

1903
U.S. establishes naval base
at Guantánamo Bay, Cuba.

1901
Cuban republic is established.

1906-1909
U.S. takes over Cuban government.

1910
Luis Muñoz Rivera becomes Puerto
Rican representative in Congress.

1898
The U.S. takes control of
Cuba and Puerto Rico.

1912
U.S. troops help put down
Cuban sugar workers' strike.

| 1895 | 1900 | 1905 | 1910 | 1915 |

Reading A Timeline What year did the United States establish a naval base in Cuba? What year did Cuba experience a sugar workers' strike?

mill owners grew very rich. They called the time "the dance of the millions."

But the dance ended as quickly as it had begun. After the war, there was too much sugar on the world market. Prices dropped to less than 4 cents by the end of 1920. Banks failed. Sugar mills closed. In the 1920s, about a quarter of Cuba's sugar mills closed.

The actions of the United States in politics and in the economy upset many Cubans. U.S. conduct created bitter memories that lasted for years.

1. What discovery wiped out yellow fever in Cuba?
2. What did the Platt Amendment add to the Cuban constitution?

2 Puerto Rico Becomes a U.S. Colony
How did the United States treat its new possession?

When the United States took over in 1898, Puerto Rico was an island of nearly one million people. It was a country of small farms. They produced many different crops. Most people were poor. Few children went to school. Only 13 percent of all Puerto Ricans could read and write.

Even with these problems, the Puerto Ricans were better off under the Spanish than the Cubans had been. In 1897, Spain had granted Puerto Rico some self-rule. The next year, Puerto Rican voters chose their first parliament. It opened just a week before the U.S. invasion. Although the parliament was sent home, most Puerto Ricans

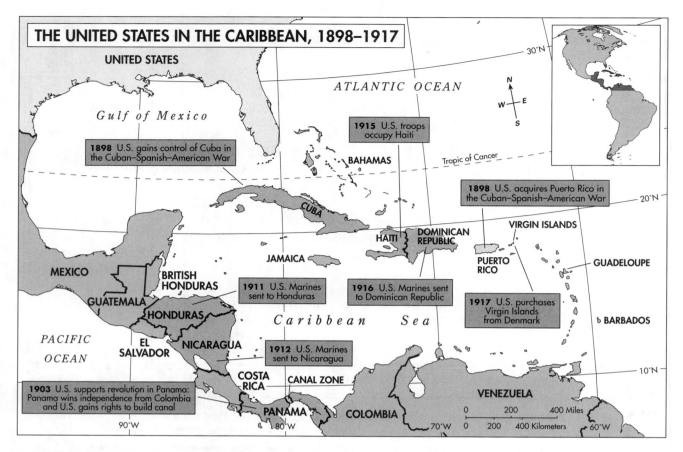

THE UNITED STATES IN THE CARIBBEAN, 1898–1917

UNITED STATES

ATLANTIC OCEAN

Gulf of Mexico

1915 U.S. troops occupy Haiti

1898 U.S. gains control of Cuba in the Cuban–Spanish–American War

BAHAMAS

Tropic of Cancer

1898 U.S. acquires Puerto Rico in the Cuban–Spanish–American War

CUBA

VIRGIN ISLANDS

HAITI

DOMINICAN REPUBLIC

JAMAICA

PUERTO RICO

GUADELOUPE

MEXICO

BRITISH HONDURAS

GUATEMALA

1911 U.S. Marines sent to Honduras

1916 U.S. Marines sent to Dominican Republic

1917 U.S. purchases Virgin Islands from Denmark

BARBADOS

HONDURAS

Caribbean Sea

PACIFIC OCEAN

EL SALVADOR

NICARAGUA

1912 U.S. Marines sent to Nicaragua

COSTA RICA

CANAL ZONE

VENEZUELA

1903 U.S. supports revolution in Panama: Panama wins independence from Colombia and U.S. gains rights to build canal

PANAMA

COLOMBIA

0   200   400 Miles
0   200   400 Kilometers

Reading a Map. When did U.S. troops occupy Haiti? What islands did the United States buy from Denmark in 1917? When did U.S. Marines invade the Dominican Republic? What countries in Central America were U.S. Marines sent to?

were pleased that the United States had arrived. They believed their lives would improve even more with U.S. help.

A U.S. colony   Life did improve for Puerto Rico. However, independence did not happen. There were two reasons for this. First, U.S. government officials felt that the Puerto Rican people had no experience in self-rule. They believed the Puerto Ricans were not ready for political freedom.

Second, the United States believed that it must control Puerto Rico for military reasons. Puerto Rico is located at the entrance to the Caribbean. The island was important to defense of the United States and its business interests in the region. So Puerto Rico became a colony of the United States.

The U.S. government tried to improve the lives of the Puerto Rican people. It built roads, bridges, and schools. However, U.S. rule brought a one-crop economy. Sugar became the island's most important product. Before long, Puerto Rico's economy depended on selling sugar to the United States.

Rules for Puerto Rico   The first U.S. government in Puerto Rico was a military one. It lasted from 1898 to 1900. A civil government began in 1900 under the **Foraker Act.** The act also set up rules. Puerto Rico would remain under the control of the United States. The President would appoint the governor and all the members of the upper house of the legislature. The lower house of the legislature would be elected by the people. The U.S. Congress could overrule the Puerto Rican legislature. There would be a Puerto Rican representative in the U.S. House of Representatives. But the person would not have a vote.

A freedom fighter   The Foraker Act angered many Puerto Ricans. It did not bring them self-government. Luis Muñoz Rivera (moo-NYOS ree-VEH-rah) decided to do something. He called it "unworthy of the United States which imposed it and of the Puerto Ricans who have to endure it."

Muñoz Rivera dedicated his life to the cause of Puerto Rican independence. In 1889, when Puerto Rico was under Spanish rule, he started a newspaper that argued for independence. He worked with Spain to gain self-government. His tactics worked. Just before the U.S. invasion, Spain had granted self-rule. After the invasion, Muñoz tried to work with the U.S. government as he had with the Spanish. In 1910, he was the Puerto Rican representative in Congress. He worked hard to have the Foraker Act changed. His efforts were successful. In 1917, a year after his death, Congress passed the **Jones Act.**

The Jones Act gave U.S. citizenship to all Puerto Ricans who wanted it. Most Puerto Ricans accepted the offer. A few refused. They believed that U.S. citizenship would make it harder for them to gain independence. The Jones Act also made it possible for Puerto Ricans to elect both houses of their legislature, not just the lower one. However, the governor and other key officials were still appointed by the U.S. President.

The new law was passed just before the United States entered World War I. Although the Jones Act did not please all Puerto Ricans, most Puerto Ricans supported the United States in the war. Nearly 20,000 Puerto Ricans served in

This postcard shows a street called "Calle de Tetuan" in San Juan, Puerto Rico. As a U.S. colony, Puerto Rico's economy came to depend on sugar cane.

the U.S. armed forces. Islanders raised $10 million in war bonds.

Statehood?   Some Puerto Ricans were more interested in economic progress than in independence. Among them was the labor leader Santiago Iglesias (ee-GLES-ee-ahs). After the war, Iglesias led a movement to have Puerto Rico made a state. He argued that statehood would give Puerto Rico greater control over its economy. It also would help to improve workers' lives.

Iglesias had a lot to complain about. Workers on tobacco farms and sugar plantations made up a large part of the population. They were very poor.

However, the island did not become a state. It remained under the control of the U.S.-appointed governors. Some of these governors named many native Puerto Ricans to government positions. Other governors, however, did not understand the island or its people. One of them declared, "There is no room on this island for any flag other than the Stars and Stripes." In the 1920s, Puerto Rican leaders asked for greater home rule from President Calvin Coolidge. Coolidge's answer was that Puerto Ricans should be grateful for what freedom they did have.

Cultural imperialism Besides political and economic reasons, many Puerto Ricans also wanted independence for cultural reasons. They accused the United States of **cultural imperialism.** That is the desire to replace the culture of a colony with the culture of the ruling country. Puerto Ricans did not want mainland U.S. culture to replace Puerto Rican culture. The longer the United States ruled, they feared, the more the island would become like the United States. In the process, Puerto Rico's folklore, literature, customs, and even language would vanish.

However, this did not happen. Few Puerto Ricans abandoned Spanish for English. The culture of Puerto Rico stayed different from that of the mainland. But the fear that it might be wiped out remained a key argument against U.S. rule.

In time, Cuba would become free. But Puerto Rico remained a part of the U.S. political system. However, Latinos of both islands came to the mainland United States to live.

1. How did U.S. rule change the Puerto Rican economy?
2. What did Puerto Ricans fear might happen as a result of cultural imperialism?

CHAPTER 8
KEY IDEAS

- After the Cuban-Spanish-American War, the United States became a power in the Caribbean. It controlled Cuba and Puerto Rico.
- Cuba became independent. But the Platt Amendment in the Cuban constitution allowed the United States to intervene.
- Unlike Cuba, Puerto Rico became a colony of the United States. In 1917, Puerto Ricans were permitted to become U.S. citizens.
- U.S. control over the Puerto Rican economy remained tight. U.S. business interests turned the island into a one-crop, sugar economy.

I. Reviewing Vocabulary

Match each word on the left with the correct definition on the right.

1. Foraker Act
2. cultural imperialism
3. Platt Amendment
4. Jones Act
5. protectorate

a. offered U.S. citizenship to Puerto Ricans
b. set up first U.S. government in Puerto Rico
c. a weak country that is under the control of a stronger country
d. replacing the customs of a colony with those of the ruling country
e. gave the United States the right to interfere in Cuba

II. Understanding the Chapter

1. What were the accomplishments of Carlos Juan Finlay and Walter Reed?
2. What was one example of the United States using the Platt Amendment to control Cuba?
3. How did the growth of the sugar industry affect Cuba's economy?
4. How did the Jones Act change the Puerto Rican legislature?
5. Why did some Puerto Ricans want independence for cultural reasons?

III. Building Skills: Reading a Map

Study the map on page 68 and answer the following questions.

1. When did the United States acquire Puerto Rico?
2. Where were U.S. marines sent in 1916?
3. What country near Cuba did U.S. troops occupy in the early 1900s?

IV. Writing About History

1. **What Would You Have Done?** If you had been U.S. secretary of state in 1901, would you have argued for or against requiring the Platt Amendment in the Cuban constitution? Explain.
2. Imagine that you are a Puerto Rican in the early 1900s. Write a short biography of Luis Muñoz Rivera that shows why he was important to Puerto Rico.

V. Working Together

1. Work with two or three classmates. Discuss the actions of the United States in Puerto Rico and Cuba after the Cuban-Spanish-American War. Then design a poster that tells how your group feels about U.S. actions in either Puerto Rico or Cuba. When you are done, display your poster in class.
2. **Past to Present** Today, the United States still controls islands in the Caribbean. With a group, decide if the United States has the right to control other countries. Present your arguments to the class.

THE UNITED STATES IS INVOLVED IN LATIN AMERICA. (1900—1920)

Why did the United States interfere in Latin America in the early years of the 1900s?

The Panama Canal was the greatest construction project of its time. Workers were brought from all over the United States and the West Indies to complete it.

Looking at Key Terms

- Panama Canal • Canal Zone • big-stick policy
- dollar diplomacy • Mexican Revolution

Looking at Key Words

- **canal:** a waterway dug by people to connect two bodies of water
- **diplomacy:** the relationships between countries
- **migrant worker:** a farm worker who travels to find work

STUDY HINT

Make a list of the U.S. Presidents mentioned in this chapter. Describe each President's policy toward Latin America and its results.

Up to his knees in mud, President Theodore Roosevelt looked around happily. In driving rain, workers moved huge piles of earth. Roosevelt made a quick speech. "You are doing the biggest thing of the kind that has ever been done, and I wanted to see how you are doing it." These workers were building the Panama Canal. The Canal was part of U.S. involvement in Latin America in the early 1900s.

1 The United States Builds the Panama Canal.

Why did the United States want to build a canal across Panama?

In 1900, traveling by sea from New York to San Francisco seemed to take forever. Ships sailed south from the United States. They traveled along the coast of South America. Then they sailed through dangerous waters at its tip. Finally, they headed north. The voyage around South America alone was over 7,500 miles (12,067 kilometers) long.

This long trip was bad for business. Shipping goods around South America was very expensive. Passengers traveling to the opposite coast of the United States spent months at sea.

The great distance also made it difficult to defend the United States. Two navies were necessary. One protected the West coast. The other guarded the East. If the route was shorter, only one navy would be needed.

"I took Panama" In 1901, President Roosevelt decided to build a **canal** across Central America. A canal is a waterway dug by people to connect two bodies of water. This canal would cut the Atlantic-to-Pacific trip in half. The canal would be located in Panama.

At the time, Panama belonged to Colombia. Roosevelt offered Colombia $10 million for the right to build the

canal. He also promised $250,000 yearly rent. Colombia wanted more.

So Roosevelt took another approach. He encouraged people in Panama to rebel against Colombia. A revolution broke out in late 1903. The U.S. gunboat *Nashville* blocked Colombia from landing its soldiers in Panama. So the rebels won. Panama declared its independence on November 3.

Only two weeks later, Roosevelt made a deal with Panama's new government. It was the same deal he had offered Colombia. The United States would build and operate the canal. Roosevelt had succeeded. He once boasted, "I took Panama." The people of Colombia were furious.

Flying death Work on the canal started in 1904. Many problems faced

Reading a Map. What lake is near the Panama Canal? Why would a Panama Canal make traveling to the U.S. west coast easier?

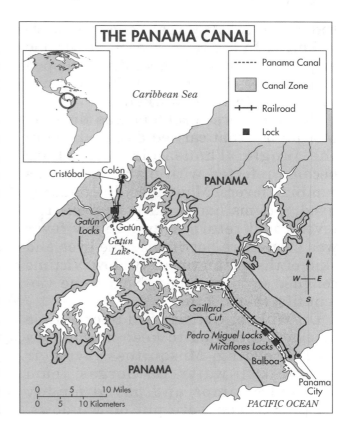

THE PANAMA CANAL

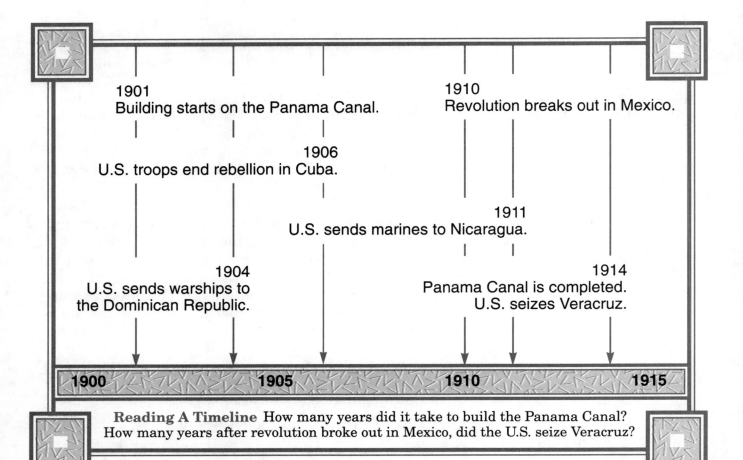

1901
Building starts on the Panama Canal.

1910
Revolution breaks out in Mexico.

1906
U.S. troops end rebellion in Cuba.

1911
U.S. sends marines to Nicaragua.

1904
U.S. sends warships to
the Dominican Republic.

1914
Panama Canal is completed.
U.S. seizes Veracruz.

1900   1905   1910   1915

Reading A Timeline How many years did it take to build the Panama Canal?
How many years after revolution broke out in Mexico, did the U.S. seize Veracruz?

the builders. The Canal Zone was mostly jungle. In the rainy season, it became an ocean of mud. Temperatures topped 120 degrees. Poisonous snakes and biting insects tortured workers.

But the worst problem was disease. Mosquitoes that carried disease lived in the jungle. Thousands of workers became infected with malaria. Victims ran high fevers. Many died. Even if they lived, victims had malaria forever. The fever could return again. Yellow fever was even more horrifying. The eyes and skin of the victim turned yellow. Victims coughed up dark blood. Next came violent fits, then death.

Dr. William Gorgas tried to end these diseases. He tried to keep mosquitoes from breeding. Mosquitoes lay their eggs in still water. So Gorgas' team drained swamps and paved muddy roads. Screens were put on windows.

They used insect spray everywhere. By 1906, these efforts had worked. The Canal Zone was safe. Workers could now concentrate on the canal.

Building the canal Engineer George W. Goethals (GOH-thahls) led the construction. About 30,000 African Americans from the West Indies made up his crew. Under his direction, they cut through miles of swamps, rivers, and mountains. They slowly worked their way across Panama.

The canal was completed in 1914. It cost 5,000 lives and $375 million. It also cost the good will of Colombia. In 1921, the United States paid the Colombian government $25 million. This was an attempt to make up for taking Panama away. But many Latin Americans were still angry with the United States.

1. Why did the United States want to build the Panama Canal?
2. List three problems facing the canal builders.

2 The United States Carries a "Big Stick."

How did the United States act as "policeman" in Latin American affairs?

President Roosevelt did not stop with the Panama Canal. He continued to use force in Latin America. Roosevelt quoted an African saying: "Speak softly and carry a big stick, and you will go far."

Latin America's police Roosevelt first used this "big-stick policy" in 1904. The Dominican Republic had a crisis. It could not pay its debts to several European countries. Roosevelt feared these countries would invade the Dominican Republic. He added a new point to his Monroe Doctrine. He said only the United States would be allowed to police the Americas.

Roosevelt moved quickly. He sent U.S. warships to the Dominican Republic. The United States took over collecting import taxes on the island. Over half were sent to Europe to pay off the debts.

Roosevelt continued to act as "policeman of the West." He stepped into Cuba in 1906. Five thousand U.S. troops ended a rebellion there and set up a new government. The United States controlled Cuba for over two years.

Dollars instead of bullets In 1909, William Howard Taft became President of the United States. He changed Roosevelt's policy. He wanted to "substitute dollars for bullets." Taft

Roosevelt first used his "big stick policy" in 1904 in the Dominican Republic. This policy added to the Monroe Doctrine. It said only the United States would police the Americas. Why would Latin Americans be upset over this policy?

Taft's "substitute dollars for bullets" caused relations to grow worse in Latin America. In 1911, Taft sent Marines into Nicaragua because it could not pay its foreign debts. This caused Latin Americans to resent the United States even more.

encouraged U.S. businesses to invest in Latin American countries. He thought this would help keep them out of debt. This policy became known as **"dollar diplomacy." Diplomacy** is the relationships between countries.

However, Taft's policy made relations worse. U.S. businesses wanted their money protected. In 1911, Nicaragua failed to pay its foreign debts. Once again the United States used force. President Taft sent in the marines. This made Latin America resent the United States even more.

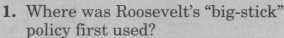

1. Where was Roosevelt's "big-stick" policy first used?
2. How did Taft change this policy?

3 The United States Invades Mexico.

How did the Mexican Revolution affect relations between the United States and Mexico?

President Woodrow Wilson took office in 1913. He did not approve of dollar diplomacy. He said he had no interest in foreign affairs. But under Wilson, relations with Latin America got worse. Wilson sent U.S. Marines to the Dominican Republic. He invaded Haiti. Wilson almost began a war with Mexico.

Revolution   In 1910, a revolution began in Mexico. Mexicans had lived for more than 30 years under dictator Porfirio Díaz (DEE-ahs). Díaz had improved Mexican industry. But only a few people benefited. Poor farmers lost their land to rich landowners.

The Mexican people revolted. Small bands attacked Mexican soldiers. They destroyed railroads and factories. Finally, in 1911, Díaz was forced to resign.

Seizing Veracruz But rebels continued to fight. President Wilson wanted the fighting in Mexico to stop. It might hurt U.S. property and businesses in Mexico. So he supported another rebel, Venustiano Carranza (kah-RRAHN-sah). Wilson hoped Carranza could control Mexico.

In 1914, Wilson ordered U.S. troops to seize the Mexican port city Veracruz. He wanted to keep shipments of weapons from reaching Carranza's enemies.

Some rebel leaders were unhappy with Carranza. They felt he would not help Mexico's poor. One of these leaders was Pancho Villa. Villa was a hero to many people in Mexico.

Villa's raid Villa had hoped the United States would help him become president of Mexico. When Wilson backed Carranza instead, Villa took revenge. In 1916, Villa's troops killed 16 U.S. mine employees in northern Mexico. Then he crossed the border into the United States and killed another 18 people.

The U.S. government was furious. Wilson sent the army into Mexico to capture Villa. However, the people of northern Mexico admired Villa. They helped hide him from the U.S. soldiers. After 11 months, the army gave up the search. But many Mexicans were angry.

1. What Mexican city did the United States capture during the Mexican Revolution?
2. What happened when President Wilson sent U.S. troops to capture Pancho Villa?

4 Mexicans Find Homes in the United States.

How did the Mexican Revolution affect immigration to the United States?

Pablo Mares (MAH-res) crossed the border into the United States. He was fleeing the fighting in the Mexican Revolution. Soon he found work in an Arizona mine. He said, "The work is very heavy, but what is good is that one lives in peace." Many Mexicans moved to the United States to find peace.

New immigrants The Mexican Revolution would improve the lives of some Mexicans. However, the fighting caused great suffering. About a million Mexicans died. Thousands fled north to the United States. (See map on page 78.) Between 1910 and 1920, the newcomers streamed across the U.S. border. They came on foot, on horseback, in wagons, and on railroad trains.

These Mexican immigrants came from very different backgrounds. Most were poor farmers. They had been forced off their land by the fighting. Some had supported one of the many different governments. Still others had money to start businesses in the United States.

Most Mexican immigrants settled in the U.S. Southwest. This area already had a large Mexican American population. The area had belonged to Mexico only about 60 years before.

Creating communities Many Mexicans who moved to U.S. cities lived in barrios. A *barrio* is a section of a city where there are large numbers of Latinos. Conditions in many *barrios* were very bad. People lived in old, overcrowded buildings. There was poor sanitation and few public services.

However, *barrio*s gave newcomers a feeling of home. Here they lived among friends and relatives from the same

Mexican communities. They formed social clubs. They visited Mexican American groceries, restaurants, and bakeries. Spanish was the language of the *barrios*.

The largest *barrio* was in Los Angeles. It had a population of 30,000 Mexican-born Americans in 1920. This was almost three times as many as in 1910. By 1925, Los Angeles had a larger Mexican population than any other city except Mexico City. Other cities with large *barrios* were El Paso and San Antonio in Texas.

Working hard   U.S. business owners saw Mexican immigrants as cheap labor. These immigrants could work in the new mines and factories of the Southwest. In addition, tracks had to be laid for the Southern Pacific and Santa Fe railroads. These railroads hired more than a thousand Mexican Americans a month.

Most Mexican immigrants were unskilled workers. They could not read or write English. They worked at the lowest paying jobs. A farm worker earned between $1.00 and $1.50 a day. The highest pay was in mine work, up to $5.00 a day. Still, these rates were much higher than what workers earned in Mexico. There the rate was about 16 cents a day.

Farm labor   In the U.S. Southwest, farms were very large. Crops were harvested at different times of the year in different regions. So Mexican American

Reading a Map. Name five cities where Mexican immigrants migrated in the United States. What southwestern state in the United States did Pancho Villa attack? In what year did the United States invade Veracruz?

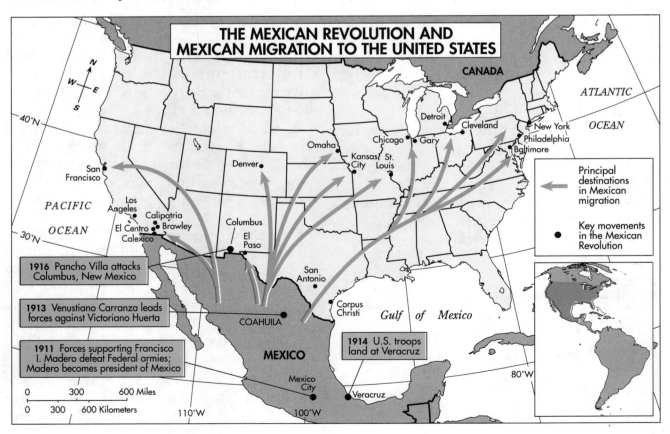

THE MEXICAN REVOLUTION AND MEXICAN MIGRATION TO THE UNITED STATES

Principal destinations in Mexican migration

Key movements in the Mexican Revolution

1916 Pancho Villa attacks Columbus, New Mexico

1913 Venustiano Carranza leads forces against Victoriano Huerta

1911 Forces supporting Francisco I. Madero defeat Federal armies; Madero becomes president of Mexico

1914 U.S. troops land at Veracruz

farm workers moved from place to place with the seasons. They became **migrant workers.** A migrant worker is a farm worker who travels to find work. They moved between California, Arizona, New Mexico, Colorado, and Texas. They harvested sugar beets, cotton, fruit, and vegetables.

Groups of migrant worker families moved from place to place. Women and children often worked with the men in the fields. The workday lasted from dawn to dark. A family might live in five different places in a year. Wages were low. Living conditions were hard. Children often could not go to school.

Unfair treatment Mexican Americans and Mexicans faced discrimination. They were paid less than others who did the same job. They were given the most dangerous jobs. When labor unions were formed in some industries, Mexican Americans were not allowed to join.

Mexican American children were forced to go to segregated schools.

Mexican immigrants were treated especially badly. Workers in the Southwest were afraid these newcomers would take their jobs away.

Seeking opportunity Gradually, Mexican Americans made their way to the United States Midwest. They worked for railroads, steel mills, and meat-packing plants there. Chicago became the largest Mexican center outside the Southwest. By 1925, 4,000 Mexican Americans lived there.

1. Why did Mexicans come to the United States from 1910 to 1920?
2. What is a migrant worker?

CHAPTER 9
KEY IDEAS

- In 1914, the United States opened the Panama Canal. It allowed ships of all nations to move quickly between the Atlantic and the Pacific Oceans.
- President Theodore Roosevelt said that only the United States would police Latin America. President William Taft tried dollar diplomacy.
- President Woodrow Wilson invaded Mexico twice in two years. This led to bad relations between Mexico and the United States.
- During the Mexican Revolution, many Mexicans settled in the United States.

REVIEWING CHAPTER 9

I. Reviewing Vocabulary

Match each word on the left with the correct definition on the right.

1. big-stick policy
2. canal
3. diplomacy
4. migrant worker
5. dollar diplomacy

a. a waterway dug by people to connect two bodies of water
b. a farm worker who travels to find work
c. the relationships between countries
d. investing in countries instead of controlling them through force
e. the use of force to get what is wanted

II. Understanding the Chapter

1. How did the United States get the right to build the Panama Canal?
2. What was President Theodore Roosevelt's policy on Latin America?
3. Why did the United States keep using force in Latin America under dollar diplomacy?
4. Why did the United States invade Mexico twice during the Mexican Revolution?
5. What kinds of jobs did Mexican immigrants find in the United States?

III. Building Skills: Analyzing a Map

Study the map on page 78. Then answer the following questions.

1. What town in the United States did Pancho Villa attack?
2. Name four cities in the U.S. Southwest many Mexican immigrants settled in.

IV. Writing About History

1. It is August 15, 1914, the day the Panama Canal was officially opened. Write an article for a newspaper covering this event. Be sure to describe the problems that the canal builders overcame.
2. **What Would You Have Done?** If you lived in Mexico during the Revolution, would you immigrate to the United States? Explain.

V. Working Together

1. Form a small group. Review the timeline on page 74. Then make your own timeline with pictures. Choose at least three events and illustrate them. Share your timelines with the class.
2. **Past to Present** With a group, research the importance of the Panama Canal today. Prepare a short presentation about your findings.

THE UNITED STATES FIGHTS WORLD WAR I. (1914—1918)

What part did the United States play in World War I?

The 369th Regiment, a segregated unit, won the highest French military medal in World War I. Not until the 1950s, did the U.S. military become desegregated.

Looking at Key Terms

- Allies • Central Powers

Looking at Key Words

- **alliance:** a group of countries that work together
- **neutrality:** not taking sides in a war
- **submarine warfare:** using submarines to sink ships bringing supplies to the enemy

- **draftee:** a person inducted into military service

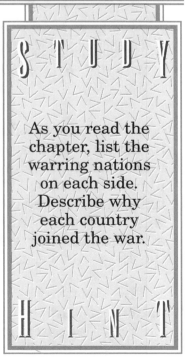

STUDY

As you read the chapter, list the warring nations on each side. Describe why each country joined the war.

HINT

In September 1918, U.S. Army Private Marcelino Serna (SER-nah) found himself on a battlefield in France. From his trench, the young Mexican American could see the German lines. From time to time, a helmeted head would pop up. Then shots were fired in his direction.

Serna waited for the right moment to shoot back. He squeezed his trigger. That instant an enemy bullet hit his cheek. He did not let the wound stop him. He pumped more bullets toward the enemy trench. Then he threw a hand grenade.

Twenty-four German soldiers climbed out of the trench. Their arms were raised in surrender. Serna marched his captives to his unit's headquarters. For his brave action, Serna received the Distinguished Service Cross. It is one of the army's highest awards. He also received a Purple Heart for being wounded. By the end of the war, he earned another Purple Heart and a medal from the French government. Private Serna was one of almost 4 million Americans who served with honor in the armed forces in World War I.

1 The United States Goes to War.

Why did the United States take part in World War I?

In the summer of 1914, war broke out in Europe. The war lasted more than four years. Most of the fighting took place in Europe. But there also was fighting in all parts of the world. So it was called the "World War." Later, after a second, similar war had broken out, the 1914 war was called "World War I."

The roots of the war The largest nations of Europe had formed **alliances** that divided them into two camps. An alliance is a group of countries that work together. In one alliance, the main members were France, Great Britain, and Russia. The members of the other were Germany, Italy, and Austria-Hungary. Austria-Hungary was an empire that ruled much of Central Europe.

A murder in June 1914 led to the war. Archduke Francis Ferdinand was shot while visiting the town of Sarajevo (sah-rah-HAY-voh). The archduke was next in line to be emperor of Austria-Hungary. The murderer was a young Serb who opposed Austrian rule of Serb territory. Serbia was an ally of Russia.

Austria-Hungary demanded that Serbia be punished. They were strongly backed by their ally Germany. When Serbia refused to meet all the demands, Austria-Hungary declared war.

Tangled alliances Now the European system of alliances led other countries to war. Russia started to help Serbia. So Germany declared war on Russia. Two days later, it also declared war on France, Russia's ally. Then Germany's armies invaded Belgium to get at France. So Great Britain, which was friendly with France and Belgium, declared war on Germany. In a few days, almost all of Europe was at war.

The two sides in the war were called the **Allies** and the **Central Powers.** The Central Powers were Germany and Austria-Hungary. The Ottoman Empire (Turkey) and Bulgaria joined the Central Powers later. The Allies at first were France, Great Britain, Russia, Belgium, and Serbia. As the war went on, they were joined by several other countries, including Italy and Japan. In 1917, the United States joined the Allies. A number of Latin American countries also joined the Allies.

The U.S. Stays Out At first, the United States tried to stay out of the

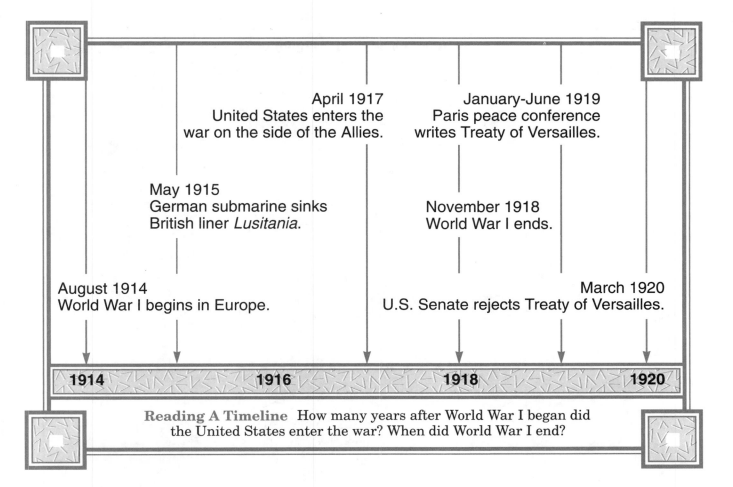

April 1917
United States enters the
war on the side of the Allies.

January-June 1919
Paris peace conference
writes Treaty of Versailles.

May 1915
German submarine sinks
British liner *Lusitania.*

November 1918
World War I ends.

August 1914
World War I begins in Europe.

March 1920
U.S. Senate rejects Treaty of Versailles.

| 1914 | 1916 | 1918 | 1920 |

Reading A Timeline How many years after World War I began did the United States enter the war? When did World War I end?

war. For more than two years, it succeeded. When the war broke out, President Woodrow Wilson proclaimed U.S. **neutrality.** That meant that the United States would not take sides in the war. Nor would it offer help to either side. It did allow U.S. companies to sell their products to countries at war. These products included weapons. The Allies bought far more from the United States than the Central Powers did.

Germany used **submarine warfare** to keep U.S. supplies from reaching Great Britain and France. Submarine warfare meant that German submarines attacked and sank cargo ships.

In some of these attacks, many American lives were lost. The attack that caused the largest loss of life was the sinking of the British ocean liner *Lusitania* in 1915. The *Lusitania* was

carrying a secret cargo of weapons. The ship blew up before many of its passengers got into lifeboats. Among the dead were 139 U.S. citizens.

No longer neutral In February 1917, German submarine attacks became more fierce. In the next two months, a number of U.S. ships were sunk. Anti-German feeling built up rapidly. Then Germany made things worse. It suggested to the Mexican government that the two countries join in a war against the United States. Mexico said no. But President Wilson would take no more from Germany. He asked Congress to declare war.

On April 6, 1917, Congress declared war on Germany. Among those voting against the war was Representative Jeannette Rankin of Montana. She had

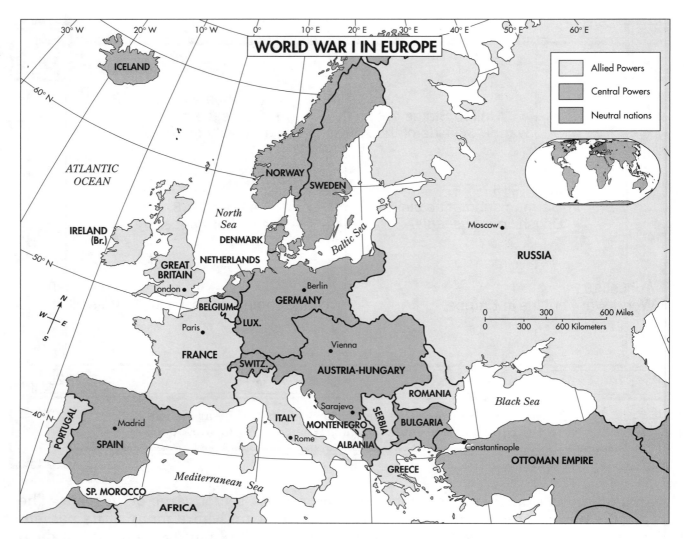

WORLD WAR I IN EUROPE

Allied Powers
Central Powers
Neutral nations

Reading a Map. This map shows the nations of Europe during World War I. Which nations were Allied Powers? Which ones were Central Powers? What countries were neutral? Which side had more countries, the Allies or the Central Powers?

been the first woman to serve in Congress. But she was not reelected.

In 1941, she returned to Congress. Later that year, Congress again voted to declare war. Her vote was the single no. Jeannette Rankin was the only person to vote against both world wars.

1. What nations made up the Allies and the Central Powers?
2. What German actions caused the United States to declare war?

2 All Americans Help in the War Effort.
How did the United States raise an army?

Soon after war was declared, Congress passed the Selective Service Act. This act required all men between the ages of 21 and 30 to register for military service. The first draft took place in early June 1917.

About 2.2 million men became **draftees.** A draftee is a person who must go into military service. In addition, many others volunteered for the army, the navy, and the Marine Corps.

By the time the war ended, the total number of Americans in military service was about 4 million.

African Americans in the service

Americans of all groups served in World War I. Yet they were not all treated in the same way. African Americans, in particular, received unequal treatment. The Marine Corps barred them from service. The navy took them only as cooks, kitchen helpers, and boiler-room workers. Only the army used them as fighting men. It did not use as many as it could have.

The U.S. Army trained more than 370,000 African American soldiers for combat. Yet three out of four spent their time in the army in labor units. They hauled supplies. They built roads. They also set up fortifications. About 100,000, however, did see combat. They served in all-African American units led mostly by white officers. Only 1,400 African Americans became officers. None reached above the rank of colonel.

Latinos and Native Americans in WW I

There were also large numbers of Latinos in the U.S. Army. When the war began, enough Puerto Rican men enlisted to form their own unit. Later, 235,000 Puerto Rican men registered for the draft. About 18,000 of these were called up for service.

Mexican Americans faced other problems during World War I. First, many U.S. citizens doubted the loyalty of Mexican Americans. This happened partly because Germany had tried to make Mexico its ally in the war. People forgot that Mexico had rejected the Germans. Anti-Mexican feelings also arose from Pancho Villa's raid on New Mexico. (See page 77.)

Yet thousands of young Mexican American men decided to serve their country. The percentage who volunteered was greater than that of any other ethnic group in the nation.

The armed services did not quite know what to do with their Latino volunteers. Many could not speak or write English fluently. Therefore, they did not finish their military training. They remained at the training centers. Some went to the front in Europe.

Most Native Americans were not U.S. citizens in 1917–1918. So they were not subject to the draft. Even so, many volunteered for service.

1. What roles did African Americans fill in the military services in World War I?
2. What problem did many Latinos face in the U.S. Army?

3 Americans See Action at Home and Abroad.

How did the U.S. people contribute to the war effort on the home front and in Europe?

"It is not an army that we must shape and train for war," said President Wilson. "It is a nation." In April, 1917, the United States was not prepared to fight. Within a year, it was ready.

Building a war machine

It was not easy to turn the U.S. economy into a war machine. Yet it was done quickly. Congress gave President Wilson the right to take over entire industries. He could also claim supplies of food and any other goods. He could control prices. Wilson gave these powers to special boards.

The results were amazing. Besides guns and tanks, the United States sent to France entire railroads and entire

During World War I, these young women worked on a farm, guiding tractors. Since many men served in the war, women were needed to take over the men's jobs. Better jobs gave women a strong sense of independence.

hospitals. In the first year of the war, more than 30 million pairs of shoes and 131 million stockings were sent to Europe. By 1918, the United States was exporting three times as much food as it had before the war.

On the home front To achieve these results, new sources of labor had to be found. Nearly four million workers had gone into military service. They had to be replaced.

In the factories and mills of the Northeast and Midwest, many of the jobs were taken by African Americans. They had just arrived from the South. Times were very hard for Southern farm workers just then. African Americans learned that the factories of Chicago, Detroit, and other cities paid good

wages. Many took advantage of the chance. Entire families moved north.

At the same time, thousands of Mexicans moved from Mexico to the U.S. Southwest. They knew that the war created new opportunities in the United States. Mexican immigrants worked in the cotton fields of Arizona. They picked sugar-beets on farms in California and Colorado. They also worked in the copper mines of New Mexico. They built railroad lines throughout the U.S. west.

The war opened new opportunities for women. Women worked in steel mills and weapons factories. They worked as lawyers and doctors for the government.

Most of the new opportunites lasted only until the end of the war. Women, African Americans and other groups were thrown out of work once the soldiers returned.

Action in Europe Meanwhile, a war was being fought in Europe. The United States entered the war in April 1917, on the side of Great Britain and France. During 1917, the main U.S. contribution to the war was at sea. The U.S. navy started chasing German submarines. In about a year and a half, more than half of Germany's submarines were destroyed. When the United States began sending large numbers of troops in 1918, not one troopship was sunk by submarines.

In July 1918, the German army began a new attack in France. The Germans hoped to knock out the British and French armies once and for all. They nearly succeeded. However, 275,000 U.S. troops arrived just in time. This was the first large group of American soldiers in Europe. They helped to turn the tide of the war at the battle of Château-Thierry (shah-TOH tee-REE). German generals later said they knew then that they

Reading a Map. What is the subject of this map? Which new nations were formed after World War I? What countries gained land? How does this map differ from the map at the beginning of the chapter?

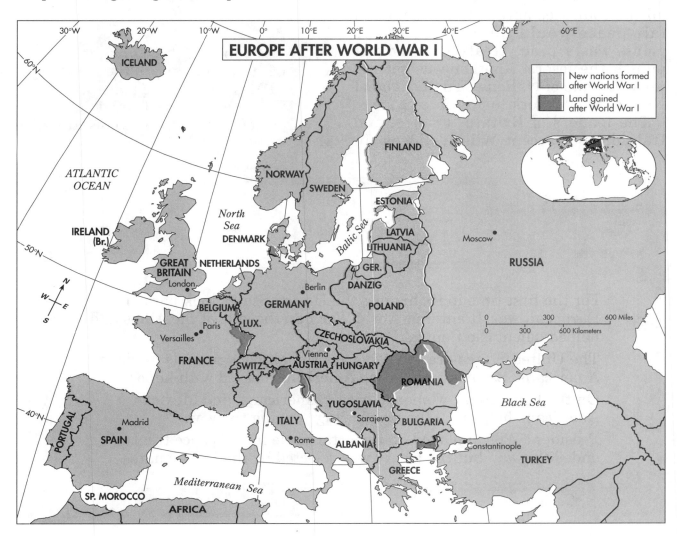

EUROPE AFTER WORLD WAR I

New nations formed after World War I

Land gained after World War I

ICELAND

ATLANTIC OCEAN

NORWAY
SWEDEN
FINLAND

North Sea
DENMARK
ESTONIA
LATVIA
LITHUANIA
Baltic Sea
Moscow

IRELAND (Br.)

GREAT BRITAIN
NETHERLANDS
London
GER.
DANZIG

RUSSIA

Berlin
BELGIUM
GERMANY
POLAND

Paris
LUX.
CZECHOSLOVAKIA
Versailles
Vienna
FRANCE
SWITZ.
AUSTRIA
HUNGARY
ROMANIA

Black Sea

YUGOSLAVIA
PORTUGAL
Madrid
ITALY
Sarajevo
BULGARIA
SPAIN
Rome
ALBANIA
Constantinople
TURKEY
GREECE

Mediterranean Sea

SP. MOROCCO
AFRICA

0   300   600 Miles
0   300   600 Kilometers

were beaten. However, the war went on for four more months.

Together the Allies pushed the German armies almost entirely out of France and Belgium. The German government asked for peace talks. On November 11, 1918, the fighting ended.

In Europe, Americans helped win the war. A number of women served as nurses with the Red Cross. African Americans, Latinos, and Native Americans fought with courage. Many won medals for their bravery, from both the U.S. and the French governments. In some cases, entire units were decorated.

Wilson's Fourteen Points   Earlier in 1918, Wilson had listed **Fourteen Points** that peace would be based on. If all the countries agreed to the points, a fair peace would follow. One of the points was a peace treaty that did not punish the losers. Another was setting up a "League of Nations." The League of Nations would work to preserve peace.

The leaders of Britain, France, and Italy did not accept Wilson's ideas. In the treaty of Versailles (vehr-SYE), they forced harsh conditions on the defeated Germans. The Allies would regret this in a few years. However, the treaty did include plans for setting up the League of Nations.

When Wilson brought the treaty home to the United States, he met a new source of opposition. A group of senators did not think that the United States should become involved in the League of Nations. The Senate refused to approve the treaty. That meant that the United States would not be a member of the League. Wilson, meanwhile, had suffered a bad stroke. He finished his term of office as a defeated and ill man.

1. What opportunities brought African Americans to the North and Mexicans to the Southwest?
2. Who prevented the United States from joining the League of Nations?

CHAPTER 10
KEY IDEAS

- For the first time in its history, the United States took part in a European war. It entered World War I on the side of the Allies and helped defeat the Central Powers.

- The United States drafted Americans of all backgrounds. African Americans, Latinos and Native Americans served with honor.

- On the home front, women, African Americans, and Mexican Americans helped fill the job shortage during the war.

- President Wilson played an important role in the peace treaty. It ended the war, but the treaty was rejected by the U.S. Senate.

REVIEWING CHAPTER 10

I. Reviewing Vocabulary

Match each word on the left with the correct definition on the right.

1. neutrality
2. submarine warfare
3. draftee
4. Allies
5. Central Powers

a. a person required to go into military service
b. Germany and its allies in World War I
c. attacks on ships bringing supplies to the enemy
d. the policy of not taking sides in a war
e. France, Britain, and their allies in World War I

II. Understanding the Chapter

1. What events led to the outbreak of World War I in Europe?
2. Why did the United States enter the war on the side of the Allies?
3. What were the roles of African Americans and Latinos in fighting the war?
4. How was the home front organized during the war?
5. What role did the U.S. Army play in the fighting in France in 1918?

III. Building Skills: Interpreting a Map

1. Using a map of Europe, explain why it was easier for the Allies to obtain supplies from the United States than it was for the Central Powers.
2. Using the same map, show how a successful German policy of submarine warfare could have harmed the Allies.

IV. Writing About History

1. If you had been president of Mexico in 1917, how would you have responded to the German invitation to go to war against the United States? Explain.
2. **What Would You Have Done?** If you had been a 21-year-old man in 1917, would you have enlisted to fight in France? Why, or why not?

V. Working Together

1. Break up into groups to research the position of the governments of (a) Austria-Hungary, (b) Belgium, (c) France, (d) Germany, (e) Great Britain, (f) Russia, or (g) Serbia. Discuss with the class what each government could have done to prevent the outbreak of the war.
2. **Past to Present** With a group research the League of Nations and the United Nations. List three ways that they are similar and three ways they are different.

Unit 3
Times of Trial
(1920s–1940s)

Chapters

11 The 1920s Are a Time of Change.
12 African American Culture Thrives in the Jazz Age.
13 A Great Depression Takes Hold.
14 The New Deal Brings New Hope.
15 The Nation Fights Another War.
16 Americans Support World War II on the Home Front.

THE 1920s ARE A TIME OF CHANGE. (1920–1929)

What changes happened in U.S. society during the 1920s?

In 1919, the Eighteenth Amendment prohibited the making or selling of alcohol. Alcohol, like this beer, was thrown into rivers or down drains.

Looking at Key Terms

- Red Scare • Jazz Age • flapper • Prohibition • speakeasies

Looking at Key Words

- **quota:** a limit
- **prosperous:** successful, especially in terms of wealth
- **tariff:** a tax on imports
- **suburb:** an area around a city that people live in
- **prohibit:** to outlaw

STUDY

Make a list of the Key Ideas on page 98. Then write an example from the chapter that supports each idea.

HINT

In 1919, Giovanni Lagomarsino needed a job. The son of Italian immigrants, he spoke perfect English. He filled out a job application at a railroad. The manager looked at his name on the form. As Lagomarsino left the office, he saw the manager tear up his application. A month later, he applied again. This time he said his name was John Lagg. He got the job. This was an example of how prejudice against immigrants grew after World War I.

1 A Slump After the War Creates Fears.

How did events after World War I lead to fear and prejudice?

After World War I, the U.S. economy suffered a depression. Returning soldiers had trouble finding jobs. Factories closed to change from making war supplies to making other goods. Europe no longer needed to buy crops from U.S. farmers. Prices of goods shot up. Wages stayed the same.

Strikes and reactions Under these conditions, workers began to organize. They formed unions. They demanded better wages and shorter hours. Business owners refused. So workers went on strike.

In September 1919, the biggest strike in U.S. history stopped the steel industry. More than 365,000 workers walked off the job. Steel companies hired armed strike breakers. Strike breakers beat workers with clubs. Twenty people were killed in the fight. In early 1920, the steelworkers' union ended the strike. None of its demands had been met. The steel companies had won.

Other strikes were more successful. Coal miners increased their wages over

25 percent. By the end of 1919, more than 3,600 strikes had taken place.

Public opinion turned against strikes. Anti-union feelings spread. Ole Hanson, the Mayor of Seattle, crushed a general strike. Governor Calvin Coolidge of Massachusetts allowed striking Boston police officers to be fired. Both became popular for these actions.

Many Americans believed workers were not acting on their own. They blamed "outsiders" for starting strikes. To them, these "outsiders" were Communists and immigrants.

Red Scare In 1917, Communists had seized control of the Russian government. They called for the workers of the world to unite and rebel. Many Americans thought strikes in the United States were the work of Communists, or "Reds." They feared that these Reds were plotting to overthrow the U.S. government.

On January 20, 1920, Attorney General A. Mitchell Palmer began a series of raids. Suspected Reds were rounded up. Thousands of immigrants were arrested. Newspapers said these "Red Raids" were a great success. However, no plot against the government was discovered. Palmer deported 550 people. Some people criticized Palmer. They said he had violated people's civil rights.

Sacco and Vanzetti Debate was even greater about a murder case. In April 1920, three robbers stole a factory payroll in South Braintree, Massachusetts. During the robbery, the paymaster and a guard were killed. Two Italian immigrants, Nicola Sacco and Bartolomeo Vanzetti, were accused of the crime.

Sacco and Vanzetti were opposed to organized government. So they were

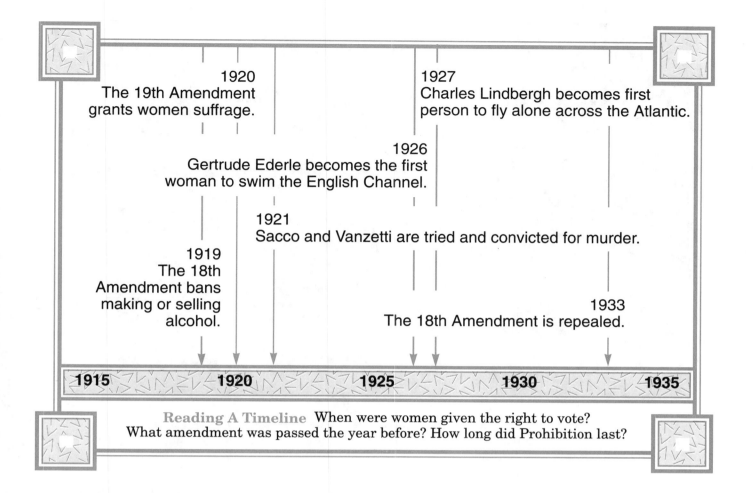

1920
The 19th Amendment grants women suffrage.

1927
Charles Lindbergh becomes first person to fly alone across the Atlantic.

1926
Gertrude Ederle becomes the first woman to swim the English Channel.

1921
Sacco and Vanzetti are tried and convicted for murder.

1919
The 18th Amendment bans making or selling alcohol.

1933
The 18th Amendment is repealed.

1915   1920   1925   1930   1935

Reading A Timeline When were women given the right to vote? What amendment was passed the year before? How long did Prohibition last?

assumed to be guilty. They were arrested for murder. In 1921, Sacco and Vanzetti were tried and convicted. They were sentenced to death.

Many people felt the trial was unjust. They said Sacco and Vanzetti were convicted because of their beliefs and because they were immigrants. Too little evidence was presented against them. Also, before the trial, the judge said he wanted to convict them. He thought they were Reds. The case was appealed. But the Massachusetts Supreme Court refused to retry Sacco and Vanzetti. They were executed in 1927.

"Different" immigrants As the Sacco-Vanzetti case shows, the Red Scare was inspired by a fear of immigrants. After World War I, Europeans began immigrating again to the United States. They came from southern and eastern Europe. They were not Protestants, like most Americans at that time. Most immigrants were Catholics or Jews. These differences fueled prejudice.

Limiting immigration The economic depression also caused anti-immigrant feelings. Jobs were scarce. Americans worried that immigrants would take away jobs. Many argued for limits on immigration.

In the early 1920s, Congress passed two laws slashing immigration. A 1921 law set temporary **quotas** on immigration. A quota (KWOH-tah) is a limit. The Immigration Act of 1924 was tougher. It lowered those limits and

Fear or prejudice against immigrants grew during the 1920s. The Ku Klux Klan was a group who attacked not only African Americans, but immigrants, Catholics, and others. Here, the Ku Klux Klan holds a parade in Washington, D.C. in 1925.

made them permanent. The laws put an end to the immigration of Asians.

The Ku Klux Klan Several groups raised fears about immigrants and other groups. The worst was the Ku Klux Klan. The Klan was formed after the Civil War. It had almost died out. But, in 1915, the Klan started growing. Now it targeted not only African Americans, but immigrants, Catholics, Jews, and labor unions as well.

The Klan used violence. As strike breakers, they beat up union members. The Klan attacked immigrants. They terrorized Catholics and Jews. Klan members murdered African Americans. Often, the Klan lynched their victims.

In 1923, the Klan was at the height of its power. It claimed over 4 million members in both the North and the South. In 1925, scandals broke out. The corruption of Klan leaders was exposed. Klan membership began to decline.

1. What were the Palmer Raids?
2. Who were Sacco and Vanzetti?

2 Business Booms in the 1920s.
Why did the U.S. economy improve in the 1920s?

Newspapers all over the country celebrated an amazing event. On November 2, 1920, 500 people heard a person read the news over a squawky box. Warren G. Harding was pronounced winner of the 1920 presidential election. This news came from a new invention—the radio. New products like the radio changed the U.S. economy in the 1920s.

Pro-business Presidents   Harding promised a return to **prosperous** times. Prosperous means successful, especially in terms of wealth. He tried to help U.S. businesses grow.

Harding cut taxes for wealthy people. He argued that if the wealthy had more money, they would invest it in businesses. Then businesses could expand and hire more workers. Workers would have more income. Some Americans disagreed with these tax cuts.

Under Harding, Congress passed an act raising **tariffs.** A tariff is a tax on imports. This act tried to protect U.S. businesses from foreign competition. Harding also cut federal spending.

Many people Harding put in power were corrupt. Several scandals broke out. In 1923, Harding died of a heart attack. Vice-President Calvin Coolidge took over. Coolidge continued Harding's pro-business plans. He was reelected in 1924.

Roaring Twenties   Between 1923 and 1929, U.S. businesses boomed. This time was called the "Roaring Twenties." American industries grew. Businesses made huge profits. To many, the 1920s were even better than times before World War I. Manufactured goods had been scarce during the war. Customers had saved their money for years. Now they spent it.

There were many jobs. Wages improved. By 1929, workers' incomes had risen by almost one third from 1900. More people could afford the products that poured from U.S. factories.

Revolution in new products Products were very different than those made just a few years before. By the

The Roaring Twenties were a time when businesses in the United States boomed. The automobile industry led the way. Cars jammed this New York City street.

late 1920s, 70 percent of U.S. homes had electricity. Americans wanted products that ran on electricity. They bought radios and refrigerators.

They also bought machines that saved labor, such as washing machines and vacuum cleaners. Time spent washing clothes could now be spent in other ways. All of these new products changed the daily life of Americans.

Effects of the car   The product that made the greatest changes in American life was the car. Henry Ford's assembly line made cars that people could afford. (See page 8.) The auto

American culture changed in the 1920s. The Jazz Age came alive with singers like Besse Smith, making this music famous around the country and the world.

rants were built on major roads. New companies produced the materials needed to build cars. Glass and rubber companies grew. Steel companies increased production. These new businesses added to the prosperity of the 1920s.

Unequal wealth Not everyone shared in this prosperity, however. Even in boom times, 10 percent of the work force was out of a job.

This percent was even greater for people of color. A 1926 report said that most Native Americans were "extremely poor." Some African Americans had found wartime jobs in the factories of the North and Midwest. But they often lost these jobs to returning white soldiers. In the early 1920s, discrimination against Mexican Americans increased. Some people argued that all Mexican immigrants should be deported.

1. Name three changes in Americans' lives that took place during the 1920s.
2. Which groups did not share in the prosperity of the 1920s?

industry took off. By the end of the 1920s, one out of five Americans owned a car.

Once people owned cars, they demanded better roads. The Federal Highway Act of 1921 encouraged road-building in the United States. Roads connected distant places as never before. People could travel much more easily. Many began moving from cities to **suburbs.** A suburb is an area in which people live around a city.

Cars also created new business opportunities. Trucks replaced shipping by train. Gasoline stations sprang up all over the country. Motels and restau-

3 Ways of Life Change.
How did American culture change in the 1920s?

Alvin "Shipwreck" Kelly started the fad. He sat on top of a flagpole as a movie stunt. Then a theater owner had him do it again to advertise the movie. Soon people all over the country were sitting on flagpoles. All the changes in the "Roaring Twenties" made people a bit dizzy. Fads were just part of the national mood.

The Jazz Age American culture changed in the 1920s. This was the **Jazz Age.** Jazz is a kind of music that was very popular then.

Jazz was created by African Americans in New Orleans in the 1880s. It blended West African rhythms and African American blues. African American musicians such as Jelly Roll Morton and Billie Holiday made jazz famous. Soon people all over the country danced to this music in hotels, clubs, and dance halls.

Jazz caused great debate. People either loved it or hated it. It captured the hearts of young people. They saw themselves as different from their parents. To them, jazz represented free-spirited, fun-loving youth. Jazz became a symbol of the new American culture in the 1920s.

Fun and games After World War I, many Americans just wanted to have fun. Play was very important to them. Movies, sports, and other entertainment occupied people's minds.

In the 1920s, movies became part of life. Actors like Rudolph Valentino, Douglas Fairbanks, and Mary Pickford became stars. They had millions of fans. In 1927, *The Jazz Singer* became the first movie with sound. In 1920, 50 million Americans went to the movies every week. By 1930, the number had doubled to 100 million.

Attendance at sports events also soared. Baseball became important. Great athletes like Babe Ruth drew huge crowds. In 1927, Ruth set a baseball record. He hit 60 home runs in a single season. Millions of people watched college football throughout the Fall. Track-and-field events were also popular. Women athletes became famous. In 1926, Americans celebrated when Gertrude Ederle became the first woman to swim the English Channel.

Hero worship The greatest hero of the age was Charles Lindbergh (LIND-berg). In 1927, Lindbergh flew alone from New York to Paris. He was the first person to cross the Atlantic alone by air.

Lindbergh was welcomed back with a parade in New York City. Congress awarded him the Congressional Medal of Honor. Babies were named after him. Songs were written about him. A new dance, "The Lindy," was created in his honor.

Changes for women For many young women, the 1920s brought new freedoms. Long skirts and long hair

The 1920s brought new freedoms to women. Here, three flappers in Harlem are dressed in short skirts and bobbed hair, the new style of the 20s.

were out. These young women were called **flappers.** They wore short skirts and silk stockings. They bobbed, or cut short, their hair. They wore makeup. They even smoked. Many people found this shocking.

But there were deeper changes as well. Women in the 1920s had new roles. During World War I, many women took over factory jobs. They lost most of these jobs when soldiers returned. Still, after the war, more women worked outside the home. They became typists, salespeople, and secretaries. Some women opened their own shops. College-educated women became teachers and social workers.

Women also gained political rights. In 1920, the Nineteenth Amendment gave women the right to vote. Women no longer had to fight for suffrage. The League of Women Voters was started to inform women about political issues. In 1924, two women were elected governors—Miriam Ferguson in Texas and Nellie Taylor Ross in Wyoming.

Prohibition   In 1919, the states adopted the Eighteenth Amendment. It **prohibited** making or selling alcohol. Prohibit means to outlaw. Alcohol companies closed. Bars shut down. The United States went "dry."

Prohibition was greatly debated. Many Americans disagreed with it. Millions broke the law. **Speakeasies,** or illegal bars, opened. People made alcohol in secret. Others smuggled it into the country. They were called bootleggers. Gangs began to organize these illegal sales. Soon, gangsters controlled most speakeasies. They made billions of dollars. They paid off corrupt officials to keep quiet. Prohibition actually encouraged crime.

By 1933, it was clear that Prohibition did not work. The Eighteenth Amendment was repealed. It was the end of an era.

1. List three activities Americans were interested in during the 1920s.
2. How did women's roles change in the 1920s?

CHAPTER 11
KEY IDEAS

- Soon after World War I, the U.S. economy suffered a depression. Many Americans felt fears about immigrants and Communists.
- Presidents Harding and Coolidge made pro-business policies. New products poured out of U.S. factories. These policies and products made the 1920s a time of great prosperity.
- In the Jazz Age, many Americans focused on having fun. Women's roles changed. Prohibition led to many people breaking the law.

REVIEWING CHAPTER 11

I. Reviewing Vocabulary
Match each word on the left with the correct definition on the right.
1. prosperous   -   **a.** a limit
2. prohibit   **b.** a tax on imports
3. quota   **c.** an area around a city that people live in
4. tariff   **d.** successful, especially in terms of wealth
5. suburb   **e.** to outlaw

II. Understanding the Chapter
1. How did workers react to difficult economic conditions after World War I?
2. What limits were put on immigration in the 1920s?
3. How did President Harding try to improve the economy?
4. What new products were produced in U.S. factories in the 1920s?
5. How did Americans entertain themselves in the 1920s?

III. Building Skills: Drawing Conclusions
Draw a reasonable conclusion for the facts below.
1. In the 1920s, half a million people were arrested for breaking Prohibition.
2. In 1929, U.S. power plants produced 19 times as much electricity as they did in 1902.

IV. Writing About History
1. **What Would You Have Done?** If you were an immigrant in the 1920s, would you change your name as Giovanni Lagomarsino did? Explain.
2. Write an article covering one event in this chapter for a 1920s magazine. Be sure to answer the questions: *who, what, when, where, why, and how.*

V. Working Together
1. Form a small group. Make a magazine using the articles you wrote for Writing About History. Include advertisements for products that first appeared in the 1920s, such as the radio. Create an exciting cover.
2. **Past to Present** In 1927, Lindbergh crossed the Atlantic. With a group, discuss how airplanes have become an important part of your lives today. List four reasons airplanes are important.

AFRICAN AMERICAN CULTURE THRIVES IN THE JAZZ AGE. (1919—1929)

In what ways did African Americans in the 1920s express their sense of pride?

The Silent March of 1917 down New York City's Fifth Avenue protested lynching, discrimination, and segregation. One of the marchers was Dr. W.E.B. DuBois.

Looking at Key Terms

- black nationalism • Harlem Renaissance

Looking at Key Words

- **casualty:** someone who has been injured or killed
- **renaissance:** rebirth
- **autobiography:** the story of one's own life written by oneself

STUDY HINT

As you are reading the chapter, answer the questions *who, what, when, where,* and *why* about the Harlem Renaissance.

On a steamy August day in 1920, 50,000 African Americans marched through Harlem. Thousands more lined the sidewalks. They cheered loudly as a man in a gold-trimmed uniform rolled past in an open car. The man was Marcus Garvey. That night, Garvey addressed 25,000 African Americans in New York City's Madison Square Garden. His words stirred African American pride.

1 Marcus Garvey Appeals to Black Nationalism.

Why were African Americans attracted to Marcus Garvey's program?

After World War I, African Americans began to focus on discrimination. W.E.B. DuBois urged African Americans to fight it hard. This battle soon became very bitter.

Race Riots   The Great Migration had left its mark. African American populations of cities in the North and Midwest steadily increased. (See page 24.)

Some whites resented these new neighbors. Many whites worried African Americans would take their jobs. Other whites did not want African Americans in their neighborhoods. Bombs destroyed the offices of Chicago real estate agents. They had sold homes in white neighborhoods to African Americans. Tensions grew between the two groups. Then, in 1919, race riots broke out across the nation.

During that summer, **casualties** mounted. A casualty is someone who has been injured or killed. Six died and 150 were injured in Washington, D.C. The toll in Chicago was 38 dead and 537 injured. By year's end, race riots had ripped through 25 U.S. cities and towns.

The Klan   The Ku Klux Klan was again threatening African Americans. (See page 94.) By day, its members held parades in Northern as well as Southern cities. The Klan put pressure on politicians to support Klan policies.

By night, Klan riders attacked African Americans in their homes. Sometimes African Americans were tarred and feathered. The number of lynchings had fallen during World War I. Now the number rose again.

A new life   African Americans were tired of these attacks. Some fought back with force. Others wanted to find political solutions. Members of the NAACP tried to change laws. However, one thing was clear. Something must be done about discrimination against African Americans.

W.E.B. DuBois fought to get African Americans to honor their African roots. These ideas were not new. In the early 1800s, Paul Cuffe wanted African Americans to go back to Africa. DuBois believed people of African descent had common interests. They should join together to struggle for freedom. This struggle would occur both in the United States and overseas.

Beginnings of a Movement   African roots inspired another African American leader—Marcus Garvey. He was one of the most important leaders of his time.

Garvey was born in Jamaica. As a young man, he traveled in Europe and the Americas. He was struck by the injustices people of African descent everywhere faced. At age 25, Garvey went to London. There he met African scholars and thinkers. They taught him about his rich African heritage.

Then in 1914, he founded the Universal Negro Improvement Association (UNIA) in Jamaica. Its goal was

Followers of Marcus Garvey, such as these Garveyite families, valued their African heritage and believed in black nationalism. Garvey's goal was economic, political, and cultural independence for people of African descent.

economic, political, and cultural independence for people of African descent.

In 1916, Garvey brought the UNIA to the United States. He opened a branch in Harlem, the African American section of New York City. Garvey decided to run the UNIA from there. This began the first powerful black nationalist movement in the United States. **Black nationalism** is the belief that people of African descent should rely on themselves. They should also be proud of their blackness and of their African roots.

DuBois and the NAACP had attracted mostly a upper and middle class following. Garvey appealed to ordinary African Americans. He offered pride and uplifting messages. The UNIA grew fast. By 1920, it claimed to have four million members.

The work of the UNIA The UNIA supported African American culture. Its

newspaper, the *Negro World,* published stories about African American leaders. Such stories were usually left out of white newspapers.

The UNIA also worked for economic independence. In 1919, Garvey founded a steamship company, the Black Star Line. He hoped it would develop business ties between Africa and people of African descent all over the world. Garvey also started the Negro Factories Corporation. It created grocery stores, laundries, a restaurant, and a publishing company.

A movement collapses Then disaster struck. Rumors began to spread. People said the Black Star Line was in financial trouble. It was true. Garvey was a poor manager. He let others run the business. They spent huge sums on leaky ships and poorly-trained crews.

The U.S. government investigated the Black Star Line. In 1922, Garvey was

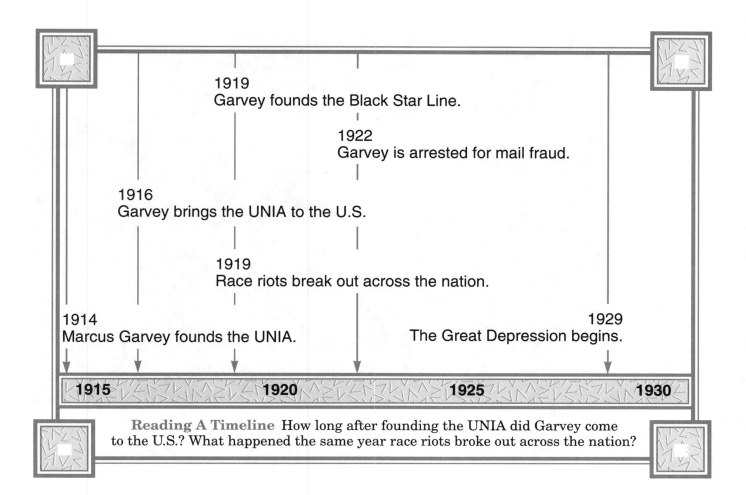

1919
Garvey founds the Black Star Line.

1922
Garvey is arrested for mail fraud.

1916
Garvey brings the UNIA to the U.S.

1919
Race riots break out across the nation.

1914
Marcus Garvey founds the UNIA.

1929
The Great Depression begins.

1915   1920   1925   1930

Reading A Timeline How long after founding the UNIA did Garvey come to the U.S.? What happened the same year race riots broke out across the nation?

arrested for mail fraud. It was not proven that Garvey meant to commit a crime. Yet, he was found guilty. He was sentenced to five years in prison. President Coolidge freed Garvey in 1927. He had served two years of his sentence. Then Garvey was deported from the United States.

Lasting effects Without Garvey, the UNIA fell apart. Yet, black nationalism did not disappear. It returned, stronger, in the 1960s. African Americans saw Garvey's great achievement. He began a movement to make African Americans a united people. "In a world where black is despised [hated]," said New York's *Amsterdam News*, "he taught them that black is beautiful."

During the 1920s, this African American pride was expressed in new ways. An explosion of African American art and culture took place in Harlem.

1. What is black nationalism?
2. Name two ways the UNIA tried to meet its goals.

2 African Americans Create the Harlem Renaissance.

What were the contributions of the artists of the Harlem Renaissance?

It was Saturday night in New York City. Taxis and limousines headed uptown. Hundreds of white people hurried to the hottest spot in town—

W.E.B. DuBois is standing to the right in the editorial office of *The Crisis*. DuBois was one of the most influential leaders of the early civil rights movement. He was one of the founders of the NAACP and was a longtime editor of *The Crisis* magazine.

Harlem. It was the place to be. White crowds cheered African American performers at the Cotton Club. They listened to jazz at the Catagonia Club. They danced the Charleston at the Savoy. Harlem in the 1920s was bursting with excitement.

African American capital of the world The Great Migration had changed New York City above 110th Street. Harlem was once an all-white neighborhood. It was now home to more than 100,000 African Americans. By the 1920s, it was the nation's largest African American community.

In the 1920s, Harlem was the cultural center for all people of African descent. It was known as the African American "Capital of the World." The greatest African American leaders, such as W.E.B. DuBois and Marcus Garvey,

lived there. The NAACP and the National Urban League had their headquarters in New York. Being part of the Harlem community gave African Americans a sense of power and pride.

Culture reborn Harlem was also the heart of a new creative movement. This was the **Harlem Renaissance.** A **renaissance** is a rebirth. In European history, it was a time when the ideas of the past were rediscovered. The Harlem Renaissance was the rebirth of African American culture. For the first time, whites appreciated African American art and literature.

African American writers, artists, and musicians were lured to Harlem in the 1920s. The *Crisis*, the NAACP magazine, offered cash prizes for excellent writing. So did the Urban League's *Opportunity*. The Harmon Foundation gave awards to

African American writers and artists. It set up exhibits of African American painters and sculptors.

Harlem's location also was an attraction. The major publishers were in New York City. Broadway theaters offered national fame for writers and performers. New York City was the center of the music business.

Most important, in Harlem, African American artists could meet and exchange ideas. This created a sense of excitement and hope. Many new talents bloomed. Some worked with common themes such as love, childhood, and grief. However, many dealt with a new

focus. They explored how it felt to be African American. African American culture inspired their work.

Writers African Americans writers burst on to the 1920s scene. They created a great body of literature. Many discussed racism and prejudice. They shared the pain of discrimination with their readers. They also shared their vision of African American pride. Novels, short stories, plays, and poetry poured out of Harlem writers.

Writers such as James Weldon Johnson, Jean Toomer, Jessie R. Fauset, and Claude McKay excelled. Zora Neale Hurston collected African American folktales. She wrote her own short stories, novels, and an **autobiography,** *Dust Tracks on a Road.* An autobiography is the story of one's own life written by oneself. Her writing celebrated being African American. Poet Countee Cullen also wrote about the African American experience. His poem "Heritage" dealt with his African roots.

Langston Hughes was one of the greatest Harlem Renaissance writers. He captured the spirit of African American music, especially jazz and the blues, in his work. He wrote fiction, autobiographies, plays, and movie scripts. But he was best known for his poetry. One famous Hughes poem was "I, Too, Sing America." In it, he demanded equality for African Americans.

Langston Hughes was one of the greatest Harlem Renaissance writers and poets. His poetry expressed the desire for African American equality.

Artists Painters and sculptors also took part in the Harlem Renaissance. Many drew inspiration from Africa and from African American history.

Artist Aaron Douglas created murals. He also illustrated the books of such writers as Hughes and Cullen. He used ideas from African sculpture. Hale Woodruff was another great mural painter. Other artists were Augusta Savage, Sargent Johnson, and Horace

Pippin. Traveling exhibitions brought their work to national attention.

Musicians In the 1920s, African American music became very popular. In 1922, Louis Armstrong brought his cornet from New Orleans to Chicago. His brilliant playing changed the sound of U.S. music. Some people mark this as the beginning of the Jazz Age.

Soon, clubs, ballrooms, and theaters dotted Harlem. In each, African American musicians played jazz and blues. Jazz greats such as Fats Waller and Duke Ellington drew huge crowds. They became world famous.

Many African American musicians became successes. Composer William Grant Still wrote operas, ballets, and movie soundtracks. Bessie Smith was called the Empress of the Blues. Her 1923 recording "Down Hearted Blues" sold more than 2 million copies. Another blues singer, Ethel Waters, won millions of fans.

Performers African American performers also got the spotlight. In the 1920s, jazz came to the stage. Broadway musicals began featuring African American actors, singers, and dancers. Shows such as *Shuffle Along* and *Hot Chocolates* became smash hits. Stars such as Florence Mills and Josephine Baker gained worldwide fame.

Paul Robeson was one of the greatest singers of his time. He also was a famous actor. Robeson thrilled audiences as Shakespeare's Othello. Robeson spoke out for African American civil rights. This made him powerful enemies. People accused him of being a Communist. The U.S. State Department called him "one of the most dangerous men in the world." They took back Robeson's passport. He was forced to live abroad. Even the stars of the Harlem Renaissance could not escape discrimination.

End of an era African American artists worked after the 1920s. But the Harlem Renaissance did not survive the decade. The economic boom of the 1920s ended. In 1929, the nation plunged into poverty. African Americans suffered with the rest of the country.

1. Name two writers of the Harlem Renaissance.
2. Who was Paul Robeson?

CHAPTER 12
KEY IDEAS

- Marcus Garvey stressed black nationalism in his Universal Negro Improvement Association. He attracted thousands of followers.
- During the Harlem Renaissance, African American artists produced great works. Many expressed pride in their African roots and in African American culture.

REVIEWING CHAPTER 12

I. Reviewing Vocabulary

Match each word or words on the left with the correct definition on the right.

1. black nationalism
2. renaissance
3. casualty
4. autobiography
5. Harlem Renaissance

a. period in the 1920s when literature and art by African Americans bloomed
b. someone who has been injured or killed
c. the story of one's own life written by oneself
d. African Americans' pride in themselves and in their African roots
e. rebirth

II. Understanding the Chapter

1. Why did race riots break out in many U.S. cities in 1919?
2. What was the goal of the UNIA?
3. What was Garvey's great achievement?
4. Why were African American artists attracted to Harlem in the 1920s?
5. What was the focus of the work of many African American writers and artists?

III. Building Skills: Finding the Main Idea

1. What is the main idea of "Beginnings of a Movement" in Section 1?
2. What is the main idea of "African American Capital of the World," in Section 2?

IV. Writing About History

1. Marcus Garvey died in 1940. Write an obituary—an article discussing his life—that could have appeared in a Harlem newspaper.
2. **What Would You Have Done?** If you had become famous during the Harlem Renaissance, would you have spoken out for African American civil rights like Paul Robeson did? Explain.

V. Working Together

1. Form a small group. Write the words "Harlem Renaissance" at the top of a sheet of paper. Then take turns writing facts about the Harlem Renaissance on the paper. Keep passing the paper around until you cannot add any more information. Compare your paper with those of other groups in the class. Add any facts that you missed.
2. **Past to Present** With a group, make a list of current writers, artists, or musicians that focus on what it is like to be African American today.

A Great Depression Takes Hold. (1929—1933)

What effect did the Great Depression have on the American people?

The Great Depression of the 1930s forced thousands of workers out of their jobs. Many had to line up in the streets just to get bread and food.

Looking at Key Terms

- Great Depression • Dust Bowl • Okies
- Arkies • Hooverville

Looking at Key Words

- **stock market:** a business where stocks, or shares of companies are bought and sold
- **depression:** a deep economic downturn
- **relief:** help given to those in poverty or need

- **breadline:** a line in which people stand to receive food
- **repatriation:** when a person is sent back to his or her own country

In the morning,
In the evening,
Ain't we got fun?

This happy song was a good symbol for the 1920s. It was a period of wealth for many people. However, in October 1929, the fun came to an end. The prosperity of the 1920s gave way to the **Great Depression** of the 1930s.

1 Millions Are Without Work.

How did people survive during the Great Depression?

The Great Depression was the worst economic crisis in U.S. history. Middle class and even rich people sank into poverty. Those who already were poor found it even harder to survive. A sad song became the symbol of the new era. "Brother, Can You Spare a Dime?" spoke for millions of Americans:

They used to tell me I was building
    a dream
And so I followed the mob.
When there was earth to plow, or
    guns to bear [carry]
I was always there
Right on the job.

Once I built a railroad, made it run
Made it race against time.
Once I built a railroad,
Now it's done.
Brother, can you spare a dime?"

The stock market crash On Thursday, October 24, 1929, the **stock market** in New York City crashed. A stock market is a place where stocks, or shares of companies, are bought and sold. When the prices of stocks rise, people who own them make money. When prices fall, people who own the stocks lose money.

Throughout most of the 1920s, stock prices rose. Beginning in 1928, they rose very quickly. People who owned stocks made a great deal of money. However, many people had bought stocks with borrowed money. If stock prices ever fell, these people would not have the money to pay their debts.

Suddenly on October 24, 1929, stock prices did fall. They fell so fast that stockholders lost over $3 billion. Never had prices fallen so far in a single day. Never had losses been so large. People called October 24 "Black Thursday."

On Tuesday, October 29, stock prices fell again. The drop in prices and the losses were even worse than those of a few days earlier. October 29 became known as "Black Tuesday." After October 1929, share prices continued to fall for almost four years. By 1932, shares were worth only one-fifth of their 1929 value. Thousands of Americans had lost most of their money.

The Great Depression The stock market crash marked the beginning of the Great Depression. A **depression** is a severe economic downturn. However, the crash was not the only cause of the depression. Large parts of the United States' economy already were in trouble by October 1929.

Prices of farm crops were very low. Many farmers had trouble paying their bills. Workers in factories earned low wages. Most could not afford the cars, radios and other products U.S. factories were building.

The stock market crash of October 1929 was the final blow that made the weak U.S. economy fall apart. Between 1929 and 1932, over 5,000 banks failed. These banks had loaned money to people and businesses. Neither group could pay their loans. Millions lost all their money. Over 100,000 businesses failed.

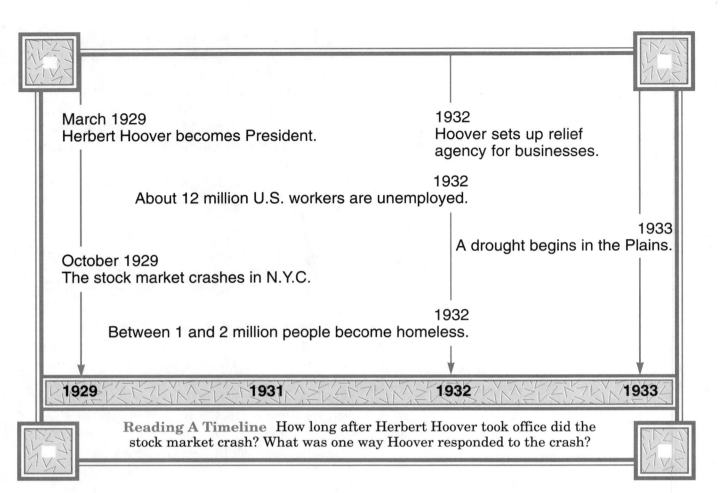

March 1929
Herbert Hoover becomes President.

1932
Hoover sets up relief agency for businesses.

1932
About 12 million U.S. workers are unemployed.

1933
A drought begins in the Plains.

October 1929
The stock market crashes in N.Y.C.

1932
Between 1 and 2 million people become homeless.

| 1929 | 1931 | 1932 | 1933 |

Reading A Timeline How long after Herbert Hoover took office did the stock market crash? What was one way Hoover responded to the crash?

As the Depression spread, millions of people lost their jobs. By 1932, about 12 million U.S. workers were unemployed. That was almost a quarter of the U.S. work force.

Unemployed and homeless During the 1930s, millions of people walked city streets looking for work. Thousands more rode railroad boxcars from state to state trying to find a job. Others simply walked from town to town. One man from Arkansas walked 900 miles (1,440 kilometers) looking for a job. Few found work. By the early 1930s, one million New Yorkers were without jobs. In Chicago, there were 660,000 jobless. In Cleveland, half of all workers could not find work.

After they lost their jobs, many people also lost their homes. Soon settlements of shacks made by the homeless appeared in U.S. cities. These shacks were built of cardboard, scrap metal, packing boxes, and tar paper. People bitterly called these settlements **Hoovervilles,** after President Herbert Hoover. Americans were angry that President Hoover's attempts to fight the Depression were failing. The largest Hooverville was in St. Louis, Missouri. Over 1,000 people lived there.

In other cities, people lived wherever they could find shelter. They lived in unused sewer pipes, under bridges, on subways, in public parks, and even in caves. During the winter, some homeless people asked to sleep in jail cells. There, at least they would be warm. By 1932, between one and two million Americans were homeless.

Hunger was even more widespread than homelessness. Millions of people had barely enough money to buy food.

Those who did not have money turned to charity. Churches and other charities opened up soup kitchens in the cities to feed the hungry. Each day millions of hungry people stood on **breadlines** to get scraps of food.

This aid, or **relief,** was not enough. People grew sick from lack of food. Children suffered the most. In New York City, one child in five was hungry. In poorer parts of the country, the situation was even worse.

Family life The Depression also weakened the confidence of the American people. Fathers who could no longer feed their families blamed themselves. Many who could not face their families left home. By 1940, over 1.5 million men had left their wives. Often, children left home so their parents would not have to feed them. About 250,000 children left home and wandered across the country.

Yet most families managed to stick together. Fathers, mothers, and children found whatever work they could to help the family. People with houses or apartments took in boarders to help meet expenses. Those with backyards planted vegetable gardens. City people grew food in vacant lots. Many wives made some extra money by making and selling baked goods or clothing. Millions of families learned to get along with what they had. They survived the Depression.

In every city, the homeless slept in sewer pipes or in huts made of tin, cardboard, and scraps of wood. This slum sprang up in an empty lot in New York City. Why do you think they were nicknamed "Hoovervilles"?

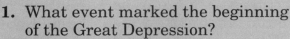

1. What event marked the beginning of the Great Depression?
2. What were Hoovervilles?

2 The Depression Hits Some Groups Hardest.

How were African Americans, Mexican Americans, and others affected by the Depression?

African Americans suffered even more than most other Americans during the Depression. One reason was that African Americans were poorer than most Americans to begin with. As the poet Langston Hughes wrote, "The Depression brought everyone down a peg or two. And the Negroes had but a few pegs to fall."

African Americans During the 1920s, over 800,000 African Americans left their homes in the South and moved to northern cities. (See Chapter 3.) Many were unskilled workers. They took jobs that others did not want. These jobs were low paying and demanded few skills. However, many lost their jobs when the Depression hit. As the last hired, African Americans often were the first fired.

The few jobs that were available often went to unemployed whites. Discrimination made the chances of finding work even slimmer for African Americans. By 1932, the jobless rate among African Americans was 50 percent. That was double the national average.

African Americans who managed to keep their jobs during the Depression also suffered. As with Americans from many other groups, African Americans with jobs had their wages cut. In some cases, employers cut wages in half. In many African American families, women worked. Many took jobs as servants in private homes where they worked for extremely low wages.

Life in the South Most African Americans during the 1930s still lived in the South. Many were tenant farmers who paid their landlords a share of their crop as rent. These farmers lived in poverty even during good times.

The tenant farmers' most important crop was cotton. But during the Depression the price of cotton dropped by two-thirds. A crop that would have brought $300 now brought $100. It became impossible to make a living on the land. In the early 1930s, the average income of African American cotton farmers was less than $200 per year.

Some African American tenant farmers moved to northern cities looking for work. Few of them found jobs. However, African American organizations provided help for the unemployed. Churches started soup kitchens and gave clothing to the needy. The National Urban League set up shelters that gave the poor food, clothing, and medical care.

The Depression increased discrimination in the United States. However, there also were examples of cooperation between whites and African Americans. In Arkansas, black and white tenant farmers organized the Southern Tenant Farmers Union. The union fought for better conditions from the landowners. It published a newspaper called the *Sharecroppers Voice*.

The landlords often used violence against the union. They hired men to break up union meetings and beat union organizers. The Southern Tenant Farmers Union won few victories. However, despite great hardship its members stuck together.

Mexican migrant workers Mexican migrant workers also suffered

Mexican American farm workers suffered greatly during the Depression. When migrant workers struck because of bad conditions, the state sent in police, rather than food. Explain the sign these women are carrying.

special hardship during the Depression. Over one million Mexicans came to the United States during the 1920s. Most of them worked as laborers on farms. They earned very low wages. When the Depression began, many of these jobs were cut.

Some Mexicans who lost their jobs decided to return to Mexico. Others, however, were sent home by force. Cities with relief programs did not want to spend money on Mexicans. The federal government called the policy of forcing Mexicans to leave the United States **repatriation.** Repatriation means to send a person back to the home country.

Altogether about 400,000 Mexicans were repatriated. Some of those sent to Mexico were children who had been born in the United States. This means they were U.S. citizens when the government sent them to Mexico.

Okies and Arkies The Depression forced another group to move. These people came from the plains of Oklahoma, Arkansas, Kansas, Texas and Missouri. The soil in this region had been used too much for farming and grazing animals. Beginning in 1933, a terrible drought began. Strong winds blew the dry, dusty soil across the plains. The dust storms were so large that they blocked out the sun. They were called "black blizzards." As one man put it, "Noon was like night." People called the region where the drought was the **Dust Bowl.** (See the map on page 114.)

Many farmers in the Dust Bowl had to leave their farms. Hundreds of thousands traveled west toward California looking for work. Entire families stuffed themselves and their belongings into creaky old cars that often broke down.

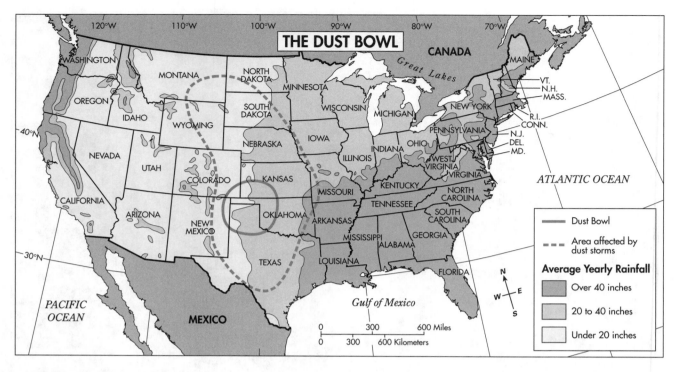

Reading a Map. What states were in the Dust Bowl? Name some other states that suffered from dust storms. Did the dust storms hit most severely in areas that got more than 40 inches of rain a year or in areas that got under 20 inches?

Families without cars climbed onto freight trains or crammed into buses. Because many migrants came from Oklahoma and Arkansas, people called all of them either "Okies" or "Arkies."

Okies and Arkies traveling west often faced discrimination. One sign on the road to California read,

"NO JOBS in California . . . IF YOU are looking for work—KEEP OUT."

Still the Okies continued westward. When they reached California, those who found jobs usually worked as migrant farm laborers.

1. What kinds of services did African American organizations offer during the Depression?
2. Who were the Okies and Arkies?

3 The Government Fails to Meet the Challenge.
Why did President Hoover refuse to aid the needy?

Herbert Hoover became President in January 1929. Before that he had been very successful in business and public service. He became a millionaire before he was 40. When he took office, Hoover said the future of the United States was "bright with hope." Like many others, he could not predict the economic crisis that would come in less than a year.

Herbert Hoover When the Great Depression hit, President Hoover was against government help for the unemployed or needy. He feared that such help would make people rely on government, not themselves. This would rob Americans of their independent spirit.

Hoover's beliefs are one reason the federal government did not act quickly to fight the Depression. Another reason is that the President did not understand how serious the situation was. Few Americans did. The country had never seen anything like the Great Depression. In the past, the country recovered from economic crises without the government's help. That did not happen after October 1929. In 1930, Hoover believed that the United States had "passed the worst." The President was wrong. Conditions only worsened with each passing day.

Hoover and the Depression At first Hoover tried to fight the Depression by making hopeful speeches to build public confidence. People called this policy "cheerleading." It failed. In 1930, Hoover tried to do more.

The federal government started projects that would give people jobs. The largest project was the huge Hoover Dam on the Colorado River. Work on the dam began in 1930. By the time it was finished in 1936, Hoover was no longer President.

In 1932, Hoover convinced Congress to set up an agency to give loans to banks, railroads, life insurance companies, and other organizations. Hoover hoped these loans would be passed on to other businesses. This would help them stay open and hire new workers. The agency helped a little but not nearly enough. When Hoover's presidency ended in March 1933, the Great Depression was as bad as ever.

1. In what year did Herbert Hoover become President?
2. What did Hoover do to try to help the economy?

CHAPTER 13
KEY IDEAS

- In October 1929, a weak U.S. economy crumbled when the stock market crashed. This marked the beginning of the Great Depression.
- Millions of Americans lost their jobs and their homes during the Great Depression. African Americans, Mexican migrant workers, and people who lived in the Dust Bowl were hit hardest.
- When the Depression first hit, President Hoover believed it would end without government help. President Hoover's attempts to end the Depression were not effective.

I. Reviewing Vocabulary

Match each word on the left with the correct definition on the right.

1. depression
2. relief
3. breadline
4. repatriation
5. stock market

a. when a person is sent back to his or her own country
b. a line on which people stand to receive free food
c. help given to those in poverty or need
d. a business where shares, or pieces, of companies are bought and sold
e. a deep economic downturn

II. Understanding the Chapter

1. Why did the stock market crash of October 1929 lead to the Great Depression?
2. What effect did the Depression have on family life in the United States?
3. Why did the U.S. government repatriate Mexican migrant workers?
4. How did the drought that began in 1933 add to the troubles caused by the Depression?
5. Why did President Hoover act slowly to fight the Depression?

III. Building Skills: Time Check

1. Which event occurred first: the stock market crash or the beginning of the drought that caused the Dust Bowl?
2. What did President Hoover do first: build the Hoover Dam or set up an agency to loan money to businesses?

IV. Writing About History

1. **What Would You Have Done?** Imagine that you are an African American tenant farmer in the South. Would you stay in the South or move to the northern cities?
2. Imagine that you are about to interview President Hoover about the Depression. List at least five questions you would ask him in your interview.

V. Working Together

1. Form a group with two or three classmates. Together, write a skit about a family who sticks together during the Great Depression. Perform your skit for the class.
2. **Past to Present** As you have read, many people became homeless during the Great Depression. Today, there are also many homeless people in the United States. With a group of classmates, discuss ways your community offers help to the homeless.

THE NEW DEAL BRINGS NEW HOPE. (1933–1938)

*How did the New Deal affect
the United States?*

President Roosevelt called his radio messages "fireside chats." They were informal talks that cheered millions of Americans who tuned in to hear them.

Looking at Key Terms

- Hundred Days • National Recovery Administration (NRA)
- Tennessee Valley Authority (TVA) • Social Security Act

Looking at Key Words

- **fireside chat:** a radio talk President Roosevelt gave to the nation
- **unemployment insurance:** a system in which the government makes payments for a certain time to people who lose their jobs
- **social security:** a government policy that provides pensions to retired people
- **welfare:** regular government payments to people who are unable to provide for their own needs
- **dictator:** a ruler who has complete control and power

STUDY

As you read through the chapter, make a list of each New Deal program. Next to each program describe what it did and who it helped.

HINT

On March 12, 1933, about 60 million Americans gathered around their radios. They already had gone through four years of hard times. They were discouraged and worried. They were about to listen to their new President, Franklin Delano Roosevelt.

Roosevelt had been in office only eight days. Yet he was already making changes. Roosevelt decided to speak to Americans in an informal, or casual, way. He called his talks **fireside chats.** The President's voice was calm and comforting. Roosevelt spoke in everyday words. This helped him win the confidence of millions of Americans. For the first time since the Depression began, the American people gained some hope.

1 President Roosevelt Launches the New Deal.
What steps did President Roosevelt take to end the Depression?

Franklin Delano Roosevelt came from a wealthy New York family. He went to an expensive private school and then to Harvard University. Although he grew up in wealth, Roosevelt did not ignore the problems of the poor. As President, he created many programs to help the poor through the Depression.

Franklin Delano Roosevelt
Franklin was a distant cousin of former President Theodore Roosevelt. Franklin admired his cousin. He followed his example by entering politics. Franklin served in the New York legislature. Then, he became assistant secretary of the navy. In 1920, he ran for Vice President but lost.

Another important influence on Franklin Roosevelt was his wife. Eleanor Roosevelt had strong views about the problems facing the United States. She spoke up for the poor and those who suffered from discrimination.

Despite Franklin's defeat in 1920, his future still looked bright. However, in 1921 disaster struck. Franklin became ill with a crippling disease called polio. His legs were paralyzed, and he never walked again. Yet polio did not stop Roosevelt. He fought to regain his strength and rebuild his body.

Reading a Chart. In what year did the percentage of unemployed nonfarm workers reach its peak? How many years did it take for the unemployed percentage to fall to below the level it was at in 1925?

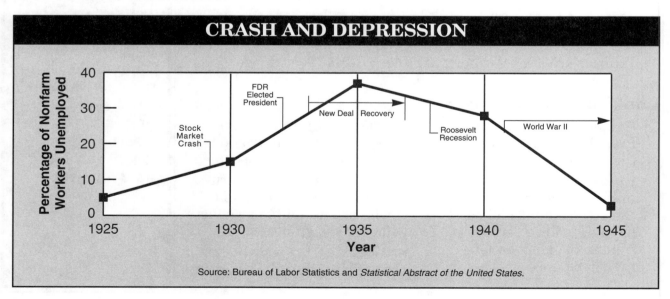

CRASH AND DEPRESSION

Percentage of Nonfarm Workers Unemployed

Stock Market Crash

FDR Elected President

New Deal | Recovery

Roosevelt Recession

World War II

Year

Source: Bureau of Labor Statistics and *Statistical Abstract of the United States.*

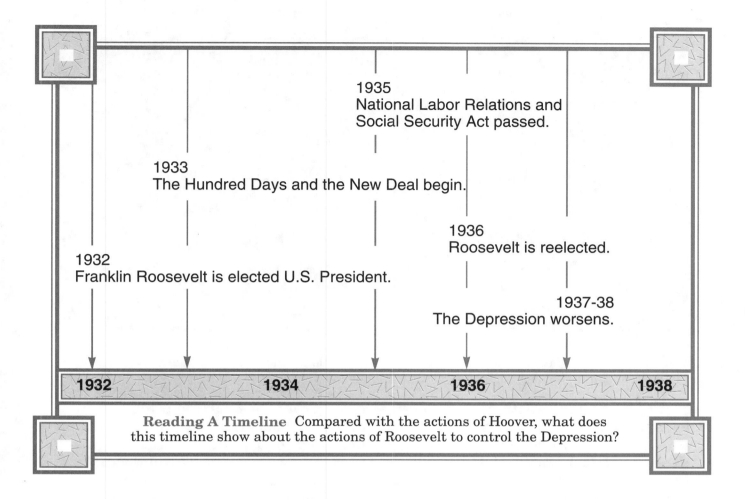

1935
National Labor Relations and
Social Security Act passed.

1933
The Hundred Days and the New Deal begin.

1936
Roosevelt is reelected.

1932
Franklin Roosevelt is elected U.S. President.

1937-38
The Depression worsens.

1932   **1934**   **1936**   **1938**

Reading A Timeline Compared with the actions of Hoover, what does this timeline show about the actions of Roosevelt to control the Depression?

Roosevelt returned to his political career. In 1928, he was elected governor of New York. During the next four years, he led the fight against the Depression in New York. In 1932, Roosevelt ran for President against Herbert Hoover and was elected. Roosevelt promised he would help the "forgotten man."

Roosevelt as President Roosevelt became President on March 4, 1933. During his campaign, he promised Americans a "New Deal." By this he meant that the government was going to try new ways to stop the Depression. In his first speech as President, Roosevelt told the American people not to be afraid. "The only thing we have to fear is fear itself," he said. He promised to act against the Depression.

The very next day the President took action. Banks all over the country were failing. Millions of people with their life savings in those banks lost all of their money. People with savings in banks that had not yet failed were worried. They wanted to take their money out. If they did, those banks would also fail.

On March 5, President Roosevelt closed all the banks. He called the closing a "bank holiday." Then, the President got Congress to pass a bill that helped the banks. That bill became law on March 9. Three days later, the President gave his first fireside chat. He explained his actions to the American people. He told them it was safe to leave their money in the banks.

The banks reopened on Monday, March 13. That day, Americans put more money into banks than they took

In 1933, two Native Americans showed support for the efforts of the National Recovery Agency to control prices and wages. Chief Little John, then 110 years old and his great-great-grandson display the "Blue Eagle," symbol of the NRA.

out. The President's actions had ended the banking crisis.

Roosevelt's Hundred Days The bank holiday marked the beginning of the **Hundred Days.** During Roosevelt's first 100 days in office, Congress passed 15 major laws. Not all of these laws worked well. Several were failures. Yet the Hundred Days showed the people of the United States that President Roosevelt was different from President Hoover. Millions of them believed that President Roosevelt really would give the nation a New Deal.

The New Deal The New Deal had three main goals. The first was to provide immediate help to millions of suffering Americans. The second was to improve the economy. The third goal was to pass new laws so that there were not so many poor people. People called these goals the "three Rs" of relief, recovery, and reform.

Several relief measures became law during the Hundred Days. One law set up a program that gave jobs to hundreds of thousands of young men. Their jobs included planting trees, fighting fires, and working to control floods.

Another law set up an agency that gave money to states to help the needy. The man in charge of this program was Harry Hopkins. He was a former social worker from New York. Hopkins wanted to get money to the states as fast as possible. In his first two hours as director, he spent over $5 million.

Two major laws aimed at economic recovery. One set up the **National Recovery Administration (NRA).** Its job was to get businesses, workers, and government to work together. The NRA set up rules to control competition between businesses. It also protected workers who wanted to organize unions. However, the NRA was not successful. It favored large businesses over small ones. Many businesses did not follow the codes.

The same law that created the NRA also created a program that spent billions of dollars on large building projects. These projects included highways, public buildings, and dams. Businesses that worked on these projects hired more workers. The most famous project was the Grand Coulee Dam on the Colorado River.

Another major law tried to help farmers by reducing the amount of crops they produced. Fewer crops would help raise prices. Then, the income of farmers would rise. The government therefore paid farmers *not* to plant crops.

The most important reform law of the Hundred Days set up the **Tennessee Valley Authority (TVA).** In 1933, the Tennessee Valley was one of the poorest regions in the United States. Flooding was a serious problem. Few of the people in the region had electricity.

Under the TVA, the government built dams on the Tennessee River. It also built dams on smaller rivers that flow into it. These dams controlled flooding and provided cheap electricity. (See the map below.) The TVA was a great success. It saved millions of acres of land. It also provided good jobs, and brought prosperity to the region.

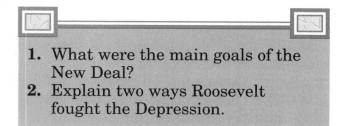

1. What were the main goals of the New Deal?
2. Explain two ways Roosevelt fought the Depression.

Reading a Map. The Tennessee Valley Authority (TVA) changed one of the poorest regions of the United States into a prosperous region. About how many states were served by the power stations of the TVA?

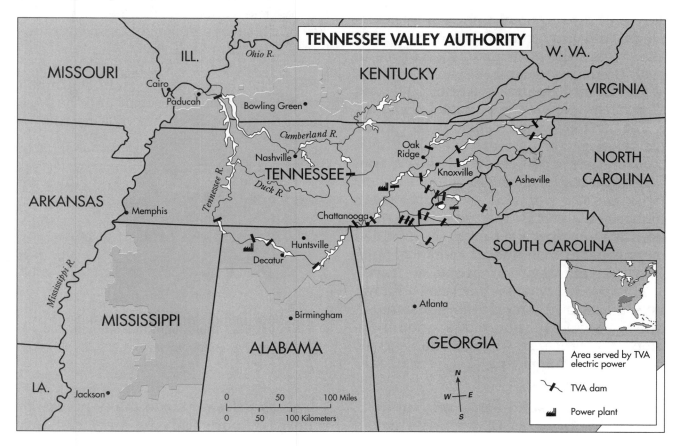

2 The New Deal Continues.

What new measures did President Roosevelt add to the New Deal?

The New Deal improved conditions for some Americans after 1933. Unemployment dropped by two million by 1935. Still, over nine million Americans were without jobs. In 1935, one worker wrote to Eleanor Roosevelt: "the forgotten man is still forgotten." Millions of others felt the same.

More new programs Roosevelt was not about to give up. "It is common sense to take a method and try it," he said. "If it fails, admit it frankly [honestly] and try another. But above all try something." He would keep trying new ways to fight the Depression.

The President introduced a new series of New Deal laws during 1935. One law put millions of people to work around the country. They built or repaired thousands of roads, hospitals, schools, airports, and playgrounds. Over the next eight years the government gave jobs to over 8.5 million people.

The **Social Security Act** of 1935 was one of the New Deal's most important reforms. It provided pensions to retired Americans. The law also set up a system of **unemployment insurance.** This protected Americans who lost their jobs. The government would give them money for a certain period of time. The **social security** system also provided payments to disabled or needy people. These payments are known as **welfare.**

This system was not perfect. It did not give all retired Americans pensions. It did not give all Americans unemployment insurance. However, it was a giant step toward improving the lives of millions of Americans.

Roosevelt's second term In 1936, Franklin Roosevelt was reelected President. The New Deal programs continued. But all the New Deal's laws and programs could not end the Depression. In fact, from 1937 to 1938 the Depression grew much worse. It lasted until the beginning of World War II (see Chapter 15). Then huge amounts of government spending for the war effort finally got the economy going.

The New Deal was not popular with all Americans. Some believed the programs would make people depend too much on the government. Others feared New Deal programs would make the government too powerful.

However, most Americans thought the New Deal was a success. It provided help to millions of Americans. The New Deal made the government take responsibility to help those in need. Its reforms reduced the differences between rich and poor.

Most important, by doing these things the New Deal made democracy stronger. During the 1930s, hard times led to the rise of **dictators** in some European countries. A dictator is a ruler who has complete control and power. Yet in the United States, the democratic system continued to work. President Roosevelt and the New Deal deserve much of the credit for this.

1. How did the New Deal help put people to work?
2. Why did some people oppose the New Deal?

3 The New Deal Includes More Americans.

What gains did immigrants and other groups make under the New Deal?

The New Deal helped many groups to take part more fully in American life.

Mary McLeod Bethune (left) was a well known educator whose lifelong work was fighting for the rights of African Americans. First Lady Eleanor Roosevelt tirelessly worked to win support from Americans for New Deal programs.

Under some New Deal programs, immigrants from southern and eastern Europe, women, African Americans, Latinos, and Native Americans were given new opportunities.

A New Deal for everyone Immigrants from southern and eastern Europe held many important government jobs during Roosevelt's presidency. These immigrants also joined the growing labor union movement.

The New Deal also provided new opportunities for women. Frances Perkins became the first woman to hold a position in the President's cabinet (see Chapter 5). She served as Secretary of Labor. Thousands of women were appointed to other government jobs. Many of these jobs involved running New Deal programs. Eleanor Roosevelt encouraged the President to hire qualified women.

African Americans and the New Deal African Americans at first were disappointed in the New Deal. Early New Deal programs allowed discrimina-

tion against African Americans. The main reason was that President Roosevelt needed white southern Congressmen to vote for these programs. To get their votes, he had to permit discrimination when the programs started operating. For example, some programs paid African American workers less than whites. Other programs forced African Americans to live in segregated, or separate, housing. African Americans working in the Civilian Conservation Corps served in segregated units.

Mary McLeod Bethune Later this situation began to change. The President named African Americans to important government posts. One of the most important of these people was Mary McLeod Bethune.

Bethune was a well-known educator from the South. Although Bethune's family was poor, they made sure that she received a good education. Bethune studied and became a teacher. But she wanted to do more. In the early 1900s, she set out to establish a school for

African Americans. Bethune had little money. She sold pies and cakes to raise funds for her school. In the end, she succeeded. Her school eventually became Bethune-Cookman College in Florida—a college that stands today.

Roosevelt appointed Bethune to head an important government office in 1935. Bethune's job was to make sure money intended for schools with African American students actually reached them. She helped over 300,000 African American young people get an education.

The New Deal did not end discrimination. But it began to move toward that goal. As singer Paul Robeson said, "Change was in the air, and this was the best sign of all."

Latinos and the New Deal The New Deal also helped Latinos. Many worked on government projects. Some Mexican American artists found jobs painting murals for public buildings.

Senator Dennis Chavez of New Mexico helped get relief to Spanish-speaking communities. Chavez was the only Latino in the U.S. Senate. However, many Mexicans living in the United States were not citizens and did not qualify for help. Roosevelt also continued the policy begun under President Hoover of sending Mexican migrant workers back to Mexico.

Native Americans and the New Deal Native Americans were another group the New Deal helped. A social worker named John Collier became head of the Bureau of Indian Affairs. He fought hard for Native American rights. Collier used the Indian Reorganization Act of 1934 to help Native Americans preserve their cultures. He also worked to stop Native American lands from being sold.

1. Who was the first woman appointed to the President's cabinet?
2. How did some New Deal programs discriminate against African Americans?

CHAPTER 14
KEY IDEAS

- President Franklin Delano Roosevelt introduced the New Deal to provide relief, recovery, and reform.
- Some New Deal programs were more successful than others at providing relief and improving the economy. However, Roosevelt kept trying new programs to improve the economy.
- Several New Deal programs tried to reform inequalities in the United States. They gave immigrants, women, African Americans, Latinos, and Native Americans new opportunities to succeed.

REVIEWING CHAPTER 14

I. Reviewing Vocabulary
Match each word on the left with the correct definition on the right.

1. welfare
2. social security
3. fireside chat
4. unemployment insurance
5. dictator

a. a ruler who has complete control and power
b. regular government payments to needy people
c. a system in which the government makes payments to people who lose their jobs
d. radio talk President Roosevelt gave
e. a government policy that provides pensions to retired people

II. Understanding the Chapter
1. How did the bank holiday help end the banking crisis?
2. What were the three main goals of the New Deal?
3. How did the government try to help farmers?
4. Why was the Social Security Act of 1935 so important?
5. How did the New Deal affect African Americans?

III. Building Skills: Reading a Map
Study the map on page 121. Then, answer the questions below.
1. Name three states the Tennessee River runs through.
2. In which states are power plants located?
3. How many states received power from the TVA?

IV. Writing About History
1. **What Would You Have Done?** Imagine that you are an adviser to President Roosevelt. Would you tell him to accept discrimination against African Americans in New Deal programs in order to get the votes in Congress necessary to pass these programs or not? Explain.
2. Create a poster encouraging people to support one of the New Deal programs. Your poster should show how the program will help people. It should also contain a sentence or two that explains the program.

V. Working Together
1. Form a group with six to eight classmates. Divide your group in two for a debate. One group will explain why the New Deal was a success. The other group will explain why the New Deal was not successful. Work with your group to list reasons to defend your position. Then, hold your debate in class.
2. **Past to Present** You have read how President Roosevelt used fireside chats to talk directly to the American people. In what way does the President speak to the American people today?

THE NATION FIGHTS ANOTHER WAR. (1933—1945)

What was the outcome of World War II?

On "D-Day," June 6, 1944, the Allied army launched the massive invasion in France to retake Europe from the Axis powers.

STUDY

On a separate piece of paper, trace the map of Europe on page 129. As you read, make notes on your map about the actions during World War II.

HINT

Looking at Key Terms

- Axis powers • Allied powers • Pearl Harbor
- D-Day • Holocaust

Looking at Key Words

- **isolationism:** a policy of staying out of world affairs
- **fascism:** a system of government ruled by a dictator who uses the military and racism to stay in power
- **anti-Semitism:** hatred of the Jewish people
- **neutral:** not taking sides in a dispute
- **draft:** to require a person to enter the military

During the 1930s, most Americans were not interested in foreign affairs. Americans were more concerned with ending the Great Depression. In 1941, all that changed. The United States entered World War II. It took four years of fighting before the world was again at peace.

1 The United States Joins the Fight.

Why did the United States join the Allies?

A feeling of **isolationism** grew in the United States during the 1930s. Isolationism is the belief that a country should stay out of world affairs. However, events in Europe and Asia would soon change the way Americans felt.

The rise of Adolph Hitler Like much of the rest of the world, Germany was hit by a depression during the 1930s. Many people in Germany became desperate. They began to trust leaders who promised to lift Germany out of the depression at any price.

Adolph Hitler was just such a leader. He and the Nazi party came to power in 1933. The Nazis believed in **fascism.** Fascism is a system of government ruled by a dictator. Fascists use nationalism, or excessive patriotism, to gain power. They also use racism.

Hitler was a racist. He believed the Germans were a superior, or better, group of people. Everybody else was inferior. Most of all, Hitler hated the Jewish people. Hatred of Jews is called **anti-Semitism.** Hitler blamed the Jews for all of Germany's problems.

Hitler's government issued laws that discriminated against Jews. The Nazis arrested many Jews and put them in prisons called concentration camps.

Many Jews fled Germany. The United States allowed about 63,000 Jewish refugees to enter between 1938 and 1939. Other countries also allowed some Jews to enter. However, most of the Jews fleeing Nazi persecution had no place to go. Anti-Semitism prevented many Jews from coming to the United States.

The Axis powers By the mid-1930s, Hitler was carrying out his plan of expansion. He sent soldiers into the western part of Germany called the Rhineland. This went against the treaty that had ended World War I. But Europe's democratic countries did nothing to stop Hitler.

In 1936, Germany signed a treaty with Italy. Italy also had a fascist government. Together Germany and Italy called themselves the **Axis powers.** A short while later, Japan joined them.

In 1938, Germany turned against two of its neighbors. First, it took over Austria. Then, Hitler demanded the western part of Czechoslovakia (chek-eh-sloh-VAH-key-ah). Czechoslovakia needed help from Britain and France to defend itself. But Britain and France simply gave in to Hitler.

While Germany upset peace in Europe, Japan did the same in Asia. Japan's goal was to conquer territory and become the most powerful country in Asia. In 1937, Japan invaded China. No country helped China.

The beginning of war The failure to stop German and Japanese invasions finally led to war. In September 1939, Germany invaded Poland. Britain and France finally declared war on Germany. World War II had begun.

Britain and France were called the **Allied powers.** The United States was officially **neutral,** or not on any side, at the start of the war. However, President Roosevelt supplied the Allies with war material. He believed a German victory would threaten the United States. Despite U.S. help, Germany defeated

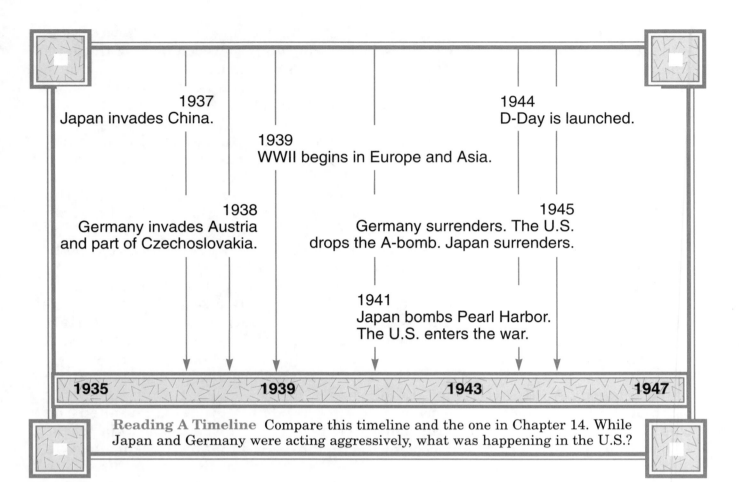

1937
Japan invades China.

1939
WWII begins in Europe and Asia.

1944
D-Day is launched.

1938
Germany invades Austria and part of Czechoslovakia.

1945
Germany surrenders. The U.S. drops the A-bomb. Japan surrenders.

1941
Japan bombs Pearl Harbor. The U.S. enters the war.

1935 **1939** **1943** **1947**

Reading A Timeline Compare this timeline and the one in Chapter 14. While Japan and Germany were acting aggressively, what was happening in the U.S.?

France in 1940. Britain now stood alone against Germany.

The German army seemed unstoppable. It had conquered most of Western Europe by June 1940. (See the map on page 129.) In June 1941, Hitler's army turned east and invaded the Soviet Union. Soon Germany controlled a large part of that country.

U.S. entry into the war In Asia, Japan controlled a large part of China as well as other territory. In 1941, the United States demanded that Japan withdraw from China. Tension between the United States and Japan increased.

Early in December, Japanese ships secretly sailed near Hawaii. On December 7, airplanes from those ships attacked **Pearl Harbor.** Pearl Harbor was the main U.S. navy base in the Pacific. In just two hours, the Japanese

destroyed most of the base and its ships. Over 2,400 Americans died.

The following day, the U.S. Congress declared war on Japan. Three days later, Germany declared war on the United States. The United States had entered World War II.

1. How did the United States help the Allies before it entered the war?
2. What event drew the United States into the war?

2 The Allies Defeat the Axis.
How did the Allies defeat the Axis?

The people of London sat quietly in underground air-raid shelters. Suddenly a loud explosion was heard. Then, the ground shook. In September 1940, the Germans began bombing raids the British called the "London Blitz." The raids continued until June 1941. The city of London was badly damaged, but not destroyed. Most important, the Nazis had not crushed the British spirit to win the war.

New weapons   The will to win was important. However, modern science also played a great role in winning the war. Both the Allies and the Axis used science to build new weapons. They built fast and powerful airplanes to bomb cities. Many people were killed in these attacks.

U.S. and British scientists developed radar to track airplanes. They came up with sonar to find submarines. Late in the war, Germany developed the world's first jet planes and large rockets. But, in 1945, the United States created the most powerful weapon ever. It was the atomic bomb.

Axis victories   The Axis powers were winning the war in 1941. They continued to win most battles during

Reading a Map. Name the main Axis powers. Name the main Allied powers. When it was at its greatest size, the Axis powers controlled territory on what continents? Where did the major Allied invasion of Europe take place?

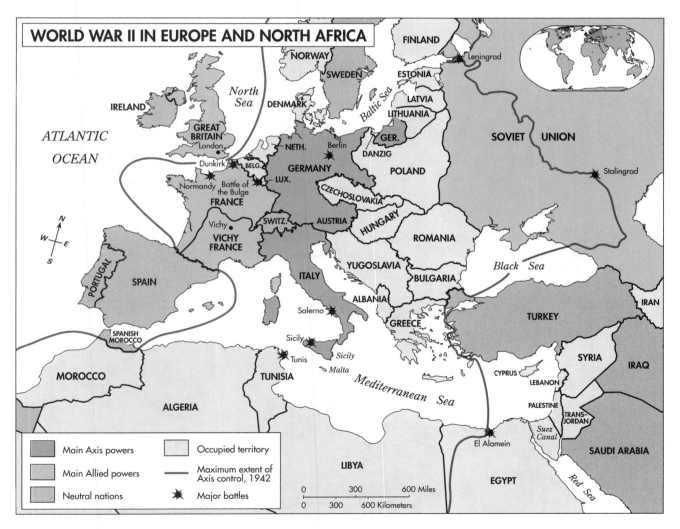

WORLD WAR II IN EUROPE AND NORTH AFRICA

■ Main Axis powers	■ Occupied territory
■ Main Allied powers	— Maximum extent of Axis control, 1942
■ Neutral nations	✸ Major battles

1942. The Germans advanced both in the Soviet Union and in North Africa.

The Japanese also advanced. They invaded the Philippines and conquered parts of Southeast Asia. They also took over many islands in the Pacific Ocean.

Allied victories By the end of 1942, the tide of battle turned against Germany. In October, the British and Americans stopped the German army in North Africa. The Soviet army stopped the Germans at the city of Stalingrad.

Nobody could stop the Japanese during 1942. However, in the spring the U.S. Navy defeated them twice in the Pacific. In early 1943, the United States began driving the Japanese back.

D-Day By 1943, Allied forces in Europe had the advantage. Then on June 6, 1944, Allied troops launched a bold plan. They crossed the English Channel and landed in France. The Allies called June 6, **D-Day.** D-Day was the largest

Reading a Map. How far east did the maximum area of Japanese control extend in 1942? Give your answers both in terms of longitude and in terms of the islands Japan did or did not control in 1942.

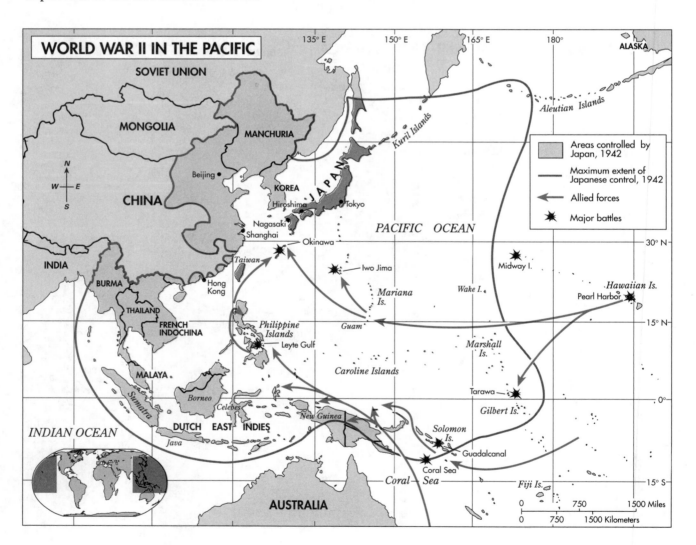

naval invasion in history. It involved over three million soldiers.

After D-Day, Allied soldiers pushed through France and eastward into Germany. Meanwhile, from deep inside their country the Soviets fought their way westward.

In 1945, the Allies closed in on Germany from the east and west. However, President Roosevelt did not live to see Germany's final defeat. He died on April 12. Vice President Harry S Truman became the new President. Germany surrendered on May 7, 1945.

The Holocaust The end of the war in Europe brought with it horrible news. During the war, the Allies had heard reports of Nazi death camps. But no one was prepared for what Allied soldiers found when they liberated the concentration camps. The Nazis had murdered six million Jews in concentration camps. The Nazis also killed millions of other innocent civilians. This terrible crime is called the **Holocaust.**

News of the Holocaust shocked people all over the world. Today, it is important to remember what happened in the Holocaust so it will not happen again.

Japanese surrender The war against Japan lasted four months after Germany surrendered. One by one the United States retook the islands the Japanese had conquered in the Pacific.

The United States finally ended the war by dropping two atomic bombs on Japan. The first bomb was dropped on the city of Hiroshima (hir-eh-SHEE-mah) on August 6, 1945. The second one was dropped on Nagasaki (nah-geh-SAH-kee) on August 9. The atomic bombs caused great loss of life and terrible destruction in Japan. Japan surrendered on September 2, 1945. World War II was over.

Dorie Miller was one of 1,000,000 African Americans who served in World War II. Miller won the Navy Cross for shooting down four Japanese planes.

1. What new weapons were developed during World War II?
2. What is the Holocaust?

3 All Americans Participate in the War.

How did Americans participate in World War II?

The United States needed a huge military force to fight the Axis. It had to **draft** millions of soldiers. When a person is drafted, he or she is required to serve in the military. More than 15 million Americans served in the U.S. military.

African Americans in the military More than one million African Americans served in the military during World War II. More than 6,000 became officers. However, the military remained segregated. More than 20 African American combat units fought in Europe. A unit of African American pilots flew fighter planes that protected U.S. bombers. It shot down 400 enemy airplanes during the war.

One of this country's first heroes was an African American named Dorie Miller. He was at Pearl Harbor working in the kitchen of a battleship. When the Japanese attack began, he ran on deck and dragged his wounded captain to safety. Then, Miller grabbed a machine gun and shot down four planes. He was awarded the Navy Cross for his bravery.

Other groups in World War II More than 500,000 Latinos served in the armed forces. They served in every branch of the military and on every bat-

tle front. Unlike African Americans, Latinos were not put in segregated units. Seventeen Mexican Americans won the Congressional Medal of Honor.

Native Americans also served in the armed forces. Among them were a group from the Navajo who served as "code talkers." Using the Navajo language, they developed a secret code the Japanese could not break. It helped send information over the radio to U.S. soldiers on many battlefields.

Thousands of Japanese Americans fought for the United States. You will read more about the discrimination Japanese Americans faced in Chapter 16.

Women also served in the military. More than 300,000 women served as nurses and in special women's units in non-combat jobs. The army called its unit the Women's Army Corps (WACs).

1. Who was Dorie Miller?
2. How did the Navajo code talkers help the U.S. military?

CHAPTER 15
KEY IDEAS

- World War II began in 1939. The Allied powers of Britain and France fought the Axis powers of Germany, Italy, and Japan.
- The Soviet Union joined the Allies in 1941. The United States joined the Allies after the attack on Pearl Harbor.
- Until 1943, the Axis were winning in Europe, Africa, and Asia. In that year, the Allies began pushing the Axis back. The Axis finally surrendered in 1945.
- Americans from all groups participated in the war effort. African Americans, Latinos, Japanese Americans, Native Americans, and women found new opportunities in the armed forces.

REVIEWING CHAPTER 15

I. Reviewing Vocabulary

Match the word on the left with the correct definition on the right.

1. draft
2. fascism
3. neutral
4. isolationism
5. anti-Semitism

   a. hatred of the Jewish people
   b. a policy of staying out of world affairs
   c. a system of government based on dictatorship, militarism, and racism
   d. not taking sides in a dispute
   e. to require a person to enter the military

II. Understanding the Chapter

1. What were Adolph Hitler's racist policies?
2. How did the world's democratic countries react to German and Japanese aggression during the 1930s?
3. What event brought the United States into World War II?
4. What was D-Day?
5. How was military service both a disappointment and an opportunity for African Americans?

III. Building Skills: Identifying Cause and Effect

1. What was the effect of Germany's invasion of Poland?
2. What caused the United States to increase aid to the Allies after 1940?
3. What was the effect of the Japanese attack on Pearl Harbor?

IV. Writing About History

1. **What Would You Have Done?** Imagine that you are a U.S. Senator in 1940. Write a speech telling whether or not you think the United States should enter the war.
2. Imagine that you are an African American serving in the military during World War II. Write two or three diary entries describing your experiences.

V. Working Together

1. Form a group with three or four classmates. Together, create a poster encouraging Americans to join the military during World War II. Your poster should point out why the war is important to the United States. Display your poster in class.
2. **Past to Present** With a group, study the maps of Europe and Asia on pages 129 and 130. Then, study a map of Europe and Asia today. What differences do you notice? What similarities?

AMERICANS SUPPORT WORLD WAR II ON THE HOME FRONT. (1941–1945)

How did World War II affect life in the United States?

One way for people on the home front to help the war effort was to collect aluminum. These New Yorkers had a party to give pots and pans.

STUDY

Create a chart with the following columns: Women, Families, African Americans, Latinos, and Japanese Americans. Write down how the war affected each group and how each group contributed to the war.

HINT

Looking at Key Terms

- victory garden
- Fair Employment Practices Commission (FEPC)
- zoot suit riots

Looking at Key Words

- **civilian:** a person who is not in the military
- **price control:** the setting of prices on certain goods and services by the government
- **ration:** to portion or limit such resources as food, clothing, or fuel
- ***bracero:*** a contract laborer from Mexico
- **internment camp:** a prison camp

As U.S. soldiers fought overseas during World War II, they often thought of family and friends they left behind. The people left at home also missed the soldiers. However, there was important work to do on the home front. In fact, work on the home front was very important to soldiers on the battlefield.

1 World War II Ends the Depression.

How did Americans on the home front contribute to the war effort?

Allied soldiers won World War II on the battlefield. But they could not have beaten the enemy without weapons and supplies. Millions of U.S. workers at home made all that the soldiers needed to fight a modern war. These workers came from all groups in U.S. society.

The war and the economy The U.S. government spent $320 billion to fight World War II. It purchased ships, airplanes, tanks, and other war supplies. These supplies were produced by U.S. factories. The factories in turn provided jobs for millions of workers.

War spending lifted the United States out of the Depression. Unemployment dropped from ten million to almost nothing. Wages went up. The income of most workers doubled.

For the first time in over a decade, people had money to spend. However, there often was nothing for them to buy. Factories were producing weapons and other war materials for the government. There were shortages of things **civilians,** or those not in the military, wanted to buy. Toasters, hair curlers, nylon stockings, and dishes were in short supply. After 1942, there were no new cars and trucks at all! The government needed car and truck factories to produce tanks and airplanes.

Price controls and rationing So few goods were available that prices rose. They rose so quickly that in 1942, the government set **price controls.** This meant that sellers could not raise their prices any more.

The government also introduced **rationing.** Rationing is when people are limited in how much of an item they can buy. The goal was to make sure that each person got their fair share. Gasoline, meat, butter, shoes, sugar, canned goods, and other products all were rationed.

Families during the war Families had to accept other hardships during the war. Many families moved to new cities or towns to get factory jobs. Cities like Los Angeles, Detroit, and Seattle grew rapidly.

Often in these and other cities, there was a shortage of housing. Schools became overcrowded. Many had to go on double session. There were blackouts of electricity. People had to practice civil defense drills in case enemy planes bombed their cities.

These problems did not stop families from working together to help the war effort. People grew their own food on small plots of land called **victory gardens.** Even people in big cities like New York grew victory gardens. Children gathered tin cans and tinfoil so the metal in them could be used to make weapons. These activities cheered people up because they felt they were helping to win the war.

1. How did war spending end the Depression?
2. What goods were rationed during the war?

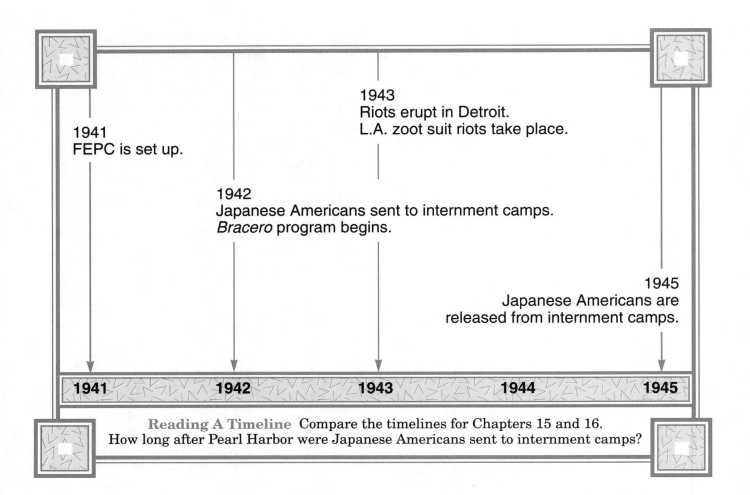

1941
FEPC is set up.

1942
Japanese Americans sent to internment camps.
Bracero program begins.

1943
Riots erupt in Detroit.
L.A. zoot suit riots take place.

1945
Japanese Americans are
released from internment camps.

| 1941 | 1942 | 1943 | 1944 | 1945 |

Reading A Timeline Compare the timelines for Chapters 15 and 16. How long after Pearl Harbor were Japanese Americans sent to internment camps?

2 The War Effort Enlists Women.

What role did women play in the war effort at home?

"Rosie the Riveter" dressed in coveralls and carried a wrench in her hand. She became an American hero during World War II. Rosie was not a real woman, however. She was a symbol. Rosie stood for the millions of women who worked in war industries. Many of these women had never worked outside the home before. The working world was a new challenge. Women met it with great energy.

Women at work World War II created a labor shortage. Fifteen million men were in the military. As a result millions of jobs opened up. Women filled many of those jobs and played a crucial role in the war effort.

About 6.5 million women joined the work force between 1941 and 1945. Many of the new women workers took jobs in factories. They also worked for the government. By 1945, women made up more than one third of the U.S. work force.

Often women worked in jobs traditionally held by men. Some worked as welders and in electronics. Others built planes and tanks. Still others drove trucks and repaired machinery.

Working women also supported their families. A soldier's pay was not enough for a family. Working women whose husbands were not in the military gave their families a second paycheck. This helped many families to live better.

Among those who gained the most were African American women. Before

World War II, they often worked on farms or as servants. After 1941, over 300,000 found jobs in factories where they earned higher wages.

Child care However, not everything was rosy for Rosie the Riveter. Working women during the war faced many problems. There were few day care centers for their children. Usually family members cared for children. But sometimes help from family members was not enough.

Working women also had problems at home. After a full day in a factory or office, they had to do housework. If they were mothers, they also had to take care of children. This meant that many women had to do two jobs.

1. Why did women join the work force in great numbers after 1941?
2. What problems did working mothers face?

The role of women changed dramatically during World War II. The demand for workers led women to join the workforce in record numbers. Here a woman works with an acetylene welding torch at a U.S. Navy shipyard.

3 African Americans and Latinos Contribute to the War Effort.

How did African Americans and Latinos help the United States win World War II?

The labor shortage created by World War II opened new opportunities for African Americans and Latinos. Millions moved from farms and small towns to cities in the North, West, and Midwest. Many made good money working in war industries. However, they still faced discrimination.

Fighting for a Double V African Americans were angry about segregation in the military (see page 132) and job discrimination. The United States was fighting for freedom abroad. But it still denied some of its citizens equal rights. African American leaders said they wanted a Double V. It meant victory over enemies abroad and over racism at home.

The man who led the struggle for equality during the war was A. Philip Randolph. Randolph was the head of the Brotherhood of Sleeping Car Porters. It was the most powerful African American labor organization in the country. Randolph demanded equality in jobs and in the military.

In 1941, Randolph began to organize a march on Washington to end discrimination. He promised "ten, twenty, fifty thousand [African Americans] on the White House lawn." Under this pressure, President Roosevelt took action. In June 1941, the President banned discrimination in war industries. He also set up the **Fair Employment Practices Commission (FEPC)** to combat discrimination.

The FEPC had some success in stopping discrimination. African Americans got better jobs in defense plants. They also were able to join labor unions.

Riots However, many problems remained. African Americans who moved to northern cities often met anger from whites. There were tensions over jobs and over housing. This tension erupted into race riots in several cities. The worst riot occurred in Detroit in 1943. It began as a fist fight between an African American and a white man. Within hours a riot swept across the city. It resulted in the deaths of 25 blacks and 9 whites.

Many people rushed to fill factory jobs during the war. However, there was also a labor shortage on the farms. Workers were needed to tend and harvest crops. To meet this shortage, the U.S. and Mexican governments set up the **bracero** program. *Braceros* were laborers from Mexico who worked on farms in the United States. Beginning in 1942, *braceros* came to the United States to harvest crops. When the harvest was over, the *braceros* returned to Mexico.

Discrimination against Mexican Americans remained, however. The so-called **zoot suit riots** were one example. A zoot suit was a style of dressing. It featured an oversized jacket and baggy pants. The style was popular with many young Latino men in the 1940s.

One summer night in Los Angeles in 1943, some white sailors complained that "zoot suiters" had attacked them. The following night hundreds of sailors roamed Los Angeles. They beat up Mexican Americans wearing zoot suits. Local police did little to stop the attacks. Finally, the military police were called in to end the riot.

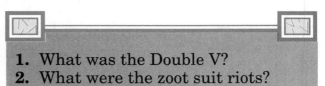

1. What was the Double V?
2. What were the zoot suit riots?

4 Japanese Americans Are Interned.

Why were Japanese Americans placed in internment camps?

They . . . built barbed-wire fences around the camp with a tower on each corner with military personnel and machine guns, rifles, and searchlights. It was terrifying because we didn't know what was going to happen to us.

This was how Ben Yorita described the camp he and his family were taken to during World War II. Yorita was not a prisoner of war captured in Europe or Asia. He was a U.S. citizen sent by the U.S. government to a prison camp. His only "crime" was that he happened to be a Japanese American.

Discrimination The worst single example of discrimination during World War II affected Japanese Americans. About 110,000 Japanese Americans lived along the U.S. West Coast. They had long been the targets of discrimination. Many businesses refused to serve Japanese Americans. Japanese

American children often were left out of school events by their classmates.

After Japan bombed Pearl Harbor in December 1941, the pressure on Japanese Americans increased. People questioned their loyalty. Mobs attacked Japanese Americans and destroyed their property.

In February 1942, President Roosevelt gave an order that all people of Japanese ancestry must leave the West Coast. They had to leave their homes whether they were American citizens or not. They were forced to live in camps in other states.

Internment Once the U.S. government gave the orders, Japanese Americans were given little time to prepare. They had to sell their property quickly because they could take only what they could carry. Often, they had to sell everything at a very low price and lose a lot of money.

Japanese Americans were taken to one of ten **internment camps.** An

Reading a Map. From what coast were people of Japanese descent evicted during World War II? Which War Relocation Authority (WRA) camps were farthest east? In what state did most of the assembly centers lie? What states had the most WRA camps?

INTERNMENT CENTERS FOR JAPANESE AMERICANS, 1942–1946

Evacuation Areas
▲ Assembly Centers
■ WRA Camps
Areas from which people of Japanese descent were evacuated, 1942

The time: June 1942. The place: Los Angeles. A Japanese American mother waits with her children to be taken to an internment camp.

internment camp is a prison camp. Most of the camps were located in far-off areas in the West. Barbed wire and soldiers surrounded the camps. Each family was given one room in a long building. Medical treatment was limited.

Despite this treatment, thousands of young men from these camps fought in the U.S. Army. They served bravely in many battles. Japanese Americans of the 442nd Regiment earned over 18,000 medals for their bravery.

In late 1945, the government closed the camps. Japanese Americans were finally allowed to go home. In 1988, the U.S. government admitted it had wronged these citizens. Each surviving person received a $20,000 payment. However, it was a small amount compared to the injustice that was done.

1. What were the internment camps?
2. When did the government admit that internment was unjust?

CHAPTER 16
KEY IDEAS

- Americans on the home front produced important war material and supplies for soldiers abroad. Americans from all groups contributed to the effort.
- Women entered the work force in great numbers during World War II. Many worked in factories and government offices.
- African Americans and Latinos found new opportunities during the war. However, they still had to combat discrimination on the home front and in the military.
- Japanese Americans were sent to internment camps during the war. Many spent years in the camps until they were closed in 1945.

REVIEWING CHAPTER 16

I. Reviewing Vocabulary
Match the word on the left with the correct definition on the right.

1. *bracero*
2. ration
3. civilian
4. internment camp
5. price control

a. a prison camp
b. the setting of prices on certain goods and services by the government
c. to portion such resources as food, clothing, or fuel
d. a person who is not in the military
e. a contract laborer from Mexico

II. Understanding the Chapter
1. Why did the U.S. government introduce price controls and rationing?
2. What hardships did families endure during the war?
3. How did women benefit from taking jobs outside the home during the war?
4. What did African American leaders mean when they said they wanted a Double V?
5. What were conditions like in internment camps?

III. Building Skills: Supporting Generalizations
Read the following generalizations. Then list two or three facts that support each one.
1. World War II changed many women's lives in the United States.
2. African Americans made some gains against discrimination during the war.
3. A shortage of labor during World War II caused changes in the U.S. work force.

IV. Writing About History
1. Write a newspaper editorial about mothers joining the work force during the World War II. Give your opinion about this issue and discuss some of the benefits and hardships working mothers face.
2. **What Would You Have Done?** Imagine that you are a Japanese American who has been sent to an internment camp. Write a letter to a friend outside the camp telling whether you would join the U.S. Army.

V. Working Together
1. Form a group of four or five students. Together, make a list of items that were rationed, banned, or were in short supply during World War II. Then, draw pictures or gather these items for a classroom display. For each item, make a card explaining why it was rationed, banned, or changed.
2. **Past to Present** How are the problems working mothers faced during World War II different from or similar to the problems working mothers face today?

Unit 4
A Challenging Period
(1945-1980)

Chapters

17 The United States and the Soviet Union Fight a Cold War.
18 The Years After World War II Bring Prosperity and Problems.
19 Five Presidents Shake Up the Nation.
20 The United States Fights a War in Vietnam.
21 Changes in the American Way of Life Take Place.

THE UNITED STATES AND THE SOVIET UNION FIGHT A COLD WAR. (1945—1962)

How did the dispute between the United States and the Soviet Union affect world politics?

Ready to touch down, a U.S. cargo plane delivers badly needed food to the people of Berlin after Soviets blockaded the city in 1948.

Looking at Key Terms
- United Nations (UN) • Marshall Plan • Berlin Blockade
- North Atlantic Treaty Organization (NATO) • Bay of Pigs
- Cuban Missile Crisis

Looking at Key Words
- **cold war:** the conflict after World War II between the Soviet Union and the U.S.
- **capitalism:** an economic system in which most businesses are owned by people
- **communism:** an economic system in which most businesses are controlled by the government
- **satellite:** a weak country under the control of a powerful country
- **blockade:** to stop anyone from coming in or going out
- **iron curtain:** the boundary between non-Communist and Communist Europe after World War II

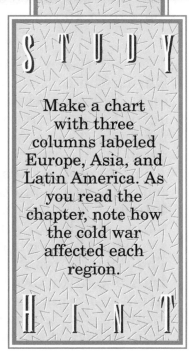

S T U D Y

Make a chart with three columns labeled Europe, Asia, and Latin America. As you read the chapter, note how the cold war affected each region.

H I N T

Just before the end of World War II, people from 50 nations met in San Francisco. They formed a new organization called the **United Nations (UN).** The UN was founded to maintain peace around the world. Member nations hoped that the UN would make it easier for nations to cooperate. The UN was able to solve some conflicts. However, it could not end the growing tension between the United States and the Soviet Union.

1 The Cold War Breaks Out.

What caused the tension between the United States and the Soviet Union?

The United States and the Soviet Union were the world's most powerful nations after World War II. During the war, the United States and the Soviet Union were allies, or partners. Soon after the war, however, the two countries became bitter enemies. The conflict between them is called the **cold war.** The cold war affected world politics for more than 40 years.

Capitalism and communism

During the cold war the United States and the Soviet Union did not fight an actual war with one another. They fought in other ways. Usually they competed to gain control of other countries.

The United States tried to persuade countries to accept democracy and **capitalism.** Capitalism is an economic system in which most businesses and land are owned by people or groups of people. The Soviet Union tried to make countries accept dictatorship and **communism.** Communism is an economic system in which most businesses and land are owned by the government.

Joseph Stalin was dictator of the Soviet Union. His goal was to establish Communist governments throughout the world. The United States led the effort to stop the Soviet Union.

Soviet control of Eastern Europe

At the end of World War II, the Soviet army stayed in much of Eastern Europe. Before the end of the war, Stalin had promised to hold free elections in the countries of Eastern Europe. After the war, he ignored his promise. Instead, the Soviets set up Communist dictatorships in these countries.

Between 1945 and 1948, the Soviets set up Communist dictatorships in Poland, Romania, Bulgaria, Hungary, and Czechoslovakia. People called the Communist-controlled countries Soviet **satellites.** A satellite is a country that is under the complete control of another country. Yugoslavia and Albania also had Communist dictatorships.

U.S. leaders feared that control of Eastern Europe made the Soviet Union too powerful. They knew that the Soviets wanted to control Western Europe too. If that happened, the Soviet Union would be a threat to the United States.

The iron curtain During 1946, Britain's leader Winston Churchill gave a speech in the United States. Churchill said there was an **iron curtain** in Europe. Behind it were the Soviet-controlled countries of Eastern Europe. The term *iron curtain* described the boundary between Western Europe and Soviet-controlled Eastern Europe.

1. What was Joseph Stalin's goal?
2. What was the iron curtain?

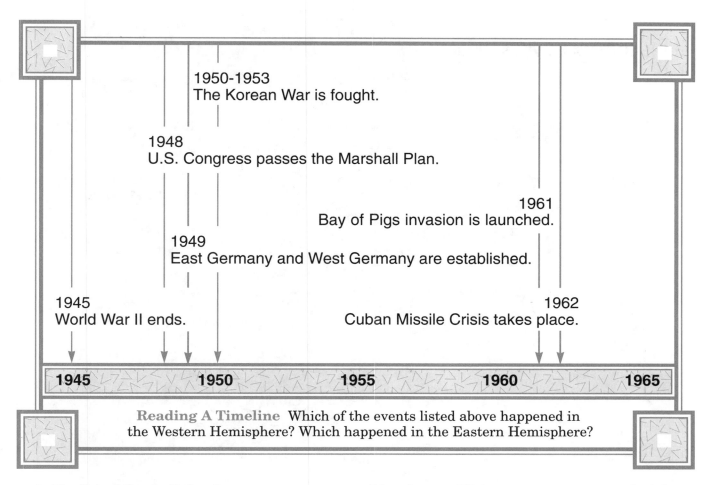

1950-1953
The Korean War is fought.

1948
U.S. Congress passes the Marshall Plan.

1961
Bay of Pigs invasion is launched.

1949
East Germany and West Germany are established.

1945
World War II ends.

1962
Cuban Missile Crisis takes place.

| 1945 | 1950 | 1955 | 1960 | 1965 |

Reading A Timeline Which of the events listed above happened in the Western Hemisphere? Which happened in the Eastern Hemisphere?

2 The United States Fights Communism.

How did the United States respond to the spread of communism?

President Harry S Truman stood before Congress in March 1947. He told Congress that the United States needed to stop the spread of communism. The countries of Greece and Turkey were in immediate danger. These countries needed help to fight communism.

Congress responded to Truman's plea. It gave Greece and Turkey $400 million in aid. This aid helped Greece and Turkey fight off communism. The idea that the United States would defend countries against communism was called the **Truman Doctrine.**

The Marshall Plan In 1947, the nations of Western Europe were in terri-ble shape. There were not enough jobs. Millions were homeless and starving. The Communist parties of Western Europe promised people a better life. If conditions did not improve quickly, there was a chance they could win the next elections.

The United States decided to help Europe rebuild. It was the best way to make sure the people of Western Europe did not turn to communism. In 1948, the United States set up the **Marshall Plan.** Under the Marshall Plan, the United States gave Western Europe $12.5 billion in aid.

The Marshall Plan was a complete success. By 1950, Western Europe had recovered from the war. The United States had saved Europe from economic collapse. It also had prevented the spread of communism to Western Europe.

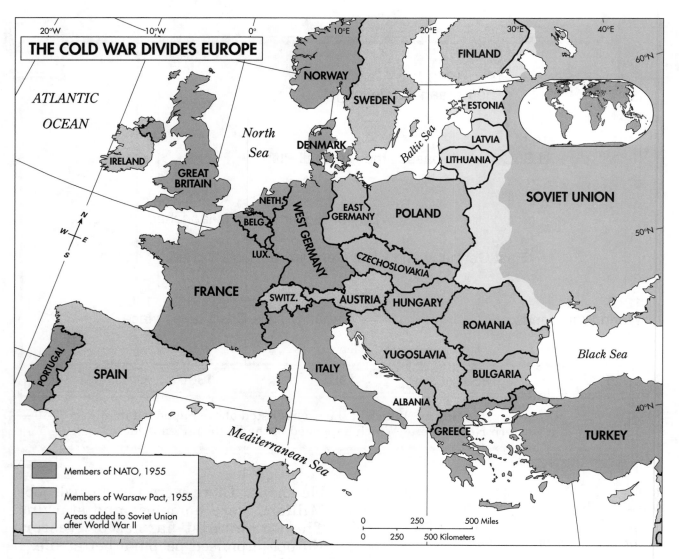

THE COLD WAR DIVIDES EUROPE

ATLANTIC OCEAN

North Sea

IRELAND

GREAT BRITAIN

NORWAY

SWEDEN

FINLAND

DENMARK

Baltic Sea

ESTONIA

LATVIA

LITHUANIA

SOVIET UNION

NETH.

BELG.

LUX.

WEST GERMANY

EAST GERMANY

POLAND

CZECHOSLOVAKIA

FRANCE

SWITZ.

AUSTRIA

HUNGARY

ROMANIA

PORTUGAL

SPAIN

ITALY

YUGOSLAVIA

BULGARIA

ALBANIA

Black Sea

Mediterranean Sea

GREECE

TURKEY

Members of NATO, 1955

Members of Warsaw Pact, 1955

Areas added to Soviet Union after World War II

0   250   500 Miles
0   250   500 Kilometers

Reading a Map. Which is further to the west, East Germany or Greece? Which European countries were neither NATO nor the Warsaw Pact? Which divided country had sections in both alliances?

Germany divided In 1948, a new crisis began. After World War II, the Allies had divided Germany into four zones. The United States, Soviet Union, Britain, and France each controlled one zone. Inside the Soviet zone was the city of Berlin, Germany's capital. Berlin was also divided into U.S., British, Soviet, and French parts.

During 1948, the Western powers introduced reforms to rebuild Germany's economy. The Soviets opposed the reforms. They wanted to keep Germany weak. In June 1948, the Soviet Union began the **Berlin Blockade.** A **blockade** attempts to stop anyone from coming in or going out of a place. The Soviet army stopped all land traffic to the western parts of Berlin. Its goal was to force the United States out of Berlin.

President Truman reacted quickly. The United States used airplanes to fly supplies over the blockade. Airplanes delivered 13,000 tons of supplies per day. An airplane landed in Berlin every

90 seconds. For almost a year, the United States supplied Berlin by airplane. In May 1949, the Soviets gave in and ended the blockade.

A few months later the Americans, British, and French combined their zones and created West Germany. The Soviets set up a new Communist satellite called East Germany. The cold war had split Germany in two.

NATO and the Warsaw Pact During the Berlin Blockade people feared that war might break out. Western leaders decided to form an organization to defend against Soviet attack. In 1949, the United States, Canada, and ten European nations formed the **North Atlantic Treaty Organization (NATO).**

The Soviet Union formed the Warsaw Pact in 1955. The Warsaw Pact was a military alliance of the Communist nations of Eastern Europe. (See the map on page 146.)

1. Why did the U.S. Congress send aid to nations in Europe?
2. What was the Berlin Blockade?

3 The Cold War Turns Hot in Korea.
What led to the outbreak of war in Korea?

Europe was not the only place the cold war was fought. The United States and the Soviet Union competed in Asia, Africa, and Latin America as well. In the Asian country of Korea, however, the cold war turned into a hot war. The United States and the Soviet Union did not fight each other directly. However, the war in Korea showed the dangers of the cold war.

Conflict in Korea At the end of World War II, the United States controlled the southern half of Korea. The Soviet Union controlled the northern half. This division was supposed to be temporary. However, cold war mistrust made it last for at least 50 years. The Soviet Union set up a Communist dictatorship in North Korea in 1948. That same year, the United States set up a non-Communist state in South Korea.

The Soviet Union supplied North Korea with weapons. In June 1950, North Korea invaded South Korea.

The United States took the Korean crisis to the UN. The UN voted to defend South Korea. The United States and several other countries sent troops to South Korea.

UN soldiers quickly defeated the North Koreans. South Korea was restored. But the UN changed its plans. Now it wanted a "unified, independent, and democratic Korea." So UN troops advanced into North Korea. However, Communist China had warned that it would get involved if North Korea was invaded. In November 1950, Communist China entered the war on the North Korean side. By the middle of 1951, the UN forces were pushed back to the original border between the two Koreas. (See the map on page 148.) The war dragged on for two more years until the two sides finally signed a cease-fire.

Results of the war The Korean War was frustrating for the American people. U.S. troops saved South Korea. But the United States and its allies did not win the war. The war ended as a draw. It cost the United States 50,000 dead and 100,000 wounded.

However, the war was a step toward ending segregation in the U.S. military. In 1948, President Truman ordered the armed forces integrated. This meant that

African Americans and whites were to fight in the same units. During the Korean War, the army took steps to carry out that order. By 1951, 30 percent of U.S. fighting units were integrated.

1. Why did the United States defend South Korea?
2. What was the result of the Korean War?

Reading a Map Which came first: the UN advance almost to the border of China or the North Korean-Chinese advance? What city lies near the armistice line?

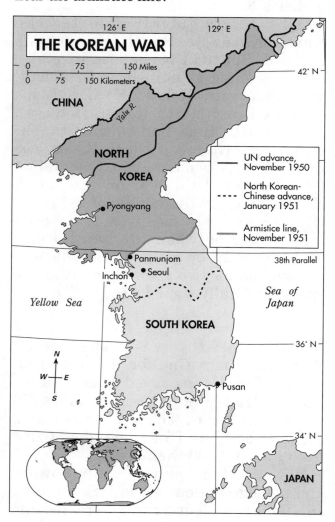

THE KOREAN WAR

0   75   150 Miles
0   75   150 Kilometers

CHINA

Yalu R.

NORTH KOREA

Pyongyang

—— UN advance, November 1950

---- North Korean-Chinese advance, January 1951

—— Armistice line, November 1951

38th Parallel

Panmunjom

Inchon   Seoul

Yellow Sea

Sea of Japan

SOUTH KOREA

42° N

36° N

34° N

126° E   129° E

N
W   E
S

Pusan

JAPAN

4 The Cold War Spreads to Cuba.

How did Cuba become involved in the cold war?

The island-nation of Cuba became part of the cold war during the 1960s. Fidel Castro led a revolution that overthrew a corrupt dictatorship in Cuba. At first, Castro enjoyed the support of the United States. However, that ended when Castro set up a Communist dictatorship. Cuba became an ally of the Soviet Union. Cuba was just 90 miles (144 kilometers) from Florida. Communism was moving closer to the United States.

The Bay of Pigs Because of Castro, many Cubans fled their homeland. They settled in the United States. (See Chapter 26.) They wanted to overthrow Castro. In 1960, the United States began training about 1,500 Cubans for an invasion of Cuba.

The invasion took place in 1961, when John F. Kennedy was President. The Cuban exiles landed in Cuba at the Bay of Pigs. They suffered a complete defeat. The **Bay of Pigs** invasion failed to remove Castro. It also embarrassed the United States.

The Cuban Missile Crisis The following year, U.S. spy planes made a shocking discovery. "It really looks mean, doesn't it?" President Kennedy asked as he studied pictures taken by the planes. The pictures showed that the Soviet Union was building nuclear missile sites in Cuba.

Kennedy knew that he must act quickly. He demanded that the Soviets remove their missiles immediately. He also blockaded Cuba so the Soviets could not send more supplies or missiles.

U.S. bombers armed with nuclear weapons were in the air and on alert. U.S. army units were stationed in

Florida. Soviet ships continued to sail toward Cuba. Soviet troops worked on the missile bases. The world stood on the brink of nuclear war.

After 13 days, the Soviets backed down. They offered to remove the missiles if the United States promised not to invade Cuba. The United States accepted the Soviet offer. The Cuban Missile Crisis was over.

After the Cuban Missile Crisis, U.S.-Soviet relations improved. The two nations signed a treaty not to test nuclear weapons in the air. They installed a direct telephone line between the White House and Soviet government headquarters. However, U.S. fears of Communist expansion soon returned. You will read about this in Chapter 20.

1. What was the Bay of Pigs invasion?
2. Why did President Kennedy blockade Cuba?

Weary American troops of the 7th U.S. Infantry Division gather round their commander to hear news of the signing of the armistice between North Korea and the United States in 1953.

CHAPTER 17
KEY IDEAS

- During the cold war, the United States and the Soviet Union competed for power in countries around the world.
- The United States fought the spread of communism in Europe.
- Cold war tensions broke out into war in Korea. The Korean war cost thousands of U.S. lives.
- The cold war came to the Americas when Fidel Castro set up a Communist government in Cuba. The United States could not remove Castro. However, it did stop the Soviet Union from building nuclear missiles in Cuba.

I. Reviewing Vocabulary

Match each word on the left with the correct definition on the right

1. capitalism
2. satellite
3. iron curtain
4. blockade
5. communism

    a. a weak country under the control of a powerful country

    b. the dividing line between East Europe and West Europe after World War II

    c. an economic system in which most businesses and land are owned by people

    d. an economic system in which most businesses and land are owned by the government

    e. to stop anyone from coming in or going out

II. Understanding the Chapter

1. What fears did the United States have about the Soviet Union after World War II?
2. What was the purpose of the Marshall Plan?
3. How did Germany and Korea become divided after World War II?
4. Why was the Korean War frustrating for the United States?
5. Why do you think people in the United States felt especially threatened by Communist government in Cuba?

III. Building Skills: Reading a Map

Study the map on page 146. Then answer the questions below.

1. List three countries that had joined NATO by 1955.
2. List three countries that had joined the Warsaw Pact by 1955.
3. Which countries became part of the Soviet Union after World War II?

IV. Writing About History

1. Write a newspaper interview in which President Truman answers questions about why he put the Truman Doctrine and Marshall Plan into practice.
2. **What Would You Have Done?** Imagine that you are an advisor to President Kennedy. What advice would you give him before the Bay of Pigs invasion? What would you tell him during the Cuban Missile Crisis?

V. Working Together

1. Work together with a group of four to five students. Create an illustrated time-line. List at least six events from the chapter in chronological order. Then, draw pictures to illustrate at least three of those events. Display your timeline in class.
2. **Past to Present** Beginning in 1989, the Soviet Union and the countries of Eastern Europe rejected communism. With a small group of classmates, choose one country in Eastern Europe. Find out what type of government that country has today. In addition, find out about U.S. relations with that country.

THE YEARS AFTER WORLD WAR II BRING PROSPERITY AND PROBLEMS. (1946–1956)

How did life in the United States change after World War II?

In 1955, Rosa Parks refused to give up her seat to a white person on a bus in Montgomery, Alabama. Her arrest sparked the civil rights movement.

Looking at Key Terms

• GI Bill of Rights • *Brown* v. *Board of Education*

Looking at Key Words

- **inflation:** a rapid rise in prices that reduces the value of money
- **veteran:** someone who has served in the armed forces
- **boom:** a period of great prosperity

- **blacklist:** a list of people or organizations under suspicion
- **boycott:** to refuse to buy, sell, or use goods from certain companies, people, or countries

STUDY
Write the questions that appear at the beginning of each section. As you read each section, answer the question. After you read the chapter, answer the question at the beginning of the chapter.
HINT

"There she is! The Statue of Liberty." Soldier after soldier happily shouted those words as their ships sailed into New York harbor in 1946. World War II was finally over. Millions of soldiers were arriving home. It was time to return to a normal peacetime life.

1 The Nation Adjusts to Peace.

What benefits and problems did peace bring to the United States?

When World War II ended the United States celebrated. People hugged and

After World War II, returning soldiers started families and the baby boom began. This boom in U.S. population filled nurseries and schools to overflowing.

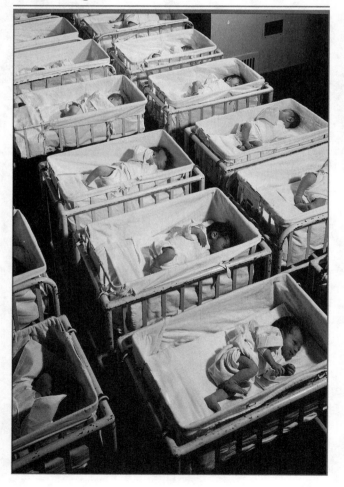

kissed each other. They danced in the streets. Drivers honked their horns as they drove through the streets.

Americans also worried about the future. They remembered the Great Depression. Only the billions of dollars spent to fight the war had ended the Depression. What would happen when that spending stopped? Where would millions of returning soldiers find jobs?

The post-war economy There were other concerns about the economy. After World War II, the government lifted the price controls that had been in place during the war. This resulted in **inflation.** Inflation is a rapid rise in prices. From 1946 to 1947 prices jumped by 33 percent.

Due to inflation, many workers went on strike for higher wages. During 1946, over 5 million workers went on strike. These strikes affected such major industries as cars, steel, and coal.

Conditions soon began to improve, however. People had saved billions of dollars from their wartime jobs. They began to buy cars, dishwashers, homes, and other things that they could not get during the war.

Consumer spending replaced government spending. Factories switched from military to consumer goods and stayed busy. The United States also sold goods to other nations. An economic **boom** began in the United States after the war. A boom is a period of great prosperity. During the 1950s, the income of the average American doubled.

Veteran's benefits The government helped returning soldiers with a law called the **GI Bill of Rights.** It gave money to **veterans** to go to school. A veteran is someone who has served in the armed forces. Many African American and Latino veterans used the GI Bill. Over eight million veterans

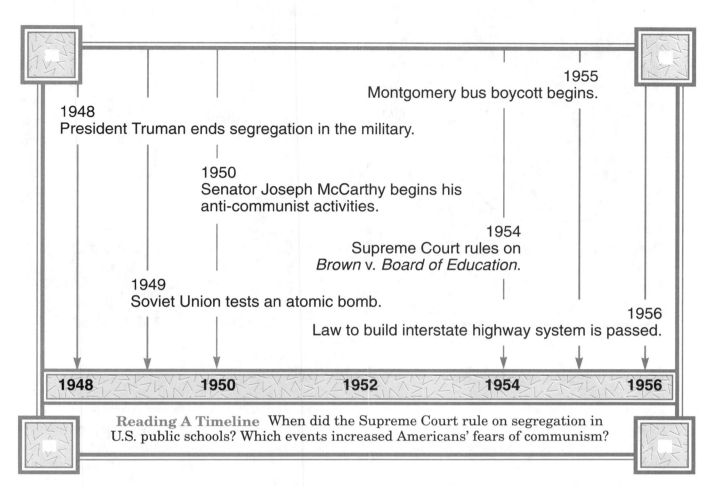

1955
Montgomery bus boycott begins.

1948
President Truman ends segregation in the military.

1950
Senator Joseph McCarthy begins his
anti-communist activities.

1954
Supreme Court rules on
Brown v. *Board of Education*.

1949
Soviet Union tests an atomic bomb.

1956
Law to build interstate highway system is passed.

| 1948 | 1950 | 1952 | 1954 | 1956 |

Reading A Timeline When did the Supreme Court rule on segregation in U.S. public schools? Which events increased Americans' fears of communism?

used the GI Bill to get an education. Over two million attended college.

The GI Bill gave veterans loans to help start businesses. It also gave them loans to buy homes. Millions of veterans bought homes in the suburbs. A suburb is a community near the outskirts of a city. After World War II, the suburbs became the fastest-growing communities in the country. By 1960, one out of four Americans lived in the suburbs.

The baby boom Americans bought homes because they had married and started raising families. In the years just after the war, a record number of Americans married. The newly married couples then had babies in record numbers. People called this sudden increase in the birth rate the baby boom.

Many of the new mothers were women who stopped working when World War II ended. After the war, more than two million women chose to leave their jobs. Another one million lost their jobs. However, the strong post-war economy soon provided many new jobs for women. By 1950, almost three million women found new jobs.

A Fair Deal President Harry Truman won a second term in 1948. He then presented his Fair Deal program. Congress passed only a few of Truman's Fair Deal laws, however. These laws raised the minimum wage and increased social security benefits. The Fair Deal also built housing for people who had low incomes.

In 1952, Dwight D. Eisenhower was elected President. Eisenhower had different ideas about the role of government than Roosevelt or Truman. He thought the government should do less

Senator Joseph McCarthy accused many high government officials of being communists. Here, he shows what he claims is a map of the U.S. Communist Party Organization. McCarthy used people's fears to start a witch hunt.

to manage the economy. However, in 1956, Eisenhower signed a law to build an interstate highway system. Over the next 20 years, the government built 41,000 miles (65,600 kilometers) of highways.

1. What benefits did veterans gain from the GI Bill of Rights?
2. What was the baby boom?

2 Fear of Communism Causes Panic.

How did the cold war affect life in the United States?

The room was crowded with senators, lawyers, reporters, witnesses, microphones, and cameras. Millions of Americans watched the scene on their televisions. A lawyer looked across a table at Senator Joseph McCarthy. "Have you no sense of decency [right or wrong], sir?" the lawyer asked angrily.

McCarthy and communism The lawyer asked that question because McCarthy had just accused yet another person of being a communist. McCarthy accused many people of being communists. He did so without proof. The people he accused often lost their jobs. They also lost friends or went to jail. That was because many Americans believed that communism threatened the American way of life.

Fear of the Soviet Union and communism began growing as World War II ended. These fears spread during the late 1940s. In the early 1950s, they ran wild. Many Americans believed untrue stories about communists inside the government. People like McCarthy spread these stories.

Cold war tensions were the main cause of America's fear of communism. Americans were angered when the Soviet Union took over Eastern Europe after 1945. They worried even more when the Soviet Union tested its first atomic bomb in 1949. Soon after, Americans found out that the Soviet

Union had spies in the United States. Spies had given the Soviet Union information about the atomic bomb.

News about spies raised fears about communism. In 1947, the movie industry in Hollywood came under attack. Actors, writers, and directors who were suspected of being communists were put on **blacklists.** A blacklist is a list of people who are considered suspicious. Blacklisted people could not find jobs.

People in other industries were also investigated. Thousands of people all over the country lost their jobs.

Senator Joseph McCarthy brought the anti-communist scare to its peak. When he began his activities in 1950, he claimed that he had a list of 205 communists in the government. Later, he changed that number several times. Yet he never proved any government worker a communist.

McCarthy's downfall Between 1950 and 1954, McCarthy was one of the most feared politicians in the United States. Then, he went too far. In 1954, he accused the U.S. Army of having communists in its ranks. A Senate committee investigated his charges. Its meetings were carried live on television.

On television, millions of Americans saw that McCarthy had no proof to back up his charges. The country turned against him. In December 1954, the Senate voted to condemn his actions. Within a few years, the communist scare was over. However, it left a deep scar on American life.

1. Who was Senator Joseph McCarthy?
2. How did the cold war affect feelings about communism in the United States?

3 The Civil Rights Movement Gets Underway.
How did the Civil Rights Movement begin?

On the cold afternoon of December 1, 1955, Rosa Parks boarded a bus in Montgomery, Alabama. Mrs. Parks was tired after working all day. Because she was an African American she sat in the "colored" section in the back of the bus. Only white people could sit in the front of the bus. That was because the buses and other public places were segregated, or separated, in Montgomery. Mrs. Parks took a seat in the first row of the "colored" section.

African Americans were forced to live under legal segregation in the South. Even drinking fountains such as this one were divided into "colored" and "white."

Elizabeth Eckford bravely passed through an ugly crowd to enter Little Rock High School. Federal troops were sent in by President Eisenhower to enforce the integration.

Rosa Parks' arrest Soon the white section of the bus filled up. The bus driver then told Mrs. Parks to give her seat to a white person. Mrs. Parks refused. She later recalled, "I don't really know why I wouldn't move. There was no plot or plan at all. I was just tired."

The bus driver said he would call the police and have Mrs. Parks arrested. "You may do that," she answered. The police came and arrested Mrs. Parks.

Segregation North and South Rosa Parks' arrest was one example of the injustices African Americans faced after World War II. In many places in the South, there were laws that segregated people. The North did not have legal segregation. However, prejudice often made segregation a fact of life. African Americans in the northern cities usually could not get housing in white neighborhoods. They often could only find low-paying jobs.

However, some progress had been made after the war. In 1947, Jackie Robinson became the first African American to play major league baseball. Other African Americans quickly joined him in the major leagues. In 1948, President Truman ordered an end to segregation in the U.S. military. He also ended segregation in the government. He appointed the first African American federal judge.

Segregation in education However, there was still much segregation as the 1950s began. This was especially true in education. Twenty-one states plus Washington, D.C. had segregated schools. Segregated schools were actually legal. In 1896, the Supreme Court had approved it in the *Plessy* v. *Ferguson* case. The Court ruled that separate school systems for whites and blacks were legal as long as they were equal. In the real world, separate schools were never equal.

By the 1950s, the NAACP wanted to convince the Supreme Court to reverse *Plessy* v. *Ferguson*. The NAACP's chief lawyer in that struggle was Thurgood Marshall. In 1954, a new case reached the Supreme Court. It was called ***Brown*** v. ***Board of Education of Topeka, Kansas.***

In this case, Oliver Brown wanted his daughter to attend an all-white school near their home. She had been traveling to a black school more than two miles (3.2 kilometers) away. All the Supreme Court justices agreed. They said segregation in all public schools was against the constitution. *Brown* v. *Board of Education* was one of the Supreme Court's most important decisions.

The court ordered school districts to integrate right away. Many did. But whites in many parts of the South did not integrate. In September 1957, a key test came in Little Rock, Arkansas. The governor of Arkansas tried to use the National Guard to stop black students from entering Central High School.

President Eisenhower acted to enforce the law. He took command of the National Guard away from the governor and sent in federal soldiers.

Boycotting the buses   Another way to fight segregation was the **boycott.** A boycott is when people refuse to buy goods or services from a certain company. After the arrest of Rosa Parks, African Americans boycotted the buses in Montgomery, Alabama. A young minister named Dr. Martin Luther King, Jr. led the boycott. King believed that the struggle against segregation had to be nonviolent. He wanted to use only peaceful methods to fight segregation.

The boycott lasted for 381 days. There were several attempts to break the boycott. A bomb exploded on the porch of Dr. King's house. The police arrested the leaders of the boycott. Still the boycott continued. As one person said, "I'm not walking for myself. I'm walking for my children and my grandchildren."

In late 1956, the Supreme Court outlawed segregation on Alabama buses. In December, Dr. King and other African American leaders boarded integrated Montgomery buses.

The successful fights against segregation in the South were only a beginning. The struggle against segregation grew during the 1960s. You will read about that effort in Chapter 23.

1. Which Supreme Court decision outlawed segregation in public schools?
2. What action sparked the Montgomery bus boycott?

CHAPTER 18

KEY IDEAS

- After World War II, the U.S. economy boomed. The GI Bill helped veterans get educations, start businesses, and buy homes.
- As a result of cold war fears, many Americans began to worry about communism in the United States. From 1950 to 1954, Senator Joseph McCarthy accused a number of people of being communists.
- African Americans began to fight for more rights during the 1950s. *Brown* v. *Board of Education* ended segregated schools. The Montgomery bus boycott ended segregation on buses.

I. Reviewing Vocabulary

Match each word on the left with the correct definition on the right.

1. boycott
2. blacklist
3. boom
4. veteran
5. inflation

a. a rapid rise in prices that reduces the value of money
b. someone who served in the armed force
c. a list of people or organizations under suspicion or disfavor
d. when people refuse to buy certain products or buy from a certain company
e. a period of great prosperity

II. Understanding the Chapter

1. How did the U.S. economy change after World War II?
2. How did events in Europe encourage a fear of communism in the United States?
3. How did the fear of communism affect people in the United States?
4. Why was the *Brown* v. *Board of Education of Topeka, Kansas* an important Supreme Court decision?
5. What effect did the arrest of Rosa Parks have on the struggle against segregation?

III. Building Skills: Time Check

1. Which came first, the Fair Deal or the election of Dwight Eisenhower as President?
2. Which came first, the Soviet Union's takeover of Eastern Europe or Senator Joseph McCarthy's accusations about communists in the United States?
3. Which came first, the arrest of Rosa Parks or the *Brown* v. *Board of Education* decision?

IV. Writing About History

1. **What Would You Have Done?** Imagine that you are Rosa Parks. Would you obey the bus driver and give up your seat on the bus? Write a diary entry that describes how you would have reacted on that day.
2. Suppose that you lived in the 1950s. Write a newspaper editorial that describes your opinion of the fear of communism in the United States.

V. Working Together

1. Choose four or five classmates to work with. Write a brief skit about the Montgomery bus boycott. In your skit, be sure to have Dr. King discuss his policy of nonviolence. Perform your skit for the class.
2. **Past to Present** Boycotts are often a good way for people to achieve their goals in a nonviolent way. With a group of classmates, find out whether there have been any boycotts that people in your community have participated in recently. Then, list other nonviolent ways people can use to achieve their goals.

FIVE PRESIDENTS SHAKE UP THE NATION. (1960—1980)

How did the federal government change the way it dealt with poverty and other social problems in the 1960s and 1970s?

President Kennedy met with the leaders of the March on Washington, including Dr. Martin Luther King, Jr. at the White House in 1963.

Looking at Key Terms

- Civil Rights Act of 1964 • Voting Rights Act of 1965
- Medicare • Medicaid

Looking at Key Words

- **assassination:** a planned murder
- **backlash:** a negative response to something that is happening
- **impeachment:** the bringing of charges against a government official

- **pardon:** an official act that wipes out the penalty for a crime
- **tyrant:** a cruel ruler
- **hostage:** a person held prisoner until demands are met

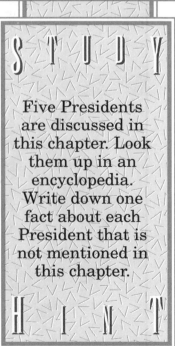

STUDY HINT

Five Presidents are discussed in this chapter. Look them up in an encyclopedia. Write down one fact about each President that is not mentioned in this chapter.

The 1960s and 1970s were a time of triumphs and tragedies. Of five Presidents who served then, two did not complete their terms of office. One was shot dead. One resigned in disgrace. During this time, the federal government took on many new jobs. It sent astronauts to the moon. It started programs to help the poor and the sick. It worked for equal rights. It tried to protect the environment. The new programs caused debate. Americans did not agree on whether the programs would help the country or hurt it.

1 President Kennedy Sets New Goals for the Nation.

What was President Kennedy's contribution to the nation?

John F. Kennedy brought a burst of energy to the White House in 1961. At 43, he was the youngest person ever elected President. He proposed a long list of new programs.

Kennedy caused mixed emotions. Many people adored him. They liked the way he played football with his brothers. They liked his Boston accent, his classy style. But many others did not like Kennedy. They called him a "spoiled rich boy."

The New Frontier   Kennedy had promised to lead the country "to the edge of a New Frontier." He wanted to fight poverty and improve education. He wanted to provide health care for the aged and to promote social justice.

His "New Frontier" programs won support from many Democrats. But others said the programs were too liberal. Conservative Democrats teamed up with Republicans to block most of the programs in Congress.

However, Congress did pass a key part of Kennedy's program. Kennedy proposed "landing a man on the moon" before the 1960s ended. The plan cost billions of dollars. Still, Congress said yes. The Soviet government already had a space program. Americans worried that the United States was falling

Reading a Chart. Which candidate won the most electoral votes? How much of the popular vote did Kennedy receive? How much did Nixon receive? Make a brief statement about the election of 1960 based on the chart below.

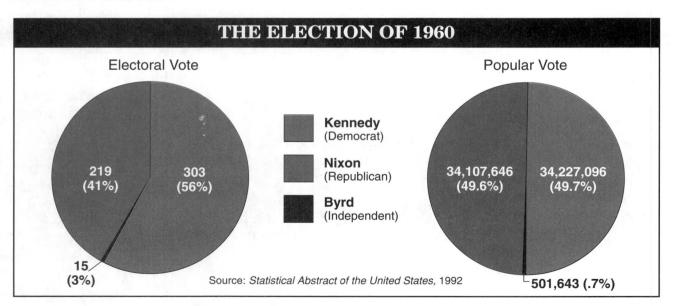

THE ELECTION OF 1960

Electoral Vote

219 (41%)   303 (56%)   15 (3%)

Popular Vote

34,107,646 (49.6%)   34,227,096 (49.7%)   501,643 (.7%)

Kennedy (Democrat)

Nixon (Republican)

Byrd (Independent)

Source: *Statistical Abstract of the United States*, 1992

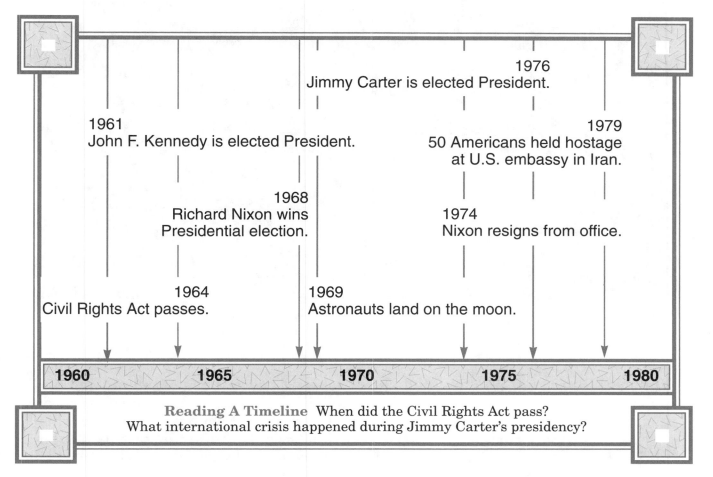

1976
Jimmy Carter is elected President.

1961
John F. Kennedy is elected President.

1979
50 Americans held hostage
at U.S. embassy in Iran.

1968
Richard Nixon wins
Presidential election.

1974
Nixon resigns from office.

1964
Civil Rights Act passes.

1969
Astronauts land on the moon.

| 1960 | 1965 | 1970 | 1975 | 1980 |

Reading A Timeline When did the Civil Rights Act pass?
What international crisis happened during Jimmy Carter's presidency?

behind. A successful moon landing would show that the United States was ahead of the Soviet Union. The space program also helped the economy. New industries developed the equipment needed for the space program.

Civil rights Kennedy spoke out for civil rights. The government went to court to back the right of African Americans to vote. To many Southern whites, this made Kennedy an enemy.

But African Americans wanted Kennedy to do more. They urged him to push for new laws for equal rights. In 1963, Kennedy proposed a sweeping civil rights bill. He said racial prejudice was a great wrong.

Death in Dallas Kennedy died before Congress could act on his civil rights bill. The date was November 22,

1963. Kennedy and his wife Jackie rode in an open car during a parade in Dallas, Texas. Shots rang out. The President slumped forward. Soon he was dead.

A government commission studied the **assassination.** An assassination is a planned murder. The commission said a lone gunman fired the fatal shots. Lee Harvey Oswald was arrested. But he never came to trial. Two days after Kennedy's death, Oswald was being moved to a new jail. A man named Jack Ruby shot and killed Oswald. Some Americans wondered if Oswald and Ruby were part of a larger plot. Even today, some Americans believe that Oswald was not acting alone.

After Kennedy's death, the country went through a period of shock and mourning. Eventually, life returned to normal. Kennedy's Vice President,

President Kennedy's Peace Corps program sent volunteers to serve all over the world. This was the first group to leave the United States. They taught for two years in schools in Ghana.

Lyndon B. Johnson, now headed the nation.

1. How did Congress respond to Kennedy's proposals?
2. What actions did Kennedy take in support of equal rights?

2 President Johnson Tries to Build the "Great Society."

What social programs did President Johnson start?

Johnson was very different from Kennedy. The Johnson family had been poor, not rich. Johnson had attended a small Texas teachers college, not Harvard. Yet Johnson succeeded where Kennedy had not. He pushed laws through Congress that brought great changes to U.S. life.

Years of service in Congress had taught Johnson the art of winning votes. He never tired of talking and persuading. He knew the names of everyone's dogs and children. He knew when to be sweet and when to talk tough. Johnson could win the votes he needed.

The Great Society Johnson's goal was to build the Great Society. He proposed many laws to do that.

First, Johnson got Congress to pass Kennedy's civil rights bill. It became the **Civil Rights Act of 1964.** The act forbid discrimination at restaurants, hotels, theaters, and ball parks. It also covered hiring and voting. It banned discrimination based on race, religion, sex, and national origin.

Next Johnson proposed a "war on poverty." Congress started ten new programs. One was a Job Corps to help unemployed young people find work. Another was Head Start. It offered early schooling to poor children.

In the presidential election of 1964, Johnson won a big victory over Republican Barry Goldwater. The Democrats increased their power in Congress. They passed Johnson's Great Society bills.

One bill started a program of federal aid to education. Before, states and local governments had paid for schools. Now, the federal government pitched in.

After new attacks on civil rights workers in the South, Johnson demanded stronger laws. Congress responded with the **Voting Rights Act of 1965.** It barred reading tests for voters. States had used such tests unfairly to keep African Americans from voting.

Congress started the **Medicare** program to help the elderly pay medical bills. Medicare was part of social security. It applied to almost everyone. The **Medicaid** program gave extra help to the poor. A new Department of Housing and Urban Development (HUD) was created. Its head, Robert Weaver, was the first African American to serve in a President's cabinet.

The shadow of Vietnam As time passed, however, a shadow fell over Johnson's Great Society. It was the shadow of Vietnam.

War had been raging in the Southeast Asian country of Vietnam since the late 1940s. Under President Johnson, the United States sent hundreds of thousands of soldiers to Vietnam. As the death count rose, the war stirred an emotional debate (see Chapter 20).

The Vietnam War hurt Johnson in two big ways. First, it drained money from his Great Society programs. Second, it turned many Americans against him. Johnson decided that he was too unpopular to win the 1968 election. He surprised everyone by announcing that he would not run.

1. List three of Johnson's programs.
2. How did the Vietnam War affect Johnson's "Great Society" programs?

Under President Johnson, Medicare was created. It helped the elderly pay medical bills. Here, retired workers picket to show their support for a Medicare bill.

3 A Scandal Leads to the Downfall of President Nixon.

Why did Watergate lead to the resignation of President Nixon?

With the Democrats divided over the Vietnam War, Republican Richard Nixon won the 1968 election. Nixon argued that the United States was wasting money on poorly-designed social programs.

Nixon achieved many successes and won strong support from voters. In 1969, U.S. astronauts landed on the

Nixon visited the Great Wall of China when he traveled to that country in 1972. The trip helped improve U.S. relations with China.

moon. When they came back, it was Nixon who greeted them.

Achievements abroad   Nixon's great love was foreign policy. He and his top adviser, Henry Kissinger, took many bold steps. In Chapter 20, you will read how they got U.S. troops out of Vietnam. Just as important were visits to China and the Soviet Union. This started a period of better relations with these Communist countries.

Communists had taken over China in 1949. For more than 20 years, the United States and China had bad relations. In 1972 Nixon flew to China. He met Chinese leaders. He visited China's Great Wall. After that, China began

buying U.S. products. Americans bought Chinese goods too. The two nations worked to resolve their differences.

Nixon also went to the Soviet Union. He signed treaties that slowed the arms race. For a few years, there was a thaw in the Cold War.

New federal powers   At home, Nixon took a conservative line. He tried to turn some federal programs over to state governments.

Yet Nixon did expand federal powers in some areas. He supported bills to promote clean air and water. In 1970, Nixon set up the Environmental Protection Agency (EPA) to fight pollution.

On civil rights, Nixon responded to a "white backlash." A **backlash** is a negative response to something. In this case, it was a response to the Civil Rights Movement. Nixon tried to please whites who thought that blacks were getting special favors. He opposed programs to bus African American children to "white" schools.

The Watergate affair   In 1972, Nixon easily won re-election. He took three out of every five votes.

A small incident during the election campaign came back to haunt Nixon. It was a burglary at the Democratic party's headquarters in the Watergate building in Washington, D.C. The burglars were working for Nixon's election campaign. An alert guard caught them in the act.

Nixon found out what had happened. He could have told his staff members to tell the truth and take their punishment. Instead, he tried to cover the facts up. His staff members destroyed evidence. They told lies to Congress and the FBI.

The truth came out anyway. Members of Congress were furious. In 1974, they started the process of **impeachment** against Nixon. Impeachment is the bringing of charges against a government official by the House of

Representatives. It is the first step in removing the official from office. The next step is conviction by the Senate. Nixon insisted: "I am not a crook." But his advisers told him he was sure to lose. So, in a dramatic television address, Nixon resigned.

Nixon never went to jail. No court ever determined whether or not he had committed a crime. President Gerald Ford, Nixon's successor, granted Nixon a **pardon.** A pardon is an official act that wipes out the penalty for a crime. Ford said he wanted to put an end to "our long national nightmare."

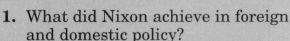

1. What did Nixon achieve in foreign and domestic policy?
2. Why did Nixon resign?

4 Troubles Hurt Presidents Ford and Carter.

Why did voters reject first President Ford and then President Carter?

During the rest of the 1970s, the United States struggled with economic woes. Voters were not happy. In 1976 they turned Gerald Ford out of office. A Democrat, Jimmy Carter, took his place. But problems at home and abroad made Carter unpopular. In 1980, the voters turned him out too.

A President who was not elected Ford was the nation's first unelected President. He had become Vice President by appointment. Nixon chose him after a scandal forced Vice President Spiro Agnew to resign in 1973. The Senate approved Ford's appointment. However, the voters had no direct say. Then Nixon stepped down. As provided by the 25th Amendment, Ford took over as President.

Ford faced deep economic troubles. In 1973, Arab nations had cut off oil sales to protest U.S. support for Israel. Oil prices shot up. Prices remained high even after the Arabs started selling oil again. The United States was in the grip of a raging inflation. Inflation is a general increase in prices which results in people being able to buy less. At the same time, business was bad.

Ford tried several programs to perk up the economy. Nothing worked. Thousands of people lost jobs. Others could not pay their bills. Unhappy voters chose Carter over Ford in 1976.

An energy crisis hit in the 1970s. People lined up at gas stations hoping to fill their tanks. In New York City and all over the country, gas lines were huge.

Carter's ups and downs Jimmy Carter too faced tough economic challenges. In 1979, oil prices soared still higher. Inflation spread through the economy. In one year, the cost of living rose by a shocking 13 percent.

Carter urged Americans to use less fuel. He turned the heat down and wore a sweater around the White House. But his talk of an "energy crisis" made many people angry. Critics said the answer to high energy prices was to find more oil.

In foreign policy, Carter had one big success. In 1978, he brought the leaders of Egypt and Israel together for peace talks. The talks took place at Camp David, in Maryland. They led to a peace treaty—the first ever between Israel and an Arab neighbor. Arabs and Israelis had fought four wars. Carter said he hoped this would be the first step to a wider peace.

Carter tried to extend the thaw in the Cold War. In 1979, he signed a new arms treaty with the Soviet Union. That December, Soviet soldiers invaded Afghanistan. Carter then put the treaty on hold. He asked Congress to boost military spending.

The worst crisis came in Iran. In 1979, a revolution rocked Iran. The shah, or emperor, had to flee. Iran's new leaders called the shah a **tyrant.** A tyrant is a cruel ruler. They blamed Americans for supporting the shah. Late in 1979, a group of Iranians seized the U.S. embassy in Teheran, the capital. They took more than 50 American **hostages.** A hostage is someone held prisoner until demands are met. For 13 long months, the crisis dragged on. A rescue mission sent by Carter ended in failure. Voters blamed Carter for the long crisis.

In 1980, Ronald Reagan, a Republican, won the presidential election. Iran released the hostages on the day when Reagan took office.

1. What problems faced Ford and Carter?
2. Why were they voted out of office?

CHAPTER 19
KEY IDEAS

- President Kennedy set new economic and civil rights goals for the nation. But before he could accomplish them, he was assassinated.
- President Johnson created many social and economic programs. Some extended civil rights of minorities. Others improved the lives of the poor.
- President Nixon acted more conservatively on issues in the United States. He eased Cold War tensions. However, a scandal forced him to resign.
- Presidents Ford and Carter tried to deal with economic troubles.

REVIEWING CHAPTER 19

I. Reviewing Vocabulary

Match each word on the left with the correct definition on the right.

1. assassination
2. hostage
3. backlash
4. impeachment
5. pardon

a. the bringing of charges against a government official
b. a negative response to something that is happening
c. a planned murder
d. an official act that wipes out the penalty for a crime
e. a person held prisoner until demands are met

II. Understanding the Chapter

1. What did President Kennedy want to accomplish?
2. What programs made up President Johnson's "Great Society"?
3. What were President Nixon's achievements abroad?
4. What problems did President Ford try to solve?
5. What crisis affected Carter's popularity in 1979?

III. Building Skills: Identifying Cause and Effect

In each of the cases below, tell which is the cause and which is the effect.

1. Nixon resigns; Watergate affair is uncovered.
2. Kennedy proposes the "New Frontier"; U.S. astronauts land on the moon.
3. Carter looses 1980 election; U.S. hostage-rescue mission to Iran fails.

IV. Writing About History

1. **What Would You Have Done?** If you were a member of Congress, would you approve President Kennedy's space program? Explain.
2. Imagine you are working for President Carter in 1979. Write a newspaper advertisement explaining how Americans should act during the energy crisis.

V. Working Together

1. Form a small group. Write dramatic newspaper headlines about the key events during the time when one of the Presidents discussed in this chapter was in office. Make a bulletin board display of your headlines.
2. **Past to Present** In 1965, President Johnson gave a speech appealing for an end to racial hatred. With a group, discuss what a President today might say about discrimination. List issues that a current President might bring up.

THE UNITED STATES FIGHTS A WAR IN VIETNAM. (1960–1975)

Why did the United States go to war in Vietnam and what was the result?

Gunfire all around, U.S. soldiers rush a wounded friend through a swamp in 1969. Thousands fought and died in the Vietnam War.

STUDY HINT

On a separate sheet of paper, make a list of the presidents from Eisenhower through Nixon. Write down how each president dealt with the issue of Vietnam.

Looking at Key Terms

- domino theory • Viet Cong • Vietnamization

Looking at Key Words

- **escalation:** a slow but steady increase in the level of warfare
- **hawk:** a war supporter

- **dove:** an opponent of war
- **amnesty:** a pardon for political offenses

Smoke and fire came out of a U.S. Navy plane over the Gulf of Tonkin. Enemy fire had scored a hit. U.S. Navy Captain Everett Alvarez, Jr. bailed out. He splashed into the water below. There, a Vietnamese fishing boat was waiting. Men pointed rifles at Alvarez and took him prisoner.

It was August 5, 1964. U.S. planes were making their first attack on North Vietnam. Alvarez, a Mexican American from California, was the first American taken prisoner in the Vietnam War.

Eight and a half years later, Alvarez came home. He was one of 591 U.S. prisoners to be released from enemy prisons. Fifty-eight thousand Americans did not come home at all. They were killed in the war.

1 The Cold War Leads the United States into War in Vietnam.

Why did a war break out in Vietnam?

Until the 1960s, few Americans had thought much about Vietnam. It was far away in Southeast Asia. But Vietnam lies just south of China. When Communists took control of China in 1949, the Cold War was at its height. U.S. leaders feared that communism would spread. They saw Southeast Asia like a string of dominoes. When one domino falls, it knocks down its neighbors. If Vietnam "fell," its neighbors would topple too. For years this **domino theory** shaped the policy of the United States. U.S. leaders tried to keep the first domino, Vietnam, from falling.

Two Vietnams Vietnam had been a colony of France. After World War II, the Vietnamese fought for independence. However, Vietnam became independent as two nations. North Vietnam had a Communist government. Its ruler was Ho Chi Minh. South Vietnam remained under French influence. It promised to hold free elections, but then refused to do so.

Opponents of the South Vietnamese government then launched a civil war. They formed groups of guerrillas. The guerillas were led by the **Viet Cong**, who were Communists.

South Vietnam asked the United States for help. President Dwight Eisenhower believed in the domino theory. He sent 1,000 military advisers to train South Vietnam's army. But South Vietnam still could not defeat the guerrillas. The fighting spread.

North Vietnam sent help to the guerrillas. The United States sent more help to South Vietnam. By 1963, President John Kennedy had increased the number of U.S. advisers to 16,700.

President Lyndon Johnson tried to force North Vietnam to stop helping the guerrillas. Undercover agents began blowing up bridges and doing other damage to North Vietnam. The American people did not know about this secret war in Southeast Asia.

A wider war Then, in August 1964, events plunged the United States into a wider war. Off the coast of North Vietnam, in the Gulf of Tonkin, the U.S. warship *Maddox* was attacked by North Vietnamese boats.

Johnson sent U.S. planes to bomb bases and oil tanks in North Vietnam. He said the United States was responding to attacks by North Vietnam. Congress quickly backed the President.

Escalation Step by step, the United States slipped into a full-scale war in Vietnam. Guerrillas attacked a base and killed U.S. military advisers. In response, Johnson ordered bombing raids. He sent the first U.S. soldiers to fight on the ground. Then the guerrillas launched new attacks. So Johnson sent more soldiers. This slow but steady rise in the level of warfare was called **escalation**.

By the end of 1965, 181,000 U.S. soldiers were in Vietnam. Three years later the figure had reached 536,000. Each week, U.S. planes brought dead soldiers home in "body bags." As the death toll rose, opposition to the Vietnam War increased.

Johnson decided in 1968 that he might not win re-election. He chose not to run at all. Richard Nixon accused the Democrats of bungling the war. He won election as president in 1968.

Reading a Map. Where is the Gulf of Tonkin located? Through which countries does the Ho Chi Minh Trail pass?

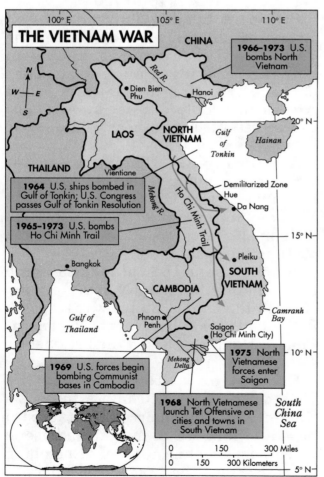

Vietnamization Nixon too believed in the domino theory. He said the United States had to "stand up to the Communists." At the same time, he wanted to end the war.

Nixon's solution was to turn the fighting over to South Vietnam's army. This policy was called **Vietnamization**. It meant that Nixon could begin bringing U.S. soldiers home. By late 1972, only 50,000 U.S. soldiers remained in Vietnam.

At the same time, Nixon stepped up air attacks. U.S. planes bombed supply routes that linked North Vietnam and South Vietnam.

Peace settlement Peace talks that began in the 1960s finally succeeded in January 1973. The United States signed agreements with North Vietnam and the guerrillas. The last U.S. ground troops came home.

However, the war continued without the United States. It finally ended in 1975. North Vietnam and the guerrillas were the winners. South and North became one nation, Vietnam. Vietnam had a Communist government.

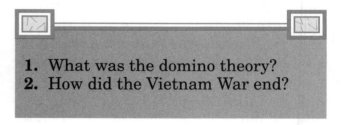

1. What was the domino theory?
2. How did the Vietnam War end?

2 Americans Are Divided on the War.
What form did opposition to the war take in the United States?

The Vietnam War sharply divided the U.S. public. Some Americans supported the war. Others criticized it. The war became the subject of bitter debate.

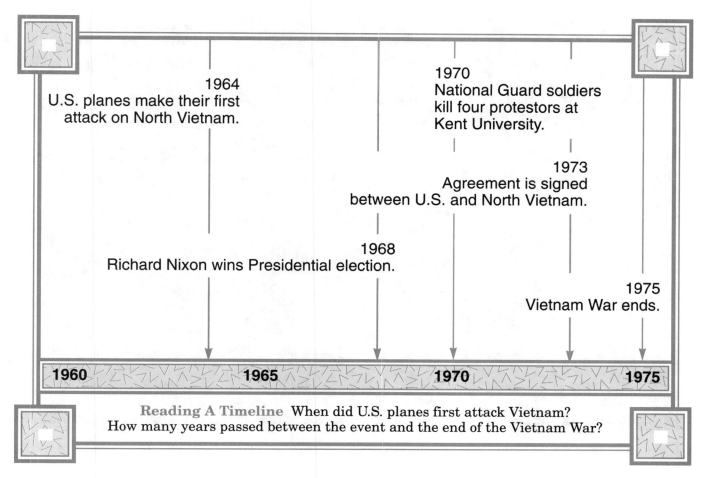

1964
U.S. planes make their first attack on North Vietnam.

1970
National Guard soldiers kill four protestors at Kent University.

1973
Agreement is signed between U.S. and North Vietnam.

1968
Richard Nixon wins Presidential election.

1975
Vietnam War ends.

1960   1965   1970   1975

Reading A Timeline When did U.S. planes first attack Vietnam? How many years passed between the event and the end of the Vietnam War?

Doves and hawks Critics and supporters of the war were given labels. **Doves** were against the war. **Hawks** were for it.

Doves argued that the war in Vietnam was a civil war. U.S. troops should not interfere. They also said that the war was hurting the United States. It was killing thousands of young Americans. And the war was a waste of money.

Hawks said that the Communist government of North Vietnam had started the war. The United States must halt the spread of communism. Hawks also said that U.S. presidents had promised to defend South Vietnam. Americans had to honor that promise. Otherwise, no one would ever trust the United States again.

Rising opposition Most Americans backed the war at first. Here and there, a few people spoke out against the war. Some college students marched in protest.

President Johnson tried not to alarm the public. He avoided asking for new taxes to pay for the rising costs of the war. U.S. planners said that the war would soon be over.

But news reports told a different story. The reports said that many South Vietnamese hated the government that the United States was backing. Despite the huge U.S. effort, victory was nowhere in sight. Many Americans began to think the U.S. government was lying about the war.

The Tet offensive Enemy attacks at the start of 1968 increased this doubt. Tet is the Vietnamese new-year holiday. On Tet, the Viet Cong attacked many cities at once. They even struck

Protests against the Vietnam War spread as the war dragged on. Thousands of demonstrators surrounded the U.S. Defense Department at the Pentagon. They were held back by armed military police.

South Vietnam's capital, Saigon. For a short time, guerrillas occupied the U.S. embassy there. U.S. and allied forces finally put down the **Tet offensive**. But it was now clear that the Viet Cong could strike anywhere. The U.S. commander asked for more soldiers.

More protests Now many more Americans protested against the war. Thousands marched in peaceful protests. Other protests turned violent. Angry students trashed college buildings. Young men burned their draft cards. Hundreds moved to Canada to avoid serving in the army.

Protests ended in bloodshed in May 1970. President Nixon had just sent ground troops into Cambodia to attack enemy supply bases. At Kent State University in Ohio, National Guard soldiers shot and killed four student protesters. Two more students died in Mississippi. There, state police fired on demonstrators at Jackson State College.

These tragedies shocked the nation. Hawks blamed the protesters. Doves blamed the war. American society was split in two.

1. Who were hawks and doves?
2. What events increased opposition to the Vietnam War?

3 Americans Look Back on the Vietnam War.

What were the long-term effects of the war?

The Vietnam War left a bad taste in everyone's mouths. But people disagreed about what had gone wrong. They drew different lessons for the future.

Drawing lessons The Vietnam War raised questions about the uses of power. Doves said that the war showed the limits of U.S. power. Despite all its firepower, the United States had not been able to win in Vietnam.

Hawks drew a different lesson. They said that the United States could have won if it had only tried harder. They accused U.S. leaders of making U.S. soldiers fight "with their hands tied behind their backs."

War's toll The war took a terrible toll. Some 11,500 women and 8,700,000 men served with U.S. forces in the war zone. More than 58,000 Americans died in the fighting.

For every American killed in the war, 3 South Vietnamese soldiers and 16 enemy soldiers died. Some 415,000 civilians were among the 1.5 million Vietnamese who died.

After the war, many Vietnamese fled their country to escape harsh conditions. Thousands came to the United States. (See Chapter 33.)

Greater involvement for people of color The Vietnam War was the first

The Women's Vietnam Veterans Memorial was unveiled in 1993. Diane Carlson, the founder of the memorial, hugged other women veterans at its dedication. It is located near the "Wall" in Washington, D.C.

U.S. war in which people of color served in large numbers in all ranks. Some of the top officers were African Americans and Latinos.

African Americans made up 10 percent of the U.S. population. Yet 20 percent of the draftees who served in Vietnam were African Americans. A larger portion of Latinos served, too. This was because most draftees were poor or working-class Americans. Middle-class youths could postpone being drafted by going to college. Often, they escaped the draft altogether. In addition, a high percentage of Americans killed in battle were African Americans and Latinos.

Healing the wounds   The Vietnam War left deep wounds on the American soul. Anger about the war died slowly. Few celebrations greeted returning Vietnam veterans. Some Americans treated them as war criminals, not war heroes.

Gradually, those who had left the country to escape the draft came home. In 1974, President Ford granted a limited **amnesty** to draft evaders. An amnesty is a pardon for political offenses.

Further healing came in 1982. On Veterans Day, November 11, the government unveiled the Vietnam Veterans Memorial in Washington, D.C. It is a long, dark granite wall. Engraved in stone are the names of all 58,000 Americans killed in the war.

In 1993, a separate memorial was put up nearby. It honored women who served in the war. One veteran who attended the dedication wiped tears from her eyes. "We were supposed to be the brave ones," she said, "and not have emotions." Now, two decades later, she could cry.

1. Which groups had a high percentage of soldiers killed in battle?
2. Name one way in which the wounds of Vietnam were healed.

CHAPTER 20
KEY IDEAS

- Cold War policies led the United States into a war in Vietnam. But the war failed to prevent Vietnam from becoming Communist.
- The Vietnam War sharply divided Americans into supporters and critics of the war. Massive protests broke out.
- The war was the first in which the U.S. military was truly integrated. It also left Americans with conflicting lessons for the future.

REVIEWING CHAPTER 20

I. Reviewing Vocabulary
Match each word on the left with the correct definition on the right.

1. dove
2. hawk
3. amnesty
4. escalation
5. domino theory

a. the idea that if one country fell to Communism, others would follow
b. a war supporter
c. a slow but steady increase in the level of warfare
d. an opponent of war
e. a pardon for political offenses

II. Understanding the Chapter
1. How did the domino theory affect U.S. involvement in Vietnam?
2. How did President Johnson try to stop North Vietnam from helping the guerrillas?
3. What was President Nixon's policy of Vietnamization?
4. How did the Vietnam War split U.S. society?
5. What lessons did Americans draw from the war?

III. Building Skills: Reading Maps
Review the map on page 170 and answer the questions below.
1. Where were U.S. ships first bombed?
2. What countries did the North Vietnamese supply route run through?
3. When did North Vietnamese forces enter Saigon?

IV. Writing About History
1. **What Would You Have Done?** Would you have enlisted in the armed forces to fight in Vietnam? Explain.
2. Write a short letter from a U.S. soldier in Vietnam to a friend who is a dove. Then write a reply explaining the friend's views.

V. Working Together
1. Form a small group. Interview someone who lived during the Vietnam War. Ask the person to tell how the war affected his or her life. Write a report. Share your report with the class.
2. **Past to Present** With a group, discuss the effect of the Vietnam War on foreign policy today. Write a paragraph on your opinion about the United States' sending troops to fight in other countries.

CHANGES IN THE AMERICAN WAY OF LIFE TAKE PLACE. (1945–1980)

What were some of the ways in which the lives of Americans changed from 1945 to 1980?

After World War II, as many as 1,500 Puerto Ricans a month came to New York. The city was a favorite location for islanders who wanted to start a new life.

Looking at Key Terms
• "baby boom" • Levittown • Sunbelt • "rock 'n' roll"

Looking at Key Words
• **hippies:** young people of the 1960s who rebelled against society

• **generation gap:** differences between parents and children

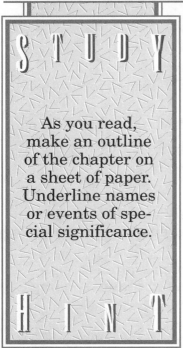

STUDY

As you read, make an outline of the chapter on a sheet of paper. Underline names or events of special significance.

HINT

Imagine yourself in the year 1945. Teenage girls faint over a singer named Frank Sinatra. Many schools require boys to wear ties and girls to wear dresses. Most Americans get their news from newspapers or from radio. Almost no one owns a television.

Now jump forward to 1980. Things are very different. Rock music has teens dancing. Blue jeans seem to be a national uniform. TV sets glow in almost every living room.

The United States faced great change in those 35 years. Suburbs grew. New styles became popular. Most of all, young people rocked the nation.

1 Large-Scale Shifts of People Take Place.

What changes occurred in where Americans lived between 1945 and 1980?

The years after World War II saw huge changes in the U.S. population. More people were born. The population shifted in two directions. Many white city residents moved to suburbs. Jobs moved with them. At the same time, large numbers of African Americans, Latinos, and new immigrants moved into cities.

The baby boom After World War II, the U.S. population exploded. Soldiers returned home and got married. They started families. The number of births jumped. This increase in birthrates was called the **baby boom**. It lasted over 20 years. It was the largest increase the United States had ever known.

Children born during this time were called baby boomers. U.S. businesses rushed to provide services for this huge new market. Thousands of new schools were built. Growing families also needed housing.

To the suburbs During the war, many young couples had lived with their parents. After the war, they could spend the money that they had saved. Now they wanted their own homes. Veterans were also able to buy homes. The government gave them low-cost loans. The demand for housing soared. Builders struggled to fill this demand.

In 1947, a builder named William Levitt had an idea. He bought farmland on Long Island near New York City. He divided it up and created a new community. He called it **Levittown.** Levitt made his houses affordable. He borrowed a trick from Henry Ford—mass production. Whole rows of houses were built with the same plan. Workers put the same toilets into the same bathrooms. They put up wall coverings that came in ready-made sheets. Houses were built in hours, not weeks.

Soon, communities had row after row of similar houses. Young families bought the houses as fast as builders could put them up. But not everyone liked the new suburbs. Some found them boring.

Some of the new suburbs were integrated. But most suburbs were not. Communities often secretly prevented home owners from selling to African Americans. Secret rules also barred groups like Italian Americans.

Heading north By 1950, a new wave of African Americans headed for Northern cities. In the South, machines that picked cotton were taking the place of human labor. There were fewer farm jobs. From 1950 to 1960, almost two million African Americans moved north. They settled in the largest of the Northern cities.

African Americans had little choice in where they lived in the 1950s. Most city neighborhoods were either all white or all black. Many neighborhoods were changing from one to the other. As whites moved out to the suburbs, African Americans moved in.

Latino migration During this same period, many Latinos were also moving to U.S. cities. Each year, 50,000 or more Puerto Ricans moved to the mainland. From Latin America, immigrants began to arrive in the United States. (You will learn more about this in Unit 5.) Some came seeking better jobs. Others sought greater freedom.

Rise of the Sunbelt In the 1970s and 1980s, other Americans were also on the move. U.S. industries were

Levittown, New York, was built as a housing project for veterans returning from World War II. The homes were mass-produced and looked very much alike.

changing. Many aging northern factories were closing. Other industries were moving south. Factory workers from the Northeast and Midwest began to move. Many resettled in the South and Southwest.

Americans were aging, too. Because of medical advances, people were living longer. Many retired people moved to a warmer climate. Hundreds of thousands settled in Florida, California, and Arizona. This area was called the **Sunbelt**. Population grew quickly there. It climbed nearly twice as fast as the total U.S. population.

This population shift changed U.S. politics. States in the Midwest and Northeast lost political power. They had fewer seats in Congress. South and Southwest states became more important. Politicians began to focus on the needs of people in these states.

1. How did Levitt create affordable houses?
2. How did the population of U.S. cities change?

2 New Styles Become Popular in the Arts.
How did television and popular music change in the years from 1945 to 1980?

Television changed American life between 1945 and 1980. At the start of the period, most people had never watched television. By the end, few people could imagine living without it.

Rise of television At first, only a few lucky families had television. Set owners would invite neighbors over for an evening in front of the tube. The black-and-white picture was often

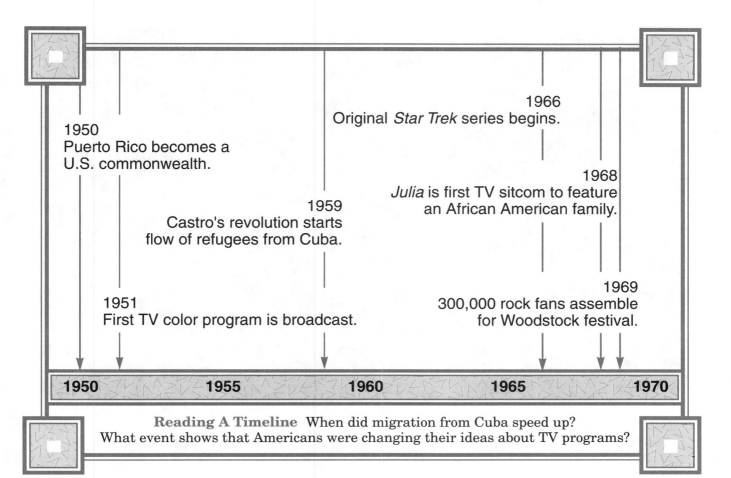

1950
Puerto Rico becomes a
U.S. commonwealth.

1966
Original *Star Trek* series begins.

1959
Castro's revolution starts
flow of refugees from Cuba.

1968
Julia is first TV sitcom to feature
an African American family.

1951
First TV color program is broadcast.

1969
300,000 rock fans assemble
for Woodstock festival.

| 1950 | 1955 | 1960 | 1965 | 1970 |

Reading A Timeline When did migration from Cuba speed up?
What event shows that Americans were changing their ideas about TV programs?

blurred by "snow." People had to squint to see the small screen. But TV was a big hit.

Television ownership soared from 14,000 households in 1947 to 30 million in 1955. Two families in every three now had sets. By 1970, TV was everywhere. More than 95 percent of all homes had a set, or even two or three.

TV as a mirror? Early 1950s TV showed a limited view of American life. It was a United States of two-parent families. Each home had two children and a dog. Fathers held jobs. Mothers stayed home to cook and clean. Many ethnic groups stayed in the background. African Americans appeared only as unimportant characters.

Slowly, American society changed, and television changed with it. By the mid-1960s, African Americans were fea-

tured performers. Singer Nat King Cole had his own show. Bill Cosby won an Emmy for his role in the *I Spy* series. But TV still did not show what African Americans, Latinos, and other groups believed and how they lived.

The power of television Television could unite Americans. It did this especially in times of crisis. When an assassin shot President Kennedy in 1963, Americans rushed to a television set. People watched TV throughout the tragic weekend. They grieved together.

TV offered Americans a front-row view of history. During the 1960s, television showed police beating civil rights demonstrators. Viewers were shocked. This helped build support for new civil rights laws.

During the Vietnam War, TV brought the sights and sounds of war into U.S.

The debate between Presidential nominees John F. Kennedy and Richard M. Nixon showed the power of television. People who watched on TV felt that the more photogenic Kennedy won; many who listened on the radio disagreed.

living rooms. It was not a pretty sight. Many people believe that television coverage helped to turn Americans against the war.

Rock 'n' roll   Perhaps television's greatest effect was on the young. Teenagers of the 1950s were the first "TV generation." They grew up watching programs like "Dick Clark's American Bandstand." Every afternoon, the program showed teens dancing to the latest music. That music was **rock 'n' roll**.

Rock 'n' roll burst onto the scene in the 1950s. Its roots were in African American rhythm and blues (R&B). Disk jockeys played tunes by African American performers such as B. B. King. Teen listeners cried for more. Before long, song writers came up with new R&B tunes. They mixed in the

amplified guitars of country-and-western music. Then they cranked up the volume. The result was rock 'n' roll.

Rock musicians became big stars. They included Elvis Presley, Chuck Berry, and Fats Domino. In the 1960s and 1970s, the Beatles were wildly popular. The Grateful Dead, the Supremes, and Carlos Santana created hit after hit. They had huge numbers of fans.

Many parents hated the new music. They blamed it for all sorts of problems in U.S. society. Teens loved it. Rock 'n' roll became a symbol of their generation.

1. Give an example of the power of television.
2. How did rock 'n' roll borrow from different musical traditions?

3 Young People Explore New and Old Ways.

How did the lives of many young people change in the years from 1950 to 1980?

The teenagers who rocked 'n' rolled were baby boomers. In fact, the word *teenager* was created for their generation. They became a strong force in American society. As they matured, they shaped U.S. culture.

Good times   The baby boomers grew up in a time when the economy was expanding. Their parents remembered the hard times of the Great Depression. To baby boomers, the 1930s were ancient history. Teens spent money on records, clothes, cars, and movies.

Baby boomers went farther in school than their parents. Four out of five now graduated from high school. Half of all high-school graduates went to college.

However, the good times were not shared equally. They affected mainly middle-class youths. Working-class kids often had limited futures. Many quit high school to take jobs. This poorer group included many African Americans, Latinos, and rural whites.

Generation gap   Some teens also tried new ways of dressing. Young men wore beards, sideburns, and long hair. Women stopped wearing makeup and dresses. Both wore sandals and faded blue jeans.

Some young people went further in rebelling against traditional values. They "dropped out" of jobs and schools. They used drugs. These people were called **hippies**. They had a way of living

In the 1960s, many young people rebelled against U.S. society and became members of the counterculture—a way of living that clashed with traditional values. These people, called hippies, promoted the ideals of peace and love.

that clashed with traditional ways. They claimed that older people did not understand them. Never before had the difference between generations—the **generation gap**—seemed so wide.

Social action Many young people worked hard for political causes. Some young people pushed conservative causes. But most were liberal.

Many students—African Americans, whites, Latinos, and others—joined the Civil Rights Movement. (See Chapter 22.) Northern African Americans and whites went south to help register African American voters. Students demanded full equality for all.

During the Vietnam War, a strong anti-war movement grew. The movement reached its peak in the late 1960s and early 1970s. Protests died out as the war ended. New economic problems were rising. Young people were more concerned about their economic futures. They became less involved in social action.

Different strokes The young people of these decades did not all fit into a single mold. Not all of them rebelled against society. Some kept their hair short and wore traditional clothes. Many fought and died in Vietnam.

Meanwhile, many young people showed a keen interest in religion. Some left the paths of their parents. They experimented with Asian religions. Among African Americans, many became Muslims. Many young people devoted themselves to traditional U.S. religions—Protestant, Roman Catholic, or Jewish. These young people drew strength from their religious faith.

Many young people based their support for the Civil Rights Movement on religious faith. Many opposed the war for religious reasons.

Others stressed a personal relation to God. Large numbers found new hope by being "born again" into a Christian faith. Churches that stressed fundamental teachings of the Bible gained many followers. Their followers became an important force in politics.

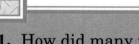

1. How did many young people rebel against traditions in the 1960s?
2. What is a generation gap?

CHAPTER 21
KEY IDEAS

- After World War II, there was a baby boom.
- Many Americans moved to the suburbs. African Americans, Latinos, and immigrants moved to the cities.
- The South and Southwest gained population and political power.
- TV attracted increasing numbers of viewers. Rock 'n' roll became the most popular form of music.
- Some young people rebelled against traditional ways.

REVIEWING CHAPTER 21

I. Reviewing Vocabulary
Match each word on the left with the correct definition on the right.

1. hippies
2. Levittown
3. baby boom
4. rock 'n' roll
5. generation gap

a. a community of mass-produced houses
b. large increase in the number of births
c. a blend of African American R&B with white country-and-western musical traditions
d. the difference between generations
e. young people of the 1960s who rebelled against society

II. Understanding the Chapter
1. What was the baby boom?
2. What major shifts in U.S. population took place between 1950 and 1980?
3. How was early TV's reflection of American life limited?
4. How were baby boomers different from their parents?
5. What kinds of social action did many young people in the 1960s take?

III. Building Skills: Cause and Effect
1. What was one cause of the high demand for housing after World War II?
2. What was one effect of the use of mechanical cotton pickers in the South?

IV. Writing About History
1. Write a poem or song about migrating to a new city or moving to the suburbs in the 1950s. Illustrate your work with a drawing.
2. **What Would You Have Done?** If you were a young person in the 1960s, what kind of social action would you have be involved in? Explain.

V. Working Together
1. With a small group, write a TV skit about one aspect of life in the United States during the 1960s. Act it out for the class.
2. **Past to Present** Many parents blamed rock 'n' roll for problems with young people in the 1950s and 1960s. With a group, discuss attacks on popular music such as rock and rap today. What points do critics make? Write a short statement of your opinion of this issue.

Unit 5
The Struggle for Equality
(1960s-1990s)

Chapters

22 African Americans Struggle for Rights and Equality.

23 African Americans Score Successes in Many Fields.

24 Women Fight for Their Rights.

25 Mexican Americans Struggle for Equal Rights.

26 A Cuban Presence Grows in the United States.

27 Puerto Ricans and Dominicans Strive to Succeed.

28 Native Americans Fight for Their Rights.

29 Americans from Asia Are a Fast-Growing Part of the U.S. Population.

30 Immigrants from Europe and the Middle East Make New Lives in the United States.

AFRICAN AMERICANS STRUGGLE FOR RIGHTS AND EQUALITY. (1960—1990s)

What were the major goals and accomplishments of the Civil Rights Movement?

In 1963, Martin Luther King Jr., led African Americans on a march in Washington, D.C., for equal rights and jobs. Some whites joined the demonstration.

Looking at Key Terms

- March on Washington • Black Muslims • Black Power
- Black Panthers • Rainbow Coalition

Looking at Key Words

- **tactic:** a way of achieving a goal
- **sit-in:** a protest in which people take a seat and refuse to leave
- **freedom ride:** a bus trip to test African Americans' rights

- **affirmative action:** a policy for correcting discrimination by increasing opportunities for certain groups

STUDY HINT

List the names of civil rights groups and leaders covered in this chapter. Write one or more events in which that group or leader took part.

In 1961, 21-year-old John Lewis stepped off a bus in Montgomery, Alabama. White men with bats tried to keep African Americans such as Lewis out of the bus station's "white" waiting room. Thirty years later, Lewis was a U.S. Representative from Alabama. He returned to Montgomery's bus station. Whites and African Americans sat together. Legal segregation was no longer an issue.

The Civil Rights Movement changed the nation. It gave new hope—and new freedoms—to African Americans. But it left many issues unsolved.

1 The Civil Rights Movement Advances.

What progress did the Civil Rights Movement make after 1960?

On February 1, 1960, four African American college students sat down at a lunch counter in Greensboro, North Carolina. The waitress refused to take their order. "This is a 'white' lunch counter," she said.

The students quietly waited to be served. They waited all day. Day after day the students came. They were using a new **tactic**. A tactic is a way of achieving a goal. This tactic was the **sit-in**. It is a protest in which people take a seat and refuse to leave.

Soon sit-ins spread to other cities. Hostile whites jeered and dumped food on the students. The students did not strike back. The Student Nonviolent Coordinating Committee (SNCC) had organized them. It taught protesters to meet violence with nonviolence.

Many civil rights groups New groups such as SNCC worked alongside older groups such as the NAACP. One key group was the Southern Christian Leadership Conference (SCLC). The

Whites poured sugar, ketchup, and mustard over the heads of sit-in demonstrators at a Jackson, Mississippi lunch counter.

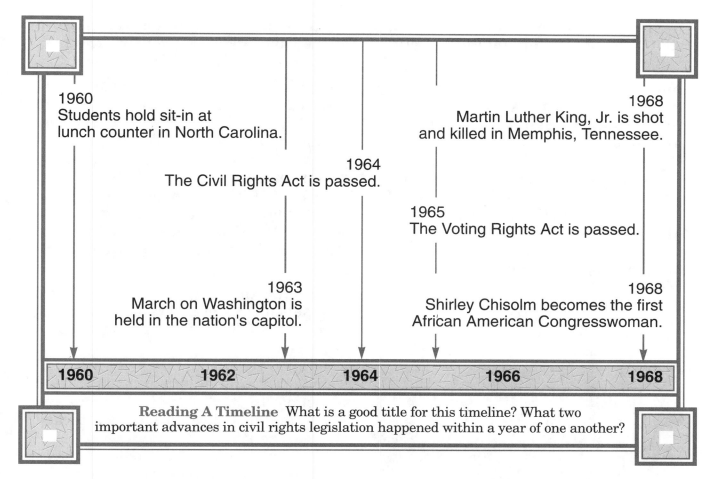

1960
Students hold sit-in at
lunch counter in North Carolina.

1964
The Civil Rights Act is passed.

1968
Martin Luther King, Jr. is shot
and killed in Memphis, Tennessee.

1965
The Voting Rights Act is passed.

1963
March on Washington is
held in the nation's capitol.

1968
Shirley Chisolm becomes the first
African American Congresswoman.

1960   **1962**   **1964**   **1966**   **1968**

Reading A Timeline What is a good title for this timeline? What two
important advances in civil rights legislation happened within a year of one another?

Reverend Martin Luther King, Jr., was one of its leaders.

Another important group was the Congress of Racial Equality, or CORE. It introduced the **freedom ride**. Freedom rides were bus trips to test civil rights laws. Federal courts ruled that buses that go between states must be open equally to all races. Freedom rides put those rulings into practice.

Starting in 1961, African Americans like John Lewis bought bus tickets. They traveled from city to city across the South. At each stop, they entered the bus station. They ordered meals. They drank from "white" fountains. They used "white" restrooms.

White mobs attacked the freedom riders. Local police looked on in silence. Sometimes police arrested the freedom riders. Finally, the federal government sent in marshals to protect the riders.

White resistance Many Southern whites resisted the Civil Rights Movement. Most did so peacefully. But a few went much further. They murdered civil rights workers. They planted bombs in African American churches. In 1963, such a bomb killed four small girls in Birmingham, Alabama.

Trouble in Birmingham Martin Luther King, Jr., led protest marches through Birmingham. The police arrested the marchers. King went to jail, but the protests continued. In one day, Birmingham officials arrested more than 900 students.

Americans saw the protests on television. Viewers saw police dogs attacking children. They saw police striking protesters with clubs. Many people felt sympathy for the protesters. The events in Birmingham upset President

Kennedy. He proposed a new civil rights bill to protect African Americans' rights.

March on Washington To rally support for the bill, civil rights leaders staged a **March on Washington**. More than 250,000 people took part on August 28, 1963. Many whites marched alongside African Americans.

Martin Luther King, Jr., gave a powerful speech. "I have a dream," he said. In his dream, race no longer mattered. African Americans and whites worked together. They ate together. They went to school together. Together, they were "Free at last!"

Reading a Chart. What trend in African American voter registration occurred in all of the states from 1960–1966? What state had the greatest increase?

AFRICAN AMERICAN VOTER REGISTRATION BEFORE AND AFTER THE VOTING RIGHTS ACT OF 1965			
	Years		Percent Increase
State	**1960**	**1966**	
Alabama	66,000	250,000	278.8
Arkansas	73,000	115,000	57.5
Florida	183,000	303,000	65.6
Georgia	180,000	300,000	66.7
Louisiana	159,000	243,000	52.8
Mississippi	22,000	175,000	695.4
N. Carolina	210,000	282,000	34.3
S. Carolina	58,000	191,000	229.3
Tennessee	185,000	225,000	21.6
Texas	227,000	400,000	76.2
Virginia	100,000	205,000	105.0

King had emerged as the central figure of the Civil Rights Movement. The next year, he won the Nobel Peace Prize.

Gains and more challenges Kennedy's civil rights bill became the Civil Rights Act of 1964. It barred discrimination in places like restaurants and hotels. It also outlawed discrimination in jobs.

In 1964, 1,000 volunteers went south. They registered thousands of new African American voters. But Ku Klux Klan members murdered three volunteers in Mississippi.

Selma In 1965, civil rights efforts focused on Selma, Alabama. Police arrested SNCC members who tried to register voters.

Then Martin Luther King, Jr., announced a 50-mile march. It started in Selma. Its goal was Montgomery, the state capital. Police on horses attacked the marchers.

President Johnson sent federal troops to protect the marchers. He pushed through a new civil rights bill. The Voting Rights Act of 1965 sent federal agents to register voters in the South.

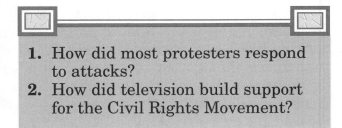

1. How did most protesters respond to attacks?
2. How did television build support for the Civil Rights Movement?

2 African Americans Explore New Paths in the Search for Equality.
How did black nationalism change the Civil Rights Movement?

Some African Americans thought the Civil Rights Movement was not moving

Martin Luther King, Jr., and other civil rights and peace movement leaders led more than 125,000 people in a parade opposing the Vietnam War. The march ended at the United Nations building where Dr. King presented a formal note of protest.

fast enough. In the late 1960s some strong new people became leaders. The Civil Rights Movement split.

Is Nonviolence Enough? Martin Luther King, Jr., insisted on nonviolence. He thought African Americans should work closely with whites. But critics said his tactics were not working. They pointed to the murders of civil rights workers. Critics agreed that laws were changing. But they said that the cost to African Americans was too high.

Critics also said many problems of African American life had not changed. Most African Americans still lived in segregated, run-down housing. African Americans earned only half as much money as whites. Their unemployment rate was double that of whites.

The Vietnam War added to African American anger. Large numbers of African Americans were fighting and dying in Vietnam. Moreover, the war was draining money from programs in African American communities.

King began to speak out against the Vietnam War. He worked for better jobs and housing for African Americans in Northern cities. But he still urged nonviolence. So new leaders arose to challenge him.

Malcolm X One of the most powerful new voices belonged to Malcolm X. He expressed the anger that many African Americans felt towards whites. He also called on African Americans to solve their own problems.

Malcolm X was a spokesperson for the Nation of Islam. This religious group was led by Elijah Muhammad. Members were known as **Black Muslims**. Muhammad taught that whites should

After Malcom X left the Black Muslims, he called himself Brother Malcolm. He urged African Americans to defend themselves in the civil rights fight.

be avoided. African Americans should separate from whites. They should control their own lives.

In 1964, after a trip to Africa and Mecca, Malcolm X split with Muhammad. He gave up the idea of complete separation. He focused on winning political power for African Americans. But he still believed there must be a revolution in U.S. society.

In February 1965, Malcolm X addressed a meeting in Harlem. Suddenly, three African American gunmen killed him. His death showed the conflict that was ripping the Civil Rights Movement apart.

Black nationalism again Malcolm X inspired a new sense of black nationalism. (See Chapter 12.) African Americans took pride in their African heritage. In the 1960s, this led to a new slogan: "Black is beautiful." African Americans began wearing African-style clothing and hairdos. They worked for African American unity in new ways.

Black Power The cry of "Black Power" rang through American cities. It was first used by a young man named Stokely Carmichael. Carmichael became head of SNCC in 1966.

To many African Americans, **Black Power** was an exciting idea. Carmichael defined it as "a call for black people to begin to define their own goals." He said SNCC should stop recruiting white members.

But the "Black Power" slogan worried many civil rights leaders. They needed white support to get civil rights bills through Congress. They urged Carmichael to stop using the phrase. He refused. The split between SNCC and other civil rights organizations widened.

Black Panthers In California, African Americans started a new political party. They called themselves the **Black Panthers**. Their goal was for African Americans to run their own communities. They started free-lunch programs and other self help programs.

Leaders of the Black Panthers considered the police to be an enemy. They claimed they had a right to self defense. So they carried guns in public. The Black Panthers became a target of police harassment. They were in several shoot-outs with the police.

Many African American leaders spoke out against the Black Panthers' use of violence. However, the Black Panthers attracted hundreds of members.

Riots in the cities African American rage often exploded on city streets. From 1964 to 1967, riots broke out in city after city. The riots arose out of African American anger against racism.

President Johnson created a group to find out the causes of the riots. In 1968, that group, the Kerner Commission, came to a frightening conclusion. "Our nation is moving toward two societies, one black, one white—separate and unequal." The commission urged Americans to remove barriers to equality. It asked for "new attitudes" and "new understanding."

Some of the deadliest riots came just weeks after the Kerner Commission made its report. On April 4, 1968, a white man shot and killed Martin Luther King, Jr., in Memphis, Tennessee. Riots broke out in 125 cities. Forty-five people lost their lives. One result was a white backlash. Whites began to show less support for the Civil Rights Movement in general.

1. How did African American protest movements change after 1965?
2. How did white Americans respond to those changes?

3 African Americans Struggle with Changing Attitudes toward Civil Rights.

How did conditions change for African Americans after the 1960s?

By 1970, the Civil Rights Movement was losing speed. African Americans were divided. Meanwhile, the white backlash made many leaders less interested in the movement. Congress showed less support for new civil rights laws. So did Presidents. The nation focused on new issues, like the Vietnam War.

During the 1970s and 1980s, the nation's mood turned conservative. Some Great Society programs were ended. Others were cut back.

Running for President African Americans kept promoting social change. Two African Americans ran for President. They were Shirley Chisolm and Jesse Jackson.

In 1968, Chisolm became the first African American woman ever elected to Congress. She ran for President in 1972. She made it as far as the first ballot of the Democratic convention. Her campaign opened people's minds to the possibility of an African American or a woman as President.

Jackson is a Baptist minister. He worked closely with Martin Luther

Marchers gathered in Washington, D.C., for the 30th anniversary of the 1963 March on Washington. Civil rights was still an issue in 1993.

King, Jr. Jackson ran in the Democratic primary elections of 1984 and 1988. He had many enthusiastic supporters. Among them were African Americans, Latinos, whites, and others. Jackson called his followers the **Rainbow Coalition**. Jackson became a prominent figure in the Democratic party. But he was not nominated.

Affirmative action   President Johnson introduced **affirmative action**. It was a policy for correcting discrimination by increasing opportunities for certain groups. Affirmative action helped African Americans get jobs and get into schools. It also helped women, Latinos, and other groups.

Many people believed affirmative action was unfair. They called it "reverse discrimination." In the early days, civil rights issues had seemed clear-cut. But affirmative action was more complex. People could not agree about these issues. Some felt that affirmative action was fair. Others did not. Debate continued into the 1990s.

Summing Up   The Civil Rights Movement had victories and setbacks.

The barriers to voting had fallen. Now politicians had to listen to African American concerns.

African Americans also became better educated. By the 1990s, 12 percent of African Americans and 22 percent of whites aged 25 or above held college degrees. The gap was narrowing.

African Americans had reached some of the highest positions in U.S. society. Colin Powell served as chairman of the Joint Chiefs of Staff. He held the nation's highest military position during the Gulf War of 1991.

Yet equality for African Americans has still not been achieved. In 1992, disturbances swept areas of Los Angeles. Many people believed these disturbances were caused by the same conditions that had caused the riots of the 1960s. Much had changed in U.S. society. But much remained to be changed.

1. How did civil rights issues become more complex after the 1960s?
2. Describe African American advances in politics.

CHAPTER 22
KEY IDEAS

- In the early 1960s, the Civil Rights Movement used peaceful protests to gain support. This resulted in the Civil Rights Act of 1964 and the Voting Rights Act of 1965.
- In the late 1960s, some African Americans turned to more militant groups such as the Black Muslims and the Black Panthers.
- From the 1970s to the 1990s, gains were made in politics, education, and economics. However, African Americans continue working toward complete equality.

I. Reviewing Vocabulary

Match each word on the left with the correct definition on the right.

1. Black Power
2. sit-in
3. affirmative action
4. tactic
5. freedom ride

a. a policy for correcting discrimination by increasing opportunities for certain groups
b. a protest in which people take a seat and refuse to leave
c. a bus trip to test African Americans' rights
d. a way of achieving a goal
e. political and economic power for African Americans

II. Understanding the Chapter

1. What tactics did African Americans use to win more rights?
2. What kinds of resistance did civil rights protesters face?
3. What were the accomplishments of Martin Luther King, Jr.?
4. What did the Kerner Commission say about the riots of the 1960s?
5. In what respect had the Civil Rights Movement succeeded by the 1990s?

III. Building Skills: Reading a Chart

Use the chart on page 188 to answer the following questions.

1. Which state had the highest number of African American voters in 1966?
2. Which state had the greatest percent increase from 1960 to 1966?

IV. Writing About History

1. **What Would You Have Done?** If you were a Supreme Court judge, would you support affirmative action? Explain.
2. Imagine that you are John Lewis. Write a speech that you might give about returning to the Montgomery bus station 30 years after your freedom ride.

V. Working Together

1. Form a small group. Research an African American leader from the 1960s to today, such as Malcolm X, Martin Luther King, Jr., or Jesse Jackson. Write a biography. Include that person's goals and achievements.
2. **Past to Present** Many Americans participated in protests for the first time in the 1960s. With a group, discuss what protest you might take part in.

AFRICAN AMERICANS SCORE SUCCESSES IN MANY FIELDS. (1950–1990s)

How have African Americans made contributions to U.S. culture, economy, and politics in recent years?

Chairman of the Joint Chiefs of Staff, General Colin Powell posed with members of the 132nd Military Police Company in Saudi Arabia.

S T U D Y

Make an alphabetical list of people discussed in the chapter. Write down facts about each one.

H I N T

Looking at Key Terms
- Black Caucus

Looking at Key Words
- **prominence:** being widely known
- **entrepreneur:** someone who manages a business
- **caucus:** a group that works together to achieve shared political goals
- **assembly:** a group that makes laws

"Say it loud, I'm black and I'm proud."
Those words from a James Brown song of the 1960s told it all. They showed the new confidence of African Americans. James Brown's song rose high on the charts. That too was important. It showed how African Americans were moving into the center of American life.

1 African Americans Contribute to the Arts and Sports.

How have African Americans helped shape U.S. popular culture?

Toni Morrison held the hand of the king of Sweden. In a long gown, she walked down a curved staircase. Morrison was in the world spotlight. Morrison was in Sweden to receive the 1993 Nobel Prize for literature. She was the first African American to win the award.

Morrison is among many who have left their mark. Over the past four decades, African Americans have gained **prominence** in the nation's—and the world's—cultural life. Prominence is being widely known.

Literature African American writers have become familiar to the American public. In the 1950s and 1960s, Ralph Ellison, Lorraine Hansberry, and James Baldwin gained fame. In 1976, Alex Haley published his book *Roots*. It tells of Haley's search for his ancestors. *Roots* begins with the capture of a young African man by slave traders. The story continues into the 1900s.

Books written by African American writers and poets have made the best-seller lists. Alice Walker's novel *The Color Purple* became a popular movie. It also brought Walker a Pulitzer Prize in 1983. Rita Dove became the U.S. poet laureate in 1993.

Music African Americans also remade the U.S. music scene. Jazz pioneers such as Dizzy Gillespie and Charlie Parker became famous. Mahalia Jackson was a leading gospel singer. In the 1960s, teens of all races rocked to the tunes of Little Richard, Aretha Franklin, Tina Turner, James Brown, Stevie Wonder, and countless others.

In the 1990s, African Americans have shaped the music world. Wynton Marsalis continues the jazz tradition. Rap artists comment on society in their music.

Dance African American dancers and choreographers—artists who design dances—have drawn wide audiences as well. Katherine Dunham and Pearl Primus were important pioneers of modern dance. The Alvin Ailey American Dance Theatre has made its mark in ballet. So has Arthur Mitchell's famous Dance Theater of Harlm.

TV and film African Americans have made strides in television and film. From 1984 into the 1990s, *The Cosby Show* featured an African American family, the Huxtables. Actor Bill Cosby played the father. It had some of the highest ratings on American television.

African Americans have starred in the movies. Sidney Poitier was an early leader. He won an Oscar in 1963 as best actor in a dramatic role. By the 1990s, stars like Whoopi Goldberg, Eddie Murphy, and Denzel Washington had achieved fame. African American directors also made a stir.

Spike Lee's 1992 film *Malcolm X* introduced the black nationalist to a new generation. Matty Rich, John Singleton, and Euzhan Palcy are other well-known African American directors.

Sports Before the 1940s, U.S. sports were not integrated. The first African American to break into major league baseball was Jackie Robinson. He started playing for the Brooklyn Dodgers in 1947.

It wasn't easy being first. Players and fans sometimes treated Robinson badly. Players called him names. Fans dumped soft drinks on him. Yet Robinson didn't fight back. He kept his cool. Robinson won the National League's "Rookie of the Year" award in 1947.

After Robinson, more African Americans became sports stars. In 1951, Althea Gibson was the first African American to play tennis at Wimbledon.

The Harlem Dance Company was founded by Arthur Mitchell. It was the first African American Classical Dance company.

She won the world singles championship there six years later. Arthur Ashe became a tennis star in the 1960s. Jim Brown was called the greatest offensive back in football's history. Early basketball stars included Oscar Robertson and Elgin Baylor. By the 1980s, African Americans such as Magic Johnson, Kareem Abdul-Jabbar, and Michael Jordan had gained worldwide fame.

Even before the Civil Rights Movement, African Americans had gained fame as boxers. Boxer Muhammad Ali (Cassius Clay) also made a stir. Ali became a hero to many young people. Once he declared: "I don't have to be what you want me to be. I am free to be who I want."

Ali lost his title in 1967. But he was not defeated in the ring. He had refused to fight in Vietnam. The war, said Ali, violated his Muslim faith. Boxing authorities took his title away. Eventually, the Supreme Court agreed with Ali. He went on to win the heavyweight title two more times. Other great African American boxers included Joe Louis and Sugar Ray Robinson.

1. In what areas have African American artists and entertainers made a mark?
2. Who was Jackie Robinson?

2 African Americans Make Economic Leaps.

What kind of economic progress have African Americans made since 1950?

In 1973, *Black Enterprise* magazine published its first yearly report. It listed the top 100 African American businesses.

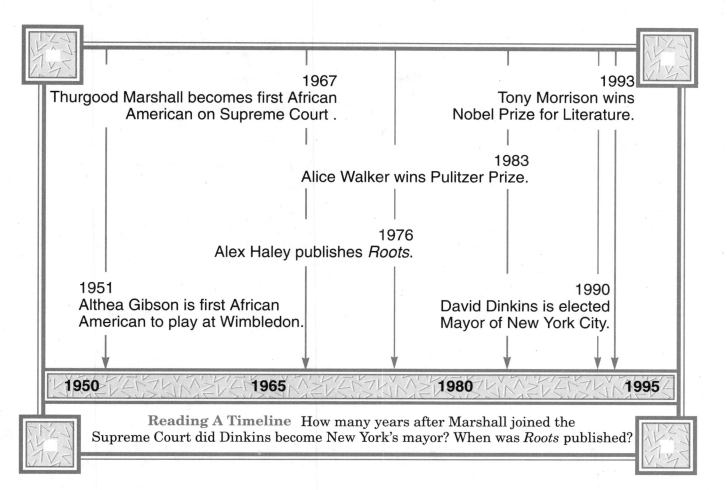

1967
Thurgood Marshall becomes first African American on Supreme Court .

1993
Tony Morrison wins Nobel Prize for Literature.

1983
Alice Walker wins Pulitzer Prize.

1976
Alex Haley publishes *Roots*.

1951
Althea Gibson is first African American to play at Wimbledon.

1990
David Dinkins is elected Mayor of New York City.

1950　　　1965　　　1980　　　1995

Reading A Timeline How many years after Marshall joined the Supreme Court did Dinkins become New York's mayor? When was *Roots* published?

Johnson Publishing Company (JPC) was the second on the list. It made about 28 million dollars in sales. Today, JPC is still on the list. Only now it is making over 261 million dollars. JPC is an example of the economic progress that African Americans have made since 1950.

Businesses African Americans became **entrepreneurs** before 1950. (See page 26.) An entrepreneur is someone who manages a business. John H. Johnson started JPC in 1942.

But after the Civil Rights Movement, many African Americans started businesses. In 1969, there were over 163,000 such companies. Some became very successful. Many were car dealerships. Others were food and beverage companies. African American-owned banks and insurance companies were also important.

Many African American businesses grew. In 1973, they made 473 million dollars. By the 1990s, sales climbed to almost 8 billion dollars. This grew twice as fast as the rest of the U.S. economy.

Today, most African American-owned businesses are small. However, new companies continue to grow quickly. The largest are now huge. Today, JPC has a staff of over 2,710 people. It has branched out into broadcasting, TV production, cosmetics, and hair care. JPC was ranked number 20 on the 1992 list of all U.S. service companies.

Prosperity for some These businesses helped increase African American income. African Americans made clear economic gains. In 1960, 10

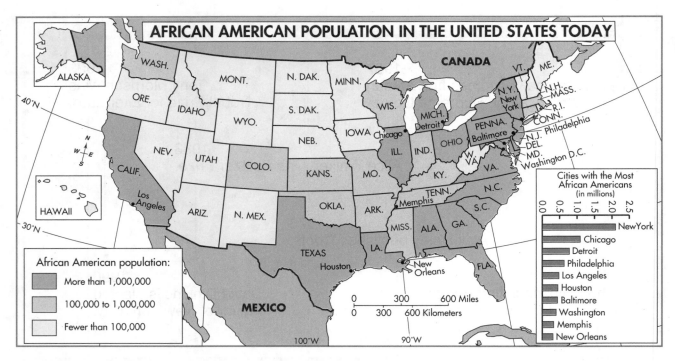

AFRICAN AMERICAN POPULATION IN THE UNITED STATES TODAY

African American population:
- More than 1,000,000
- 100,000 to 1,000,000
- Fewer than 100,000

Cities with the Most African Americans (in millions)
- New York
- Chicago
- Detroit
- Philadelphia
- Los Angeles
- Houston
- Baltimore
- Washington
- Memphis
- New Orleans

Reading a Map. According to the map, what city has the highest population of African Americans? Which region has the lowest population of African Americans? Explain why the African American population is distributed this way.

percent of African American families had incomes qualifing them as "middle class." By the 1980s, 25 percent did. Nearly 11 percent earned between 50,000 dollars and 99,000 dollars. Many African Americans became managers and professionals. In the 1990s, over 16 percent of African Americans were managers or professionals.

Yet African Americans knew their gains might not last. During a recession in the early 1990s, African American unemployment rates soared. Also, African American families still had lower incomes than other families. It was clear that African American economic progress must continue.

1. How has Johnson Publishing Company changed since 1973?
2. What economic problems still face African Americans?

3 African Americans Fill Political Offices.

What gains did African Americans make in holding political offices?

In the world of politics, too, African Americans were making gains. The biggest advances came at local and state levels. But nationally, too, African Americans advanced.

Members of Congress   For many years, African Americans had moved into large cities. This created areas of African American voting power. In the 1950s, more African Americans were elected to Congress. Three African Americans won seats in 1954. It was the first time that this happened in the 20th century.

During the 1960s, voting rights spread in the South. (See Chapter 22.) This gave African Americans new power. In 1968, African Americans won

10 seats in Congress. They hadn't done that well since Reconstruction.

African American members of Congress created a **Black Caucus**. A **caucus** is a group whose members work together to achieve shared political goals. The group focused on issues affecting African Americans. By the 1990s, the Black Caucus had 40 members.

Other national positions Presidents began appointing African Americans to top government posts. The first African American to serve in a president's cabinet was Robert C. Weaver. He became head of the Department of Housing and Urban Development in 1966. (See page 163.)

In 1967, Thurgood Marshall became the first African American to serve on the Supreme Court. Marshall had been the NAACP's chief lawyer. He started many law suits that ended official segregation. As a Supreme Court justice, Marshall pushed for equality. He often stood against a conservative Court majority. Marshall retired in 1991. President Bush appointed another African American, Clarence Thomas, to take Marshall's seat on the Court.

Local and state offices African American gains came fast at the local and state level. African American candidates did best in places where many African Americans lived.

As late as 1966, whites headed the governments of all big Northern cities. But that changed. By 1973, African Americans became mayors in cities as

Joycelyn Elders was the Surgeon General nominee in 1993. Here, she waits with Congresswoman Carol Moseley-Braun before the start of Elders' Senate Labor Committee hearing on Capital Hill. Elders delivered a dramatic opening address.

large as Detroit, Los Angeles, Newark, Cleveland, and Washington, D.C. In the South, New Orleans had an African American mayor.

More advances came in the years that followed. African American mayors included Walter Washington in Chicago, Andrew Young in Atlanta, and David Dinkins in New York City.

African Americans won at the state level, too. By 1973, more than 200 African Americans were in 37 state **assemblies**. An assembly is a group that makes laws. In the 1990s, some 500 African Americans were in state assemblies. In 1990, L. Douglas Wilder became governor of Virginia. He was the first African American to be elected governor of a state.

The number of African American elected officials continues to grow. In 1964, African Americans were elected to less than 300 posts. Today, this has risen to more than 8,000.

Increased influence   The Civil Rights Movement's voting drives let more African Americans vote. This increased African American political influence. Today, politicians know "the African American vote" can make a difference. African Americans do not always vote for candidates of their own race, any more than other Americans do. They back candidates whose policies they like. Both major parties design their policies to attract more African American votes.

1. What does the Black Caucus focus on?
2. What helped give African Americans greater political influence?

CHAPTER 23
KEY IDEAS

- African Americans have greatly affected U.S. literature, music, dance, television, and film. They have also become famous in sports.
- The number of African American–owned businesses has grown. This has brought prosperity to some African Americans. However, African American economic progress must continue.
- Increasing numbers of African Americans have held political offices. African American votes have also become more important to all politicians.

REVIEWING CHAPTER 23

I. Reviewing Vocabulary

Match each word on the left with the correct definition on the right.

1. caucus
2. prominence
3. assembly
4. Black Caucus
5. entrepreneur

a. being widely known
b. someone who manages a business
c. a group in Congress that works to advance African American goals
d. a group whose members work together to achieve shared political goals
e. a group that makes laws

II. Understanding the Chapter

1. How have African Americans contributed to the arts in the United States?
2. Why is Jackie Robinson important?
3. What kinds of African American–owned businesses have grown large?
4. How has the economic status of African Americans improved?
5. What political gains have African Americans made since 1950?

III. Building Skills: Making Judgments

Explain whether you agree or disagree with these statements.

1. Racial prejudice is no longer a problem for African American athletes.
2. Unemployment is the most important economic problem for African Americans.
3. Involvement in politics is the best way in which African Americans can improve their economic conditions.

IV. Writing About History

1. **What Would You Have Done?** Imagine yourself as Jackie Robinson in 1947. Other players and fans are mistreating you. Will you fight back? Explain.
2. Write a paragraph about an African American writer or entertainer that you especially like. Tell why you think that person is important.

V. Working Together

1. Form a small group. Together, create a list of goals that you think the Black Caucus might want to achieve. Present your list to the class.
2. **Past to Present** Alex Haley's book *Roots* inspired many people to trace their own roots. With a group, discuss what you know about your family history. Can you see how each person's roots fit into U.S. history?

WOMEN FIGHT FOR THEIR RIGHTS. (1950–1990s)

How did American women seek a more equal place in American life?

In 1981, women demonstrated at the Lincoln Memorial in an attempt to get the Equal Rights Amendment ratified.

Looking at Key Terms

- National Organization for Women (NOW)
- women's liberation • Equal Rights Amendment (ERA)

Looking at Key Words

- **restriction:** something that puts limits on a person or group
- **feminism:** the movement to gain equal political, eco-nomic, and social rights for women
- **liberation:** the act of becoming free

STUDY

Write down the main idea of each section of the chapter in a sentence. After the class discussion, add supporting details to each sentence.

HINT

In 1959, Ruth Bader Ginsburg graduated from Columbia University in law. She was tied for first in her class. Ginsburg then applied to law firms for a job. But she was turned down by all of them. Ginsburg was rejected because she was a woman and a mother. She finally found a job, but she never forgot this experience. As a lawyer, Ginsburg brought cases of discrimination against women to trial.

Many women in the United States have faced discrimination. In the 1960s, women resumed their struggle for equal rights. These efforts resulted in changes in U.S. society. Women have risen to important positions. In 1994, Ginsburg became a U.S. Supreme Court justice.

1 Women Face Unequal Treatment.

Why were many women unhappy with their roles in society in the 1950s and 1960s?

In the 1950s, the role of women was clear. They must be wives and mothers. However, U.S. society was changing. Many women did not fit the ideal. While television showed them as happy housewives, many were working outside the home. Many women started to question how society viewed them.

Women in the workforce At the end of World War II, many women lost high-paying jobs. Some women became homemakers again. Others went back into "female" jobs. They worked as waitresses, typists, and nurses.

The percentage of women holding jobs shrank. But the percentage did not fall below what it had been before World War II. By 1950, the number of women workers was growing again.

Getting educated Women in the postwar years were better educated than ever before. In 1940, half of all women went no farther than ninth grade. By 1966, half of all women finished high school. By the 1990s, 80 percent of women graduated from high school. This was equal to the percent of men graduating.

More women went on to college. In 1940, less than 4 percent of women finished four years of college. By 1970, about 8 percent did so. By 1990, almost 20 percent finished college.

Unequal pay As they gained more education, women sought better jobs. In the past, most job-holding women had come from the working class. Now, more and more middle class women held jobs.

Some took jobs that had been performed by men. But women usually were paid less than men, even when they did the same work. A woman bank teller made 15 dollars less a week than a male bank teller. A woman laundry worker averaged 49 cents an hour less than a man. Overall, women made only 60 dollars for every 100 dollars that men made. Some women began to question these differences.

Many restrictions Women also faced many **restrictions**. A restriction is something that puts limits on a person or group. Women had trouble borrowing money to buy cars or houses. Lenders said that women would not be able to pay off their loans. Women also had problems getting credit cards. Usually the first question they were asked was: "How much does your husband make?"

Even in legal matters a woman was not equal. Wives often needed their husband's permission to sign a contract or to buy property. In some states, women could not serve on juries.

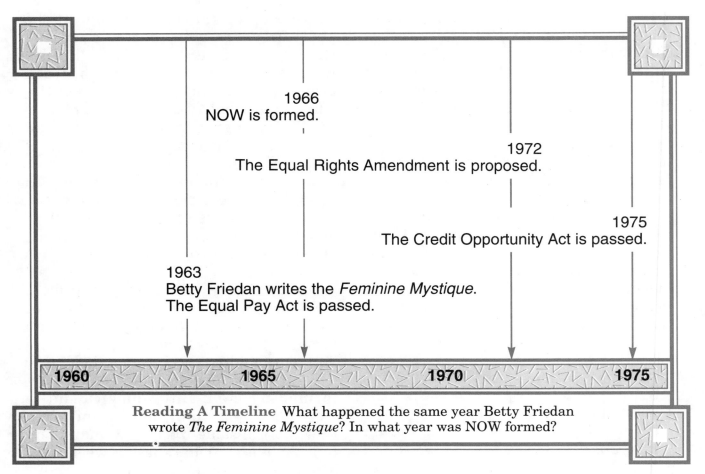

1966
NOW is formed.

1972
The Equal Rights Amendment is proposed.

1975
The Credit Opportunity Act is passed.

1963
Betty Friedan writes the *Feminine Mystique*.
The Equal Pay Act is passed.

| 1960 | 1965 | 1970 | 1975 |

Reading A Timeline What happened the same year Betty Friedan wrote *The Feminine Mystique*? In what year was NOW formed?

"Is this all?" With the growth of suburbs (see page 177), many women's lives changed. Couples often moved away from their relatives. In the past, relatives had helped take care of children. Now many young mothers were alone in the suburbs. They had to raise children by themselves. This put great pressure on women.

Many women began to question their roles. Some had high levels of education. Others had worked during the war. But now the total burden of raising children fell on them. And they were not able to follow a career. Many asked themselves, "Is this all?"

Among the homemakers who asked this question was Betty Friedan. Although trained as a psychologist, she had given up her career. She was raising three children. She began thinking about women's roles.

During the late 1950s, Friedan conducted a survey. She asked women who had graduated from college what they were doing now. Friedan also asked if they were happy. She found that many women were not happy.

Friedan then wrote a book, *The Feminine Mystique* (1963). It attacked the belief that women could only find happiness as wives and homemakers. Friedan urged women to expand their roles in society.

1. How did education for women change after World War II?
2. What problems did women face in the 1950s and 1960s?

2 The Women's Rights Movement Gets Under Way.

How did women organize to get their rights?

Thousands of women read *The Feminine Mystique*. Many agreed with Friedan's views. Women began debating how to change U.S. society.

New beginnings This was not the first time that American women had fought for their rights. In the late 1800s and early 1900s, women focused on their right to vote. (See Chapter 6.) The movement to gain equal political, economic, and social rights for women is called **feminism**. Many women started calling themselves feminists.

Feminists looked to the Civil Rights Movement for ways to fight discrimination. Some had already been involved in the civil rights struggle. They used their experiences to begin to organize women.

National Organization for Women In 1966, Friedan and 300 others started an organization. They called it the **National Organization for Women,** or NOW. Friedan called NOW "a civil rights movement for American women." NOW welcomed male as well as female members. By the early 1990s, NOW claimed 280,000 members.

NOW worked to change laws. It filed court cases against companies that dis-

A housewife shows off her new dishwasher in this typical 1950s advertisement. Newspapers, magazines, and television were filled with images of women in traditional roles. But many women started questioning these roles in the 1960s.

Some women argued that just changing laws that discriminated against women was not enough. They wanted women's liberation. This rally was held in 1978 to push for full equal rights for women.

criminated against women. NOW also asked Congress for new laws to help women and families.

Changing laws Even before NOW was founded, Congress had considered women's concerns. Many new laws resulted. The Equal Pay Act of 1963 and other laws required employers to treat women fairly. No longer could employers pay women less than men for the same work. Employers could not advertise separate jobs for women and men.

Women also gained new economic rights. A 1975 law barred lenders from discriminating against women. Other laws made it easier for women to rent or buy a place to live.

Women's liberation Some women argued that changing the laws was not enough. Instead of just civil rights, they wanted **women's liberation**. **Liberation** is the act of becoming free.

The women's liberation movement tried to change people's beliefs. It attacked the idea of women as "the weaker sex." Feminists explored new roles for women. They demanded that "male" jobs such as police officers be open to women. They pointed out that women could work at full-time jobs and still be good mothers.

Different perspectives Like the Civil Rights Movement, the women's movement split into many parts. Feminists disagreed about how to achieve the goals of the women's movement.

Many women felt that the women's movement did not represent them. They said that it was made up of mostly middle-class women. Working-class women often did not feel included. The focus on opening more jobs did not apply to them. Many already had jobs. They wanted to improve their conditions.

Many African Americans, Latinas, Native Americans, and others felt left out. Some leaders of the women's movement were from these groups. But the vast majority were white. Some women of color rejected fighting for their rights as women. They believed that civil rights for their whole group was more important.

Many women were opposed to the goals of the women's movement. They argued that women's roles as wives and mothers were very important. They felt there was nothing more important than providing secure, loving homes for their children. They argued that the women's movement put down motherhood. Many women said they did not want to be the same as men. Instead, the differences between men and women should be respected.

The Equal Rights Amendment In 1972, Congress proposed the **Equal Rights Amendment** (ERA). The ERA had first been proposed in the 1920s. It called for total equality for men and women under the law.

Many states quickly ratified it. But strong opposition to the ERA emerged. Critics, including many women, feared that the ERA would hurt rather than help women. Opponents blocked further approvals. Only 35 of the necessary 38 states had ratified when the deadline came. So the ERA died.

Issues today Women's issues have continued to stir debate. Perhaps the most controversial issue is abortion. Many women's groups support "choice." This is the right of a woman to have an abortion. In 1972, the Supreme Court agreed to that right. Opponents say that abortion is murder. A "pro-life" movement began to fight abortion.

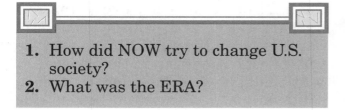

1. How did NOW try to change U.S. society?
2. What was the ERA?

3 Women Take More Important Roles in Society.

What roles do women play in U.S. society today?

After President Clinton announced her nomination as Supreme Court justice, Ruth Bader Ginsburg made a speech. "My law school class in the late 1950s numbered over 500. That class included less than 10 women. Today, few law schools have female enrollment under 40 percent." This example shows the great changes that had taken place in less than 50 years. Women now contribute to every part of U.S. life.

Opening up jobs More women now work outside the home. Over half of all

Reading a Chart. How many more women were working outside the home in 1990 than in 1960?

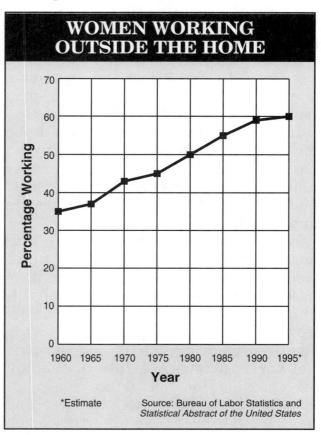

WOMEN WORKING OUTSIDE THE HOME

*Estimate   Source: Bureau of Labor Statistics and *Statistical Abstract of the United States*

In 1993, Ruth Bader Ginsburg became the second woman to serve as a Supreme Court justice. Ginsburg is shown here with the first two women to serve on the Senate Judiciary Committee, Dianne Feinstein and Carol Moseley-Braun.

women hold jobs. These jobs have become more varied. One goal of the women's liberation movement was ending the difference between "women's work" and "men's work." By law, jobs today are open to all qualified people.

Increasing numbers of women have moved into professional jobs. In the past, a woman lawyer or manager was unusual. But not any more. Women now hold 48 percent of the jobs as managers and professionals.

Women have also moved into other jobs once considered "men's work." Some women work in steel mills. Others have become police detectives and firefighters. Women have become prominent TV newscasters. In the 1990s, Connie Chung became one of the highest-paid network anchors. Elizabeth Watson even became Houston's police chief.

In the early 1990s, the air force and navy for the first time allowed women into combat positions. A woman flight instructor in the navy marveled at the changes. "When I joined in 1974," she said, "women didn't even work on planes. Being a pilot was an option I didn't even think about. It's remarkable, the changes I've seen."

Women in office   Women have also become important in politics. In 1984, for the first time, one of the major parties nominated a woman for Vice President. She was Geraldine Ferraro, a Democrat. But the party lost the election.

The Congress of 1993-1994 had a record number of women—48 in the House and 7 in the Senate. Both California senators were women— Barbara Boxer and Dianne Feinstein. Carol Moseley Braun of Illinois was the only African American in the Senate.

At the state and local levels, women politicians have done even better. Ella

Grasso in Connecticut and Ann Richards in Texas were among the women elected as governors. By the 1990s, women held about 20 percent of the seats in state legislatures. In Washington, they held almost 40 percent.

New groups have formed to train women for political campaigns. They also help pay the costs of running for office. The National Women's Political Caucus and the Women's Campaign Fund are two groups that back candidates from both major parties.

Women are also being appointed to high offices. In 1981, Sandra Day O'Connor became the first female Supreme Court justice. A decade later Ginsburg joined the Court. Jeane Kirkpatrick and Madeleine Albright were U.S. Representatives to the United Nations. Hillary Rodham Clinton promoted health-care reform in the 1990s.

Remaining differences However, for all the changes, women and men are not yet equal. Women's pay still lags behind men's. But the gap is getting smaller. By 1992, women's earnings rose to 75 dollars for every 100 dollars that men earned.

Pay levels aside, women have a harder time advancing within a business. Many rise to a certain level and then are stopped. Most companies are controlled by men at the top.

Women still find it hard to juggle careers and children. Fathers now often share the role of care-giver. But divorced and single mothers have fewer choices. Many working parents depend on day-care centers. Some employers now offer day care near the workplace.

Laws have been passed to help working parents. President Clinton signed the Family Leave Act into law in 1993. It provides 12 weeks of unpaid time off after the birth or adoption of a child.

1. How have women's roles in politics changed?
2. What problems do women face today?

CHAPTER 24
KEY IDEAS

- In the 1950s and 1960s, many women began to question their roles in U.S. society.
- In the 1960s, women began to organize to fight for equal rights. Some women also tried to change people's beliefs about women.
- Today, women are playing more important roles. However, women still do not earn as much as men.

REVIEWING CHAPTER 24

I. Reviewing Vocabulary

Match each term on the left with the correct definition on the right.

1. ERA
2. restriction
3. liberation
4. NOW
5. feminism

a. something that puts limits on a person or group
b. the act of becoming free
c. the movement to gain equal political, economic, and social rights for women
d. a proposed amendment for total equality between men and women
e. an organization that fights for equal rights for women

II. Understanding the Chapter

1. How have women's roles in the workforce changed since World War II?
2. Why did some women in the 1950s and 1960s question their roles in society?
3. How did NOW and the women's liberation movement try to change conditions for wome
4. What happened to the Equal Rights Amendment?
5. How successful have women been in gaining equality in pay?

III. Building Skills: Fact versus Opinion

Label which statements below are fact and which are opinion.

1. Women and men who do the same job should have equal earnings.
2. In general, men make more money than women.
3. A higher proportion of women hold jobs now than in the 1950s.
4. Existing laws give women all the protection they need.

IV. Writing About History

1. **What Would You Have Done?** If you had been a member of your state legislature in 1975, would you have voted to ratify the ERA? Explain.
2. Interview an adult woman about the women's liberation movement. How did the movement affect her own life? Did she support or oppose it? Write a newspaper story about the interview. Use direct quotes where possible.

V. Working Together

1. Form a small group. Create posters showing the important roles that women in U.S. society play today. Include politicians, homemakers, business leaders, and professionals.
2. **Past to Present** Study the graph on page 207. With a group, discuss how you think the graph will look in the year 2150. Make a graph for the group that shows your predictions.

MEXICAN AMERICANS STRUGGLE FOR EQUAL RIGHTS. (1950—PRESENT)

How did Mexican Americans work to win greater rights?

César Chávez fought for the rights of migrant farm workers. When he died in 1993, he was still working for his farm workers union.

Looking at Key Terms

- *La Causa* • *El Movimiento*
- Immigration Reform and Control Act of 1986 • NAFTA

Looking at Key Words

- **migrant worker:** a farm worker who travels to find work
- **recognize:** to agree that a union can represent workers in a company
- **Chicana or Chicano:** American of Mexican descent
- **bilingual:** in two languages

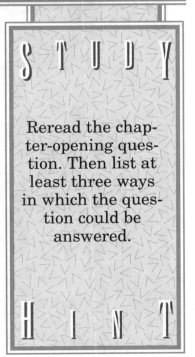

STUDY

Reread the chapter-opening question. Then list at least three ways in which the question could be answered.

HINT

In 1962, César and Helen Chávez and their eight children settled in Delano, California. That town was in the heart of a rich farming area. Much of the work on the valley's farms was done by Mexican and Mexican American workers. César and Helen Chávez, too, took jobs on one of the valley's farms.

The Chávezes had another job as well. They wanted the farm workers to form a union. Thousands of workers said yes. Many scribbled notes to the Chávezes. "I hope to God we can win!" one said.

1 Farm Workers Form a Union.

How did migrant farm workers win greater rights in the 1960s?

In the 1960s, Mexican American farm workers worked in the fields for 14 to 16 hours a day. For such work, they might be paid only five dollars. From this money, they had to buy food and pay rent for run-down shacks.

From farm to farm Many Mexican Americans were **migrant workers** in California, Arizona, New Mexico, and Colorado. A migrant worker travels from place to place as crops ripen.

Often, whole families worked side by side in the fields. Because they moved so often, few children of migrant workers stayed in one school for long. César Chávez, for example, had gone to 30 schools before he dropped out at the end of the 8th grade.

These conditions left Mexican Americans poorer than most U.S. citizens. In 1960, Mexican American families

In 1988, Dolores Huerta, one of the founders of the United Farm Workers, led a rally in San Francisco to protest dangerous pesticides on grapes. With her is Maria Elena Chávez, 16, the daughter of César Chávez.

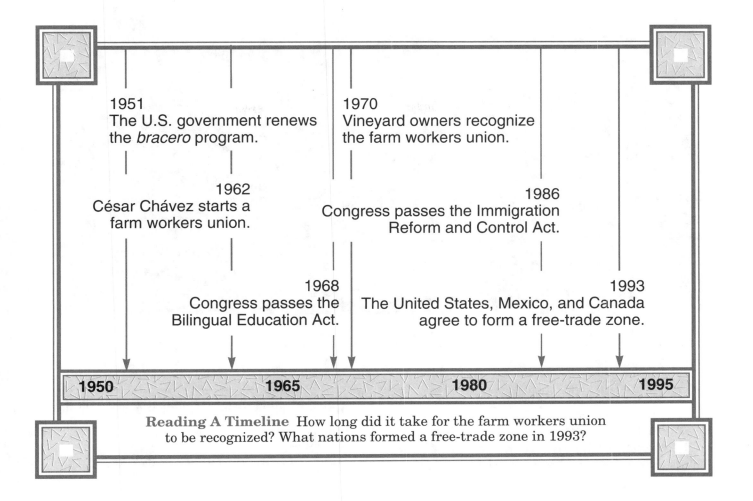

1951
The U.S. government renews the *bracero* program.

1970
Vineyard owners recognize the farm workers union.

1962
César Chávez starts a farm workers union.

1986
Congress passes the Immigration Reform and Control Act.

1968
Congress passes the Bilingual Education Act.

1993
The United States, Mexico, and Canada agree to form a free-trade zone.

1950   1965   1980   1995

Reading A Timeline How long did it take for the farm workers union to be recognized? What nations formed a free-trade zone in 1993?

earned only two thirds of what Anglo families earned.

The U.S. government had helped create these conditions. After World War II, the government continued the *bracero* program. (See Chapter 16.) In fact, U.S. farm owners brought in more Mexican workers after the war than during it. They paid the *braceros* very low wages. This kept wages low for *all* farm workers. When farm workers tried to organize unions for better pay, owners often replaced them with *braceros*.

A growing union   These were some of the problems César Chávez thought a farm workers' union would solve. In 1962, he formed such a union. He was helped by Helen Chávez. Another important leader was Dolores Huerta, a former migrant worker and teacher.

The union slowly grew. Many farm workers pinned their hopes for better lives on the union. They called it *La Causa*, "The Cause."

The union got some help in its early days. It and many other labor unions had called for a stop to the *bracero* program. In 1964, the U.S. government finally ended it. Farm owners could no longer rely on *braceros* to break strikes.

But the farm owners still disliked the farm workers' union. They refused to **recognize** it. This meant that they would not accept that the union stood for all the workers on their farms.

¡Viva la Huelga!   In September 1965, a group of Filipino grape pickers went on strike near Delano. They asked Chávez if the union would back them. Chávez put the question to union mem-

In 1979, César Chávez met with members of the United Farm Workers outside a U.S. Senate committee hearing in Salinas, California. There, he called for a national boycott of lettuce.

bers at a rally. They answered, *"¡Viva la Huelga!"* ("On with the strike!")

Soon the strike spread to other farms. Chávez then set out to make *La Causa* a national issue. He won the support of church leaders and people in the Civil Rights Movement. He held marches and huge rallies. He asked people across the nation not to buy grapes picked by non-union workers.

In 1970, the vineyard owners finally recognized the union. Chávez, Huerta, and the union went on to new battles. For example, they tried to force lettuce growers to sign contracts. They won some of these battles and lost others. But *La Causa* had begun a struggle to gain full civil rights for all Latinos.

1. What were conditions like for Mexican American farm workers in the 1960s?
2. What was *La Causa?*

2 Mexican Americans Expand the Civil Rights Movement.

How did Mexican Americans fight for their civil rights?

César Chávez had started the push for full Latino rights. Other Mexican Americans joined in the struggle. They called their campaign for rights ***El Movimiento,*** or The Movement.

A name of pride Many Mexican Americans of the 1960s showed a new pride in their heritage. Some began to call themselves ***Chicanas*** or ***Chicanos*** to express their pride.

Radical action Most workers in *El Movimiento* followed Chávez's path of nonviolence. A few, however, took up violent means. Reies López Tijerina [tee-huh-REE-nuh] of New Mexico was one of these.

Mexican War of 1846–48. The governments of both the United States and Mexico refused to study the matter. Tijerina then took more violent steps. In 1966, his group took over part of a national forest in New Mexico. In 1967, Tijerina led an attack on a jail in a New Mexican town to free members of his group being held there.

Tijerina went to prison for two years. After his release, he again worked to improve conditions for Mexican Americans. Only now, he called for non-violent change.

Organizing Other Mexican Americans followed different paths to improve lives for their people. In Colorado, Rodolfo "Corky" Gonzales started a movement in 1965. This movement had two goals. One was to build pride in Latino culture. The other was to start Chicano self-help programs. The movement set up a ballet company, a day-care center, and a weekly newspaper.

In Texas, José Angel Gutiérrez [goo-tee-AIR-es] pushed for change through voting. He started a new political party. Soon, the party had candidates on state and local ballots in the Southwest.

By the 1970s, more and more Latinos were winning state and national offices. They included governors Jerry Apodaca in New Mexico, Raúl Castro in Arizona, and U.S. Senator Joseph Montoya of New Mexico.

Other achievements *El Movimiento* increased respect for Latino culture in the United States. It also helped open new doors to Latinos in business and education. For example, in 1968 Congress passed a law aiding students who did not read or speak English well. Under it, school districts set up **bilingual** classes. That is, classes would be offered both in English and in the students' native language.

José Gutiérrez started La Raza Unida, a chicano political party in Texas. Beginning in 1970, Mexican Americans had gained political power in that state.

1. How did José Angel Gutiérrez attempt to improve conditions for Mexican Americans?
2. What was one sign of increasing Latino influence in the 1970s?

3 Mexican Americans Face New Challenges.
What issues concerned Mexican Americans as a new century approached?

Mexican Americans built on the advances of *El Movimiento* after the 1970s. In addition, there were many more people of Mexican background in the United States. Today, there are over

13 million people of Mexican background here. They are the sixth largest of all ethnic groups in the nation.

A growing influence The role of Mexican Americans in politics has grown. Many were elected to office. Other Mexican Americans have been named to key posts. In 1993, President Bill Clinton named two Mexican Americans to his Cabinet. Henry Cisneros of Texas became Secretary of Housing and Urban Development. Federico Peña of Texas took over as Secretary of Transportation.

Mexican American influence can be seen and heard everywhere. Reporters like María Hinojosa (hee-noh-HOH-suh) file stories on national networks. Actors like Edward James Olmos, Emilio Estévez, and Charlie Sheen star on TV and in movies. Latino musicians play to larger audiences than ever before.

Immigration Even as Mexican Americans became more accepted on the national scene, they still had special concerns. One of these was immigration.

Mexicans had long moved north across the border to the United States. They came seeking jobs and better lives. Some of these Mexican immigrants entered the country illegally.

Many U.S. citizens worried about illegal immigration. They feared that the newcomers would take jobs from citizens and hold down wages.

In 1986, Congress passed the **Immigration Reform and Control Act**. This act pardoned many illegal immigrants. However, it set heavy fines for businesses that used illegal workers.

The new act made more than two million Mexicans legal immigrants. Yet some critics feared that the law might harm all Latinos. They said that business owners were afraid of hiring illegal

In 1993, U.S. Secretary of Transportation Federico Peña and county Supervisor Yvonne Brathwaite Burke showed the proposed route of the Metro in Los Angeles.

immigrants. So employers might not hire *any* Latinos.

New trade policies Despite the new law, Mexicans kept coming to the United States. Mexico did not have enough jobs for all of its workers. What jobs there were did not pay as well as those in the United States.

The United States and Mexico tried to set up new ways of doing business with each other. The U.S. government thought that if there were more jobs in Mexico, fewer Mexicans would come to this country illegally. It also believed that Mexican workers with better jobs would buy more goods from the U.S. That would help this nation's economy.

Under one plan, U.S. companies built assembly plants in Mexico. U.S. companies shipped unfinished goods to the plants. Mexican workers finished the goods. Then the products were shipped back to the United States for sale.

The first plants opened in 1965. By 1990, there were more than 1,000 of them, with over 450,000 workers.

In 1993, the United States and Mexico worked out a new plan to aid business growth. Those countries and Canada signed the North American Free Trade Agreement **(NAFTA).** Under NAFTA, goods can go from one country to another without any tariffs, or taxes. Without tariffs, the prices of goods are lower. Also, the agreement allows businesses to set up factories in other member countries.

Not all people were happy with NAFTA. Some U.S. workers worried about their jobs. They feared that businesses would move factories to Mexico. Some poor Mexicans feared that they would suffer as well.

It is not clear how well NAFTA will work. What is certain is that Mexico and Mexican Americans will play a larger part in U.S. affairs in the 21st century.

1. In what ways can the influence of Mexican Americans be seen in U.S. life today?
2. Why did some U.S. workers object to NAFTA?

CHAPTER 25
KEY IDEAS

- Mexican Americans such as César Chávez and Dolores Huerta worked for years to build a union for migrant farm workers. The union won better conditions for workers.
- In the late 1960s, the Mexican American civil rights movement grew. *Chicanos* and *Chicanas* expressed pride in their heritage. They took a more active part in politics.
- Mexican Americans' influence on life in the United States has continued to grow in recent years.

REVIEWING CHAPTER 25

I. Reviewing Vocabulary
Match each word on the left with the correct definition on the right.

1. migrant worker   a. an American of Mexican descent
2. *Chicano*   b. the struggle to build a union for farm workers
3. recognize   c. in two languages
4. *La Causa*   d. a person who harvests crops in different places
5. bilingual   e. to admit that a union can represent workers in a company

II. Understanding the Chapter
1. How was the *bracero* program harmful to Mexican American farm workers?
2. How did César Chávez try to force farm owners to deal with *La Causa*?
3. How was *El Movimiento* similar to the African American Civil Rights Movement?
4. What did the Immigration Reform and Control Act of 1986 do?
5. How would both the United States and Mexico benefit if economic conditions improved in Mexico?

III. Building Skills: Sequencing
Rewrite the following events in the order in which the events took place:

Congress passes Immigration Reform and Control Act. Canada, Mexico, and the United States form a free trade zone. The U.S. government renews the *bracero* program. César Chávez begins to organize farm workers in California.

IV. Writing About History
1. **What Would You Have Done?** Imagine that you are a migrant farm worker in California in 1965. Your boss said that any of his workers who join the union will be fired. Will you join anyway? Explain.
2. Write a proposal for a program to build pride in Latino culture.

V. Working Together
1. Form a group. Imagine that you are members of the farm workers' union in its early days. Design posters or think of songs and skits that might persuade people to join the union. Present your material to the class as a whole.
2. **Past to Present** Unions like *La Causa* were started so members could work to improve their situations. With a group, discuss what union you would start today. What changes would you fight for?

A Cuban Presence Grows in the United States. (1959—Present)

How did Cubans who fled communism in their homeland build new lives in the United States?

In the 1950s, many Cubans, like these in Brooklyn, protested U.S. support of the dictator of Cuba, Juan Batista.

Looking at Key Terms
- "Little Havana"

Looking at Key Words
- **political exile:** person who leaves a country for political reasons
- **boat lift:** operation designed to bring refugees to safety by sea
- **multinational:** company with businesses in more than one nation
- **embargo:** an order preventing trade with another nation

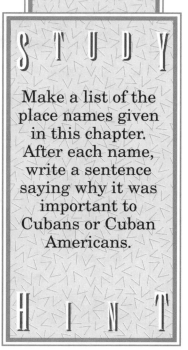

STUDY

Make a list of the place names given in this chapter. After each name, write a sentence saying why it was important to Cubans or Cuban Americans.

HINT

On New Year's Day in 1959, Cubans filled the streets of Havana. They sang and danced and cheered. A revolution had just thrown out dictator Fulgencio Batista (bah-TEES-tah). One Cuban woman later recalled that day: "It was like looking at a whole country caught up in a new beginning. We hoped to set up a democratic government respected by the people and respected by the world. It was a magic moment. But the dream soon went sour."

1 Many Cubans Flee Communist Rule in Their Homeland.

Why did thousands of Cubans come to the United States after 1959?

Fidel Castro led the revolution that threw Batista out. After the revolution, Castro became Cuba's new leader. Castro soon began to turn Cuba into a communist country. This angered U.S. leaders. Tensions between Cuba and the United States led to the Bay of Pigs invasion in 1961. These tensions also caused the Cuban Missile Crisis in 1962. You read about these events in Chapter 17.

A time of changes Castro brought great changes to Cuba. At first, some of these changes were positive. Over 300,000 people joined teaching groups. They taught people in the country to read and write.

However, Castro's programs soon split the Cuban people. Castro took land from the wealthy. But he also took land from people who were middle class.

Castro also wanted the government to control Cuba's economy. The govern-

Reading a Map. In the 1960s and 1970s, the United States was actively involved in events that affected Cuba. What Caribbean countries were involved in the U.S. invasion at the Bay of Pigs?

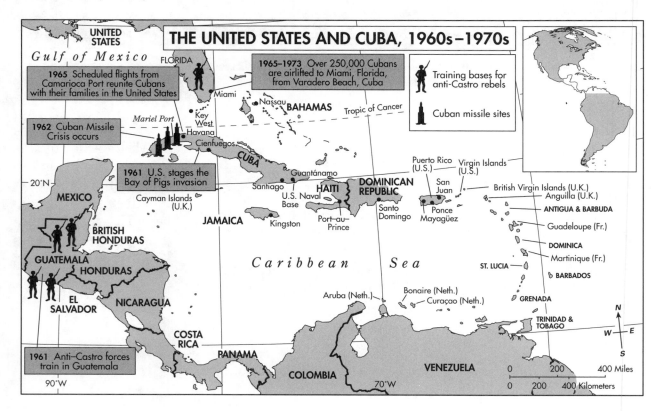

THE UNITED STATES AND CUBA, 1960s–1970s

1965 Scheduled flights from Camarioca Port reunite Cubans with their families in the United States

1965-1973 Over 250,000 Cubans are airlifted to Miami, Florida, from Varadero Beach, Cuba

Training bases for anti-Castro rebels

Cuban missile sites

1962 Cuban Missile Crisis occurs

1961 U.S. stages the Bay of Pigs invasion

1961 Anti-Castro forces train in Guatemala

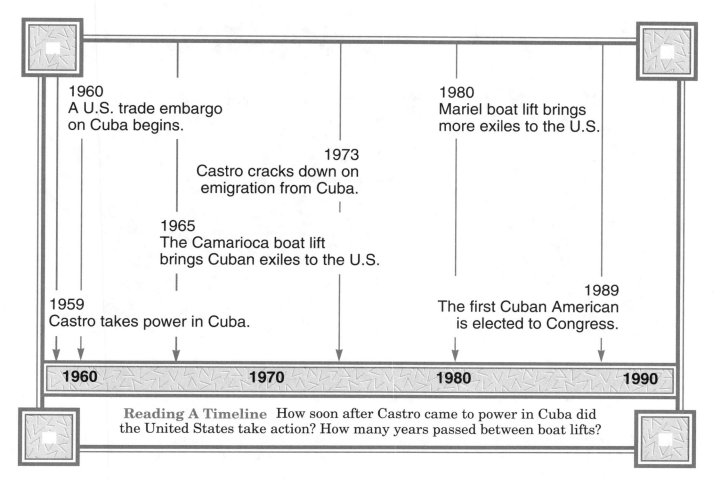

1960
A U.S. trade embargo on Cuba begins.

1973
Castro cracks down on emigration from Cuba.

1965
The Camarioca boat lift brings Cuban exiles to the U.S.

1959
Castro takes power in Cuba.

1980
Mariel boat lift brings more exiles to the U.S.

1989
The first Cuban American is elected to Congress.

1960   1970   1980   1990

Reading A Timeline How soon after Castro came to power in Cuba did the United States take action? How many years passed between boat lifts?

ment took over many private businesses. Many Cubans who had no ties to Batista lost their businesses.

Many other Cubans at first supported Castro. They had hoped the revolution would bring democracy. They did not want communism. But Castro brought in Communist ideas. Many Cubans began to be worried. Also, Castro threw into prison many who disagreed with his ideas. Hopes of a new democracy soon died.

Leaving Cuba By mid-1959, some Cubans had begun to leave their homeland. They became **political exiles**, people who leave a country for political reasons. Many of them wanted to take Cuba back from Castro. Some of them took part in the Bay of Pigs invasion. Others raised funds and looked for other ways to get rid of Castro.

Many of the early exiles were wealthy or middle class. Many made their livings as doctors, lawyers, or business owners. At first, Castro permitted the exiles to go. Between his takeover in 1959 and the Cuban Missile Crisis in 1962, about 150,000 exiles left Cuba.

After the missile crisis, Castro changed his policy. Cuba's economy needed the skills that many exiles had. Also, the flight of so many Cubans made Castro's government look bad in the eyes of other nations. Castro tried to stop people from leaving the island. In the next three years, only 30,000 left.

New waves of exiles Castro's policy on exiles changed several times over the years. In 1965, Cuba and the United States made an agreement. Castro would let Cubans with relatives in the

In the Spring of 1980, thousands of Cuban refugees left the port of Mariel near Havana and sailed to the United States. This 118-foot Panamanian ship *Red Diamond* carried about 850 refugees to freedom near Key West, Florida.

United States leave, but only if those relatives came to the island to get them.

The reaction surprised everyone. Hundreds of boats of all sizes left Florida. They sailed to Cuba. Thousands left the island in this **boat lift**. A boat lift is an operation designed to bring refugees to safety by sea.

Soon after the boat lift, a regular airlift was set up between Cuba and the United States. Some 2,800 flights carried exiles to new lives outside Cuba. By 1973, the loss of exiles was too much for the island's economy. Castro again stopped people from leaving. By that time, though, over 500,000 exiles had left. That was one tenth of Cuba's people!

People continued to leave Cuba, but in smaller numbers. Often, they risked their lives in tiny boats or rafts. Not until 1980 did Castro permit large numbers of Cubans to leave again.

In that year, a group of Cubans took shelter in Peru's embassy in Havana. They asked for shelter there until Castro would let them leave the island. Castro then made a surprise announcement. He said they could go. He also said any other Cubans who wished to leave should go to the embassy. Some 10,000 Cubans rushed to the building.

As the number of hopeful exiles grew, Castro made another announcement. Cubans in the United States could come to the port of Mariel to pick up relatives who wished to leave.

Once again, thousands of small boats sailed the 90 miles that separated Cuba from the United States. Once again, thousands of Cubans climbed aboard those boats to seek new lives. In all, over 125,000 Cubans left in this Mariel boat lift.

These people were different from earlier exiles. They were mostly members of the working class. About seven out of ten had factory jobs. Also, many were of African ancestry.

Like earlier Cuban exiles, some settled in South and Central America. A small number made their way to Europe. The largest part, however, came to the United States. The largest part of these settled in Florida. Most of these made their homes in or near Miami.

1. What kinds of changes did Castro's programs bring to Cuba?
2. Describe the first exiles to leave Cuba.

2 Cuban Exiles Make New Homes in the United States.

Where did Cuban exiles settle in the United States?

In 1959, Miami, Florida, was a quiet city best known as a vacation spot. That year though, the first exiles from Castro began to arrive. They helped turn Miami into a booming business center. Today, many people call it the "Capital of Latin America."

Settling in Miami Cuban exiles settled in Miami for one main reason. It was the closest big city to Cuba. Just 200 miles separated the exiles from their homeland. Many hoped that they would be in Miami just a short while. They thought Castro would soon be thrown out. Then they could return.

But Castro held on to power. Soon, more exiles joined the earlier ones in Miami. By 1973, over 300,000 Cubans made the city their home.

Most Cubans settled in a Miami neighborhood called Little Havana. Little Havana became the center of Cuban life in the United States. *Calle Ocho* (KAH-yeh OH-choh) was the heart of Little Havana. *Calle Ocho*

means Eighth Street. There, Cuban restaurants served foods of the island. People played dominoes in the park. Others sipped cups of thick, strong Cuban coffee. News stands carried papers and magazines written in Spanish. Anti-Castro slogans in Spanish were painted on the walls of many buildings.

A changing city The arrival of so many Cubans had a huge impact on Miami. One exile explained what their coming meant. She said, "The migration of the 1960s made Miami a big city. In the 1970s, the hard work of the Cuban people turned it into a great city."

As you have read, many of the early Cuban exiles had skills and education. They used these to make a living in the United States. Many started businesses that served other Cuban people. Some of these firms expanded to do business with other parts of Latin America.

As these businesses grew, Miami became a Latin American boomtown. Today, the city is headquarters for more than 250 **multinationals**. These are companies with businesses in more than one nation. Latin American business leaders now invest more than one billion dollars a year in the city.

Today, more than 600,000 Cuban Americans live near Miami. This is more than half of all the nation's Cuban Americans. Many live in the city. Others have settled in Dade County, the county around Miami.

Many Cuban exiles have now become U.S. citizens. In recent years, they have shown their growing political power. In 1985, for example, they helped elect Xavier Suárez mayor of Miami. He was the first Cuban American mayor of a major U.S. city. In 1989, voters in Dade County sent Ileana Ros-Lehtinen to the U.S. House of Representatives. She

A section of Miami, Florida, known as Little Havana, is filled with Spanish-speaking people. It is the center of the Cuban community in the United States.

became the first Cuban American and the first Latina to serve in Congress.

Cuban Americans today Today, there are over one million Cuban Americans in the United States. They make up the nation's third largest Spanish-speaking group.

Not all Cuban Americans live in Miami. Some moved west or north. Most, however, chose to live in cities. Today, many Cuban Americans live in New York City, Chicago, and Los Angeles. The largest Cuban American center outside of Miami is in Union City, New Jersey. Over 100,000 Cuban

Americans have settled there. They have helped bring new life to the streets of this city.

Cuban Americans today hold many different jobs. About three in ten are lawyers, doctors, teachers, and business people. Others have jobs as mechanics, service workers, and crafts people. Ties among Cuban Americans are strong. Many Cuban Americans work for Cuban American business people.

Among Latino groups, Cuban Americans have the highest average income. More than 83 percent of Cuban Americans aged 25 to 34 have graduated from high school. Almost a fourth of these have completed four or more years of college.

A changing world What does the future hold for Cuban Americans? Much depends on what happens in Cuba.

Castro remains in power there. Cubans continue to flee from his rule. Some leave on special flights to the United States. Others continue to risk their lives to escape. Some of these steal airplanes and flee to Florida. Others sail on rafts made of inner tubes and tree branches.

Why are people willing to risk so much? Life is very hard in Cuba. The United States continues an **embargo** on Cuba begun in 1960. This means that U.S. citizens and businesses cannot sell goods to Cuba or buy goods from it. Before Castro's revolution, the United States had been Cuba's main trading partner. Loss of this business has hurt Cuba's economy badly.

After the embargo took effect, the Soviet Union became Cuba's main economic backer. With the breakup of the Soviet Union in 1991, Cuba lost this support. Economic conditions grew worse on the island. Today, there are shortages in everything from food to clothing to gasoline.

Castro is almost 70 years old. Many people wonder how long he can hold power. If he dies or is overthrown, many exiles hope to return to Cuba. They would like to build a democracy there. "Next year in Havana," many of these exiles say.

But many Cubans no longer think of themselves as exiles. Many of them are not sure they would return to Cuba. This is especially true of those raised in the United States. In one survey, only 40 percent of those 34 years old or younger said they would go back to Cuba. They are now proud Cuban Americans. They have built homes and lives that mix Cuban and U.S. ways.

1. Where did most Cuban exiles in the United States settle?
2. What kinds of jobs do most Cuban Americans hold today?

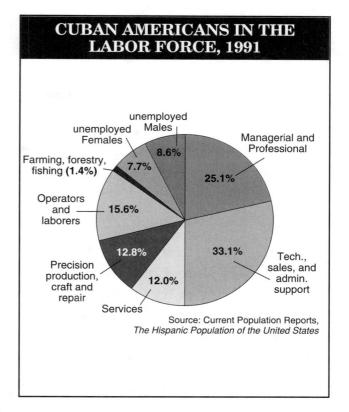

CUBAN AMERICANS IN THE LABOR FORCE, 1991

unemployed Males 8.6%
unemployed Females 7.7%
Farming, forestry, fishing (1.4%)
Operators and laborers 15.6%
Precision production, craft and repair 12.8%
Services 12.0%
Tech., sales, and admin. support 33.1%
Managerial and Professional 25.1%

Source: Current Population Reports, *The Hispanic Population of the United States*

Reading a Chart. What does this chart show? Most Cubans earn their living in what field? What percent have jobs in service industries?

CHAPTER 26
KEY IDEAS

- After Fidel Castro came to power in Cuba, he set up a communist government. Thousands of Cubans escaped to the United States.
- The first group of exiles were mostly middle-class people. Many of the later immigrants were working-class people
- Most of the Cubans settled in the Miami region of Florida. They made the area a center of Latino culture.
- Many Cuban Americans established businesses and worked in professions. As a group they earned more than any other Latinos in the United States.

REVIEWING CHAPTER 26

I. Reviewing Vocabulary

Match each word on the left with the correct definition on the right.

1. embargo
2. boat lift
3. multinational
4. Little Havana
5. political exile

   a. operation designed to bring refugees to safety by sea
   b. company with businesses in more than one nation
   c. home of many Cuban Americans
   d. person who leaves a country for political reasons
   e. order preventing trade with another nation

II. Understanding the Chapter

1. Why were many Cubans unhappy with Castro's revolution?
2. Why did Castro try at several points to stop emigration from Cuba?
3. How did exiles in the 1980 boat lift differ from earlier Cuban exiles?
4. How did the arrival of Cuban exiles in Miami change the city?
5. What factors have added to Cuba's economic problems since the 1959 revolution?

III. Building Skills: Reading a Map

Study the map on page 220. Then answer the questions below.

1. What U.S. city is closest to Cuba?
2. About how far is it from Miami to Havana?
3. What part of Cuba is under U.S. control?
4. Where did anti-Castro forces train?
5. From what ports shown on the map did boat lifts of exiles leave Cuba?

IV. Writing About History

1. **What Would You Have Done?** Imagine that you are a Cuban high school student in 1960. Your father is a doctor and your mother is a lawyer. Businesses owned by several of their friends have been taken over by the government. The friends are going to leave Cuba for the United States. Your mother and father wonder if they should go to. They ask you what you think. What would you say? Explain your answer.
2. Write a newspaper story describing one of the major boat lifts from Cuba to the United States.

V. Working Together

1. Form a small group. Together, design a poster that might be placed in a Miami park honoring Cuban exiles who settled in that city. The poster might use text, key dates in the arrival of the exiles, or pictures illustrating key events. When you have finished, show your design to the class.
2. **Past to Present** The U.S. embargo on trade with Cuba is still in effect. With a group, discuss the embargo. Do you think it is the right thing to do? List the reasons for your group's opinion. Then present the list to the class.

PUERTO RICANS AND DOMINICANS STRIVE TO SUCCEED. (1950s–1990s)

How did people from Puerto Rico and the Dominican Republic build new lives on the U.S. mainland?

This building housed an early Puerto Rican Merchants Association office. The association worked to promote businesses within the community.

Looking at Key Terms

- Operation Bootstrap • Young Lords • Washington Heights

Looking at Key Words

- ***autonomismo:*** Spanish for self-rule
- **commonwealth:** a self-governing nation with strong political and economic ties to another nation

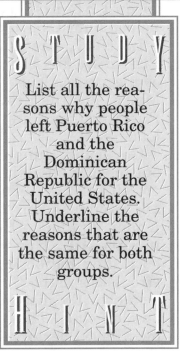

STUDY

List all the reasons why people left Puerto Rico and the Dominican Republic for the United States. Underline the reasons that are the same for both groups.

HINT

On July 25, 1952, two flags flew over historic El Morro fortress in Puerto Rico. They were the flags of the United States and Puerto Rico. But for the first time in 54 years, the U.S. flag was not above the flag of Puerto Rico. Instead, the two flags flew side by side. The position showed a change in the relationship between Puerto Rico and the United States.

1 Life Changes in Puerto Rico.

What changes happened in Puerto Rico after World War II?

The United States had ruled Puerto Rico since the Spanish-Cuban-American War of 1898. As you read in Chapter 8, the island was a colony of the United States. But many Puerto Ricans were unhappy with rule by the United States. They wanted to govern themselves.

A new form of government After World War II, Luis Muñoz Marín (mah-REEN) led the struggle for self-rule. His father, Luis Muñoz Rivera, had fought to end Spanish rule. Now, the son helped limit U.S. rule.

In 1947, the U.S. Congress gave Puerto Ricans the right to elect their own governor. The voters elected Muñoz Marín. For the first time in 400 years, Puerto Ricans had chosen their own leader.

Governor Muñoz Marín quickly set out to work on a plan of *autonomismo*, or self-rule. In 1950, the U.S. Congress approved his plan. It took effect in 1952. Under it, Puerto Rico became a **commonwealth**. This meant it was a self-governing nation. However, it still had strong ties to the United States.

Puerto Ricans could now elect their own officials. They could also fly their own flag. Puerto Ricans remained U.S. citizens. They could be drafted into the military, but they did not pay federal income taxes.

Not all Puerto Ricans liked the new plan. Some wanted Puerto Rico to be completely independent. Others wanted it to become a state of the United States. Debate over the plan was often angry at that time. It still goes on today.

A new economic plan Muñoz Marín believed that the years that Puerto Rico had been a colony had been harmful. Living conditions were poor for many people.

Muñoz Marín created a program to improve the economy. He called his program **Operation Bootstrap**.

Under the plan, he invited U.S. companies to build factories in Puerto Rico. This would provide jobs. It would also help change the island's economy from farming to industry.

The plan changed Puerto Rico. In 1952, there were only 82 factories on the island. By 1970, there were more than 1,000. Change also came in the form of new highways, housing projects, and schools.

The great migration Under the plan, wages in Puerto Rico rose. Unemployment dropped. But there were still more jobs and higher wages on the U.S. mainland. Many Puerto Ricans decided to try to build better lives there.

The big move to the mainland started after World War II. Low airline fares made the trip quicker and cheaper than by boat. In the 1950s and 1960s, about 50,000 Puerto Ricans came to the mainland each year. By 1980, 1.4 million people had taken part in this "great migration."

Most newcomers settled in New York City. As early as 1970, the number of Puerto Ricans living there had reached 820,000. This was double the population

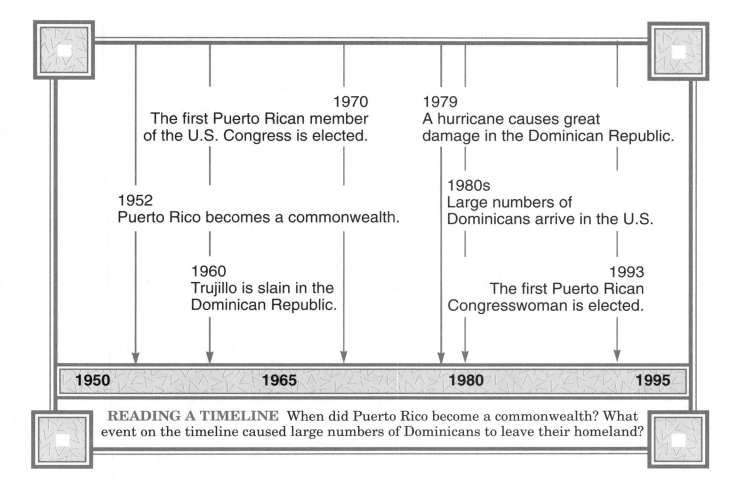

1970
The first Puerto Rican member of the U.S. Congress is elected.

1979
A hurricane causes great damage in the Dominican Republic.

1952
Puerto Rico becomes a commonwealth.

1980s
Large numbers of Dominicans arrive in the U.S.

1960
Trujillo is slain in the Dominican Republic.

1993
The first Puerto Rican Congresswoman is elected.

1950   1965   1980   1995

READING A TIMELINE When did Puerto Rico become a commonwealth? What event on the timeline caused large numbers of Dominicans to leave their homeland?

of San Juan, the island's largest city. Some people even called New York City the "Puerto Rican capital of the world."

But Puerto Ricans did not come just to New York City. They also lived in barrios, or neighborhoods, in Philadelphia, Pennsylvania; Newark, New Jersey; and other cities. The largest community outside of New York grew up in Chicago, Illinois. Today, over 200,000 Puerto Ricans live there.

1. What factors led to the "great migration" from Puerto Rico after World War II?
2. Where did most Puerto Ricans who came to the mainland settle?

2 Puerto Ricans Meet New Challenges.

What patterns of life took shape among Puerto Ricans on the mainland?

Puerto Ricans who moved to the mainland hoped for better lives. But they had to start at the bottom of the economic ladder. In the 1950s, 92 percent of mainland Puerto Ricans worked at unskilled or semiskilled jobs. They earned low wages. But Puerto Ricans found many ways to improve conditions for themselves.

Organizations offer help. The Puerto Rican government itself offered aid to islanders on the mainland. In 1948, the government opened a branch in New York City. It acted as an employment office, translator, and guide to city

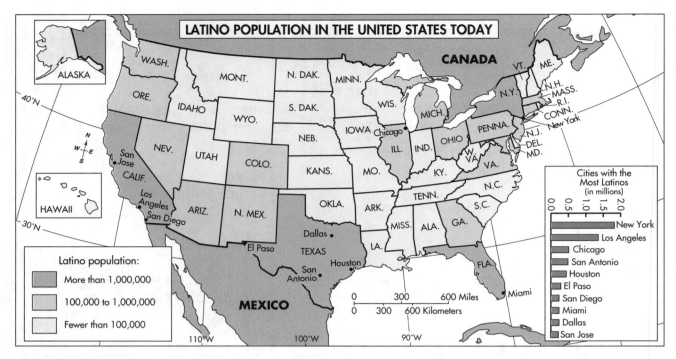

LATINO POPULATION IN THE UNITED STATES TODAY

CANADA

ALASKA

HAWAII

Latino population:
- More than 1,000,000
- 100,000 to 1,000,000
- Fewer than 100,000

MEXICO

Cities with the Most Latinos (in millions)

New York
Los Angeles
Chicago
San Antonio
Houston
El Paso
San Diego
Miami
Dallas
San Jose

Reading a Map. What does this map show? Name the states with the greatest Latino populations? What geographical fact explains why these states have such large Latino populations?

services. The office also worked for passage of laws to help Puerto Ricans on the mainland.

Puerto Ricans started other organizations to improve their lives. The Puerto Rican Forum struggled to find ways of overcoming poverty among islanders in mainland cities. An organization called ASPIRA ("Hope") was founded in 1969. It aimed to improve educational opportunities among Latinos.

One success is Lida Viruet (vee-RWET). In September 1989, Viruet brought her two daughters to the mainland. She wanted a better life. Although she was a skilled computer programmer, she did not speak English well. Viruet worked several part-time jobs to support her family. Then she went back to college and took courses in English and community health. Today she teaches people with disabilities. Most important to Lida Viruet is that her children finished college.

Fighting discrimination Puerto Ricans on the mainland had to struggle with another problem. Many were of African or Native American ancestry. Often, they were victims of discrimination.

Some Puerto Rican groups tried to fight this racism. One group was the **Young Lords**. They pushed for full civil rights for Puerto Ricans. They also tried to better conditions in the *barrios*. Often, they used demonstrations, sit-ins, and other forms of direct action.

Puerto Ricans today Puerto Ricans are the second-largest Latino group in the nation. They make up 11 percent of all Latinos. Puerto Ricans have spread out across the nation. In the 1950s, over 80 percent of mainland Puerto Ricans lived in New York City. Today, less than 50 percent do.

Puerto Ricans have made important gains. Today, nearly 15 percent of mainland Puerto Ricans hold skilled or professional jobs. About 55 percent of Puerto Ricans between ages of 25 and 34 are high school graduates. The number of college graduates continues to rise.

Puerto Ricans on the mainland have gained political power. In 1970, Herman Badillo became the first Puerto Rican elected as a voting member of Congress. In recent years, Puerto Ricans such as José Serrano of New York City and Luis Gutiérrez of Chicago held seats in the House of Representatives. In 1993, Nydia Velázquez (veh-LAHS-kes) became the first Puerto Rican woman in Congress.

Nydia Velázquez represents the 12th district of New York. Velázquez is the daughter of a sugar cane worker and his wife. In the 1970s, Velázquez moved to the New York City district she now represents. Her first job was teaching at Hunter College. She also worked for organizations that helped the Puerto Rican community. In Congress, Velázquez has fought to end poverty in her district and others.

Issues on the island People in Puerto Rico did not agree on how to make the island's economy strong while keeping its own culture. One battle was over the use of English. One party wanted schools to teach both English and Spanish. Another party disagreed. It felt that Spanish should remain the official language because it was a key part of the Puerto Rican identity.

Meanwhile, the status of Puerto Rico remains an important issue. Should the island remain a commonwealth? Should it be a state? Should it be independent? In 1993, Puerto Ricans voted to keep the island a commonwealth.

Puerto Ricans on the mainland remain interested in island issues. They are proud of their island and its traditions. They are also proud of what they and the island have contributed to the culture of the United States.

1. What was the aim of the Young Lords?
2. How has Puerto Rican settlement on the mainland changed in recent years?

At a New York Puerto Rican Day parade, these Puerto Ricans challenge others to register to vote with the word "Atrévete—Dare to."

These Dominicans are celebrating a holiday in the Jackson Heights section of Queens, New York. Dominicans maintain strong ties to their homeland.

3 Dominicans Come to the United States.

Where did most Dominicans in the United States settle?

Puerto Ricans were not the only people from the Caribbean to come to the U.S. mainland. In the 1960s, large numbers of people from the Dominican Republic began to arrive as well.

Times of uncertainty From 1930 to 1961, the Dominican Republic was controlled by one man, Rafael Trujillo (troo-HEE-yoh). He ruled as a dictator. Trujillo used the nation's economy to make himself and his friends wealthy. He punished those who disagreed with him. Some he put in prison. Others were tortured to death.

Everything began to change in 1961. In May of that year, an unknown gunman killed Trujillo. Political unrest followed. In 1965, U.S. President Lyndon Johnson sent in U.S. marines to end a revolution. Then, Joaquín Balaguer (bah-lah-GHER) was elected president in 1966.

The political scene grew calmer in the late 1960s and early 1970s. Then in 1979, a huge hurricane did over $1 billion of damage to the island.

The years of unrest and disaster hurt the island's economy. By the 1980s, the nation owed $4 billion to other countries. Prices soared. Almost a fourth of all Dominicans had no jobs.

Coming to New York The problems led many Dominicans to leave the island. Soon after Trujillo's death, at least 20,000 people a year were leaving. Many of the first to go were members of the middle class.

Most Dominicans who came to the United States settled in New York City's **Washington Heights**. This is a neighborhood in upper Manhattan. There, Dominican *bodegas,* or grocery stores, sell Dominican specialties. Restaurants such as Las Tres Marias serve *sancocho,* a tasty Dominican stew.

Dominican groups formed to aid the newcomers. For example, the Northern Manhattan Coalition for Immigrant Rights handles problems with city, state, and national governments. The Dominican Small Business Association helps the many Dominicans who have set up their own businesses.

Dominicans continue to come to the United States in large numbers today. By the 1990s, they had become one of the nation's fastest growing immigrant groups. At least 20,000 enter the United States each year. They are the largest foreign-born group in New York City. Over 700,000 now live in the New York area alone.

Dominicans in the United States keep ties to their homeland strong. In a recent year, they sent almost $800 million back to family members on the island. But for many, ties to the United States are growing stronger. More and more Dominicans are becoming U.S. citizens. They proudly call themselves Dominican Americans.

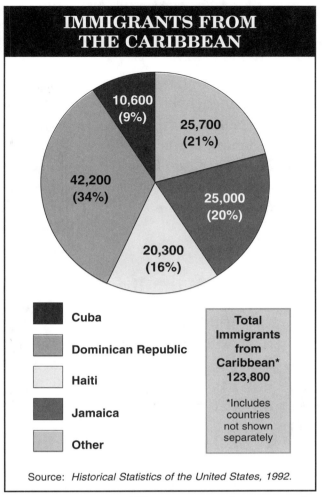

IMMIGRANTS FROM THE CARIBBEAN

- 10,600 (9%)
- 25,700 (21%)
- 25,000 (20%)
- 20,300 (16%)
- 42,200 (34%)

- Cuba
- Dominican Republic
- Haiti
- Jamaica
- Other

Total Immigrants from Caribbean* 123,800

*Includes countries not shown separately

Source: *Historical Statistics of the United States, 1992.*

Reading a Chart. What country has sent the most immigrants to the United States? the fewest?

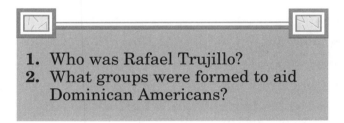

1. Who was Rafael Trujillo?
2. What groups were formed to aid Dominican Americans?

CHAPTER 27
KEY IDEAS

- After World War II, Puerto Rico became a commonwealth, a self-governing nation with strong ties to the United States.
- After the war, 2 million Puerto Ricans came to the mainland.
- Puerto Ricans today are the nation's second-largest Latino group.
- Political unrest, natural disaster, and economic problems started a large immigration from the Dominican Republic to the United States.
- Today, Dominicans are the nation's seventh-largest immigrant group.

I. Reviewing Vocabulary

Match each word on the left with the correct definition on the right.

1. commonwealth
2. Young Lords
3. Washington Heights
4. Operation Bootstrap
5. *autonomismo*

a. group that took direct action to improve conditions for mainland Puerto Ricans
b. self-rule
c. neighborhood in upper Manhattan where many Dominicans settled
d. self-governing nation with ties to another nation
e. plan to improve Puerto Rico's economy

II. Understanding the Chapter

1. How did the relationship between the United States and Puerto Rico change after World War II?
2. How did Governor Muñoz Marín try to improve Puerto Rico's economy?
3. What is one issue Puerto Ricans debate today?
4. What led many Dominicans to leave their homeland after 1960?
5. What was the status of Dominican immigration in the 1990s?

III. Building Skills: Reading a Chart

Study the chart on page 233. Then answer the following questions.

1. What groups does the chart give information about?
2. Immigrants from the Dominican Republic are what percent of the total Caribbean immigrant group?
3. Immigrants from what nation are 16 percent of the total Caribbean immigrant population?

IV. Writing About History

1. **What Would You Have Done?** Imagine that you are a member of the Puerto Rican legislature in the 1990s. How would you vote on the question of whether English and Spanish or just Spanish is allowed in the island's schools? Explain.
2. Write a letter that a Dominican immigrant to the United States in 1980 might have sent to a friend back home explaining why he or she decided to leave the island.

V. Working Together

1. With two or three classmates, plan an illustrated timeline titled "Puerto Ricans and Dominicans, 1945 to the Present." Discuss what events should appear on the timeline. Draw it on pieces of paper. Display the finished timeline to the class.
2. **Past to Present** Puerto Ricans still debate the question of statehood, commonwealth status, or independence for the island. With a group, decide what should happen to Puerto Rico. Then report the group's decision and five best reasons.

NATIVE AMERICANS FIGHT FOR THEIR RIGHTS. (1950—PRESENT)

How did changing government policies affect the lives of Native Americans in recent years?

In the 1960s, the same spirit that stirred African Americans and Latinos to fight for their rights rose up among Native Americans.

Looking at Key Terms

- "Red Power" • American Indian Movement

Looking at Key Words

- **termination:** a bringing to the end, conclusion

STUDY

Set up two columns labeled "Advances" and "Setbacks." As you read the chapter, list events that aided or harmed Native Americans.

HINT

In 1961, Herbert Blatchford, Clyde Warrior, Melvin Thom, and other Native Americans started something new. It was the National Indian Youth Council (NIYU). The members were young and had college educations. They called for **"Red Power."** That meant the power of Native Americans to take charge of their own lives. During the 1960s, Native Americans renewed their long struggle for full rights.

1 Native Americans Face More Government Policy Changes.

Why did Native Americans renew their fight for equal rights?

For a brief time in the 1930s and 1940s, it seemed that things might improve for Native Americans. A new law, the Indian Reorganization Act, was passed. The law let many Native American nations set up their own governments. Under the law, Native Americans got back some reservation lands that they had lost.

A new policy Soon, however, Native Americans faced a major setback. Once again, other people wanted Native American lands.

During World War II, the United States could not get supplies of oil and natural resources from other lands. The U.S. government needed steady supplies of these resources. Also, the war had been very costly for the U.S. government. It wanted to cut down on its spending.

So in the late 1940s, the U.S. government began a new policy toward Native

Reading a Chart. What is this chart about? How does Native American unemployment compare to unemployment for other U.S. citizens? Overall, how does the quality of life compare for the two groups?

QUALITY OF LIFE FOR NATIVE AMERICANS COMPARED TO OTHER U.S. CITIZENS

	Native Americans/ Eskimo/Aleut	Other U.S. Citizens
Birthrate	28.8 births/per 1,000	15.9 births/per 1,000
Deathrate	11.0 infant deaths/per 1,000 live births	10.0 infant deaths/per 1,000 live births
Life Expectancy	71.5 yrs.	75 yrs.
Population	1,959,234 (.8% population)	248,710,000 (population)
Average Family Income	$19,865	$21,800
Unemployment *(Males)* *(Females)*	15.4% 13.1%	6.4% 5.7%

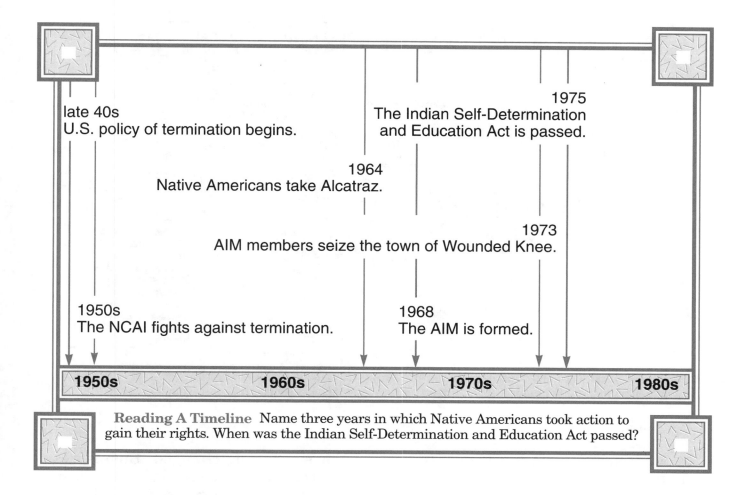

late 40s
U.S. policy of termination begins.

1975
The Indian Self-Determination
and Education Act is passed.

1964
Native Americans take Alcatraz.

1973
AIM members seize the town of Wounded Knee.

1950s
The NCAI fights against termination.

1968
The AIM is formed.

1950s — **1960s** — **1970s** — **1980s**

Reading A Timeline Name three years in which Native Americans took action to gain their rights. When was the Indian Self-Determination and Education Act passed?

Americans. The U.S. government called the policy **termination.** "Termination" means "ending." The policy would help the United States to gain supplies of natural resources and to cut spending. However, the policy would do little to help Native Americans.

The new policy was aimed at ending federal programs for Native Americans. It shifted those programs to the states. State governments then controlled Native American lands within their borders. Often, they sold the rights to resources on these lands to businesses.

Termination's effects Under termination, Native Americans once again lost control of large chunks of their lands. As a Blackfoot woman said, "We had to sell our land. The [U.S. government] is starving us to get our land."

The businesses bought leases to drill oil or mine coal or cut lumber on Native American property. Often, these business would ruin the land. In return, Native Americans received small payments or nothing at all.

The U.S. government also hoped that Native Americans would leave their reservations. The government wanted Native Americans to look for jobs in the cities. It set up a program to help them to find jobs and places to live.

Many Native Americans did move. By the late 1960s, over half of all Native Americans lived off the reservations. Some found city jobs. Others found unemployment, poverty, and discrimination.

Response Most Native Americans strongly opposed termination. A Blackfoot leader explained why. He said,

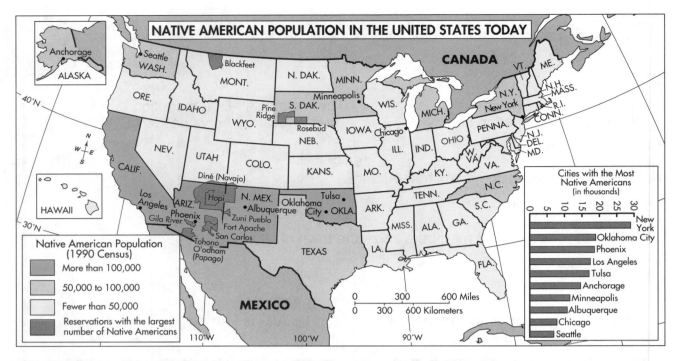

NATIVE AMERICAN POPULATION IN THE UNITED STATES TODAY

Native American Population
(1990 Census)
- More than 100,000
- 50,000 to 100,000
- Fewer than 50,000
- Reservations with the largest number of Native Americans

Cities with the Most
Native Americans
(in thousands)

New York
Oklahoma City
Phoenix
Los Angeles
Tulsa
Anchorage
Minneapolis
Albuquerque
Chicago
Seattle

Reading a Map. What is shown in this map? Name three states that have the largest reservations. What two cities have the largest Native American populations?

"In our Indian language, the only translation for termination is to 'wipe out' or 'kill'. . . . How can we plan our future when the Indian Bureau is trying to wipe us out as a race?"

In 1944, representatives from many Native American peoples had formed the National Congress of American Indians. It was the first truly national Native American group. The congress fought hard against termination. Other groups formed later. Together, they worked for years to get improvements.

By the 1960s, the protests were finally being heard. Under Presidents Kennedy and Johnson, the termination program ended.

A new U.S. Commissioner of Indian Affairs, Philleo Nash, took office. He backed new measures to strengthen Native American nations. He also tried to make sure that Native Americans got a fair share in President Johnson's War on Poverty programs (see Chapter 19).

Not everything changed. Businesses still controlled a lot of Native American lands. However, the government told the companies to pay Native Americans more.

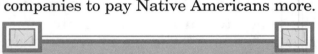

1. What were the aims of the U.S. government's termination policy?
2. How did Native Americans feel about the termination policy?

2 Native Americans Take Direct Action.
How did Native Americans fight for their rights?

By the 1960s, the government programs had worsened conditions many Native Americans faced. The United States was the richest, most powerful nation on earth. But the reservations often seemed as poor as some undeveloped country.

Poverty was common on the reservations. Native Americans earned 75 percent less than other Americans. There were few jobs. Unemployment ran ten times higher than in the rest of the nation. Many people on reservations lived in rundown houses or shacks. Their homes often had no running water or indoor plumbing.

The poverty took a heavy toll among Native Americans. The death rate among Native Americans was much higher than that of other Americans. Compared to the national average, many more Native American babies died before they completed their first year of life. An average American could expect to live about 75 years. For a Native American, the figure was 71.5 years.

Beginnings of protest Conditions like these called for change. In 1961, some 500 Native Americans gathered in Chicago. They were members of 67 Native American nations. President Kennedy had asked for the meeting. He wanted Native Americans' ideas on how conditions might be improved. The meeting drew up a "Declaration of Indian Purpose." It said that Native Americans had to play roles in all government policies that touched their lives.

Yet the meeting left some younger Native Americans unhappy. They felt that stronger actions were needed. Soon, they were calling for "Red Power."

Direct action Soon, Native American groups across the nation were taking action to win their rights. Native Americans in the state of Washington held "fish-ins" to protest the loss of fishing rights promised under old treaties. In 1964, Native Americans briefly took over the old federal prison on Alcatraz Island in San Francisco Bay. They said

that treaties had promised the U.S. government would give unused land to Native Americans.

In 1968, a new Native American group formed. It was the **American Indian Movement** (AIM). AIM soon became the strongest voice for Native American rights.

In 1972, over 500 AIM members came to Washington, D.C. They were part of a protest called "The Trail of Broken Treaties." They demanded new treaties with the federal government. As part of the protest, they took over the Bureau of Indian Affairs.

An even larger protest came in the following year. AIM members seized the town of Wounded Knee on the Pine Ridge Reservation in South Dakota. The place had special meaning to Native Americans. In 1890, U.S. troops had killed over 250 Sioux at Wounded Knee.

AIM members demanded a greater say in how the reservation was run. Members of 64 different Native Americans nations joined AIM at Wounded Knee. Soon, U.S. law officers and troops surrounded the town. Gunfire crackled. More than 300 federal officers kept up the siege. For ten weeks, the AIM members held out. Finally, they surrendered. They won few of their demands.

Changing laws Direct "Red Power" actions like these continued through the 1970s. Native American protests brought some changes. In 1968, for example, Congress passed a law that gave Native Americans full civil rights. But the law had little effect on the lives of most Native Americans.

Some laws did help. In 1975, the Indian Self Determination and Education Act gave Native Americans a role in shaping federal housing, schooling, and job-training programs for the reservations. Other laws supported Native American culture.

In 1978, the U.S. Congress passed a law that protected special Native American forms of worship.

Richard Nixon and Jimmy Carter also worked to correct the wrongs of the termination policy. The Presidents backed new programs to help economic development on reservations.

Progress in the courts Native Americans also used the nation's courts to improve conditions for themselves. They argued that the U.S. government or the states had broken earlier treaties. Sometimes they asked for land to be returned to them. Sometimes they asked for money as damages.

The siege at Wounded Knee brought attention to the needs of Native Americans. Supporters from many states tried to bring supplies. They were turned away.

Native Americans scored some major victories in these cases. In Maine, the Penobscot people won the return of 300,000 acres of land and a fund of 27 million dollars. The Penobscot used the money to build a cassette tape plant that brings in 11 million dollars a year.

In Taos, New Mexico, Native Americans saw Blue Lake littered with cans, bottles, and trash. To them, it was as if garbage had been piled in a church. They decided to fight to regain control of Blue Lake. It took years of work. But in 1971, Native Americans in Taos won back the lake that was a holy place in their religion. Other groups won cases in California, Arizona, Washington, Alaska, and Wisconsin.

In the 1980s and 1990s, Native Americans have faced new problems. President Reagan seemed to favor going back to the old policies. Under Reagan, U.S. programs for Native Americans suffered deep cuts. Native Americans were also hurt by the economic slump in the late 1980s and early 1990s.

Native Americans today Over 2 million Native Americans live in the United States today. About a third of them are on reservations. Many have found new ways to better their lives. Some Native Americans have increased production of resources from their lands. They receive larger payments for these resources.

Other peoples moved into manufacturing. The Choctaw of Mississippi, for example, make electrical appliances and auto parts. The Passamaquoddy of Maine produce fertilizer. The Zuñi of New Mexico craft traditional silver and turquoise jewelry. It sells to a growing U.S. market.

Some Native Americans have decided to bring tourists to their lands. The Mescalero Apache of Arizona run a large ski resort. Other peoples in many states have opened gambling casinos. These casinos bring in millions of dollars. This money aids Native Americans in building for the future.

Native Americans still debate what course is best. Some believe that Native Americans should mix more completely into U.S. society. They should become doctors, teachers, and business people.

Others feel that Native Americans must make strong efforts to keep old ways alive. They feel that these ways have value, not only for Native Americans, but for the nation as well.

Whatever course Native Americans wish to follow, they do share one belief. They have the right to choose that course for themselves.

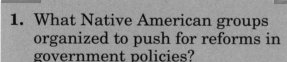

1. What Native American groups organized to push for reforms in government policies?
2. How have different Native American groups aided themselves in recent years?

A Cherokee, Mary Ross is an advanced systems engineer. Because women are valued members of Cherokee society, Ross was confident that she could succeed as a rocket designer.

CHAPTER 28
KEY IDEAS

- After World War II, the U.S. government began a policy called termination. Its purpose was to end federal programs.

- Under termination, Native American peoples lost much reservation land. Many Native Americans moved to cities.

- In the 1960s, groups such as AIM formed to push actively for reforms. They wanted Native Americans to have greater control over federal policies.

- In recent years, different Native American groups have started many projects to improve their economic conditions.

REVIEWING CHAPTER 28

I. Reviewing Vocabulary

Match each word on the left with the correct definition on the right.

1. AIM
2. Indian Self Determination and Education Act
3. termination
4. National Indian Youth Council
5. National Congress of American Indians

a. a federal policy toward Native Americans from the late 1940s to the 1950s
b. an organizer of the "Trail of Broken Treaties" protest
c. the first national organization of Native American peoples
d. a measure giving Native Americans a greater say in the running of reservations
e. a group that pushed for reform and "Red Power"

II. Understanding the Chapter

1. Why did the U.S. government begin a policy of termination in the late 1940s?
2. What effects did termination have on Native American lands?
3. What kinds of changes did groups like AIM push for?
4. (a) What kinds of cases have Native Americans brought to the courts in recent years? (b) What results have they achieved in those cases?
5. What differences exist among Native Americans about what course they could best follow in the future?

III. Building Skills: Fact Versus Opinion

Label each statement below **"F"** for fact or **"O"** for opinion.

1. Native Americans lost control of some reservation lands during termination.
2. To live happier lives, Native Americans should return to older ways.
3. The "Red Power" protests of the 1960s and 1970s were a waste of time and effort.
4. Today, about a third of the nation's Native Americans live on reservations.

IV. Writing About History

1. **What Would You Have Done?** Imagine that you are a Native American delegate to a 1961 meeting in Chicago. The meeting is to draw up a "Declaration of Indian Purpose." Write three things that you believe the declaration should contain. Give your reasons for thinking that these things are important.
2. Design a poster that might have been used in one of the "Red Power" protests discussed in this chapter. Create a slogan that will make your point.

V. Working Together

1. With two or three students, design a monument that you think could be set up at Wounded Knee, South Dakota. Share your group's plan with the class.
2. **Past to Present** With a group, discuss the methods Native Americans used to improve their conditions. Think about something in your school or community that you would like to improve. Create a plan of action. Use methods borrowed from Native Americans to make the changes you want.

AMERICANS FROM ASIA ARE A FAST-GROWING PART OF THE U.S. POPULATION. (1940s—PRESENT)

What factors have contributed to the growth in immigration from Asia in recent years?

Asian Americans, like these Korean picnickers, belong to the fastest-growing ethnic or cultural group in the United States.

Looking at Key Terms
- McCarran-Walter Act • Immigration Act of 1965
- Civil Liberties Act of 1988

Looking at Key Words
- **naturalize:** make a native of one country into a citizen of another country
- **proportion:** the share in relation to the whole

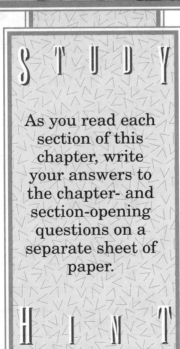

STUDY

As you read each section of this chapter, write your answers to the chapter- and section-opening questions on a separate sheet of paper.

HINT

Prejudice against Asians had deep roots in the United States. In 1790, Congress had passed a law about how immigrants could **naturalize**, or become citizens. According to that law, only "whites" could be naturalized citizens. That meant that Asians immigrants could not become citizens.

Many other examples of discrimination followed. In 1882, a U.S. law cut off immigration from China. Later laws cut off immigration from Korea, the Philippines, and India. Then, during World War II and the Cold War, things began to change.

Today, Asian Americans belong to the fastest-growing cultural group in the United States. From 1960 to 1985, their number increased 577 percent.

1 U.S. Policy Changes Encourage Immigration from Asia.

Why did U.S. policies toward immigration from Asia change?

After World War II ended, the Cold War began. The United States and the Soviet Union both searched for friends around the world. Laws that showed prejudice toward Asians were embarrassing to the U.S. government. Pressure grew to change those laws.

In 1946, Congress voted to let immigrants from India into the United States. The law also said that they could become naturalized citizens. In 1952,

Reading a Chart. Between 1961–1970, what nation sent the most immigrants to the United States? How many Filipinos came between 1971–1980? What country sent fewer people to the United States in 1981–1990 than in 1971–1980?

Asian Immigration to the United States, 1961–1990
(IN THOUSANDS)

Country	1961–1970	1971–1980	1981–1990
Cambodia	1.2	8.4	116.6
China (Mainland)	96.7 (includingTaiwan)	202.5	373.6
Taiwan			15.2
Hong Kong	25.6	47.5	63.0
India	31.2	176.8	261.9
Philippines	101.5	360.2	495.3
Thailand	5.0	44.1	64.4
Vietnam	4.6	179.7	401.4
Japan	38.5	47.9	43.2
Laos	0.1	22.6	145.6
Korea	35.8	272.0	338.8

Source: *Statistical Abstract of the United States, 1992.*

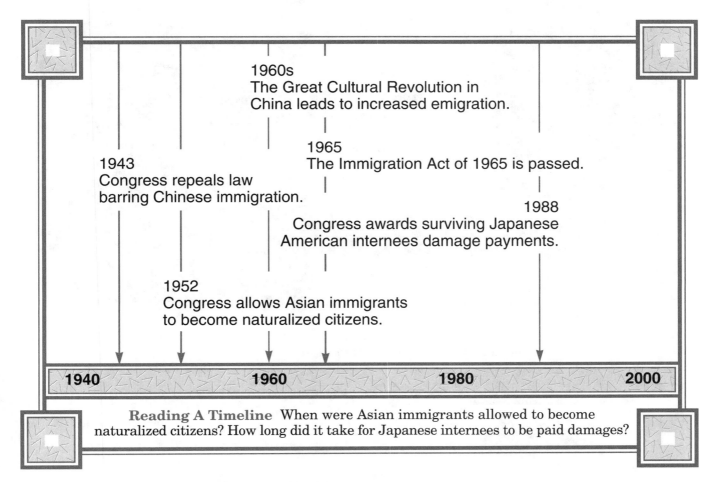

1960s
The Great Cultural Revolution in China leads to increased emigration.

1965
The Immigration Act of 1965 is passed.

1943
Congress repeals law barring Chinese immigration.

1988
Congress awards surviving Japanese American internees damage payments.

1952
Congress allows Asian immigrants to become naturalized citizens.

1940   1960   1980   2000

Reading A Timeline When were Asian immigrants allowed to become naturalized citizens? How long did it take for Japanese internees to be paid damages?

Congress passed the **McCarran-Walter Act**. This allowed immigration from most of Asia. The McCarran-Walter Act also overtuned the 1790 law that said only "whites' could become citizens. Yet Congress kept strict limits on immigration from Asia.

A new immigration act Then Congress made a major shift in immigration policy. It passed the **Immigration Act of 1965**. This act did away with the huge differences between how many immigrants from Europe and from Asia could enter the United States. Under the act, about 20,000 immigrants from each Asian country could enter the United States each year.

Now, immigration from Asia began to rise. Before the act passed, Asian Americans made up less than 1 percent of the U.S. population. By 1990, they made up 3 percent. By 2050, this **proportion** will be even higher. Proportion means the share in relation to the whole. Asian Americans will make up 10 percent of the U.S. population.

Immigrants are now arriving from many Asian nations. In 1960, 97 percent of Asian immigrants came from just three nations—Japan, China, and the Philippines. By 1990, large numbers of immigrants from Vietnam, Korea, India, Cambodia, and Laos had come to the United States.

The kinds of people coming to the United States from Asia changed, too. Once, Asian immigrants were mostly men. Now, whole families were traveling here. In earlier times, Asian immigrants thought that they would return to their home countries after earning some money. Now, many arrived with the idea of staying and building new lives in the United States.

Chinese American Maya Lin designed the Vietnam Veterans memorial in her early twenties. Lin says that the polished, black granite wall inscribed with the names of the 58,000 Americans who died in the war is Asian in its simplicity.

1. How did the McCarran-Walter Act affect immigration to the United States?
2. What led to a great increase in the number of Asian immigrants to the United States?

2 An End to Exclusion Brings Many Chinese to the United States.

Where have most recent Chinese immigrants to the United States settled?

The Chinese were among the first Asians to immigrate to the United States. They have contributed in many ways to American life and culture.

Years of discrimination In the 1800s, the Chinese helped build the railroads of the U.S. West. They also played key roles in making farming important in California (see Chapter 2). But prejudice against the Chinese grew. In 1882, Congress passed a law that sharply cut Chinese immigration. Not until World War II was that law repealed.

Even then, the number of Chinese immigrants remained low. A new law set a limit of 100 Chinese immigrants a year. In the same year, 6,524 Polish immigrants entered the United States.

Other factors also kept immigration from China low. A civil war there ended in a victory for Chinese Communists in 1949. This took place during the "Red Scare" of the Cold War years (see Chapter 17). U.S. officials feared that immigrants might be Communists.

An opening door Change did come. Cold War tensions eased. Then, the McCarran-Walter Act of 1965 increased immigration from China.

The law was passed at a time when there was trouble in China. Many people left China. First, they made their way to Hong Kong or Taiwan. But many went on to the United States.

By the 1970s and 1980s, immigrants were still leaving China. Now, however, they were hoping to make a better life in the United States.

New lives in the United States
The new immigrants brought great changes to the Chinese community in the United States. In 1960, over 60 percent of the Chinese in the United States had been born in the United States. Twenty years later, over 60 percent had been born in Asia.

Most of the new immigrants settled in old Chinese communities. Over 60 percent lived in California and New York. They brought new life to the old Chinatowns of New York City, San Francisco, and Los Angeles. The populations of these Chinatowns grew. Some new communities began as well. Flushing, in New York City, and Monterey Park, outside Los Angeles, are two places that have large Chinese American populations today.

The new Chinese immigrants often faced hard conditions. Housing was often run-down. It was also very crowded and very expensive. Most Chinese did not speak English well. They ended up having to take jobs in or near Chinatowns. Many worked in restaurants or clothing factories there. However, heavy competition for jobs helped keep wages low.

Still, ties remain strong among Chinese American families. Many immigrant parents stress to their children the importance of doing well in school. They see education as a means for their children to better their lives and take a full share in the opportunities that the United States offers.

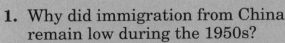

1. Why did immigration from China remain low during the 1950s?
2. What conditions did new immigrants from China find when they arrived in the United States?

3 Many Changes Affect the Lives of Japanese Americans.

How have Japanese Americans fared after the internment during World War II?

Like the Chinese, Japanese in the United States had long known prejudice and discrimination. Japanese immigration had begun in the late 1800s. But in 1907–1908, the United States and Japan reached an agreement that shut off immigration almost completely. Japanese Americans then faced internment camps during World War II (see Chapter 16). Internment ended early in 1945. Japanese Americans then had to pick up the pieces of their lives.

After the war Internment had angered Japanese Americans. Some lost faith in this country and decided to go back to Japan. Of the 120,000 who had been interned, about 4,700 returned to Japan after the war. Some found a hard life in Japan. Many then returned to the United States.

Most Japanese Americans chose to remain in the United States. Internment had cost them heavily. They had lost homes and businesses. Many Japanese Americans had to start all over again in low-paying jobs as they struggled to rebuild their lives.

Fighting back Some Japanese Americans fought to correct these wrongs. They pushed for an end to state laws that limited their right to own land. Slowly, states repealed those laws.

They also fought for repayment for losses during the war. In 1948, they won a partial victory. The U.S. government paid out some 38 million dollars in damages. But this was only a tenth of the amount Japanese Americans were seeking.

This naturalization ceremony took place on San Francisco's Angel Island. Known as the Ellis Island of the West, Angel Island was the port of entry for almost one million Asian and Pacific Rim immigrants between 1910 and 1940.

Righting a wrong Many Japanese Americans were not satisfied. They wanted the U.S. government to admit that internment had been wrong. In 1976, President Gerald Ford officially canceled the wartime internment order. He stated that internment had been unjust.

Congress then set up a committee to study the internment. In 1983, the committee issued a report. It said that internment had been an injustice. The committee advised payments of 20,000 dollars to each surviving internee.

In 1988, Congress acted on the report. It passed the **Civil Liberties Act of 1988**. The act approved payments to the internees. For most Japanese Americans the amount of the payments did not matter. What was important was the admission that "Japanese Americans were and are loyal Americans." They had suffered a terrible wrong.

Declining immigration After the war, the United States and Japan became close allies. But immigration from Japan never became heavy. After Japan rebuilt from the damage of World War II, its economy boomed. Businesses there had plenty of jobs.

Today, immigrants from Japan make up less than 2 percent of the Asian immigrants who come to the United States. Many Japanese who do come to the United States are business people working for branches of Japanese companies here.

1. What financial losses did interned Japanese Americans suffer during World War II?
2. What did the Civil Liberties Act of 1988 do?

4 Korean and Filipino Immigrants Build New Lives in the United States.

Why have many Koreans and Filipinos moved to the United States in recent years?

The first wave of Korean immigrants came to the United States early in the 1900s. About 8,000 went to Hawaii.

There they worked on sugar plantations. By the 1920s, changing conditions in Korea and changing immigration laws in the United States ended this. It would be over 40 years before a second group of Korean immigrants reached the United States.

A changing Korea After World War II, Korea had been split into two countries. One part, North Korea, was ruled by Communists. The other, South Korea, had free enterprise. The two countries fought a bloody struggle early in the 1950s. (See Chapter 17.) Korea had long been a farming nation. After the Korean War, South Korea began to change to a modern, industrial power.

But South Korea was one of the most densely populated countries on earth. There were not enough jobs for all its people. Also, the jobs did not pay well. After the Immigration Act of 1965, many Koreans began to move to the United States.

Koreans in the United States In less than 15 years, the Korean population in the United States rose from less than 10,000 people to over half a million. Most of these immigrants settled in Los Angeles and New York City.

Most Koreans who have come to the United States have been well educated. Over half have college degrees. Many are doctors, engineers, or professionals in their homeland. Most did not find similar jobs in the United States. They did not speak English well enough to follow their careers here.

But many of these immigrants came to the United States with some money. They used this money to open shops or businesses here. Many of these businesses served the growing Korean American community.

Reading a Map. Which states have the largest Asian American populations? What geographical reason can explain why so many Asian Americans live there?

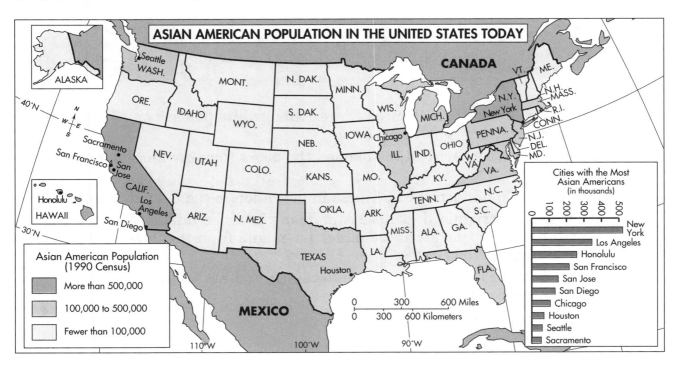

Often, whole families worked in these businesses. They hoped to send their children to college. Some of those children have become doctors, engineers, or professionals here. Korean families have struggled to make such dreams come true.

Great Progress for Filipino Immigrants Filipinos are people from the Philippine Islands. Filipinos make up the largest of all recent Asian immigrant groups. Close to a million Filipinos have entered the United States since 1965.

Political reasons drove many Filipinos to the United States in the 1970s and 1980s. The government of Ferdinand Marcos jailed many opponents. In recent years, many Filipinos have come to the United States for economic reasons. "There are a large number of well-educated people in the Philippines," one government official says. "They can't find jobs here. The job situation is much better in the United States."

In general, Filipinos have not developed their own neighborhoods in older sections of cities. Rather, they tend to mix in, throughout cities and suburbs.

Most of the recent Filipino immigrants have their roots in large cities. There are many professionals among them. Many are engineers, teachers, and lawyers. A large number are involved in medical care. Many doctors and nurses all over the United States have Filipino roots. For example, Filipinos are staff doctors in every major hospital in northern New Jersey and the New York City region.

1. Where have most recent Korean immigrants to the United States chosen to live?
2. Why have many Filipinos come to the United States in recent years?

CHAPTER 29
KEY IDEAS

- After World War II the United States changed its policies on Asian immigration from Asian countries.
- The Immigration Act of 1965 opened the doors to many more Asian immigrants.
- Trouble in China increased Chinese immigration to the United States.
- After a long struggle, Japanese Americans interned during World War II gained apologies and damage payments from the government of the United States.
- Koreans and Filipinos have come to the United States in large numbers since 1965.

I. Reviewing Vocabulary

Match each word on the left with the correct definition on the right.

1. proportion
2. Civil Liberties Act of 1988
3. McCarran-Walter Act
4. naturalize
5. Immigration Act of 1965

a. a law that allowed Asian immigrants to become citizens

b. a law that led to a great increase in immigration from Asian nations

c. the share in relation to the whole

d. to make a native of one country into a citizen of another country

e. a law that approved payments to interned Japanese Americans

II. Understanding the Chapter

1. What effect did the Cold War have on U.S. policies toward immigration from Asia?
2. (a) How have the types of Asian immigrants to the United States changed in recent years? (b) How have their reasons for coming changed?
3. Why have many recent Chinese immigrants stayed in low-paying jobs?
4. Why has immigration from Japan remained low in recent years compared with that from other Asian nations?
5. How have many Korean immigrants earned their livelihoods in the United States?

III. Building Skills: Reading a Chart

Study the chart on page 244. Then answer the following questions.

1. What does the chart show?
2. How did immigration from China change during this period?
3. From what nation did immigration increase at the lowest rate?

IV. Writing About History

1. **What Would You Have Done?** Imagine that you are a Japanese American who was interned during World War II. Write a letter to your representative in Congress asking the U.S. government to admit that it made a mistake in interning Japanese Americans.
2. Imagine that you are a recent immigrant from one of the Asian countries discussed in this chapter. Write a letter to a friend or relative in your home country explaining why that person should or should not come to the United States to live.

V. Working Together

1. With a group, plan an illustrated storybook for elementary students. Your book will tell about the experiences of one person from an immigrant group as he or she begins a new life. Your teacher will give your storybook to an elementary class.
2. **Past to Present** With a group, research other Asian immigrants to the United States in the late 1900s. Make a map of Asia that shows the countries that the immigrants came from.

IMMIGRANTS FROM EUROPE AND THE MIDDLE EAST MAKE NEW LIVES IN THE UNITED STATES.

(1945—PRESENT)

How did immigration from Europe and the Middle East change after World War II?

St. Patrick's Day parades show how immigrant groups, like these Irish Americans, honor their heritage yet are full members of U.S. society.

S T U D Y

Make a list with three columns: "Immigration in the 1920s," "Immigration after World War II," "Fall of Communism." Explain how the periods affected immigration.

H I N T

Looking at Key Terms

- Displaced Persons Act of 1948

Looking at Key Words

- **displaced persons:** people who are forced out of their homelands by war

- **mosque:** Islamic house of worship

Europe had long been the place where most U.S. immigrants had their roots. In 1940, for example, about seven out of every ten immigrants came from Europe. Very few immigrants were from the Arab world. That picture would change after World War II.

1 Immigration from Europe Continues.

Why did immigration from Europe slow down after World War II?

Many Americans thought that World War II would bring floods of new immigrants from Europe. World War II had left much of Europe in ruins. Millions had died in the war. Others had lost their homes and their jobs. Old governments had gone. New governments took charge. Many of these governments were run by Communists. It was a time of great unrest.

People who had been forced out of their homelands by the war were known as **displaced persons**. Many displaced persons wanted to move to the United States. They hoped to build new lives.

However, the United States at this time had strict immigration laws. Those laws had been passed in the 1920s (see Chapter 11). The laws had limited immigration from Eastern and Southern Europe. They set strict quotas, or limits, on the number of immigrants from those areas. But now Southern and Eastern Europe had millions of displaced persons.

These problems bothered many Americans. President Truman called on Congress to "find ways to fulfill our responsibility to end this suffering." Congress listened and soon passed a new law.

The **Displaced Persons Act of 1948** let 100,000 people a year into the United States. Between 1948 and 1952, about 450,000 displaced persons entered the country. About 30 percent of them were Jews who had survived the Nazi Holocaust.

Cold War years As you have read in Chapter 17, soon after World War II, the United States and the Soviet Union began the struggle that was known as the Cold War. Communist governments had taken over most of the nations of Eastern Europe. The United States accepted people fleeing from communism. From 1953 to 1956, the United States took in over 200,000 refugees from Eastern Europe.

In 1956, the people of Hungary rose in revolt against Communist rule. Soviet tanks soon crushed the revolt. But many Hungarians fled their country. About 40,000 came to the United States.

The Cold War brought great changes to immigration. The old quota system from the 1920s discriminated against people of color. At the same time, the United States was seeking allies among people of color in Asia, Africa, and the Middle East. This system embarrassed Americans.

Finally, Congress ended the old quota system. As you have read in Chapter 29, Congress passed the Immigration Act of 1965. Lawmakers thought that the new law would cause immigration from Europe to boom. They were in for a great surprise.

Changing patterns The Immigration Act of 1965 brought many new immigrants from Asia and Latin America. But immigration from Europe did not increase. Instead, it dropped steadily.

There were a number of reasons for this drop. A main reason was that Communist governments often refused to let people leave their countries.

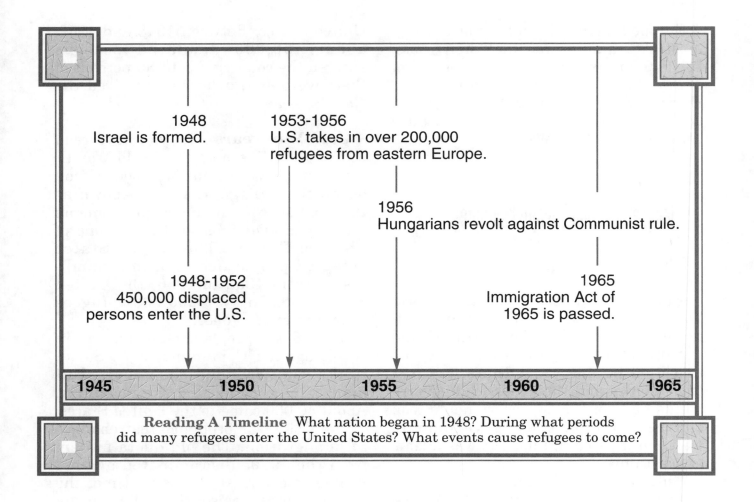

1948
Israel is formed.

1953-1956
U.S. takes in over 200,000
refugees from eastern Europe.

1956
Hungarians revolt against Communist rule.

1948-1952
450,000 displaced
persons enter the U.S.

1965
Immigration Act of
1965 is passed.

| 1945 | 1950 | 1955 | 1960 | 1965 |

Reading A Timeline What nation began in 1948? During what periods
did many refugees enter the United States? What events cause refugees to come?

Another reason was the recovery of Europe's economies. Business boomed in many nations. Once, European workers had come to the United States because they could not find jobs in their homelands. Now, factories in Europe had more and more goods. There were more jobs than workers.

The fall of communism   Changes in recent years have affected immigration to the United States. In the late 1980s, Communist governments fell all over Eastern Europe. The Soviet Union broke apart. (See Chapter 32.) Economic conditions were bad. Many people tried to come to the United States. Russians, for example, are now building new communities in the Brighton Beach section of New York City. Another growing Russian community is in Hollywood, California.

Will immigration from Europe continue to fall? Or will it begin to grow again? This is uncertain. If the former Communist nations prosper, chances are good that immigration will stay low. But if hard times continue, European immigrants may again try to better their lives in the United States.

Remembering roots   When recent immigrants looked at the experiences of earlier immigrants, they were hopeful. Many earlier immigrants had succeeded in building better lives.

Earlier immigrants had faced discrimination. Many had tried to learn English as they struggled to make their livings. Often they were forced to take low-paying jobs. They had to live in crowded, run-down neighborhoods.

But many of those earlier immigrants improved their lives. They formed groups to help them adapt to life in the United States. They learned English and won better jobs. As they prospered, many bought homes in the cities or the suburbs. Many saw their children graduate from high school and go to college.

The descendants of these earlier immigrants still have strong ties to their roots. Irish Americans closely follow news from Ireland. Polish Americans send aid back to Poland as that nation tries to build its economy. Jewish Americans are concerned with events in Israel.

The descendants of European immigrants have kept their customs and cultures alive in the United States. Many cities still have Little Italys. Shops and markets in such neighborhoods sell foods and products from the "old country." Newspapers in Polish, Russian, German, and Hungarian offer news of events in the home country. Holidays like Columbus Day offer Italian Americans the chance to celebrate their roots. German Americans celebrate Steuben Day with parades. Jewish Americans remember the horror of the Holocaust at the Holocaust Museum in Washington, D.C.

Sveta Kirilova on the left is a Russian immigrant. She works in a New York deli. Although the Communist government has fallen, Kirolova still worries about her parents in St. Petersburg. She is not sure the new Russian government will be better.

Donna Shalala, with Jesse Jackson, is the first Arab American woman to serve in the U.S. Cabinet. She is the Secretary of Health and Human Services.

1. How did the United States attempt to aid people made homeless by World War II?
2. Why did immigration from Europe fall in the 1950s and 1960s?

2 Arab American Communities Grow.

How have Arab Americans made their mark on the United States?

The first immigrants from the Arab world arrived in this country long before World War II. The first large group of Arab immigrants arrived between 1880 and 1914. Most of these immigrants came from Lebanon. Lebanon was then a part of Syria. Most of these early immigrants were Christian Arabs.

Early in the 1900s, they were joined by Muslim Arabs. In those years, about 100,000 Arabs came to the United States from the Middle East.

Many of the Christian Arabs did not take jobs in the nation's growing industries. Instead, some traveled from town to town selling goods. Others settled down and opened shops. Some of these small stores grew into huge clothing businesses. The Farah and Haggar companies are two such companies. Joseph Haggar came to the United States from Lebanon in 1908. He sold clothes for a number of years. Then in 1926, he moved to Dallas, bought some sewing machines and began a business to make work pants. Like Henry Ford, Haggar set up an assembly line. But Haggar's assembly line made men's pants. Today, the Haggar company is the world's largest maker of men's slacks.

Many of the Muslim Arabs who arrived in the United States before World War II found work in the growing automobile industry. Muslim Arab communities grew up near automobile plants. Such cities as Toledo, Ohio, and Detroit, Michigan, attracted many Arab immigrants. The Arab community that formed in Dearborn, Michigan, is one of the nation's largest.

World War I brought an end to this first wave of immigration. The immigration laws of the 1920s set low limits on how many people could enter the United States from the Middle East.

New waves of immigrants Immigration from the Middle East remained low until well after World War II. In 1948, the Jewish state of Israel was formed in the area that the Arabs called Palestine.

Many Arabs left Israel when the Jewish state was formed. They fled to Lebanon, Jordan, Syria, and Egypt. Some later came to the United States. Israel and its Arab neighbors clashed in wars in 1948, 1967, and 1973. Many left to escape the fighting.

Middle Easterners today Today, Americans of Arab background number from 3.5 to 6 million. Middle Easterners in the new wave of immigration have settled all across the United States. Dearborn, Michigan, remains a favorite spot for newcomers. Almost one out of five people in the city of Dearborn has Arab roots. But other important Arab American communities have sprung up in New York, New York; Jersey City, New Jersey; Washington, D.C.; and Glendale, California.

This Arab American family lives in Brooklyn, New York. Over 3.5 million people of Arab descent live in the United States. Although Arab Americans have absorbed much from their American surroundings, they still take pride in their roots.

George Fawzi owns two shoe stores in the Detroit area. His first store was a small shop on Warren Street in East Dearborn, Michigan. Warren Avenue is a wide street with many small shops. Many of the stores are owned by Arab American business people.

George's father was born in Palestine and moved to Jordan during the 1960s. George was born in Jordan. He moved to Dearborn with his parents and two sisters in 1981. He explained:

> I spoke almost no English when I arrived here. I learned English mostly in high school. Then I worked my way through college by selling in a shoe store. After studying finance, I decided to start my own business. Today, I am most interested in getting other Arab Americans involved in our community.

Most of the new Middle Eastern immigrants are Muslims. They have built **mosques**, Islamic houses of worship, in cities all across the United States. Today, Islam is the second-largest non-Christian religion in the nation, after Judaism. Soon it will be the largest.

The new immigration has created new pride among Arab Americans. They are proud of the accomplishments of people like Donna Shalala. She is Secretary of Health and Human Services under President Clinton. They are also proud of the many contributions that Middle Easterners have made to art, literature, and science.

Yet there is some uneasiness along with the pride. Tensions remain high in the Middle East. Acts of terrorism still shake the region.

Arab Americans fear that such acts will lead to prejudice against Arab Americans. This is why Arab American groups work to remind the American people of the many contributions that Arab Americans are making to the United States.

1. How did most early Arab immigrants to the United States make their livings?
2. Of what religion are most recent arrivals from Arab lands?

CHAPTER 30
KEY IDEAS

- After World War II, the United States passed special laws to let in European immigrants fleeing communism.
- As European nations rebuilt after World War II, immigration to the United States from those nations declined.
- Between 1880 and 1914, a first wave of immigration brought some 100,000 people to the United States from the Middle East.
- Political unrest in several Middle Eastern nations contributed to increased immigration from that region after World War II.

REVIEWING CHAPTER 30

I. Reviewing Vocabulary

Match each word on the left with the correct definition on the right.

1. displaced person
2. immigrant
3. quota
4. Displaced Persons Act
5. mosque

a. an Islamic house of worship
b. someone forced from his or her homeland by WW II
c. a measure under which 450,000 immigrants entered the United States between 1948 and 1952
d. a person who settles permanently in another country
e. a limit on how many people from a particular group can enter the country

II. Understanding the Chapter

1. How did the Cold War affect immigration to the United States from Europe?
2. Why did European immigration to the United States begin to fall off after the 1950s?
3. What changes in recent years have led to a rise in immigration from Eastern Europe?
4. What are some events that have contributed to Arab immigration to the United States since World War II?
5. How have current events in the Middle East affected the lives of Arab Americans?

III. Building Skills: Supporting Statements

List the facts in this chapter that support each statement below.

1. The Displaced Persons Act increased immigration to the United States.
2. Many Jews settled in the United States after World War II.
3. The Immigration Act of 1965 did not result exactly as expected.

IV. Writing About History

1. **What Would You Have Done?** If you were an editor of a newspaper in 1952, would you support the Displaced Persons Act? Remember that many of your readers are European immigrants or the children of such immigrants. Explain.
2. Imagine that you are a recent Egyptian immigrant to the United States. Write a letter to a friend or relative back in Egypt saying whether they should or should not move to the United States.

V. Working Together

1. With a group, plan an Immigrant Appreciation Day celebration. Draw up a schedule of events and activities. Together, plan and write a short speech that would be an appropriate opening to the celebration.
2. **Past to Present** President Truman felt that the United States had a "responsibility" to accept displaced persons after World War II. With a group, discuss whether the United States has a responsibility to accept immigrants from places torn apart by war. Write a paragraph stating your opinion.

Unit 6
Facing a Changing World
(1980-Present)

Chapters

31 New Leaders Search for New Solutions.

32 The United States Is Challenged by World Problems.

33 New Immigrants Make the United States a More Diverse Nation.

34 The United States Faces Challenges.

35 Science Changes the Way Americans Live.

36 The American People Face the 21st Century.

NEW LEADERS SEARCH FOR NEW SOLUTIONS. (1981—PRESENT)

How did the policies of Presidents Reagan and Bush differ from the policies of President Clinton?

Ronald Reagan was elected President in 1980. He is one of only three presidents to receive over 500 votes in the Electoral College.

Looking at Key Terms
- Sunbelt

Looking at Key Words
- **landslide:** an overwhelming victory in an election
- **social programs:** government programs that aid needy groups of people
- **conservatism:** a political theory that favors less government activity
- **budget deficit:** the debt created when a government spends more money than it takes in
- **recession:** a sharp downturn in business

The late 1970s was a difficult time for the nation. The economy was not doing well. High inflation meant high prices for food, clothing, and other items. Inflation is a rapid rise in prices. Interest rates on bank loans were high. Thus it was hard to borrow money. President Jimmy Carter was not able to improve the economy. This cost him the 1980 election. Republican Ronald Reagan became the 40th President of the United States.

1 The United States Turns More Conservative.

What steps did President Reagan take to deal with the nation's problems?

Ronald Reagan had run for governor of California in 1966. At the time, his opponent made fun of him. Reagan had once been a popular movie actor. The opponent asked what a former movie actor knew about running one of the biggest states in the country.

Reading a Chart. What does this chart show? From 1985 to 1990, what was the only year in which the deficit decreased? Is the deficit increasing or decreasing?

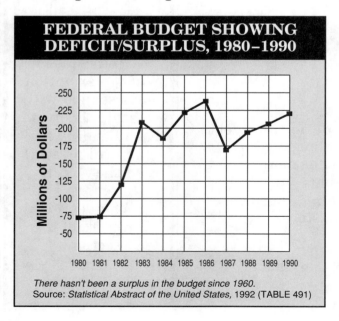

FEDERAL BUDGET SHOWING DEFICIT/SURPLUS, 1980–1990

Millions of Dollars

-250 -225 -200 -175 -150 -125 -100 -75 -50

1980 1981 1982 1983 1984 1985 1986 1987 1988 1989 1990

There hasn't been a surplus in the budget since 1960.
Source: *Statistical Abstract of the United States, 1992* (TABLE 491)

Reagan had the last laugh. He won the election in a **landslide**. A landslide is a political term for an overwhelming victory in an election. Reagan served two terms as governor. In 1980, he ran for President of the United States and won. At age 69, he was the oldest person ever elected to that office. Reagan was a charming person. His manner appealed to both young and old Americans. For example, early in 1981, Reagan was wounded during an assassination attempt. But, he did not lose his sense of humor. He told the surgeons who operated on him that he hoped they were all good Republicans. Reagan recovered and was more popular than ever. In fact, Reagan was one of the most popular Presidents of modern times.

Reagan was popular not just because of his charm. His ideas about government also fit the mood of the country. In the 1980s, many U.S. citizens became less interested in the drive for social justice that had happened in the 1960s. They resented having to pay high taxes to support **social programs**. These are government programs that aid needy groups of people. Building public housing is a social program. Aiding unemployed people is another social program.

Reagan's ideas were part of a new mood of **conservatism** in the nation. Most conservatives believe in reducing the size of government. They also want to give business more freedom.

Reagan believed that his main job was to "get the government off the backs of the people." The federal government was spending 120 billion dollars per year on social programs in 1981. Reagan felt that the state and local governments should pay for many social programs. He got Congress to cut back some programs and end others. These cuts hurt the poor, including many Latinos and African Americans.

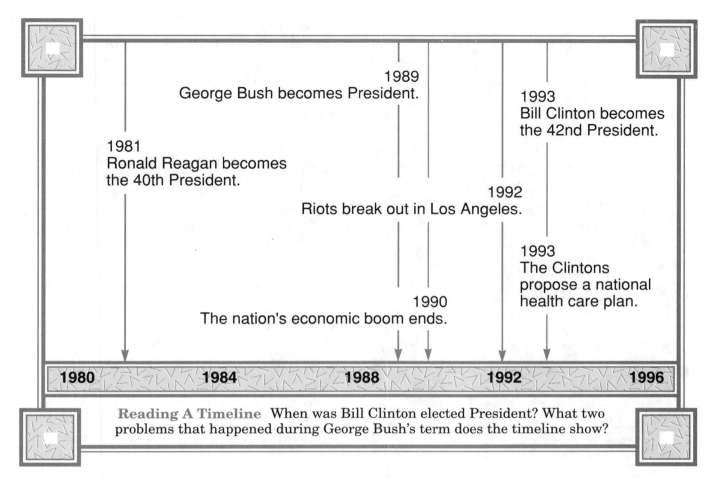

1989
George Bush becomes President.

1981
Ronald Reagan becomes
the 40th President.

1993
Bill Clinton becomes
the 42nd President.

1992
Riots break out in Los Angeles.

1993
The Clintons
propose a national
health care plan.

1990
The nation's economic boom ends.

| 1980 | 1984 | 1988 | 1992 | 1996 |

Reading A Timeline When was Bill Clinton elected President? What two problems that happened during George Bush's term does the timeline show?

Reagan also wanted to cut taxes. He believed that lower taxes would lead people to invest more money in business. Businesses would then be able to grow and hire more workers. The economy would improve.

More money for the military Reagan was able to cut taxes. The tax cuts meant that the government had less money coming in. He also cut spending for social programs. However, President Reagan did not cut spending for defense. He almost doubled defense spending between 1981 and 1987. He felt that the country had to be strong to meet the threat of the Soviet Union. Reagan called that country the "evil empire."

This spending forced the government to borrow billions of dollars to pay its bills. This created a **budget deficit**. A budget

deficit is created when a government spends more money than it takes in.

The economy booms During Reagan's time in office, the country had a long economic boom. Middle-class and wealthy Americans were doing well. However, the poor did not enjoy the good times. Most Latinos and African Americans did not share in the boom. Many were jobless. Many found themselves locked in the inner cities. Others were victims of high crime rates there.

The boom was not spread out equally across the United States. It was especially strong in the **Sunbelt**. The Sunbelt is a term for the South and Southwestern parts of the United States. At the same time, the older cities of the Northeast and the Midwest went into a long decline. Their factories

Sandra Day O'Connor was the first woman appointed to the Supreme Court. Although she is conservative, she has favored affirmative action and some women's rights issues.

were old. They could not compete with newer plants in other regions.

New Directions Reagan found another way to carry out his conservative ideas. He was able to appoint three new Justices to the Supreme Court. All three were conservatives like himself. One of these Justices was Sandra Day O'Connor. She became the first woman Supreme Court justice. Reagan also appointed three women to Cabinet-level positions. No other President before him had named so many women to Cabinet-level positions.

When Reagan left office in 1989, the nation's economy was booming. However, the budget deficit was huge. Controlling this deficit would be one of the central issues faced by the new President, George Bush.

1. What were Reagan's policies toward business?
2. Who is Sandra Day O'Connor?

2 George Bush Tries to Become "the Education President."

What were President Bush's goals for the United States?

George Bush came to the White House after a long career in public service. Bush joined the Navy at 18 during World War II. As a young Navy fighter pilot, he won medals for heroic action. Bush moved to Texas after college and founded his own oil company. He entered politics. In the 1960s, he was elected to the House of Representatives from Texas. In the 1970s he served the United States at the United Nations and in China. Later he became director of the Central Intelligence Agency (CIA). From 1981 to 1989, he was Ronald Reagan's Vice-President.

"The Education President" Bush promised to continue Reagan's economic policies. He promised to cut the deficit and not raise new taxes to do it. He also wanted to improve the U.S. education system. He called himself "the Education President" and met with educators to improve schools.

Bush never really became "the Education President" in the minds of the American people. He always seemed to be caught up in some other crisis. Many Americans thought he was more interested in foreign affairs than in issues in the United States. He discovered that it would take a lot of money to improve education. There was not much federal money available. He said that the job of improving schools would have to be largely carried out by the local and state governments.

A bad recession   In the last year of Bush's term, the nation entered a serious **recession**. A recession is a downturn in business. Large numbers of savings banks began to fail. Savings banks fail when they aren't repaid money that they have lent. These banks then can't pay back people who put money in the banks. The government took over hundreds of the banks to keep them alive. This cost the taxpayers billions of dollars.

The economic boom had ended by 1990. More and more Americans did not have work. Critics warned that a lack of government action to aid the poor was adding to the anger among these groups.

That anger exploded into violence in Los Angeles in April 1992. Four white police officers had been charged with beating an African American man named Rodney King. A videotape of the beating convinced many people that the officers were guilty. Then a jury decided that the officers were not guilty. This led to days of violence in Los Angeles. The violence brought new calls for programs to aid the poor.

Bush's popularity fell. Many people believed that he had not lived up to his promises to improve public schools and the economy. Some Americans also felt that he broke his promise when he approved new taxes in 1989.

George Bush, here at a Head Start Center in Maryland, promised more money for education. But he thought local and state governments should pay for improving schools.

Bush ran for a new term in 1992. He hoped that U.S. victories against Iraq (see Chapter 32) would overshadow the problems of home. But he lost. The people wanted a change. They elected a new President who promised to restore the economy and improve people's lives.

1. What experience did George Bush bring to the presidency?
2. What was Bush's attitude towards education?

President Bill Clinton worked to improve social problems. Here, Clinton, Elie Wiesel, and Harvey Meyerhoff light an eternal flame outside the U.S. Holocaust Museum. The museum honors those who died in the Holocaust.

3 Bill Clinton Charts a New Direction for Americans.

What did President Clinton do about the deficit and health care?

In 1963, 17-year-old Bill Clinton went to Washington, D.C., with an Arkansas youth group. He met and shook hands with President John Kennedy. It was a turning point for the young man. Later, Clinton said that it was when he shook hands with the President that he decided to go into public service. He still proudly displays a picture of himself shaking hands with President Kennedy.

Thirty years later, Bill Clinton was elected President. Like Kennedy, he was one of the youngest persons to be elected President.

Like Reagan and Bush, Clinton also had to deal with problems of the grow-ing national debt. Clinton's goal was to reduce the debt. He also wanted to get the U.S. economy moving. Clinton proposed a program that would cut spending by nearly five hundred billion dollars over four years. The plan called for more taxes, especially for the wealthiest Americans. It included an energy tax on gasoline and other fuels. "This economic plan can't please everybody. But if it is taken as a whole, it will help all of us," Clinton said.

A National Health Plan   Clinton also wanted to make the federal government more active in social programs. Health care was at the top of his list of concerns. "All of our efforts to make the economy stronger will fail unless we also take bold steps to reform our health-care system," he said.

The cost of health care has increased steadily over the past 30 years. In 1965 the United States spent 42 billion dollars on health care. In 1992 it spent 820 billion dollars! Health insurance was so expensive that 37 million Americans in 1992 could not afford any insurance. Without insurance, these Americans were sometimes not able to get the medical treatment they needed.

Clinton's wife, Hillary Rodham Clinton, was put in charge of developing a health-care plan. Mrs. Clinton had been a successful lawyer in Arkansas before her husband became President. In her new role, Hillary Rodham Clinton traveled the country meeting with Americans to try to develop the best plan possible.

In 1993, the Clintons proposed a national health-care plan. The program called for giving medical insurance to all Americans, even poor ones. The program would partly be paid for by new taxes.

Some people in Congress opposed the Clinton plan. They thought it would be too costly. Others said it would take away Americans' rights to choose their own doctor. Although many Americans had doubts about parts of the Clinton plan, most agreed something had to be done about health care.

President Clinton wanted to use government to solve social problems. Whether he would be able to complete his goals was unclear. Only one thing was certain. The problems that faced Presidents Carter, Reagan, Bush, and Clinton would not simply go away. It would take hard work and cooperation among Americans to solve them.

1. What goals did President Clinton set for himself?
2. What role did Hillary Rodham Clinton play in developing Clinton administration programs?

CHAPTER 31
KEY IDEAS

- President Ronald Reagan cut government spending for social programs. He also reduced taxes. At the same time, he greatly increased spending for the military. This led to a large budget deficit.

- President George Bush believed in many of the same conservative ideas as Reagan. However, he was more interested in improving education.

- Bill Clinton was one of the youngest Presidents to hold office. He got Congress to pass a deficit program. He also worked for the passage of a national health-care system.

I. Vocabulary

Match each word on the left with the correct definition on the right.

1. budget deficit   **a.** the states of the South and Southwest

2. Sunbelt   **b.** an overwhelming election victory

3. social programs   **c.** a sharp downturn in business

4. recession   **d.** government programs that aid needy groups of people

5. landslide   **e.** the shortage that results when the government spends more money than it takes in

II. Understanding the Chapter

1. How did President Reagan reduce the role of government in the United States?

2. Why did some critics feel Reagan's economic policies were unfair?

3. Why was President Bush unable to become "the Education President"?

4. How did President Clinton propose reducing the growing national deficit?

5. Describe the Clinton health-care plan. Why did some people oppose it?

III. Building Skills: Summarizing

On a separate sheet of paper, write two or three sentences that summarize each of the topics below.

1. The reasons that Ronald Reagan was one of the most popular Presidents.

2. The difficulties that led President Bush to lose the presidency after only one term.

3. The ways in which President Clinton tried to reduce the deficit and improve the lives of Americans.

IV. Writing About History

1. What Would You Have Done? Imagine that you were elected President in 1980. How would you improve the economy? Would you cut social programs, reduce the military budget, or do something else? Explain your reasons.

2. Create a campaign poster for either Bill Clinton or George Bush in the 1992 election. In your poster explain why people should vote for your candidate.

V. Working Together

1. Form a group with two or three classmates. Choose one of the three Presidents discussed in this chapter. Create a dramatic skit, a mural, or an oral report about an incident in this President's life.

2. Past to Present In a group, discuss whether or not the medical care that Americans receive is good. Then write a brief newspaper editorial supporting or criticizing the health-care plan of President Clinton.

THE UNITED STATES IS CHALLENGED BY WORLD PROBLEMS. (1980—PRESENT)

How did the United States respond to world issues in the 1980s and 1990s?

Israel and the Palestine Liberation Organization signed a peace accord. Clinton watched Yitzhak Rabin and Yassar Arafat shake hands.

Looking at Key Terms

- Operation Desert Storm • Sandinistas
- Contras • Iran-Contra scandal

Looking at Key Words

- **free-market economy:** an economy in which there is little government control
- **free-trade zone:** a place where there are no taxes on trade between countries

- **trade deficit:** when a country spends more to buy goods and services from other countries than it gets by selling goods and services to those countries

STUDY

Look at the chapter timeline. On a separate piece of paper, write down how the events are related.

HINT

In the early 1980s, Cold War tensions rose. President Reagan called the Soviet Union an "evil empire." The United States built up its military strength.

Five years later, the mood had changed. Reagan made his first visit to Moscow, the Soviet capital. He walked through Red Square with the leader of the Soviet Union, Mikhail Gorbachev (GOR-buh-chof). He spoke to Soviet students at Moscow State University:

You are living in one of the most exciting times in history. It is a time when the first breath of freedom stirs the air. The heart beats to the rhythm of hope.

What had happened to turn the Soviet Union from an enemy to a friend?

1 The United States Sees the Soviet Union Collapse.

What was the effect of the breakup of the Soviet Union?

In 1985, Mikhail Gorbachev came to power in the Soviet Union. The country was in serious trouble. The old Communist system was not working. Many people did not have enough food or good housing. Gorbachev knew he had to improve the Soviet economy. He had to give greater freedom to the Soviet people.

The communist economy of the Soviet Union controlled almost all business. Gorbachev tried to make the Soviet

Reading a Map. What former Soviet Republics border China? What countries share a south and southwestern border with Turkmenistan?

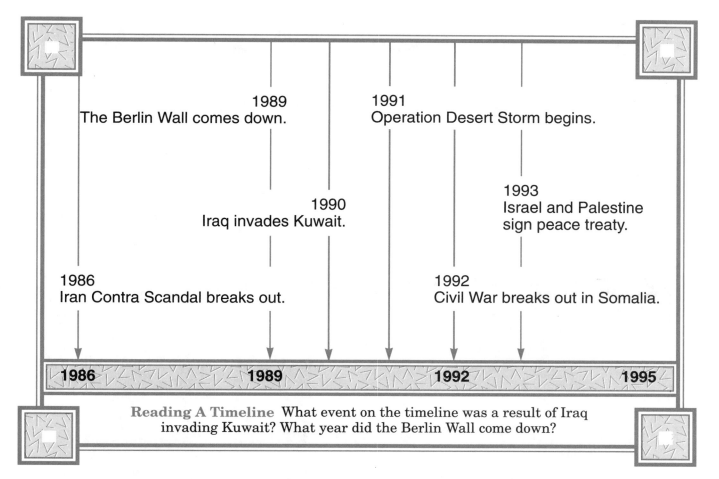

1986	**1989**	**1992**	**1995**

1986
Iran Contra Scandal breaks out.

1989
The Berlin Wall comes down.

1990
Iraq invades Kuwait.

1991
Operation Desert Storm begins.

1992
Civil War breaks out in Somalia.

1993
Israel and Palestine sign peace treaty.

Reading A Timeline What event on the timeline was a result of Iraq invading Kuwait? What year did the Berlin Wall come down?

Union more like a **free-market economy**. In a free-market economy, people make, sell, and buy things freely. There is little government control. The United States, Western Europe, and Latin America have free-market economies.

The Soviet Union spent a fortune on military weapons. This hurt its economy. To stop the arms race, Gorbachev tried to build better relations with the West. He met with President Reagan several times. In 1987, the two leaders signed a treaty. They agreed to destroy many of their missiles. Gorbachev then cut the Soviet armed forces. He pulled troops and tanks out of Eastern Europe.

New democracies Without Soviet support, Eastern European governments began to crumble. All over Eastern Europe, people were unhappy with communism. In 1989, Poland broke free. It became the first Communist country to elect a non-communist government. Other countries followed.

In late 1989, the Berlin Wall came down. The Communist government of East Germany fell. East Germans were free to cross into West Germany. Within a year, East and West Germany again became one nation, Germany.

The fall of the Soviet Union Gorbachev's changes could not save the Soviet Union. The economy got worse. Conflicts broke out between different groups within the Soviet Union. People in the republics demanded independence.

The Soviet Union was not one nation. It was made up of 15 "republics." People in the republics spoke different languages and had different religions. Only communist power had held the Soviet Union together.

On Christmas Day 1991, Gorbachev resigned. The Soviet Union was no more. The republics became independent. The largest republic was Russia. Boris Yeltsin was its president.

When the Soviet Union collapsed, the United States became the only superpower in the world. Many Americans believed the United States did not need to worry about world events anymore. New events quickly proved them wrong.

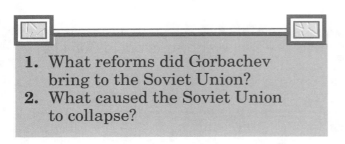

1. What reforms did Gorbachev bring to the Soviet Union?
2. What caused the Soviet Union to collapse?

2 The Middle East and Africa Demand U.S. Attention.

Why did the United States become involved in conflicts in the Middle East and Africa?

The "Screaming Eagles" of the U.S. 82nd Airborne Division sped towards Iraq. In assault helicopters, they flew through black skies and pouring rain. After flying nearly 170 miles, they destroyed a highway. It linked Iraq's capital, Baghdad, with an important port. Iraq's army was cut in two. The 82nd Airborne Division was part of a UN force. They were dealing with a crisis in the Middle East.

Invasion of Kuwait The Middle East had been a world trouble spot for many

Reading a Map. What country suffered a famine, causing UN forces to distribute food? Where did Middle East peace talks begin in 1991?

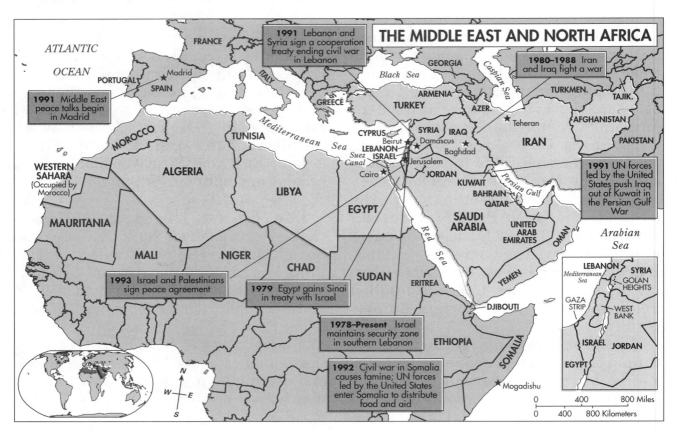

years. In August 1990, another conflict started. Saddam Hussein, dictator of Iraq, invaded the tiny country of Kuwait. It had valuable oil wells. Within days, Iraq controlled all of Kuwait.

The United States feared that Saddam might next invade Saudi Arabia. Saudi Arabia is one of the world's largest producers of oil. The United States and the UN sent 500,000 troops to Saudi Arabia. They warned Iraq to leave Kuwait.

President Bush gave Saddam a deadline for leaving Kuwait. Saddam had to get out by January 15, 1991. If he refused, UN troops would attack Iraq.

Operation Desert Storm   The January 15 deadline came and went. Saddam's troops remained in Kuwait. The UN attack began. It was called **Operation Desert Storm**. The UN forces were led by Americans. Missiles and planes hit targets in Iraq. Ground troops moved into Kuwait. After a few days of combat, Iraq's armed forces were destroyed. Half-starved Iraqi soldiers surrendered to UN troops. The UN troops freed Kuwait and took control of southern Iraq. Although Saddam was defeated, he stayed in power. He continued to stir up trouble in the Middle East.

Peace in the Middle East   In other parts of the Middle East, the United States also acted as a world leader. For years, U.S. Presidents had worked for peace between Israel and the Arab nations. In the late 1980s, President Bush got peace talks started between Israel and the Palestinians. Palestinians were Arabs who had lived in the area that became Israel.

In August 1993, news of an agreement between Israel and the Palestinian Liberation Organization (PLO) shocked the world. The PLO had led the fight against Israel. Under the

agreement, Palestinians would have self-rule within Israel. In September 1993, Israeli and Arab leaders traveled to Washington, D.C. They signed a peace agreement at the White House. It was a first step toward peace.

Starvation in Somalia   A very different problem arose in the East African nation of Somalia. A civil war led to a breakdown of government in 1992. Millions of Somalis fled to the countryside to escape the fighting. The food supply ran short. People started dying of hunger.

The United States and the UN sent troops to Somalia's capital, Mogadishu (moh-guh-DEE-shoo). Their mission was to help supplies reach the starving people. The troops tried not to fight with the different sides. But Somalis from one group killed some American soldiers. UN soldiers were also killed.

Americans were disturbed by the deaths in Somalia. Many questioned the U.S. role as a world peace-maker. Public opinion turned against the mission. The U.S. government pulled the American soldiers out of Somalia.

1. What caused Desert Storm?
2. Why did the United States send troops to Somalia?

3 Latin America Challenges the United States.
How did the United States respond to Latin America in the 1980s and 1990s?

In the 1980s, a civil war broke out in Nicaragua. It ended with a new government. The winners called themselves **Sandinistas** (san-duh-NEEST-uhz). The Sandinistas tried to make major

In 1991, a military coup overthrew Haiti's first democratically elected President. Now, hundreds of Haitians seek refuge in the United States.

weapons to Iran. The money made from the weapons sales was then secretly given to the Contras.

When news of these secret deals broke, several top Reagan aides resigned. Some were put on trial for breaking the law. The affair became known as the **Iran-Contra scandal**.

Invasion of Panama   In the 1980s, the country of Panama was ruled by its army. The United States discovered that the leader, General Manuel Noriega (noh-ree-AY-gah) was involved in the drug trade. In 1989, Noriega threw out a democratic election. Then he made himself dictator. The United States protested, but Noriega refused to listen.

In late 1989, the United States invaded Panama. Noriega was captured. He was put on trial in Miami. He was found guilty and sent to prison. The United States said it had hurt the drug trade. But many Latin Americans were angry. The United States had used force again.

Haitian coup   The nation of Haiti has close ties with the United States. During the 1980s and 1990s, large numbers of Haitians came to the United States. They have continued to be concerned with events in Haiti. There, military rule was replaced in 1990. Haitians looked forward to democratic government. Jean-Bertrand Aristide (ar-uh-STEED) was elected president of Haiti. Soon after, the military overthrew Aristide. He fled to the United States.

President Clinton was unsure how to act. He wanted Aristide back in power. But, he did not want to use force. Some Americans, especially Haitian Americans, demanded Aristide's return to power. Others argued that U.S. troops should not be involved. They wanted the U.S. government to focus on problems at home. How would the United States act? This question would be a major U.S. concern in the 1990s.

changes in their country. They were also unfriendly to the United States.

President Reagan provided weapons and training to the **Contras** of Nicaragua. The Contras were Nicaraguans who wanted to overthrow the Sandinistas.

Congress debated aid to the Contras. Opponents claimed that the United States had no right to help overthrow another country's government. Supporters warned that Nicaragua would become a center for communism in Central America. The opponents won. In 1988, a law was passed ending all aid to the Contras.

Aides to President Reagan paid no attention to this law. A plot started in the White House. Americans sold

1. Who did the United States support in Nicaragua?
2. Why did the United States invade Panama?

4 U.S. Power in Trade Is Threatened.

How have other countries challenged U.S. leadership in world trade?

Thirty years ago the United States was a world leader in trade. Today foreign countries such as Germany, Taiwan, and Japan have joined the U.S. as leading world traders. They sell high quality goods cheaply. By the late 1980s, Japan sold more than 25 percent of all cars in the world. It also sold 90 percent of all TVs.

At the same time, Americans were buying more foreign-made goods. This has led to a **trade deficit**. A trade deficit means that a country spends more to buy from other countries than it gets by selling to them. In the early 1990s, the trade deficit was over $108 billion dollars. The U.S. government tried to cut this deficit. It feared the economy would suffer if it was not lowered.

Free trade The North American Free Trade Agreement (NAFTA) went into effect in 1994. It was an attempt to deal with the trade deficit. (See Chapter 25.) NAFTA makes all of North America a **free-trade zone**. In a free trade zone, there are no taxes on trade between countries. In the past, U.S. goods sold in Mexico and Canada had taxes added to their price. People in these countries often did not buy American goods. Because of the tax, the goods were often too expensive.

NAFTA became a hot issue. Supporters said the treaty allowed U.S. goods to be sold to a larger market. Opponents said more American jobs would move to Mexico. In November 1993, Congress passed NAFTA by a narrow margin. It would take several years to see the results of the agreement.

1. What is a trade deficit?
2. What is NAFTA?

CHAPTER 32
KEY IDEAS

- The Soviet Union collapse in 1991 ended the Cold War. This left the United States as the only superpower.
- During the late 1980s and early 1990s, the U.S. government used force in Panama, Kuwait, and Somalia. However, trouble in Nicaragua and Haiti divided public opinion.
- In recent years, U.S. trade has been threatened by countries in Asia and Europe. Congress passed NAFTA to try to solve this problem.

I. Reviewing Vocabulary
Match each word on the left with the correct definition on the right.

1. communist economy
2. Contras
3. trade deficit
4. free-market economy
5. free-trade zone

a. rebels who wanted to overthrow the Communist government of Nicaragua
b. an economy where there is a great deal of government control
c. an economy in which there is little government control
d. a place where there are no taxes on trade between countries
e. when a country spends more to buy goods and services from other countries than it gets by selling to them

II. Understanding the Chapter
1. What events led to the collapse of the Soviet Union and the end of communism in Eastern Europe?
2. Why did the United States invade Panama?
3. How did the United States and the UN get Iraq out of Kuwait?
4. Why was President Clinton unsure about how to act toward Haiti?
5. What solutions did the U.S. government try to cut the trade deficit?

III. Building Skills: Making a Chart
Use the information in this chapter to complete the following chart.

Comparing Crises In The World

Country	Crisis	U.S. response

IV. Writing About History
1. Do you think the United States should use force in its role as world leader? Write a letter to the U.S. President explaining your opinion.
2. **What Would You Have Done?** If you were a member of the Senate at the time of the vote on NAFTA, would you support or oppose it? Explain.

V. Working Together
1. With a group, create a map of the world showing countries where the United States got involved in the 1980s and 1990s.
2. **Past to Present** With a group, choose one of the crises discussed in this chapter. Research how past events helped to create this crisis and what solutions may be found. Share your findings with the class.

NEW IMMIGRANTS MAKE THE UNITED STATES A MORE DIVERSE NATION. (1970—PRESENT)

Why were immigrants from Asia, and South America now coming to the United States in large numbers?

Duyen Baccam, a refugee from Laos, celebrated Thanksgiving with family and friends in Iowa. The feast had Laotian and American dishes.

Looking at Key Terms

- Shining Path

Looking at Key Words

- **refugee:** a person who is forced to flee his or her homeland

- **boat people:** immigrants who come to the United States in open boats

In 1977, Dang Trinh Le (dahng trihn lay) and her family fled Vietnam in a small boat. They left behind almost all their possessions. They left their house and their land. They took only a small amount of cash. It was hidden in an old family clock. They spent some time in the Philippines. Then they spent two years in Hawaii. In 1981, Le, now 14 years old, went to live in Boston. Her father had been a lawyer in Vietnam. Now he decided to open a restaurant with his brother in Boston. Le, her parents, four sisters, and two brothers arrived in Boston on a cold day in February. The future seemed as bad as the weather. They had little money.

These Vietnamese Americans bargained over fish in New Orleans, Louisiana. About 4,000 Vietnamese refugees live in this area.

Except for the father, they barely understood English. They knew little about the culture.

By 1994, their situation looked quite different. The restaurant was successful. The three oldest children, including Le, had college degrees. All had good jobs. Three others were in college. The youngest child was in her senior year of high school. Le said:

It was really hard at first. I didn't have any friends. I couldn't understand my teachers or the other kids in school. And I hated the cold. I wanted to go back to Vietnam, but we couldn't. We had lost everything when we left.

I think I felt better when I found a few kids in my school also had just come to the United States. Then I began to understand the language better.

Finally I realized I didn't have any choice. The United States was my home. It took about a year and a half, before I started to think of myself not as Vietnamese, but American.

1 Vietnamese Escape from Communism to the United States.

How did Vietnamese refugees reach the United States?

Le was not alone. Throughout American history, tens of millions of people have come here as immigrants. They have felt strange and lonely at first. Often, they wanted to return to their homeland. Some did return. But most remained in the United States.

Until 1965, most of these immigrants came from Europe. But then large numbers of immigrants began arriving from

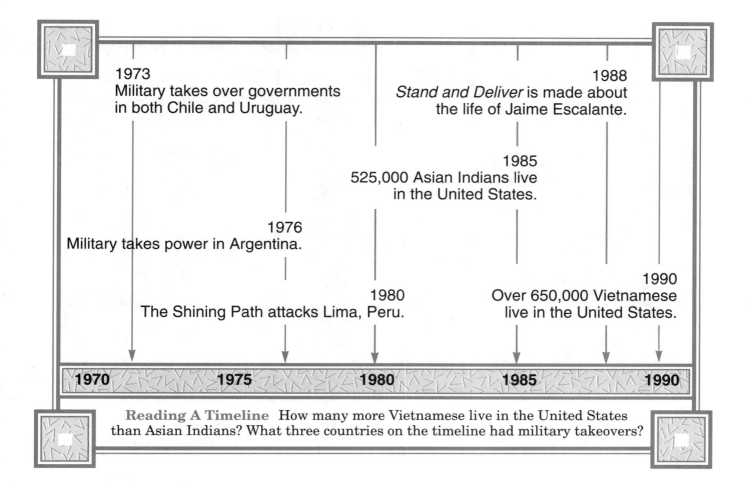

1973
Military takes over governments in both Chile and Uruguay.

1988
Stand and Deliver is made about the life of Jaime Escalante.

1985
525,000 Asian Indians live in the United States.

1976
Military takes power in Argentina.

1980
The Shining Path attacks Lima, Peru.

1990
Over 650,000 Vietnamese live in the United States.

1970   1975   1980   1985   1990

Reading A Timeline How many more Vietnamese live in the United States than Asian Indians? What three countries on the timeline had military takeovers?

Asia and Latin America. In that year, Congress passed a new immigration law. It allowed more people to come to the United States from places other than Europe. In the 1980s, more than seven million immigrants entered the United States. Almost half came from Latin America. Another 37 percent came from Asia. Only one out of ten came from Europe.

In the early 1900s, when immigrants from Europe were pouring into the United States, people called the nation the Land of Promise. Le's story shows that many immigrants still think of the United States in that way.

Vietnamese in the United States
For the Vietnamese, it had been a long, hard journey to the United States. By 1975, the long Vietnam War had ended.

(See Chapter 20.) The Communists took control of all Vietnam. Thousands of South Vietnamese fled their country to escape communism. Many of these **refugees** found a home in the United States. Refugees are people who are forced to leave their homes and move to another place. Usually they must leave because of war.

Just before the Communists took over, the United States flew nearly 100,000 Vietnamese out of the country. One Vietnamese woman recalled the confusion at the airport.

All of these people were trying to get on the plane. It didn't matter if you had a ticket. I saw people pushing to get in. Women and children could not get on. The shelling came closer. Finally, the pilot had to

This group of Southeast Asian refugees are attending a meeting of Commission on Human Rights. Community outreach and self-help programs are organized to make Asian refugees feel welcome in the United States.

leave. The plane took off with people still hanging at the open door. Two or three fell into the sea and died.

Then the Communists were in full control of Vietnam. Many Vietnamese still wanted to leave. Many of them left in open boats. They were called **boat people**. Some were picked up in the water by U.S. ships. Others died when their boats were wrecked by storms. Some were attacked by pirates. A woman who survived an attack remembered the voyage with bitter memories.

One person was killed after being hit with an iron bar. Another had her finger cut off because she was unable to pull off her wedding ring.

When everything was looted, the pirates hurried to go. They released the men they had moved to their

ship, and pushed them back to our boat. Some fell into the water and drowned with their hands tied behind their backs.

The Vietnamese suffered much to get to the United States. Once here, they worked hard to succeed in their new lives. The first Vietnamese to arrive had some advantages. They were mostly well-educated city people who could speak English. Many settled in California and found jobs in computer science and technology.

"Get rid of the Vietnamese"
Later Vietnamese immigrants had little education. Some were fishers. Many of the Vietnamese settled along the coast of the Gulf of Mexico from Florida to Texas. There they could work on fishing and shrimp boats.

Local fishers often resented them. They thought the Vietnamese would take away their jobs. Some put bumper stickers on their cars that read: "Save Your Shrimp Industry. Get Rid of the Vietnamese." Some Vietnamese were even threatened with violence. In other places, however, the local people came to admire the Vietnamese fishers. They found them honest and hard working. Some Americans even let them take over the shrimping in their area.

Some Southeast Asians had few skills to help them succeed in the United States. The *Hmong* are a simple people who lived in the hills of Vietnam and Laos. Many of them fought for the United States during the Vietnam War.

By 1990, about 90,000 Hmong had come to the United States. Many Hmong do not speak English. They had no written language of their own until 1950. Unlike many Vietnamese, the Hmong have not become a part of American society as quickly as other groups.

By 1990 there were over 650,000 Vietnamese in the United States. They had overcome many barriers. They became successful and respected Americans.

1. What event in 1975 brought many Vietnamese to the United States?
2. How did later immigrants from Vietnam differ from earlier Vietnamese immigrants?

2 Indians from Asia Find Opportunity in the United States.

Why did Asian Indians enter the United States in the 1970s?

Americans from Asia are not alike. They are a diverse group. "There is no such thing as an Asian American," says Amy Lan, a Los Angeles maker of films. "We come from China, Japan, India, Vietnam, Korea, and the Philippines. We are as different as Russians are from English."

Asians from India have a very different culture from Asians from Vietnam. In 1965 there were only 10,000 Asian Indians living in the United States. By 1985, there were 525,000. What happened to cause such a great increase?

By the 1960s, India had a large, well-educated, middle class. However, the Indian economy was not growing fast enough. Each year, millions of Indians finished their education. But the economy did not create enough jobs for them. Many educated people could not find good jobs in India. Some of them came to the United States to find new opportunities and new lives.

Finding new work Many of the Indian immigrants did not find work in their profession. Instead, they had to try other work. Many opened travel agencies, diners, and clothing shops. Today Asian Indians own 15,000 motels in the United States.

Many Asian Indians are happy in their new homeland. They learn the customs of the United States even while they keep their Indian cultures alive. Some speak only their native language at home. They teach their children Indian customs. They wear traditional Indian clothes.

Other Indian immigrants are bothered by the differences in the American way of life from the life they knew in India. Says one Indian woman doctor:

I sometimes would like to move back to India. I am getting old and I am afraid my children will grow up and will not be near me. In India, children take care of their parents. This doesn't happen in this country.

Asian Indians celebrate the Hindu festival of Ganesha in Flushing, Queens, a part of New York City. Asian Indians have joined American society, but have still managed to keep their Indian traditions alive.

1. What did Asian Indians do for a living when they came to the United States?
2. How is American society different from Indian society?

3 Newcomers Arrive from South America.

Why did large numbers of South Americans come to the United States in the 1980s and 1990s?

There were few immigrants to the United States from South American countries until the 1970s. Then economic hard times drove many South Americans to the United States. Political unrest grew. In 1973, the military took over governments in both Uruguay and Chile. In 1976, the military took power in Argentina.

Citizens who disagreed with the government of Argentina were arrested. Many of them were never seen again. This became known as Argentina's "dirty war." It caused 75,000 Argentines to flee to the United States. A brutal government in Chile caused many people to move to the United States. Other South American countries had different problems. In 1980, a group of terrorists called the **Shining Path**, attacked Lima (LEE-muh), the capital of Peru. Over the next 13 years 25,000 people were killed in Peru. In Colombia, drug gangs fought with the government. Many Colombians fled the violence.

To Freedom Recently, South American nations have made great strides toward democracy. In 1989, for example, Chile held its first free democratic election in more than ten years.

Still, people from South America continue to come to the United States. Usually they come to the United States to get better jobs. Experts believe that there will be more than one million people with South American roots in the United States by the year 2000. Together with other Latino groups, they are changing the face of the United States.

Jaime Escalante In 1964, a Bolivian math teacher named Jaime Escalante (HAH-meh es·kah-LAHN-teh) settled in southern California. Escalante did not have a degree from an American college. Therefore, he was not allowed to teach in this country.

But Jaime Escalante was not a person to give up easily. He worked as a cook and a janitor to pay for night school. As he worked, he studied English. Then he earned an engineering degree. High-paying job offers came his way. But Escalante took the job he loved most—teaching young people.

In 1974 he got a job teaching math at a high school in East Los Angeles. Most of the students were poor and Latino. Escalante made math fun and challenging. His students were surprised to find that they wanted to learn in his class. One year, 18 of Escalante's students passed the Advanced Placement calculus exam. Escalante was named one of the best teachers in the United States. In 1988 a movie, *Stand and Deliver*, was made about his life.

Escalante had a saying for his students: "Raise your sights." Many South Americans have accepted his challenge. About seven out of every ten South Americans graduate from high school here. More than two in ten have graduated from college. South Americans have very high rates of employment.

Reading a Chart. What country had the highest increase in immigration from 1961 to 1990? What three countries had a decrease in immigration from 1961 to 1980? What happened to immigration in these countries after 1980?

(IN THOUSANDS)

South American Immigration to the United States, 1961–1990

Country	1961–1970	1971–1980	1981–1990
Argentina	42.1	25.1	25.7
Brazil	20.5	13.7	23.7
Chile	11.5	17.6	23.4
Colombia	70.3	77.6	124.4
Ecuador	37.0	50.2	56.0
Guyana	7.1	47.5	95.4
Peru	18.6	29.1	64.4
Venezuela	8.5	7.1	17.9
Source: *Statistical Abstract of the United States, 1992.* Table 8			

Bolivian American Jaime Escalante urged his Latino students to "raise your sights." Many did by passing the AP calculus exam!

Many South American immigrants live in large cities. Los Angeles, Chicago, New York, and Miami all have large South American populations.

The largest group of South Americans in the United States lives in Jackson Heights in Queens, New York. Here you can find restaurants, shops, and travel agencies representing nearly every country in South America. The streets are alive with the sounds of Latino music. Each immigrant group speaks Spanish with a slightly different accent from the others. It is an exciting place to live and work.

Like the other new immigrants, the South Americans have enriched the United States with their own culture. They have also drawn strength and support from their adopted country.

1. What problems at home drove many South Americans to come to the United States?
2. Who is Jaime Escalante?

CHAPTER 33
KEY IDEAS

- In 1965, Congress passed a new immigration law. It allowed more people to come to the United States from places other than Europe.
- After the Communist victory in Vietnam, thousands of Vietnamese immigrated to the United States.
- Many Asian Indians immigrated, looking for greater economic opportunities.
- Political and economic problems caused many South Americans to come to the United States.

I. Reviewing Vocabulary
Match each word on the left with the correct definition on the right.

1. boat people   **a.** caused 75,000 Argentines to flee
2. refugee   **b.** the capital of Peru
3. "dirty war"   **c.** immigrants who come to the United States in open boats
4. Lima   **d.** a terrorist group in Peru
5. Shining Path   **e.** a person forced to flee his or her homeland

II. Understanding the Chapter
1. Why did large numbers of Vietnamese begin coming to the United States in the 1970s?
2. Why have some Americans resented Vietnamese immigrants?
3. What reasons brought large numbers of Asian Indians to the United States?
4. What events in South America caused thousands to immigrate to the United States?
5. Where did many South Americans settle in the United States?

III. Building Skills: Reading a Time Line
Study the time line on page 279. Then answer the following questions:

1. In 1990, how many Vietnamese lived in the United States?
2. On the time line, what was the last South American country to have political problems?

IV. Writing About History
1. **What Would You Have Done?** If you were a Vietnamese American fisher and you were threatened, how would you have acted? Explain.
2. Write a skit about a teenager whose family immigrated from India. Show why they immigrated and how life is different in the United States.
3. Imagine that you are a reporter for your school paper. You are going to interview Jaime Escalante. Write a list of questions that you would like to ask him.

V. Working Together
1. Form a small group. Create a display about one group of immigrants. Include charts, graphs, original art, maps, and newspaper clippings.
2. **Past to Present** With a group, discuss the reasons that people have for immigrating to the United States. What reasons did early settlers have? What reasons do immigrants today have? List these reasons on a chart. Put a check next to reasons that are the same.

THE UNITED STATES FACES CHALLENGES. (1990—PRESENT)

What are Americans doing about some of the major problems facing the United States?

Habitat for Humanities volunteers like former President Jimmy Carter travel to cities and rural areas to build and repair homes for the poor.

Looking at Key Terms

- Environmental Protection Agency
- Habitat for Humanity • AIDS

Looking at Key Words

- **landfill:** an area where garbage is dumped
- **pollution:** waste that makes the air, water, or land unhealthy
- **acid rain:** harmful rain caused by factory wastes in the air

- **recycle:** to use again
- **poverty line:** the income below which people are considered poor by the U.S. government
- **addict:** a person who depends on drugs

In 1986, a barge left New York City and moved down the eastern coast of the United States. The barge tried to unload its cargo at many ports. Each time, it was turned away. It traveled for a year before it found a place to unload its cargo.

The cargo that so many cities and towns did not want was garbage. New York City's **landfills**, areas where garbage is dumped, had no more room. The city had no place to put its garbage. So it tried to find some room in other landfills. But wherever the barge docked, communities were facing the same problem. Americans create huge amounts of trash each year. Where are Americans going to put this trash? This is just one of the issues challenging Americans today.

1 Americans Try to Improve Their Environment.

What are Americans doing to reduce pollution of the air, water, and land?

One of the most serious problems facing the United States is **pollution**. Pollution is created by waste from products. These wastes make the air, water, or land dirty and unhealthy. Air is polluted by fumes from cars and smoke from factories. Streams, rivers, and lakes are polluted by factory waste that is dumped into the water. The trash in landfills leaks into water supplies. Then the water becomes polluted. It is not safe to drink. Fish and other sea life die. Beaches are forced to close because the water is unsafe to swim in.

Pollution can also come from the sky. **Acid rain** is rain that has small amounts of acid in it. It is caused by factory wastes that are sent into the air. When it rains, the acid falls to the ground in the rain. Acid rain can travel in clouds over long distances. It can fall as much as 2,500 miles (4,000 kilometers) away from the source.

Acid rain falling in bodies of water may kill fish. It can also ruin soil and destroy trees.

Americans take action Until 1970, most Americans weren't aware how pollution was hurting their environment. In that year, people around the world held the first annual "Earth Day." People all over the United States heard about problems with the environment. The American people began to be concerned. They demanded that their government take action.

In July 1970, President Nixon created the **Environmental Protection Agency** (EPA) to enforce new laws. The Clean Air Act of 1970 limited the amount of pollution in car exhausts. The Clean Water Act of 1972 set high standards for drinking water.

The concern with the environment continued into the 1990s. In 1993, President Clinton signed a law that limits the use of certain chemicals in manufacturing. In the same year, major U.S. car makers set a goal of making cars that get 80 miles (128 kms.) to the gallon of fuel. Such a car would further cut down on exhaust fumes. Researchers are also working on cars that run on electricity, not gas.

Recycling One way all Americans can help the environment is to **recycle**. To recycle is to use again. Recycling programs collect cans, bottles, newspapers, and other items. Then they are processed so that they can be used again. Many towns give home owners crates for items to be recycled. The items are picked up by trucks and brought to recycling centers. Recycling cuts down on garbage. It prevents landfills from filling up quickly. Recycling also saves valuable natural resources.

1. What damage can be caused by acid rain?
2. What is the goal of the EPA?

2 Poverty and Homelessness Remain Problems.

What is being done to help the poor and the homeless in the United States?

Karen Benari shivers in the winter morning air. She and her mother try to wake up her two brothers. They are

Reading a Chart. Scientists are researching solutions for a number of environmental issues. What are some things that are at risk? What are some actions being taken to deal with the problems of toxic waste?

The Global Environment

Issue	Concern	Action
Deforestation Destruction of forests	Tropical rain forests of Brazil and other nations around the equator are cleared every day for farming. Wood is used as fuel and to make goods. **At Risk:** Clean air, normal climate conditions, public health	In the rain forests fuels and fuel burning devices reduce the need to use trees as fuel. People have started new industries that do not use rain forest land for farming.
Greenhouse Effect Gradual warming of the Earth's atmosphere	All nations burn fuel. The use of fuel has risen since the Industrial Revolution of the late 1700s. The burning fuel lets off large amounts of carbon dioxide. Some scientists say this raises the global temperatures. **At Risk:** Clean air, normal climate conditions, public health	Scientists are researching how serious the problem is. Ways of lowering carbon dioxide fumes and increasing fuel ability are being made.
Hole in the Ozone Break in the Earth's natural atmospheric shield	Damaging chemicals threaten the ozone's ability to block out the harmful rays of the sun. These chemicals are used in foam spray cans and as cooling devices in air conditioners and refrigerators. **At Risk:** Normal climate conditions, public health	Officials of the United States and 22 other nations have signed a treaty agreeing to decrease these harmful chemicals. A total ban is due for the year 2000.
Toxic Waste Poisonous garbage	Some results of industrial production, making weapons, and nuclear power plants leak into the soil, ground water, lakes, and rivers. **At Risk:** Healthy soil, safe water, wildlife populations, public health	"Superfund" groups have given hundreds of millions of dollars to clean up the worst dump sites. Scientists are researching and developing safe ways of dumping.

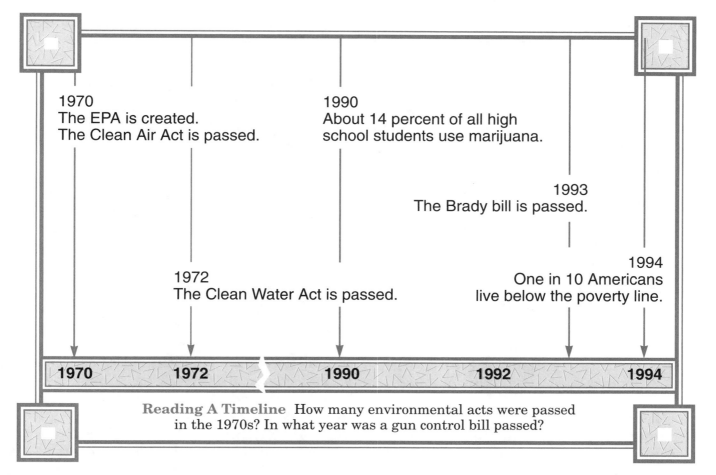

1970
The EPA is created.
The Clean Air Act is passed.

1990
About 14 percent of all high
school students use marijuana.

1993
The Brady bill is passed.

1972
The Clean Water Act is passed.

1994
One in 10 Americans
live below the poverty line.

| 1970 | 1972 | 1990 | 1992 | 1994 |

Reading A Timeline How many environmental acts were passed in the 1970s? In what year was a gun control bill passed?

sleeping in cardboard boxes under a bridge. Later, Karen's family will go to a homeless shelter. There, they will wait for their one hot meal of the day.

Two years ago, Karen's father lost his job. His company put in machines that could do his work faster. The father got a few small jobs in the neighborhood, but then the job supply dried up. Soon after, Karen's father left them.

When the family could not pay their rent, they moved to a cheaper apartment. Then the money ran out. The family was forced out onto the streets. During winter, they sleep in a homeless shelter. But as soon as it is warm enough, they move outside. The homeless shelter is dangerous. Karen has little hope that her family will ever be stable again.

The United States is the richest nation in the world. Still, about one out of ten Americans lives in poverty. Many Americans believe that poverty is the nation's greatest problem.

Poverty The U.S. government counts how many Americans are poor. It figures out a minimum amount a person can earn in order to survive. This amount is called the **poverty line**. In 1994, the poverty line for a family of four was about $14,500. About ten percent of all Americans were living below the poverty line in 1994. This means that a huge number of Americans could not care for their families. Experts say this number will probably grow.

Some Americans are more likely to be poor than others. Women and children are more heavily affected. More than one in five children in the United States lives below the poverty line. People of color are also more likely to face poverty. About a third of the poor are African Americans. Others are Latino and Asian. However, most of the poor people are white.

The homeless crisis   Among the poorest of the poor are thousands of Americans without homes. The homeless can be found in every city across the United States. Many of the homeless are families with young children.

The number of homeless people in the United States is hard to pin down. Some people think there are half a million homeless Americans. Others say there are three million. Nearly a fifth of the homeless have part-time or full-time jobs. One cause of homelessness is the lack of low-cost housing in the United States. Other causes are unemployment, mental illness, and drug abuse.

Helping the homeless   There are many programs to help the homeless. In some cities, empty apartments are offered to families for a little money or even for free. The families agree to repair the buildings.

One group that works with the poor to build and fix up homes is called **Habitat for Humanity**. Each year, thousands of volunteers travel to cities and rural areas. There they build new homes or repair existing ones. The most famous Habitat for Humanity volunteer is former President Jimmy Carter. He is a spokesperson for this group.

Anti-poverty efforts   Poor people also need new skills to help them find work. Education gives students the skills necessary to compete in a changing world. But only about seven of every ten American students graduate from high school. Even many who do graduate do not have good reading and writing skills. These students find it difficult to hold jobs in the business world. Businesses require good reading and writing skills.

1. What is the poverty line?
2. List two causes of homelessness.

3 Americans Fight Against Drugs and Crime.
How are Americans trying to reduce crime and drug use?

In the cities, Americans are building islands of hope. They rent an empty lot and clean it up. Then they build a house and plant gardens around it. In Puerto Rican neighborhoods, these projects are called *casitas*. Today, *casitas* show hope.

They also show pride in the Puerto Rican heritage. Musicians perform *plenas* (PLEH-nahs), a kind of musical newspaper. The words from one *plena* warn young people to stay away from crack.

> *Be careful of crack,*
> *You shouldn't smoke it.*
> *This sorry atrophy [waste],*
> *If you do not look out,*
> *Will crack you.*

The *casitas* help fight drugs and crime. These are serious problems facing the United States.

Drugs   Drug use has become a major concern since the 1980s. One survey found that some 75 million Americans 12 years and older had used illegal drugs at least once. In 1990, about 14 percent of all high-school students used marijuana. Two percent said they used cocaine.

A person who takes drugs can become an **addict**. An addict is a person who depends on drugs. A person who

People across the country have been protesting drug use in their communities. In New York, people gathered outside St. Patrick's Cathedral to take part in a vigil against drugs. What are some actions that have been taken to prevent drug use?

becomes an addict often changes behavior. Addicts do things they normally might not do. They take risks another person would not take.

Drug abuse affects all aspects of life. Employees who use drugs have more accidents at work. They also have trouble producing good work. Families are hurt by drug abuse. Parents who use drugs are more likely to neglect their children. Drugs can also lead to physical abuse. Drug abuse costs the United States over 58 billion dollars a year in lost work, in health care, and in deaths.

AIDS Another serious problem in part caused by drugs is the spread of **AIDS**. AIDS stands for Acquired Immune Deficiency Syndrome. It is caused by a deadly virus. The disease damages the body's ability to fight illness. The virus can enter the body in a number of ways. One way is through sexual contact with someone who is infected. Another way is by sharing needles while taking drugs.

Today, there is no cure for AIDS. There is also no medicine to prevent it. Scientists are trying to find a cure for it. But they have not been successful. Meanwhile AIDS continues to spread. Millions of people throughout the world continue to die from the disease.

Crime Crime is directly connected to drugs. In three of the largest U.S. cities, more than seven out of ten men arrested tested positive for drugs. Almost half of all women arrested tested positive. Experts estimate that up to 80 percent of all crimes are drug related.

Rival gangs of drug dealers shoot it out in city streets. Many of those killed are innocent bystanders. To pay for drugs, addicts often turn to crime. Many addicts are young people who use guns to rob.

Crime statistics for youths are huge. Between 1982 and 1991, the number of arrests of youths for murder rose 93 percent. Many of their victims were also young people. In just one year in the early 1990s, 5,300 children and teenagers were killed by gunfire in the United States. Murder is now the third leading cause of death for elementary- and middle-school children.

Gun control More and more Americans want to stop the killing. The problem is that Americans do not agree on how to do this. Some call for stricter gun laws. Others patrol their neighborhoods against crime.

In recent years, the campaign against guns has grown stronger. In November 1993, President Clinton signed a law requiring a five-day waiting period for anyone buying a handgun. More and more states are banning automatic and semi-automatic weapons.

Preventing crime and drug abuse Gun control is only one way that has been suggested to stop crime. People in communities across the United States are working to clean up their neighborhoods. People in Denver, Colorado, have organized groups to police their own neighborhoods. In Providence, Rhode Island, one group calls police on cellular phones to tell them about drug sales under way.

Another way to prevent crime is to fight drug use. The U.S. government is spending more on anti-drug programs. More money is now being used for drug-treatment centers. Drug-education programs have been set up in many schools. These teach young people the dangers of drugs.

1. List three effects of drug abuse.
2. How is crime connected to drugs?

CHAPTER 34
KEY IDEAS

- Pollution of the air, water, and land is a major problem facing the United States. The U.S. government has taken steps to protect the environment.
- Millions of Americans live below the poverty line. Government and private efforts are being made to improve these people's lives.
- Drug abuse and crime are growing problems. Americans have begun programs to fight these threats.

I. Reviewing Vocabulary

Match each word on the left with the correct definition on the right.

1. landfill
2. addict
3. recycle
4. poverty line
5. pollution

    a. a person who depends on drugs
    b. waste from products that make the air, water, or land dirty
    c. an area where garbage is dumped
    d. the income below which people are considered poor by the U.S. government
    e. to use again

II. Understanding the Chapter

1. How does pollution harm the air and water?
2. In what ways does recycling help protect the environment?
3. What have the government and private groups done to help the homeless?
4. How does drug use hurt our society?
5. What is one way in which Americans have tried to prevent crime?

III. Building Skills: Summarizing

Write a three- or four-sentence paragraph that summarizes each of these topics.

1. Government actions to improve the environment
2. Who the poor are in the United States
3. Growth of drug abuse and crime in the United States

IV. Writing About History

1. **What Would You Have Done?** If a friend offered to sell you drugs, would you turn him or her in? Explain your answer.
2. Create a poster urging people to recycle. Be sure to include the reasons that recycling would help the environment.

V. Working Together

1. Have a class Awareness Day focusing on the environment, the poor and homeless, or the dangers of drugs. Work in small groups to create murals, skits, and group discussions. Invite guest speakers to your class on this day.
2. **Past to Present** Pollution has been a problem since the Industrial Revolution. With a group, discuss problems with the environment a hundred years ago. Compare with problems today. Write a paragraph describing how you imagine that pollution will be handled in the future.

SCIENCE CHANGES THE WAY AMERICANS LIVE. (1990—PRESENT)

What changes has science brought to the lives of Americans in recent years?

On this assembly line, robots do much of the work of building cars. With automation, robots are being used for jobs once done by people.

Looking at Key Terms

• virtual reality • network • information highway

Looking at Key Words

- **computer:** a machine for storing and using information
- **program:** a series of instructions for a computer
- **automation:** the use of machines to do jobs that were once done by humans
- **modem:** a device to send information between computers over the telephone
- **laser:** a powerful beam of light that can be used to perform surgery
- **organ transplant:** an operation in which a body organ, such as the heart, is taken from a body and put in a living person
- **satellite:** an object that circles Earth or another body in space

Mike Horn straps on his helmet and gloves. Instantly, he is no longer in the crowded mall. Instead, he is transported to a sunny field. Above him soars a flying dinosaur. He lifts his finger and lightening cracks. The dinosaur falls to the ground.

Seem like science fiction? Think again. This is **virtual reality.** Virtual reality is a way of using computers and videos that let people act in made-up scenes. The U.S. Air Force uses it to train pilots and astronauts. It is one of many new ideas that scientists are working on in the United States. Science has changed American life since the beginning of the Industrial Revolution (see Chapter 1). Today, science continues to transform Americans' lives.

1 Computers Create a Revolution.
What changes have computers made in our lives?

In 1946, scientists showed an amazing new invention. It was one of the world's first **computers**. Computers are machines that store and use information. The 1946 computer was called ENIAC (EE-nee-ack). ENIAC was a monster of a

Reading a Chart. How much did the percentage of computer use in schools increase from 1981 to 1989? What is the importance of computers to the future?

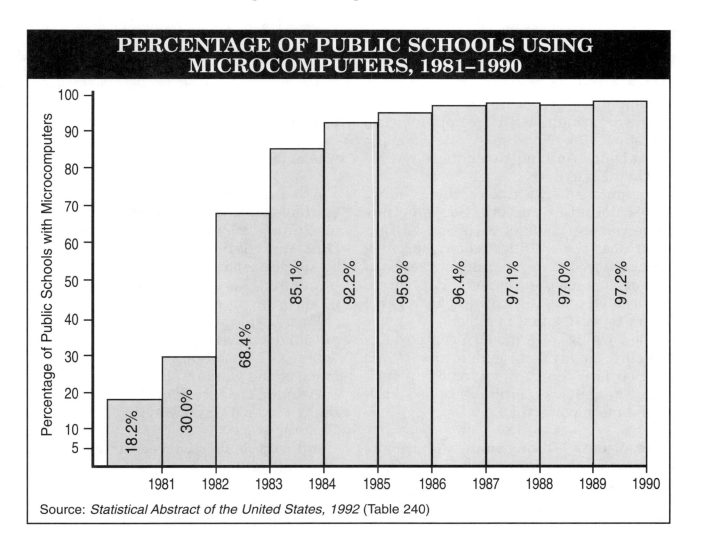

PERCENTAGE OF PUBLIC SCHOOLS USING MICROCOMPUTERS, 1981–1990

Percentage of Public Schools with Microcomputers

- 1981: 18.2%
- 1982: 30.0%
- 1983: 68.4%
- 1984: 85.1%
- 1985: 92.2%
- 1986: 95.6%
- 1987: 96.4%
- 1988: 97.1%
- 1989: 97.0%
- 1990: 97.2%

Source: *Statistical Abstract of the United States, 1992* (Table 240)

At a Consumer Electronics Show in Chicago, people are able to experience virtual reality. Kimberly Chun shows Edward J. Trager III how to use five-ounce sunglasses to see big screen television images. With the glasses, the TV images seem real.

machine. It took up 2,000 square feet and weighed 50 tons. But its memory could store only about 20 words.

Computers today Today's computers make ENIAC seem as old as Mike Horn's dinosaur. A little computer chip can store 800,000 words in its memory. It is about a million times more powerful than ENIAC.

Computers do two kinds of things. First, they calculate numbers. Second, they make certain kinds of decisions. A computer does these things when you put a **program** into it. A program is a series of instructions for the computer. A program might tell a computer how to play a game or how to teach a math problem.

The "brains" of a modern computer is the chip. Today's chips are tiny. Chips may be less than a quarter of an inch long. This allows computers to be smaller and more powerful.

New uses Today many Americans work with computers at home. Many more work with computers on the job or at school. Computers have become a part of our everyday lives. At school, you may learn a language or do math problems on a computer. At home, you may play games on a computer.

Workers use computers to write checks, design buildings, or keep schedules. When you call up a friend on the phone, a computer puts through your call. The book you are reading right now was made with the aid of a computer.

Automation In industry, computers have another use. They help control machines. They also speed up **automation**. Automation is the use of machines to do jobs that were once done by humans. It lets companies make more goods or provide more services.

Many people are worried that automation will put Americans out of work. Giant robot machines now do much of the work of putting cars together. Wouldn't Henry Ford be surprised to see a modern-day assembly line? (See Chapter 1.)

Industry leaders agree many factory jobs will be lost. However, automation will create new jobs, they argue. Businesses will expand. High-paying jobs such as managers, machine repair,

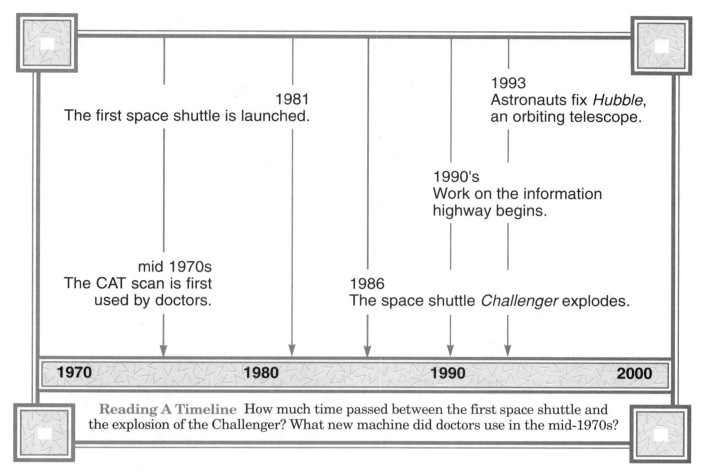

1981
The first space shuttle is launched.

1993
Astronauts fix *Hubble*,
an orbiting telescope.

1990's
Work on the information
highway begins.

mid 1970s
The CAT scan is first
used by doctors.

1986
The space shuttle *Challenger* explodes.

| 1970 | 1980 | 1990 | 2000 |

Reading A Timeline How much time passed between the first space shuttle and the explosion of the Challenger? What new machine did doctors use in the mid-1970s?

and computer programmers will increase. To have these jobs, people need higher education.

Information highway Computers have grown more powerful. But the real power of computers lies in their working together. Computers that are linked together are called a **network**. A network can be connected with wires. Or computers can be linked through **modems**. A modem is a device that sends information between computers over the telephone.

Scientists are working on creating a worldwide network. Anyone with a computer could call in and link up with any other person with a computer. Computers will also be hooked up to telephones, televisions, and video systems. This project has been called the **information highway**.

Using the information highway, we may be able to choose from 500 TV channels. We will be able to order food from supermarkets and have it billed to our accounts. We could order movies on the television simply by punching numbers into the computer.

This will be only be the beginning. Scientists are working on computers that will answer spoken commands. Other computers may be able to "think" in a way similar to the human brain. Today's computers are much more powerful than ENIAC. But tomorrow's computers will make today's seem like toys.

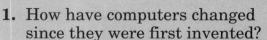

1. How have computers changed since they were first invented?
2. What is a network?

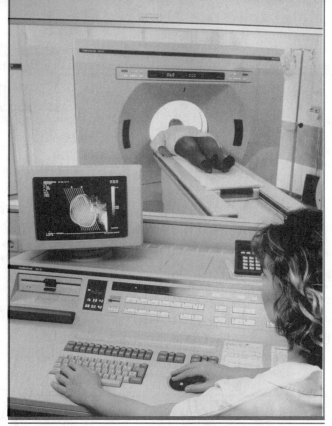

Doctors have used the CAT scan since the mid-1970s. A CAT scan is a type of X-ray that allows doctors to see inside a patient's body without surgery.

2 Advances in Medicine Save Lives.

How has medical science improved the quality of life?

A doctor hurries to see her patient in the emergency room. The patient has a high fever, an infection, and terrible stomach pain. All signs point to surgery. But the patient is an elderly woman who had a recent heart attack. She may die on the operating table. So the doctor insists on a CAT scan. This is a special way of seeing inside the patient's body.

When the tests come back, the doctor is relieved. It is an infection of the large intestine. The patient does not need surgery. She can be given medicine to control the infection. Soon, the patient has fully recovered. The CAT scan may have saved her life.

Living longer Advances in medicine have helped Americans live longer. In 1900, the average American could expect to live about 50 years. Today, this has risen to about 75 years. Medicine can now cure or prevent many serious diseases that killed people in 1900.

New tools New machines help doctors identify disease. A CAT scan is a kind of X-ray. The patient gets into a large machine shaped like a tube. A computer-guided scanner then moves around the patient. It takes pictures from different angles. A computer inside the scanner creates a single picture. This allows doctors to see a much clearer picture than a single X-ray gives.

Another tool is optical fibers. These are glass tubes so narrow they can be threaded through a person's vein. A tiny camera in the fiber takes pictures of the body. These are later arranged by computer. Doctors can clearly see where a problem is. Then they can act to correct it.

New tools also help doctors treat disease. A **laser** is a powerful beam of light. It can cut through the strongest steel. Lasers can be used to perform some kinds of surgery. The laser beam can enter the body and destroy diseased tissue. At the same time, it will not harm healthy tissue. Lasers can also seal wounds. They can clear blocked blood vessels. Lasers are used to operate on human eyes. Surgery that was considered very dangerous a few years ago can be done safely now with lasers.

New treatments Over the past ten years, many lives have been saved with **organ transplants**. When an organ such as the heart, lung, or liver fails, the patient will die. However, sometimes new organs can replace the failed ones. This operation used to make headlines. Today transplants have almost become common.

New research has also helped save lives. Diet and exercise have been shown to be important. Scientists have discovered that a healthy diet can help extend a person's lifetime. They recommend that Americans eat more fresh vegetables and fruit. These foods contian valuable vitamins and minerals.

What next? Soon, advances only dreamed about will be a reality. Scientists are working on mechanical body parts such as artificial eyes. They are also trying to find a vaccine for cancer and AIDS. Medical breakthroughs will continue to help Americans live longer, healthier lives.

1. What does a CAT scan do?
2. What are three new advances in medicine.

3 Space Travel Aims High.

What has the United States achieved in space travel?

Humans on the moon? For most of history, this seemed impossible. Yet in July 1969, billions of people around the world watched it on television. U.S. Astronaut Neil Armstrong walked on the moon. Then they heard his voice from 240,000 miles away. "That's one small step for a man. One giant leap for mankind." Today space travel has become so everyday that people hardly take notice.

Space shuttle program Twenty years ago, things were different. The first space craft were very expensive. They cost the U.S. government billions of dollars. These craft also could not be used more than once. Then in 1981, U.S. scientists sent the **space shuttle** into flight. It was the first craft that could be used again. The space shuttle could stay in space for a week or more.

For nearly five years, the space shuttles made successful missions. Then in January 1986, the space shuttle *Challenger* exploded. The seven crew members were killed. The explosion was caused by a fuel leak. Scientists worked for 32 months to make the next shuttle safe. Today the space shuttle continues to be a key part of the U.S. space program.

The Hubble is a giant telescope in space that studies the universe. Other spacecraft send us weather reports, business information, and live television broadcasts.

Other spacecraft The government has also put **satellites** into space. A satellite is something that circles Earth or another body in space. Satellites are very useful. Some give information about the weather. They tell of the approach of hurricanes and blizzards. Weather satellites have saved hundreds of lives because people could prepare for storms. Scientists use satellites to study pollution. Some satellites help to spot forest fires.

Businesses also use satellites. Telephone companies use them to send calls around the world. Live TV broadcasts are also beamed by satellite. Other satellites can show the location of natural resources, such as oil deposits.

The space debate The U.S. space program has made great discoveries about the planet and the universe. It has also led to many useful inventions. Nonstick pans, velcro, and latex paints come from materials invented for the space program. Many advances have also been made in medicine, computers, and communication.

However, many people question the price of these discoveries. The U.S. gov-ernment spends about 7.5 billion dollars per year on the space program. Some Americans argue that this money should be spent on other programs. They feel that problems such as poverty and homelessness should be solved first.

Other Americans strongly support the space program. They believe that it will lead to more great discoveries. These might save millions of dollars or even millions of lives.

Into the future Although the debate still goes on, the U.S. space program also continues. In the 21st century, scientists hope to send astronauts to Mars. They are working on spacecraft that will travel billions of miles away. They will explore areas we do not even know about today. We have only begun to explore the vastness of space.

1. How was the space shuttle an improvement over earlier space craft?
2. Name three uses of satellites.

CHAPTER 35
KEY IDEAS

- Computers have speeded up the way people organize informations and solve problems. They have also led to many new jobs. It has also led to many new ways of doing things, both in business and at home.
- Medical science has developed new tools and treatments. Americans are living longer than ever before.
- The U.S. space program has made amazing discoveries about our planet. It has also led to new inventions.

I. Reviewing Vocabulary
Match each word on the left with the correct definition on the right.

1. satellite
2. laser
3. automation
4. computer
5. modem

   a. a powerful beam of light that can be used to perform surgery

   b. a device that sends information between computers over the telephone

   c. something that circles Earth or another body in space

   d. the use of machines to do jobs that were once done by humans

   e. a machine for storing and using information

II. Understanding the Chapter
1. How have computers both taken away jobs and provided new ones?
2. What is an information highway?
3. How have medical advances changed Americans' lives?
4. What benefits have come from the U.S. space program?
5. Why is the U.S. space program the subject of debate?

III. Building Skills: Understanding Charts
Read the chart on page 295 and answer the following questions.
1. What percent of public schools had microcomputers in 1981?
2. How much did this percentage change between 1989 and 1990?
3. In what year was there the largest increase in this percentage?

IV. Writing About History
1. **What Would You Have Done?** Imagine that you own a company that is thinking of automating. Your workers are against the use of computers. They say that computers will take away their jobs. What will you do? Write a two paragraph letter responding to your workers.
2. Imagine you are a scientist running tests on board the space shuttle. Write your impressions in a journal entry.

V. Working Together
1. Form a small group. Create a television program that presents exciting new breakthroughs in computers, medicine, and space travel.
2. **Past to Present** New technology often presents new problems or challenges. With a group, discuss any issues that might come from the advances in technology covered in this chapter. Write a paragraph explaining one such issue and give your opinion about a possible solution.

THE AMERICAN PEOPLE FACE THE 21ST CENTURY (1990—PRESENT)

What changes can the people of the United States expect as they enter a new century?

The United States is a land of many different cultures. This cultural diversity challenges Americans to appreciate and respect all people.

Looking at Key Terms

- melting pot • mosaic

Looking at Key Words

- **diversity:** a wide range of differences
- **retirement:** the time when a person stops working for a living
- **disabilities:** physical or mental conditions, such as blindness, deafness, or muscular problems.

STUDY

Copy the key ideas on page 308. Under each idea, write the facts from the chapter that support it.

HINT

Imagine you could step back into time to the year 1900. You would find the cities of the United States very different than they are today. Of course, there would be no sign of any of this century's inventions. They hadn't been invented yet. People would still be riding horses on unpaved streets. There would be no television or radio. There would be very few telephones. People would look at you in a funny way if you started talking about computers. Space flight? That would be for science fiction!

But it is not just the old technology that might surprise you about the cities of 1900. You'd probably also be surprised by the people of American cities. There would be little of today's **diversity**. Diversity is a wide range of differences. The people would have backgrounds mostly from Northern and Western Europe. If you walked the streets of American cities, you would see few people who were not white. Unless you lived in the South, you'd see few African Americans. You'd see very few Asians, unless you lived in San Francisco or Seattle. You'd see hardly any Latinos, unless you lived in the southwestern United States.

American cities have changed as the American people have changed. Why is the American city of today so different from that of 1900? How have these changes affected our nation? The answers to these questions will tell you a lot about what American life will be like in the 21st century.

1 The United States Has More Diversity Than Any Other Nation.

How have Americans changed in the decades since 1900?

The 1900 census identified about nine out of ten Americans as white. People of color made up only one in ten. This figure included African Americans, Asians, and Native Americans.

Ninety years later, the United States had a very different look. The United States had 249 million people. The part listed as white had dropped to 71 percent. African Americans were now 12 percent of all Americans. Latinos made up 9 percent. Asians were 3 percent.

The great immigration   Much of the change was due to immigration. The U.S had seen two great waves of immigration in the 1900s. One came in the first 20 years, from 1900 to 1920. Large numbers of people came to the United States. Most of them were from Southern Europe or Eastern Europe. (see Chapter 2). Then, for about 50 years, immigration dropped off (see Chapter 11).

Immigration rose again in the late 1970s. It grew stronger in the 1980s. More than eight and a half million immigrants came to the United States in the 1980s. By 1990, more than 21 million Americans had been born outside the United States. Immigration continues strong in the 1990s.

The United States today   Like earlier immigrants, many recent immigrants came here to escape poverty. Others wanted to leave political unrest.

However, there were major differences between the two waves of immigrants. Immigrants at the beginning of the century were mainly from Eastern and Southern Europe. Most of the new immigrants came from Asia, Latin America, and the Caribbean. More than half were from Latin America and the Caribbean. About half the Latin Americans came from Mexico.

Yet the fastest-growing group were not Mexicans. They were people from Asia. The number of Asian Americans doubled in the 1980s. Thousands fled

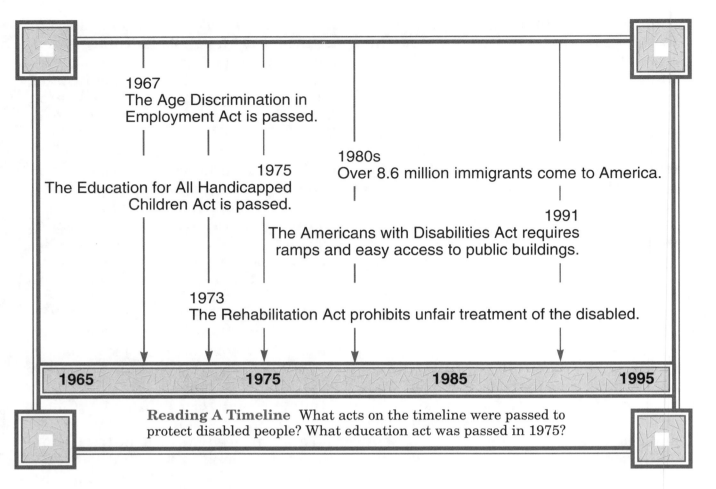

1967
The Age Discrimination in Employment Act is passed.

1980s
Over 8.6 million immigrants come to America.

1975
The Education for All Handicapped Children Act is passed.

1991
The Americans with Disabilities Act requires ramps and easy access to public buildings.

1973
The Rehabilitation Act prohibits unfair treatment of the disabled.

| 1965 | 1975 | 1985 | 1995 |

Reading A Timeline What acts on the timeline were passed to protect disabled people? What education act was passed in 1975?

from wars in Southeast Asia. Many others came here from the Philippines and India. Usually, they came here for better economic opportunities.

1. What is one cause of the great diversity in the United States?
2. What is the fastest-growing group of immigrants to enter the United States?

2 New Voices Speak Up.

How are the elderly and the disabled working for their rights?

As the century draws to a close, Americans are changing in many ways. The U.S. population is growing, but it is growing slowly. In general, Americans are marrying later in life. They are also having fewer children. There are also more elderly Americans.

A new force In 1900, there were 2.5 million people in the United States over the age of 65. By the year 2000, there will be almost 35 million Americans over 65. Today, one in every eight Americans is more than 65 years old. Early in the next century, one in five will be in that group.

There are more elderly because people are living longer today. Better health care and better food have helped many Americans live longer.

The role of the elderly has changed, too. In the early years of the United States, older people had a great deal of power. They were the heads of their families. They remained the heads as long as they lived. They worked as long as they stayed healthy. There was no such thing as forced **retirement**. Retirement is the time when a person stops working.

The first retirement law was passed in 1792. It gave a small pension to Americans who had fought in the Revolution. Since that time, other pension laws have been passed. The most important was Social Security, passed in the 1930. Social Security provides pensions to most Americans of retirement age (see Chapter 14).

Many people are happy to retire. But others do not want to stop working. Social security does not give many people enough money to live on. Also, not all people have company pensions.

About 30 years ago, the elderly began to join together to protect their rights. They put pressure on the government. Their main goal was the right to work as they got older. A 1967 law kept employers from discriminating against elderly job applicants or workers. A 1978 law raised the retirement age from 65 to 70 for people who work for private companies.

With a longer life ahead of them, elderly people are looking for ways to enrich their lives. They are looking for interesting activities. For example, the Foster Grandparent Program allows elderly people to help care for children from poor families. Many elderly people also do volunteer work in hospitals, schools, and libraries.

The disabled   Another group that has fought for its rights is disabled people. People with **disabilities** have physical or mental conditions. There are 35 million disabled Americans. They want everyone to know that they are far from helpless. About five million people with disabilities are employed.

These people are not asking for much. They just want the chance to live as normal a life as possible. That means getting a decent job. It also means being able to go to school or to the movies.

Many people with disabilities have spoken out for their rights. They won new rights in several laws that were passed in the 1970s. A 1973 law bans unfair treatment of disabled people in government programs. For example, a building built with government funds has to have an elevator and a ramp for wheelchairs. A 1977 law said that all disabled students have the right to free public education.

The Americans with Disabilities Act of 1991 requires owners of public places to provide an easy way in. Restaurant owners have to build ramps at entrances.

A lot of people think that a ramp into the kitchen is enough. They think it doesn't matter how you get into the building, as long as you can get into it. But shouldn't we be able to go to a restaurant through the front door with everybody else?

Reading a Chart. What age group has the smallest total population? What group has the fewest number of males?

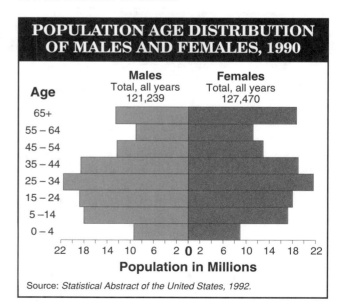

POPULATION AGE DISTRIBUTION OF MALES AND FEMALES, 1990

Source: *Statistical Abstract of the United States, 1992.*

People with disabilities have overcome a number of stereotypes in American society. Americans have come to realize that disabled people are far from helpless. They want a chance to lead a normal life like everyone else.

The speaker is violinist Itzhak Perlman. Perlman was disabled by polio at the age of four. He walks with crutches and leg braces. He plays the violin sitting down. Yet he is considered one of the world's great musicians.

Like Perlman, other people with disabilities have talents to contribute to society. They just need the chance to express these talents.

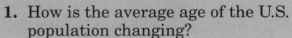

1. How is the average age of the U.S. population changing?
2. What did the Americans with Disabilities Act of 1991 do?

3 Is the United States Like a Melting Pot or a Mosaic?

If Americans have so many different backgrounds, what unites them into one nation?

The official motto of the United States is "E Pluribus Unum." This Latin phrase means "from out of many, there is one." The history of the United States shows how people from many nations came together to make one nation.

The immigrants who poured into the United States in the late 1800s and early 1900s were expected to fit in. Americans expected that the immigrants would change their cultures to fit into the larger "American culture." At the time, people thought of the United States as a big melting pot. Melting pot is a term taken from industry. In a factory melting pot, different metals are heated to a high temperature. At this heat, they all mix together. When this mixture cools, it forms a new metal, known as an alloy.

In the American melting pot, the same thing was supposed to happen. People from many different lands and cultures came together. They were supposed to lose their "foreign" ways and become "American." All Americans would be similar in culture and customs.

It has not worked that way. Today we can see that all Americans have not "melted" into one culture. Americans have kept part of their original culture. They have also accepted pieces of culture that Americans everywhere have.

People have discarded the old melting pot idea. They have a new image. That image is a **mosaic**. Mosaic is a picture or design made up of many small pieces of glass or stone. Each of the small pieces may be beautiful. But all the pieces put together are a work of art.

In the same way, the United States is made up of many small pieces. These pieces are our different peoples and cultures. Taken together, all these pieces creates something larger, something beautiful. It is the culture of today's United States.

In a melting pot, each group is supposed to lose its culture and become like everyone else. In a mosaic, each group keeps much of its culture. At the same time, it contributes to a larger culture, that of the United States.

You can see pieces of the mosaic in any large American city. Walk down a street and you will see restaurants and shops representing many different ethnic groups. People in a neighborhood may speak the language of their homeland. They may speak English in the way of their culture. Their dress may reflect their homeland. They are proud of their differences, but they are also proud to be Americans.

Reading a Map. What does this map show? What states share a border with Mexico? What country is 90 miles south of Florida? What lakes create a natural border with Canada? How far is it from Los Angeles, California to Washington, D.C.?

Strength in diversity When the United States became a new nation in 1776, it was already a very diverse nation. Many Americans had their roots in West Africa, Northern Europe, and Western Europe. Native Americans practiced many different cultures. During the 1800s, many Latino people became citizens of the United States as the country expanded. From 1820 to 1990, about 59 million people immigrated to the United States. These people came from all over the world.

The mixing of all these people is a major part of U.S. history. Many times, they did not mix happily. We have seen many examples of deadly conflict between Americans. We have also seen examples of injustice. We have seen that Americans sometimes discriminated against each other. Indeed, discrimination certainly exists today. However, diversity has also made the United States great.

In other places in our world, diversity is not a strength. Many nations are being torn apart by hatred between people of different ethnic groups. By contrast, the mixing of cultures is one of the great stories of American history. The United States is the most diverse nation on earth. With all the conflict, we are stronger because we are diverse.

The United States draws strength from its diverse population. The response to our diversity expands our legal and democratic traditions. New opinions and ideas are heard and considered and adopted. U.S. culture is enriched by Latino, African, Asian, European, and Native American contributions to music, literature, and the arts. Diversity also strengthens the U.S. economy and helps American business succeed. Through diversity, the promise of the United States is forever renewed.

1. Give an example of diversity in the United States.
2. What is the difference between a melting pot and a mosaic?

CHAPTER 36
KEY IDEAS

- The United States is the most varied nation in the world because the cultural backgrounds of its people so diverse.
- The elderly have organized to protect their rights. People with disabilities have also begun working for fair treatment.
- The idea of a mosaic describes the United States well. Each person's differences are added to make up the whole united nation.

I. Reviewing Vocabulary

Match each word on the left with the correct definition on the right.

1. diversity
2. melting pot
3. mosaic
4. retirement
5. disability

a. a work of art or anything made up of smaller pieces
b. a wide range of differences
c. physical or mental condition
d. an idea that all immigrants would lose their culture and become "Americans"
e. the time when a person stops working for a living

II. Understanding the Chapter

1. How has the population of the United States become more diverse?
2. How is today's immigration different from the immigration of the early 1900s?
3. What is a goal for which the elderly have fought?
4. What rights for disabled Americans have become law?
5. How is the United States today more like a mosaic than a melting pot?

III. Building Skills: Reading a Time Line

Study the time line on page 304. Then answer the following questions:

1. How long after the Rehabilitation Act was the Americans with Disabilities Act passed?
2. When was the last great wave of immigration in the United States?
3. What one event shows improvements for elderly Americans?

IV. Writing About History

1. Write a short story about a time traveler who comes from 1900 to today. Include a discussion of how the population of the United States has changed.
2. **What Would You Have Done?** Imagine that you were Itzhak Perlman. You wanted to go to a special restaurant. But the only way that you could get into the restaurant was through a kitchen ramp. What would you do? Explain your answer.

V. Working Together

1. Form a small group. Create a bulletin-board display showing the mosaic of people and cultures in the United States today.
2. **Past to Present** With a group, discuss how the role of the elderly has changed since the 1900s. Write a paragraph about how this role might change in the future.

Glossary

acid rain harmful rain caused by factory wastes in the air (p. 287)

addict a person who depends on drugs (p. 290)

affirmative action a policy for correcting discrimination by increasing opportunities for certain groups (p. 192)

agriculture the science of farming (p. 28)

alliance a group of countries that work together (p. 82)

amnesty a pardon for political offenses (p. 174)

anti-Semitism hatred of the Jewish people (p. 127)

assassination a planned murder (p. 161)

assembly a group that makes laws (p. 200)

autobiography the story of one's own life written by oneself (p. 105)

automation the use of machines to do jobs that were once done by humans (p. 296)

autonomismo a Spanish word meaning "self-rule" (p. 228)

backlash a negative response to something that is happening (p. 164)

barrio a section of a city where large numbers of Latinos live (p. 33)

bilingual in two languages (p. 215)

blacklist a list of people or organizations under suspicion or in disfavor (p. 155)

blockade to shut off a place to stop anyone from coming in or going out (p. 146)

boat lift operation designed to bring refugees to safety by sea (p. 222)

boat people immigrants who come to the United States in open boats (p. 280)

bodega a Spanish word meaning "a small grocery store" (p. 33)

boom a period of great prosperity (p. 152)

boycott to refuse to buy, sell, or use goods from certain companies, people, or countries (p. 157)

bracero a contract laborer from Mexico (p. 138)

breadline a line in which people stand to receive food (p. 111)

bribery making illegal payments to officials (p. 49)

budget deficit the debt created when a government spends more money than it takes in (p. 263)

canal a waterway dug by people to connect two bodies of water (p. 73)

capitalism an economic system in which most businesses and land are privately owned (p. 144)

casualty someone who has been injured or killed (p. 101)

caucus a group that works together to achieve shared political goals (p. 199)

Chicana or *Chicano* American of Mexican descent (p. 214)

civilian a person who is not in the military (p. 135)

cold war the conflict after World War II between the Soviet Union and the United States (p. 144)

colonialism taking over of foreign countries as colonies (p. 57)

commonwealth a self-governing nation with strong political and economic ties to another nation (p. 228)

communism an economic system in which most businesses and land are controlled by the government (p. 144)

compromise an agreement that gives each side part of what it wants (p. 62)

computer a machine for storing and using information (p. 295)

conservation preservation of natural resources (p. 50)

cultural imperialism the desire to replace the culture of a colony with that of the ruling country (p. 70)

depression a deep economic downturn (p. 109)

dictator a ruler who has complete control and power (p. 122)

diplomacy the relationships between countries (p. 76)

disabilities physical or mental conditions, such as blindness, deafness, or muscular problems (p. 305)

discriminate to treat a person or group unfairly (p. 11)

displaced persons people who are forced out of their homelands by war (p. 253)

diversity a wide range of differences (p. 303)

dove an opponent of war (p. 171)

draft to require a person to enter the military (p. 131)

draftee a person inducted into military service (p. 84)

embargo an order preventing trade with another nation (p. 224)

entrepreneur someone who manages a business (p. 197)

escalation a slow but steady increase in the level of warfare (p. 170)

fascism a system of government ruled by a dictator who uses the military and racism to stay in power (p. 127)

feminism the movement to gain equal political, economic, and social rights for women (p. 205)

fireside chat a radio talk President Roosevelt gave to the nation (p. 118)

free-market economy an economy in which there is little government control (p. 271)

free-trade zone a place where there are no taxes on trade between countries (p. 275)

freedom ride a bus trip to test African Americans' rights (p. 187)

general strike a strike of all workers in the same industry (p. 43)

generation gap difference between parents and children (p. 182)

ghetto a separate section of Eurpean cities where Jews were forced to live (p. 17)

hawk a war supporter (p. 171)

hippies young people of the 1960s who rebelled against society (p. 181)

hostage a person held prisoner until demands are met (p. 166)

impeachment the bringing of charges against a government official (p. 164)

imperialism building of empires (p. 60)

industrial working in industry such as manufacturing (p. 18)

inflation a rapid rise in prices that reduces the value of money (p. 152)

internment camp a prison camp (p. 139)

iron curtain the boundary between non-Communist and Communist Europe after World War II (p. 144)

isolationism a policy of staying out of world affairs (p. 127)

landfill an area where garbage is dumped (p. 287)

landslide an overwhelming victory in an election (p. 262)

laser a powerful beam of light that can be used to perform surgery (p. 298)

lector a reader hired by cigar workers to read to them as they worked (p. 35)

liberation to make free (p. 206)

lynch to murder by a mob (p. 25)

migrant worker a farm worker who travels to find work (p. 79, 212)

modem a device that sends information between computers over the telephone (p. 297)

monopoly complete control of a whole industry (p. 9)

mosque Islamic house of worship (p. 258)

multinational company with businesses in more than one nation (p. 223)

naturalize make a native of one country into a citizen of another country (p. 244)

neutral not taking sides in a dispute (p. 127)

neutrality not taking sides in a war (p. 83)

organ transplant an operation in which a body organ, such as the heart, is taken from a body and put in a living person (p. 298)

pardon an official act that wipes out the penalty for a crime (p. 165)

persecution harsh treatment of people because of their religion, race, or political ideas (p. 17)

political exile person who leaves a country for political reasons (p. 221)

pollution waste that makes the air, water, or land unhealthy (p. 287)

poverty line the income below which people are considered poor by the U.S. government (p. 289)

prejudice an unfair opinion about a person made without knowing much about that person (p. 20)

price control the setting of prices on certain goods and services by the government (p. 135)

primary election an election that lets voters choose their party's candidates for office (p. 50)

program a series of instructions for a computer (p. 296)

prohibit to outlaw (p. 98)

prominence being widely known (p. 195)

proportion the share in relation to the whole (p. 245)

prosperous successful, especially in terms of wealth (p. 95)

protectorate a weak country under the control of a stronger country (p. 65)

quota a limit (p. 93)

ration to portion or limit such resources as food, clothing, or fuel (p. 135)

recall a special election that allows voters to remove an elected official from office (p. 50)

recession a sharp downturn in business (p. 265)

recognize to agree that a union can represent workers in a company (p. 213)

recycle to use again (p. 287)

refugee a person who is forced to flee his or her homeland (p. 279)

relief help given to those in poverty or need (p. 111)

renaissance rebirth (p. 104)

repatriation when a person is sent back to his or her own country (p. 113)

reservoir a place for collecting fresh drinking water (p. 13)

restriction something that puts limits on a person or group (p. 203)

retirement the time when a person stops working for a living (p. 305)

satellite a weak country under the control of a powerful country (p. 144)

satellite an object that circles Earth or another body in space (p. 300)

segregation separation of one group from others by law (p. 24)

sharecropper a person who farms a plot of land owned by another in exchange for a share of the crop (p. 24)

sit-in a protest in which people take a seat and refuse to leave (p. 186)

social programs government programs that aid needy groups of people (p. 262)

social security a government policy that provides pensions to retired people (p. 122)

stock market a business where stocks, or shares of companies, are bought and sold (p. 109)

strike refusal to work until demands are met (p. 40)

submarine warfare using submarines to sink ships bringing supplies to the enemy (p. 83)

suburb an area around a city that people live in (p. 96)

suffrage the right to vote (p. 52)

sweatshop a crowded room in which dozens of workers make clothing or other products (p. 11)

tactic a way of achieving a goal (p. 186)

tariff a tax on imports (p. 95)

tenement a rundown building divided into many small apartments (p. 13)

termination a bringing to the end, conclusion (p. 237)

trade deficit when a country spends more buying goods and services from other countries than it gets by selling to them (p. 275)

trust a group of corporations managed by a single board of directors (p. 50)

tyrant a cruel ruler (p. 166)

unemployment insurance a system in which the government makes payments for a certain time to people who lose their jobs (p. 122)

union workers organized to protect their rights and improve work conditions (p. 40)

urban having to do with a city (p. 18)

veteran someone who has served in the armed forces (p. 152)

welfare regular government payments to people who are unable to provide for their own needs (p. 122)

Index

Abbott, Robert S., 26
Abdul-Jabbar, Kareem, 196
Abortion, as woman's issue, 207
Acid rain, 287
Addams, Jane, 50
Addiction, drugs, 290-291
Affirmative action, 192
Afghanistan, 166
African Americans
  affirmative action, 192
  in arts, 29, 97, 105-106, 195
  Black Nationalism, 102, 190
  businesses of, 26, 197-198
  Civil Rights Movement, 27-28,
  101-103, 155-157, 186-192
  discrimination against, 24-25
  educational progress of, 28
  and Great Depression, 112
  and Harlem Renaissance, 103-104
  Jim Crow laws, 24-25
  job discrimination, 11-12, 51, 96
  and Ku Klux Klan, 94, 101
  migration from South to North,
  24-26, 86, 101, 177
  and New Deal, 123-124
  newspapers of, 26
  in politics, 198-200
  Presidential candidates, 191-192
  and Progressives, 50-61
  scientific discoveries of, 28-29
  segregation of, 24-25, 156-157
  sharecropping in South, 24
  in sports, 196
  and television, 179, 195
  tenant farmers, 112
  and Vietnam War, 173-174
  and World War I, 85
  and World War II, 132, 137-138
  See also Civil Rights Movement
Aging of population, 304-305
  and employment discrimination, 305
  and retirement, 305
  and Sunbelt, 178
Agnew, Spiro, 165
Agriculture
  African American contributions, 28-29
  migrant workers, 78-79
Aguinaldo, Emilio, 57, 58
AIDS, 291
Ailey, Alvin, 195
Airplane, Lindberg's flight, 97
Albright, Madeleine, 209
Ali, Muhammad, 196
Alliances, World War I, 82
Allies
  World War I, 82, 83, 88
  World War II, 127-128, 129, 130-131
American Federation of Labor (AFL), 41
American Indian Movement, 239
Americans with Disabilities Act of
  1991, 305
Amsterdam News, 103
Anthony, Susan B., 52
Anti-Semitism, and Hitler, 127, 131
Apodaca, Jerry, 215
Appliances, labor-saving, 95
Arabs
  Camp David peace talks, 166
  communities in U.S., 257
  immigration to U.S., 256-258

oil embargo, 165
Aristide, Jean-Bertrand, 274
Arizona, 37
Arkies, 113-114
Armenian immigrants, 18, 19
Armstrong, Louis, 106
Armstrong, Neil, 299
Artists, African Americans, 105-106
Ashe, Arthur, 196
Asians
  immigrant groups in U.S., 244
  percentage of U.S. population, 245
  post-World War II immigration,
  244-245
  See also specific groups
ASPIRA, 230
Assassination, of Kennedy, 161
Assemblies, function of, 200
Assembly line, 8
Atchison, Topeka, and Santa Fe
  Railway, 35
Atomic bombs, 131
Austria-Hungary, in World War I, 82
Autobiography, 105
Automation, computers, 296-297
Automobiles
  effects of, 95-96
  mass production of, 8
Autonomismo, 228
Axis, 127, 129-130

Baby boom
  characteristics of generation, 181-182
  post-World War II, 153, 177
Backlash, 164
Badillo, Herman, 231
Baker, Henry, 29
Baker, Josephine, 106
Balaguer, Joaquín, 232
Baldwin, James, 195
Bank failures, 109
Bank holiday, 119
Barrios, 33
  Mexicans, 77-78
  Puerto Ricans, 229, 230
Baseball, 97
Batista, Fulgencio, 220
Baylor, Elgin, 196
Bay of Pigs, 148, 220, 221
Beatles, 180
Belgium, in World War I, 82
Berlin Blockade, 146-147
Berry, Chuck, 180
Bethune, Mary McLeod, 123-124
Big-stick policy, 75
Birmingham civil rights march, 187-188
Black Caucus, 199
Black Enterprise, 196-197
Blacklists, 155
Black Muslims, 189-190
Black Nationalism, 102
Black Panthers, 190
Black Power, 190
Black Star Line, 102
Black Thursday, 109
Black Tuesday, 109
Blatchford, Herbert, 236
Boat lift, Cubans, 222
Boat people, 280
Bodegas, 33, 232

Bootleggers, 98
Born again, 182
Boxer, Barbara, 208
Boxer Rebellion, 60
Boycotts, by African Americans, 157
Bracero program, 138, 213
Brandeis, Louis, 45
Braun, Carol Moseley, 208
Breadlines, 111
Bribery, 49
Brighton Beach, 254
Brotherhood of the Sleeping Car
  Porters, 137
Brown, James, 195
Brown, Jim, 196
Brown, Oliver, 156
Brown v. Board of Education of
  Topeka, Kansas, 156-157
Brown, William Wells, 29
Budget deficit, 263
Bulgaria, 144
  in World War I, 82
Bureau of Indian Affairs, 124
Bush, George, 264-265

Calle Ocho, 223
Camp David peace talks, 166
Canals
  function of, 73
  Panama Canal, 73-74
Capitalism, nature of, 144
Carmichael, Stokely, 190
Carnegie, Andrew, 9
Carranza, Venustiano, 77
Carter, Jimmy, 165-166, 240, 290
Carver, George Washington, 23, 28-29
Casitas, 290
Castro, Fidel, 148, 220-225
Castro, Raúl, 215
Catagonia Club, 104
CAT scan, 298
Catt, Carrie Chapman, 52, 53
Central Powers, 82, 83
Challenger, 299
Chateau Thierry, battle of, 87
Chávez, César, 212-214
Chávez, Dennis, 124
Chávez, Helen, 212, 213
Chesnutt, Charles W., 29
Chicago, 18, 40, 41
Chicago Defender, 26
Chicanos, 214
Child care, and World War I, 137
Child labor, 10-11, 44
Child labor laws, 11, 45, 50
China
  communism, 164, 169, 246
  exclusionary laws for immigrants,
  21, 244
  and imperialism, 60
  Nixon and opening of, 164
  Open Door Policy, 60, 61
Chinatowns, 247
Chinese Americans
  current status of, 247
  discrimination against, 21, 246
  during Gold Rush, 16, 19-20
  settlements in U.S., 247
Chinese Exclusion Act, 21
Chisolm, Shirley, 191

Chung, Connie, 208
Churchill, Winston, 144
Cigar factories
  and Cubans, 34-35
  lectores, 35
  and Puerto Ricans, 33
Cincinnati, 18
Cisneros, Henry, 216
Cities
  African Americans settlement in, 25-26
  immigrants settlement in, 18-19
  improvements in, 12-13
  tenements, 13
  See also specific cities
Civilians, 135
Civil Liberties Act of 1988, 248
Civil Rights Act of 1964, 162, 188
Civil Rights Movement, 27-28, 51,
  101-103, 155-157, 186-192
  Birmingham protest marches, 187-188
  Black Panthers, 190
  Black Power, 190
  boycotts by African Americans, 157
  Congress of Racial Equality, 187
  freedom rides, 187
  and Kennedy, John F., 161
  Malcolm X, 189-190
  march on Washington, 188
  and Martin Luther King, 187-189
  National Association for the
    Advancement of Colored People
    (NAACP), 27-28
  race riots, 191
  and Rosa Parks, 155-156
  school desegregation, 156-157
  Selma march, 188
  sit-ins, 186
  Southern Christian Leadership
    Conference, 186-187
  student participation in, 182
  Universal Negro Improvement
    Association, 101-103
  and white backlash, 164
  white resistance to, 186, 187
Clark, Dick, 180
Clean Air Act of 1970, 287
Clean Water Act of 1972, 287
Cleveland Gazette, 26
Clinton, Bill, 216, 266-267, 274, 287, 292
Clinton, Hilary Rodham, 209, 267
Cold War, 144-149
  Berlin Blockade, 146-147
  and Cuba, 148-149
  and Eastern Europe, 144
  end of, 270-272
  and immigration, 253
  iron curtain, 144
  Korean War, 147-148
  Vietnam War, 169-174
Cole, Nat King, 179
Collier, John, 124
Colombia, 282
Colonialism, 57
Color Purple, The (Walker), 195
Commonwealth, of Puerto Rico, 228
Communism
  China, 164, 169, 246
  and Cold War, 144-149
  and collapse of Soviet Union, 270-272
  Cuba, 220-225
  in Eastern Europe, 144, 253
  McCarthy era, 154-155
  and Marshall Plan, 145
  nature of, 144

Red Scare, 92, 93
  and Truman Doctrine, 145
Computers, 295-297
  functions of, 296-297
  history of, 295-296
  and information highway, 297
Congress, African American mem-
  bers, 198-199
Congress of Racial Equality, 187
Conservation, Progressive era, 50
Conservatism, Reagan administra-
  tion, 262-263
Coolidge, Calvin, 70, 92, 95
Cosby, Bill, 179, 195
Cosby Show, The, 195
Cotton Club, 104
Crime, 291-292
  and drug problem, 291-292
Crisis, The, 104
Cuba
  Bay of Pigs, 148, 220, 221
  boat lift, 222
  and Castro, 220-225
  communism, 220-225
  Cuban Missile Crisis, 148-149, 220, 221
  current economic status, 224
  independence from Spain, 35, 65
  political exiles from, 220-223
  U.S. control of, 65-67, 76
  U.S. embargo on, 224
Cuban Americans
  and cigar factories, 34-35
  current status of, 224
  in Miami, 223
  settlement in Key West, 34
Cuban-Spanish-American War, 32,
  35, 57, 65
Cuffe, Paul, 101
Cullen, Countee, 105
Cultural imperialism, 70
Czechoslovakia, 144
  and World War II, 127

Dance, African American contribu-
  tions, 195
Dance Theater of Harlem, 195
D-Day, 130-131
Dearborn, 257
Declaration of Indian Purpose, 239
Deforestation, 288
Department of Housing and Urban
  Development, 163, 199
Depression, 109, 135
  See also Great Depression
Dewey, George, 57
Díaz, Porfirio, 76
Dinkins, David, 200
Disabled persons, 305-306
  legislation related to, 305
Discrimination
  and African Americans, 24-25
  and Chinese Americans, 21, 246
  and immigrants, 11-12
  and Japanese Americans, 138-139,
  247
  and Puerto Ricans, 230
  and Vietnamese, 280-281
Displaced persons, 253
Displaced Persons Act of 1948, 253
Diversity, in United States, 303-304,
  306-308
Dollar diplomacy, 76
Dominican Republic, 75
  political unrest, 232

Dominicans, 232-233
  in New York City, 232-233
Dominican Small Business
  Association, 233
Domino, Fats, 180
Domino theory, 169
Douglas, Aaron, 105
Doves, on Vietnam War, 171, 173
Draftees, 84, 131
Drug problem, 290-291
  anti-drug programs, 292
  and crime, 291-292
DuBois, W.E.B., 27, 101, 104
Dunham, Katherine, 195
Dust Bowl, 113-114

Eastern Europe
  immigration from, 254
  iron curtain, 144
  satellites, 144
East Germany, 147
Ederle, Gertrude, 97
Edison, Thomas, 8
Education, 28, 264-265
Egypt, 257
Eighteenth Amendment, 98
Eisenhower, Dwight D., 153-154, 169
Elections, primary election, 50
Electricity, 12-13, 95
El Grito de Lares, 32, 33
Ellington, Duke, 106
Ellison, Ralph, 195
El Morro, 228
El Movimiento, 214-215
El Paso, 78
Embargo, on Cuba, 224
ENIAC, 295-296
Environment
  acid rain, 287
  deforestation, 288
  greenhouse effect, 288
  landfills, 287
  legislation related to, 287
  ozone depletion, 288
  recycling, 287
  toxic waste, 288
Environmental Protection Agency
  (EPA), 164, 287
Equal Pay Act of 1963, 206
Equal Rights Amendment, 207
Escalante, Jaime, 283, 284
Escalation of Vietnam War, 169-170
Estévez, Emilio, 216

Factory Investigating Commission,
  44-45
Fads, 96
Fairbanks, Douglas, 97
Fair Deal, 153
Fair Employment Practices
  Commission, 138
Family Leave Act, 209
Family life
  in Great Depression, 111
  during World War II, 135
Fascism, 127
Fauset, Jessie R., 105
Feinstein, Diane, 208
Feminine Mystique (Friedan), 204, 205
Feminism, 205-207
Ferdinand, Francis, 82
Ferguson, Miriam, 98
Ferraro, Geraldine, 208

Filipino Americans
  current status of, 250
  reasons for immigration, 250
Finlay, Carlos Juan, 65
Fireside chats, 117, 118
Flappers, 98
Foraker Act, 32, 68-69
Ford, Gerald, 165, 248
Ford, Henry, 8, 95, 177
Foster Grandparents Program,
  305
Fourteen Points, 88
France
  in World War I, 82, 87
  in World War II, 127
Franklin, Aretha, 195
Freedom rides, 187
Free-market economy, 271
Friedan, Betty, 204

Garvey, Marcus, 101-103, 104
General strike, 43
Generation gap, 181-182
Gentlemen's Agreement, 62
Germany
  Berlin Blockade, 146-147
  East, 147
  unification of, 271
  West, 147
  in World War I, 82, 87-88
  in World War II, 127-132
Ghettos, 17
GI Bill of Rights, 152-153
Gibson, Althea, 196
Gillespie, Dizzy, 195
Ginsburg, Ruth Bader, 203, 207
Girls Bill, 45
Goethals, George W., 74
Gold, discovery of, 16
Goldberg, Whoopi, 195
Goldman, Emma, 10
Goldmark, Josephine, 45
Goldwater, Barry, 162
Gómez, José Miguel, 66
Gompers, Samuel, 41
Gonzales, Rodolfo "Corky," 215
Gorbachev, Mikhail, 270
Gorgas, Dr. William, 74
Grand Coulee Dam, 121
Grasso, Ella, 208-209
Grateful Dead, 180
Great Britain
  in World War I, 82
  in World War II, 127, 128-129
Great Depression
  and African Americans, 112
  and Dust Bowl, 113-114
  family life during, 111
  homelessness, 110-111
  and Hoover, 114-115
  and Mexican Americans, 112-113
  stock market crash, 109
  unemployment, 110-111
Great Migration, 24, 101, 104
Great Society, 162-163
Greece, 145
Greenhouse effect, 288
Guam, 35
  U. S. control of, 65
Guantanamo Bay, 35
Guerrillas, 169-170
Gulf of Tonkin, 169
Gun control, 292
Gutiérrez, José Angel, 215

Gutiérrez, Luis, 231

Habitat for Humanity, 290
Haiti, coup of 1990, 274
Haley, Alex, 195
Hampton Institute, 28
Hansberry, Lorraine, 195
Hanson, Ole, 92
Harding, Warren G., 94-95
Harlem Renaissance, 103-104
Harmon Foundation, 104-105
Hawaii, 128, 248
Hawks, on Vietnam War, 171, 173
Hay, John, 60
Haymarket Riot, 40-41
Head Start, 162
Health care, Clinton plan, 266-267
Hinojosa, María, 216
Hippies, 181-182
Hiroshima, 131
Hitler, Adolph, 127
Hmong, 281
Ho Chi Minh, 169
Holiday, Billy, 97
Hollywood, 254
Holocaust, 131
Homelessness
  Great Depression, 110-111
  1990s, 289-290
Hoover Dam, 115
Hoover, Herbert, 110, 114-115, 120
Hoovervilles, 110
Hopkins, Harry, 120
Hostages, in Iran, 166
Howard University, 28
Huerta, Dolores, 213
Hughes, Langston, 105, 112
Hull House, 50
Hundred Days, of Roosevelt, 120
Hungarians, immigration to U.S., 253
Hungary, 144
Hunger, in Great Depression, 111
Hurston, Zora Neale, 105
Hussein, Saddam, 273

Iglesias, Santiago, 69
Immigration
  Arabs, 256-258
  Asian immigrants, post-World
  War II, 244-245
  Chinese immigrants, 16-17, 19-20, 21,
  246-247
  and Cold War, 253
  Cubans, 34-35, 220-225
  discrimination by unions, 42-43
  displaced persons, 253
  Dominicans, 232-233
  employment discrimination, 92
  eras of, 303
  Europeans, 17, 253-255
  exclusionary laws, 21
  Filipinos, 250
  and growth of cities, 18-19
  Indians (Asian), 281
  Irish immigrants, 16
  Japanese immigrants, 20
  Koreans, 249-250
  legislation, 93-94, 216, 245, 246,
  249, 253
  and naturalization, 244-245
  nineteenth century, 16-17
  Puerto Ricans, 33, 178, 228-231
  quotas (1920s), 93-94, 253
  reasons for, 17-18

refugees, 279-280
  self-help groups of, 19
  South Americans, 282-284
  twentieth century, 18-21
  Vietnamese, 278-281
  See also specific immigrant groups
Immigration Act of 1924, 93-94
Immigration Act of 1965, 245, 249
Immigration Reform and Control Act,
  216
Impeachment, and Nixon, 164-165
Imperialism
  and China, 60
  cultural imperialism, 70
Imports, tariffs, 95
Indian Reorganization Act of 1934,
  124, 236
Indians (Asian), immigration to U.S.,
  281
Indian Self Determination and
  Education Act, 239
Industrialism
  child labor, 10-11
  and discrimination against
  immigrants, 11-12
  and immigration, 18
  mass production, 8
  and rise of millionaires, 8-10
  and working conditions, 10, 11-12
Inflation
  1970s, 165, 166
  post-World War II, 152
Information highway, 297
Initiative, 49
International Ladies Garment
  Worker's Union, 43
Internment, of Japanese Americans,
  139-140, 247-248
Interstate highway system, 154
Iran-Contra scandal, 273-274
Iran hostage crisis, 166
Iraq, Operation Desert Storm, 273
Irish immigrants, 16
Iron curtain, 144
Israel, 257
  Camp David peace talks, 166
Italy
  in World War I, 82
  in World War II, 127

Jackson Heights, 284
Jackson, Jesse, 191-192
Jackson, Mahalia, 195
Jackson State College, 172
Jacksonville, 34
Japan
  exclusionary law for immigrants,
  62, 247
  Gentleman's Agreement, 62
  takeover of Korea/China, 59-60
  war with Russia (1905), 61
  in World War I, 82
  in World War II, 128, 130, 131, 132
Japanese Americans
  discrimination against, 138-139, 247
  immigration to U. S., 20, 247, 248
  internment of, 139-140, 247-248
  labor organization, 42-43
  payments to internees, 248
  and school segregation, 62
  and World War II, 132, 138-140
Japanese-Mexican Labor Association,
  43
Jazz, 195

Jazz Age, 97, 106
Jazz Singer, The, 97
Jews
  and Hitler, 127, 131
  persecution of and immigration, 17-18, 127
Jim Crow laws, 24-25
Job Corps, 162
Johnson, James Weldon, 105
Johnson, John H., 197
Johnson, Lyndon B., 162, 188, 191, 232, 238
  Great Society, 162-163
  and Vietnam War, 163, 169, 170
Johnson, Magic, 196
Johnson Publishing Company, 197
Johnson, Sargent, 105
Johnson, Tom, 49
Jones Act, 32, 69
Jones, Mary Harris (Mother Jones), 10-11
Joplin, Scott, 29
Jordan, 257, 258
Jordan, Michael, 196
Jungle, The (Sinclair), 10

Kelley, Florence, 45
Kelly, Alvin "Shipwreck," 96
Kennedy, John F., 148, 160-161, 188, 238, 239
  assassination of, 161, 179
  and civil rights movement, 161
  New Frontier, 160-161
  and Vietnam War, 169
Kent State University, 172
Kerner Commission, 191
Key West, Cubans in, 34
King, B.B., 180
King, Dr. Martin Luther, Jr., 157, 187-189, 191
King, Rodney, 265
Kirkpatrick, Jeane, 209
Kissinger, Henry, 164
Knights of Labor, 40
Korea, immigration from, 249
Korean Americans, current status of, 249-250
Korean War, 147-148, 249
Ku Klux Klan, 94
  and African Americans, 101
  targets of, 94
Kuwait, 273

La Causa, 213
La Follette, Robert, 49
Landfills, 287
Landslide, 262
Larrazolo, Octaviano, 37
Lasers, medical uses, 298
Las Gorras Blancas, 36
Latin America
  big-stick policy in, 75
  dollar diplomacy in, 76
  Iran-Contra scandal, 273-274
  Panama, invasion of, 274
  Panama Canal, 73-74
  in World War I, 82
Latinos. See individual groups
League of Nations, 88
League of Women Voters, 98
Lebanon, 256, 257
Lectores, 35
Lee, Spike, 195
Levittown, 177

Levitt, William, 177
Lewis, Edmonia, 29
Lewis, John, 186, 187
Lindberg, Charles, 97
Little Havana, 223
Little Richard, 195
Lockwood, Belva Ann Bennett, 51
London Blitz, 129
Los Angeles, 78
Louis, Joe, 196
Lusitania, 83
Lynching, of African Americans, 25, 26, 27, 50-51

McCarran-Walter Act, 245, 246
McCarthy, Joseph, 154-155
McCoy, Elijah, 8
McKay, Claude, 105
Maddox, 169
Magellan, Ferdinand, 57
Maine, 35
Malaria, 74
Malcolm X, 189-190
Malcolm X, 195
Mares, Pablo, 77
Marshall Plan, 145
Marshall, Thurgood, 156, 199
Mass production, 8, 177
Medicaid, 163
Medical science, 298-299
  diagnostic tools, 298
  lasers, 298
  organ transplants, 298-299
Medicare, 163
Mexican Americans
  in *barrios,* 77-78
  discrimination against, 79, 96
  El Movimiento, 214-215
  employment of, 78, 79, 86
  as farm workers, 78-79, 212-213
  free trade policy, 217
  and Great Depression, 112-113
  illegal immigration, 216-217
  labor organization, 42-43
  migrant workers, 78-79, 212-213
  and New Deal, 124
  in politics, 216
  repatriation of, 113
  union for farm workers, 213-214
  in World War I, 85
  in World War II, 132
  zoot suit riots, 138
Mexico
  bracero program, 138, 213
  Mexican Revolution, 76-77
  U.S. gains New Mexico, 35-37
Miami, 223
Migrant workers, 78-79, 212-213
Military
  Americans in World War I, 84-85
  segregation in, 147-148, 156
Miller, Dorie, 132
Mills, Florence, 106
Mitchell, Arthur, 195
Modems, 297
Mogadishu, 273
Monopoly, 9
  government regulation of, 50
Monroe Doctrine, 75
Montoya, Joseph, 215
Moon exploration, 299
Morgan, Elizabeth, 41-42
Morrison, Toni, 195
Morton, Jellie Roll, 97

Mosques, 258
Mother Jones, 10-11
Movies
  African American contributions, 195
  post-World War I, 97
Muckrakers, 48
Muhammad, Elijah, 189-190
Muller v. Oregon, 45
Muñoz Marín, Luis, 228
Murphy, Eddie, 195
Music
  African American contributions to, 29, 97, 106, 195
  jazz, 97, 106, 195
  rock 'n' roll, 180
Muslims, Middle Eastern immigrants, 257, 258

Nagasaki, 131
Nash, Philleo, 238
Nashville, 73
National American Women Suffrage Association, 52
National Association for the Advancement of Colored People (NAACP), 28, 51, 101, 102, 104, 156
National Congress of American Indians, 238
National Indian Youth Council, 236
National Organization for Women (NOW), 205-206
National Recovery Administration (NRA), 120-121
National Urban League, 104, 112
National Women's Political Caucus, 209
National Women's Trade Union League, 43
Native Americans
  American Indian Movement, 239
  current status of, 240-241
  laws related to, 239-240
  National Congress of American Indians, 238
  and New Deal, 124
  poverty of, 96
  Red Power, 236, 239
  reservations, conditions on, 238-239
  termination policy, 236-238
  and World War I, 85
  and World War II, 132
Naturalized citizens, 244
Nazi Party, 127, 131, 132
Negro Factories Corporation, 102
Negro World, 102
Networks, computers, 297
New Deal, 118-124
  and African Americans, 123-124
  goals of, 120-121
  and Mexican Americans, 124
  National Recovery Administration (NRA), 120-121
  and Native Americans, 124
  public opinion about, 122
  Roosevelt's Hundred Days, 120
  Social Security Act of 1935, 121
  Tennessee Valley Authority (TVA), 121
  and women, 123
New Frontier, 160-161
New Mexico, 35-37
Newspapers, of African Americans, 26
New York Age, 26

New York City, 18, 229, 232-233, 247
Nicaragua, 76, 273
Nineteenth Amendment, 53, 98
Nixon, Richard, 163-165, 240, 287
  foreign policy achievements, 164
  and impeachment, 164-165
  and Vietnam War, 170
  and Watergate, 164
Noriega, Manuel, 274
North American Free Trade
  Agreement (NAFTA), 217, 275
North Atlantic Treaty Organization
  (NATO), 147
Northern Manhattan Coalition for
  Immigrant Rights, 232-233
Nuevomexicanos, 35-37

Ocala, 34
O'Connor, Sandra Day, 209, 264
Oil companies, 9
Oil embargo, 165
Okies, 113-114
Olmos, Edward James, 216
Open Door Policy, 60, 61
Operation Bootstrap, 228
Operation Desert Storm, 273
Opportunity, 104
Organ transplants, 298-299
O'Sullivan, Mary Kenney, 43
Oswald, Lee Harvey, 161
Ozone depletion, 288

Palcy, Euzhan, 195
Palestine, 257, 273
Palestinian Liberation Organization
  (PLO), 273
Palmer, A. Mitchell, 92
Panama, invasion of, 274
Panama Canal, 73-74
  and Colombia, 73
Pardon, of Nixon, 165
Parker, Charlie, 195
Parks, Rosa, 155-156
Paul, Alice, 53
Pearl Harbor, 128, 139
Peña, Federico, 216
Perkins, Frances, 44-45, 123
Perlman, Itzhak, 306
Persecution, and immigration, 17
Peru, 282
Philippines, 35
  and Spain, 57
  U.S. control of, 57-59, 65
  and World War II, 130
Pickford, Mary, 97
Pippin, Horace, 105-106
Platt Amendment, 35, 65
Plenas, 290
Plessy v. Ferguson, 156
Poitier, Sidney, 195
Poland, 144
  and World War II, 127
Political exiles, from Cuba, 220-223
Pollution, 287
Poverty
  Americans, 289-290
  poverty line, 289
Powell, Colin, 192
Prejudice, against immigrants, 20-21
Presley, Elvis, 180
Price controls, 135
Primary election, 50
Primus, Pearl, 195
Program, computer, 296

Progressives, 48-51
  and African Americans, 50-61
  conservation activities, 50
  government reforms of, 49-50
  settlement houses, 50
  trust busting of, 50
  and women's movement, 51-53
  worker protection reforms, 50
Prohibition, 98
Provident Hospital, 29
Puerto Rican Forum, 230
Puerto Ricans
  current status of, 230-231
  discrimination against, 230
  in New York City, 228-229
  organizations for aid to, 229-230
  on U.S. mainland, 33, 178, 228-231
  in World War I, 85
Puerto Rico
  as commonwealth, 228, 231
  cultural imperialism issue, 70
  freedom fighting, 69
  Operation Bootstrap, 228
  as Spanish colony, 32, 67
  statehood issue, 69-70, 231
  as U.S. colony, 67-70
  U.S. control of, 32-33, 68

Radar, 129
Radio, 94-95
  fireside chats, 118
Ragtime, 29
Rainbow Coalition, 192
Randolph, A. Philip, 137-138
Rankin, Jeanette, 83-84
Rationing, 135
Reagan, Ronald, 166, 262-264,
  273-274
Recall, 50
Recession, nature of, 265
Recreation, post-World War I, 97
Recycling, 287
Red Power, 236, 239
Red Scare, 92, 93, 246
Reed, Walter, 65
Referendum, 50
Reform
  child labor laws, 10-11, 44, 50
  muckrakers, 48
  Progressives, 48-51
  of working conditions, 42, 44-45
Refugees, 279-280
Relief, 111
Religion, and baby boomers, 182
Reservoirs, 13
Restrictions, 203
Retirement, legislation related to, 305
Rhineland, 127
Richards, Ann, 209
Rich, Matty, 195
Riots
  race riots, 101, 138, 191
  Vietnam protests, 172
  zoot suit riots, 138
Rivera, Luis Muñoz, 69
Roaring Twenties, 95, 96
Robertson, Oscar, 196
Robeson, Paul, 106, 124
Robinson, Jackie, 156, 196
Robinson, Sugar Ray, 196
Rockefeller, John D., 9
Rock 'n' roll, 180
Romania, 144
Roosevelt, Eleanor, 118, 123

Roosevelt, Franklin D., 127, 131, 139
  background of, 118-119
  New Deal, 118-124
Roosevelt, Theodore, 50, 58, 61, 62,
  73, 118
Roots (Haley), 195
Ros-Lehtinen, Ileana, 223
Ross, Nellie Taylor, 98
Ruby, Jack, 161
Russia
  war with Japan, 61
  in World War I, 82
Russians, immigration to U.S., 254
Ruth, Babe, 97

Sacco, Nicolo, 92-93
St. Louis, 18
San Antonio, 78
Sandinistas, 273-274
San Francisco, 18
Santana, Carlos, 180
Sarajevo, 82
Satellites, 144, 300
Saudia Arabia, 273
Savage, Augusta, 105
Segregation
  of African Americans, 24-25, 156-157
  of Japanese, 62
  in military, 147-148, 156
Selective Service Act, 84
Self-help groups, of immigrants, 19
Serbia, 82
  in World War I, 82
Serrano, José, 231
Settlement houses, 50
Seventeenth Amendment, 50
Shalala, Donna, 258
Sharecroppers, 24
Sharecroppers Voice, 112
Sheen, Charlie, 216
Sherman Anti-Trust Act, 50
Shining Path, 282
Sinclair, Upton, 10
Singleton, John, 195
Sit-ins, 186
Smith, Bessie, 96, 106
Social programs, 262
Social Security Act of 1935, 122
Social security system, 122, 305
Somalia, starvation in, 273
South America, political unrest in, 282
South Americans, immigration to
  U.S., 282-284
Southern Christian Leadership
  Conference, 186-187
Southern Tenant Farmers Union, 112
Soviet Union
  Afghanistan invasion, 166
  collapse of, 270-272
  satellites of, 144
  spies of, 155
  See also Communism
Space program, 160-161
  cost of, 300
  future view, 300
  moon exploration, 299
  satellites, 300
  space shuttle program, 299
Space shuttle program, 299
Spain
  Cuban independence, 35, 65
  and Philippines, 57
  Puerto Rico as colony, 32
  U.S. war with, 32, 35, 57-58

Speakeasies, 98
Spelman College, 28
Sports
 African Americans in, 196
 post-World War I, 97
Stalin, Joseph, 144
Standard Oil Company, 9
Stand and Deliver, 283
Stanton, Elizabeth Cady, 52
Steel companies, 9
Steffens, Lincoln, 48, 49
Still, William Grant, 106
Stock market crash, 109
Strikes
 farm workers, 213-214
 general strike, 43
 nature of, 40
 steel industry, 92
Student Nonviolent Coordinating
 Committee, 186
Suárez, Xavier, 223
Submarine warfare, 83
Suburbs, 96
 post-World War II, 153, 177
Suffrage movement, 52-53
Sugar, and Cuba, 66-67
Sunbelt, 263-264
 growth of, 178
Sweatshops, 11
 reform of, 42
Syria, 257

Taft, William Howard, 57, 75-76
Tanner, Henry Ossawa, 29
Tariffs, 95
Television, 178-180
 African Americans on, 179, 195
 as mirror of society, 179
 power of, 179-180
 rise of, 178-179
 and rock 'n' roll, 180
Tenant farmers, 112
Tenements, 13
Tennessee Valley Authority (TVA), 121
Termination policy, Native Americans,
 236-238
Tet offensive, 171-172
Thomas, Clarence, 199
Thom, Melvin, 236
Tijerina, Reies López, 214-215
Toomer, Jean, 105
Toxic waste, 288
Trade
 free-trade zone, 275
 leaders in world trade, 275
 trade deficit, 275
Trail of Broken Treaties, 239
Triangle Shirtwaist Company fire,
 43-45
Trujillo, Rafael, 232
Truman Doctrine, 145
Truman, Harry S., 131, 145, 146-147,
 153, 156, 253
Turkey, 145
 in World War I, 82
Turner, Tina, 195
Tuskegee Institute, 27, 28
Typewriter, and female employment, 51

Unemployment
 Great Depression, 110-111
 during World War II, 135
Unemployment insurance, 122
Union City, 224

Unions, 40-45
 American Federation of Labor (AFL),
 41
 anti-union sentiment, 92
 discrimination against immigrants,
 42-43
 Haymarket Riot, 40-41
 Knights of Labor, 40
 and strikes, 40
 Women's Alliance, 41-42
 women's organizations, 42
United Nations (UN), 144
Universal Negro Improvement
 Association, 101-103
Urban League, 104
Urban nation, and immigration, 18

Valentino, Rudolph, 97
Van Vorst, Marie, 10
Vanzetti, Bartolomeo, 92-93
Velázquez, Nydia, 231
Versailles, Treaty of, 88
Victory gardens, 135
Viet Cong, 169, 171-172
Vietnamese, 278-281
Vietnam Veterans Memorial, 174
Vietnam War, 169-174
 and African Americans, 173-174, 189
 American opposition to, 171, 172
 casualties of, 173
 causes of, 169
 escalation of, 169-170
 and Johnson, 163
 memorial to, 174
 peace settlement, 170
 protests against, 172, 182
 Tet offensive, 171-172
 Vietnamization, 170
Villa, Pancho, 77, 85
Virtual reality, 295
Voting, Nineteenth Amendment, 53, 98
Voting Rights Act of 1965, 163, 188

Wake Island, U. S. control of, 65
Walker, Alice, 195
Walker, Madame C.J., 26
Waller, Fats, 106
War on poverty, 162, 238
Warrior, Clyde, 236
Warsaw Pact, 147
Washington Bee, 26
Washington, Booker T., 23, 27
Washington, Denzel, 195
Washington Heights, 232
Washington, march on, 188
Washington, Walter, 200
Watergate, 164
Waters, Ethel, 106
Watson, Elizabeth, 208
Weaver, Robert C., 163, 199
Welfare, 122
Wells, Ida B., 27
West Germany, 147
Wilder, L. Douglas, 200
Williams, Dr. Daniel Hale, 29
Wilson, Woodrow, 53, 76, 83, 85, 88
Women
 athletes, 97
 education of, 203
 employment of, 51, 203, 207-208
 Equal Rights Amendment, 207
 feminism, 205-207
 and New Deal, 123
 in 1920s, 97-98

 in politics, 208-209
 post-World War II position, 203-204
 Progressive era, 51-53
 suffrage movement, 52-53
 unequal pay, 203, 209
 unionization, 41-42, 43
 voting rights, 52-53, 98
 women's liberation movement,
 206-207
 during World War I, 86
 during World War II, 132, 136-137
Women's Alliance, 41-42
Women's Army Corps (WACs), 132
Women's Campaign Fund, 209
Wonder, Stevie, 195
Wood, Leonard, 65
Woodruff, Hale, 105
Working conditions
 child labor, 10-11, 44
 factories of early 1900s, 10, 11-12
 reform laws, 42, 44-45
 and rise of unions, 40-45
 and Triangle Shirtwaist Company
 fire, 43-45
World War I
 action in Europe, 87-88
 and African Americans, 85
 Allies, 82
 Americans in military service, 84-85
 Central Powers, 82
 end of, 88
 home front activities, 86-87
 and Latinos, 85
 and Native Americans, 85
 origins of, 82
 post-war economy, 92
 submarine warfare, 83
 U.S. entry into, 83-84
 U.S. neutrality, 83
 U.S. war machine, 85-86
World War II
 and African Americans, 132, 137-138
 Allies, 127-128
 Americans in military service, 131-132
 atomic bombs, 131
 Axis, 127, 129-130
 D-Day, 130-131
 economic effects, 135
 family life during, 135
 and Hitler, 127
 and Holocaust, 131
 and Japanese Americans, 132, 138-140
 and Mexican Americans, 132
 and Native Americans, 132
 post-war economy, 152
 U.S. entry into, 128
 weaponry of, 129
 women during, 132, 136-137
Wounded Knee, 239
Writers, African Americans, 105, 195

Ybor City, 34
Ybor, Vicente Martinez, 34
Yellow fever, 65
Young, Andrew, 200
Young Lords, 230

Zoot suit riots, 138